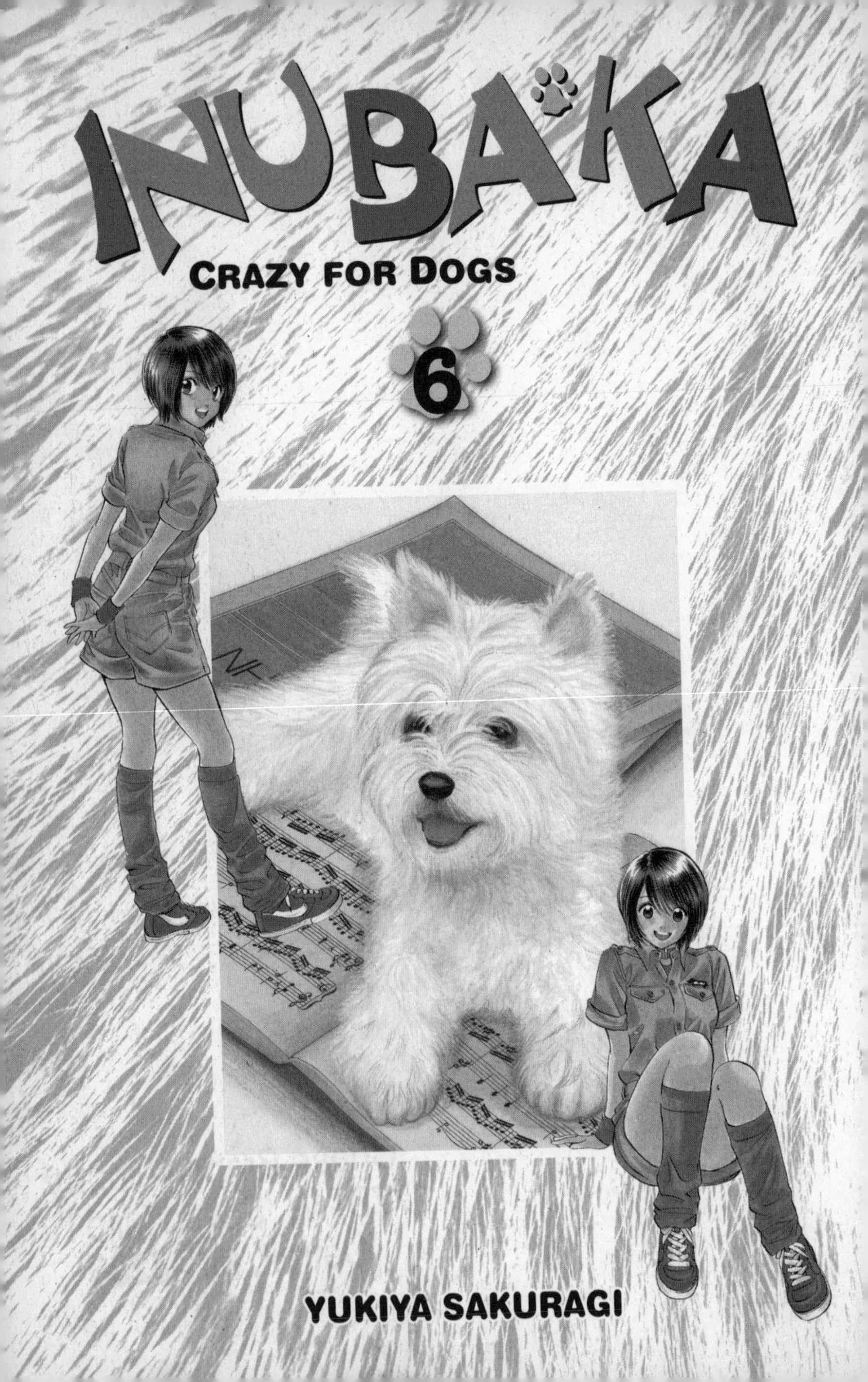
INUBAKA
CRAZY FOR DOGS
6
YUKIYA SAKURAGI

Contents

Story thus far

Teppei is the manager of the recently opened pet shop Woofles. He intended to breed his black Labrador Noa with a champion dog, but instead Noa was "taken advantage of" by an unknown and unfixed male dog!

The unknown dog's owner was Suguri Miyauchi and her dog was a mutt named Lupin. Suguri is now working at Woofles to make up for her dog's actions.

Suguri's enthusiasm is more than a little unique. She has eaten dog food (and said it was tasty), caught dog poop with her bare hands, and caused dogs to have "happy pee" in her presence. Teppei is starting to realize that Suguri is indeed a very special girl.

In volume 5 Suguri met Henry, a German shepherd separated from his owner who was hospitalized after an accident. They entered a dog agility contest to restore Henry's broken spirit. Together they faced a tough rival and a traumatic memory that haunted Henry. Overcoming all of this, Henry and Suguri eventually won the cup by moving up from second place after the winner was disqualified for being too hard on his dog. Henry went back to his owner, and Suguri's life went back to normal, but...?

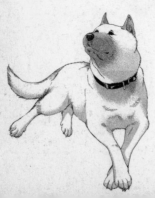

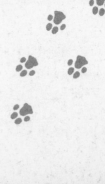

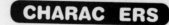

CHARAC ERS

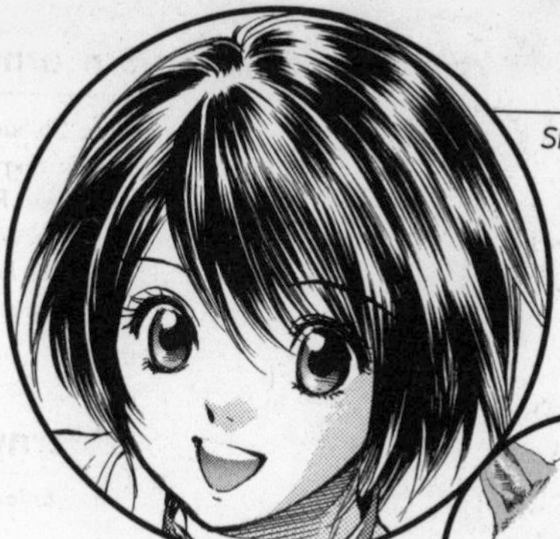

Suguri Miyauchi

She seems to possess an almost supernatural connection with dogs. When she approaches them they often urinate with great excitement! She is crazy for dogs and can catch their droppings with her bare hands. She is currently a trainee at the Woofles Pet Shop.

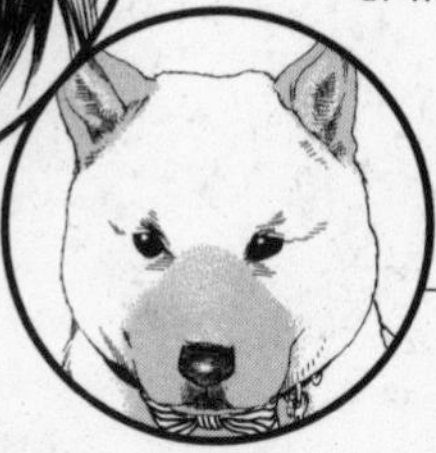

Lupin

♂ *Mutt (mongrel)*

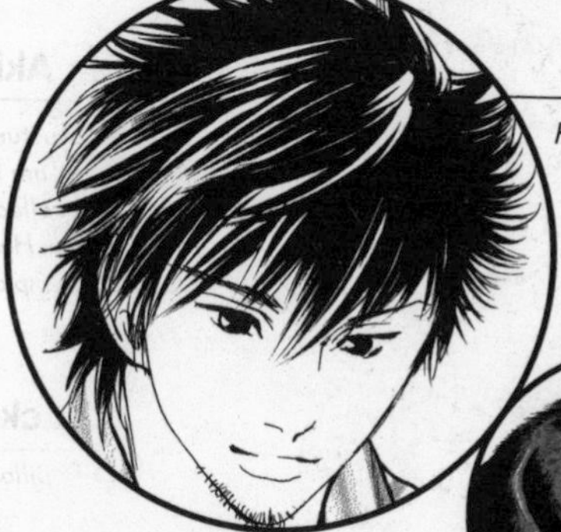

eppei Iida

He is the manager of the recently opened pet shop Woofles. He is aware of Suguri's special ability and has hired her to work in his shop. He also lets Suguri and Kentaro crash with him.

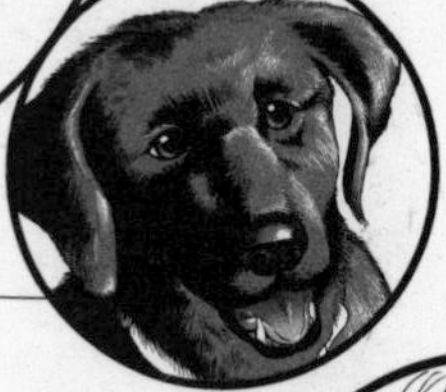

Noa

♀ *Labrador retriever*

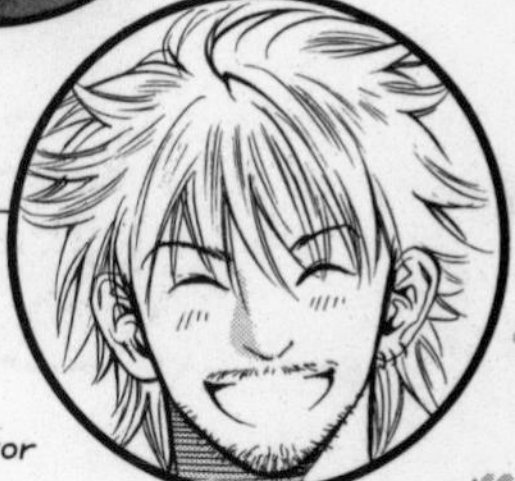

Kentaro Osada

A wannabe musician and buddy of Teppei's from high school. Teppei saved Kentaro when he was a down-and-out beggar. He has a crush on the piano instructor Kanako, but not her dog...

Melon
🐾 Chihuahua

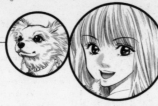

Chizuru Sawamura

She adopted a Chihuahua, Melon, after her long-time pet Golden Retriever Ricky alerted her that he was ill. She works at a hostess bar to repay Melon's medical fees.

Kanako Mori

She teaches piano on the second floor of the same building as Woofles. Her love for her dog, Czerny, is so great that it surprises even Suguri!

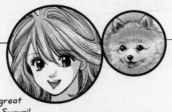

Czerny
🐾 Pomeranian

Zidane
🐾 French bulldog

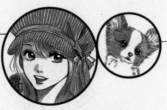

Hiroshi Akiba

Pop-idol otaku turned dog otaku. His dream is to publish a photo collection of his dog, Zidane. He is a government employee.

Mari Yamashita

She is a model whose nickname is Yamarin. She decided to keep an unsold Papillon, Lucky, who was her co-star in a bread commercial.

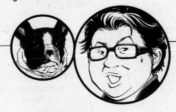

Lucky
🐾 Papillon

Kim

A Korean friend of Kentaro. He had a phobia of dogs, but he has been working hard to get over it in order to get close to Suguri, whom he has a crush on. He bought a Shiba dog!

Chanta
🐾 Shiba

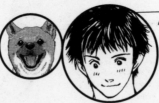

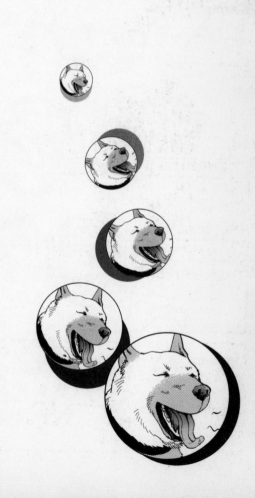

CHAPTER 53: A "POOR LITTLE THING"

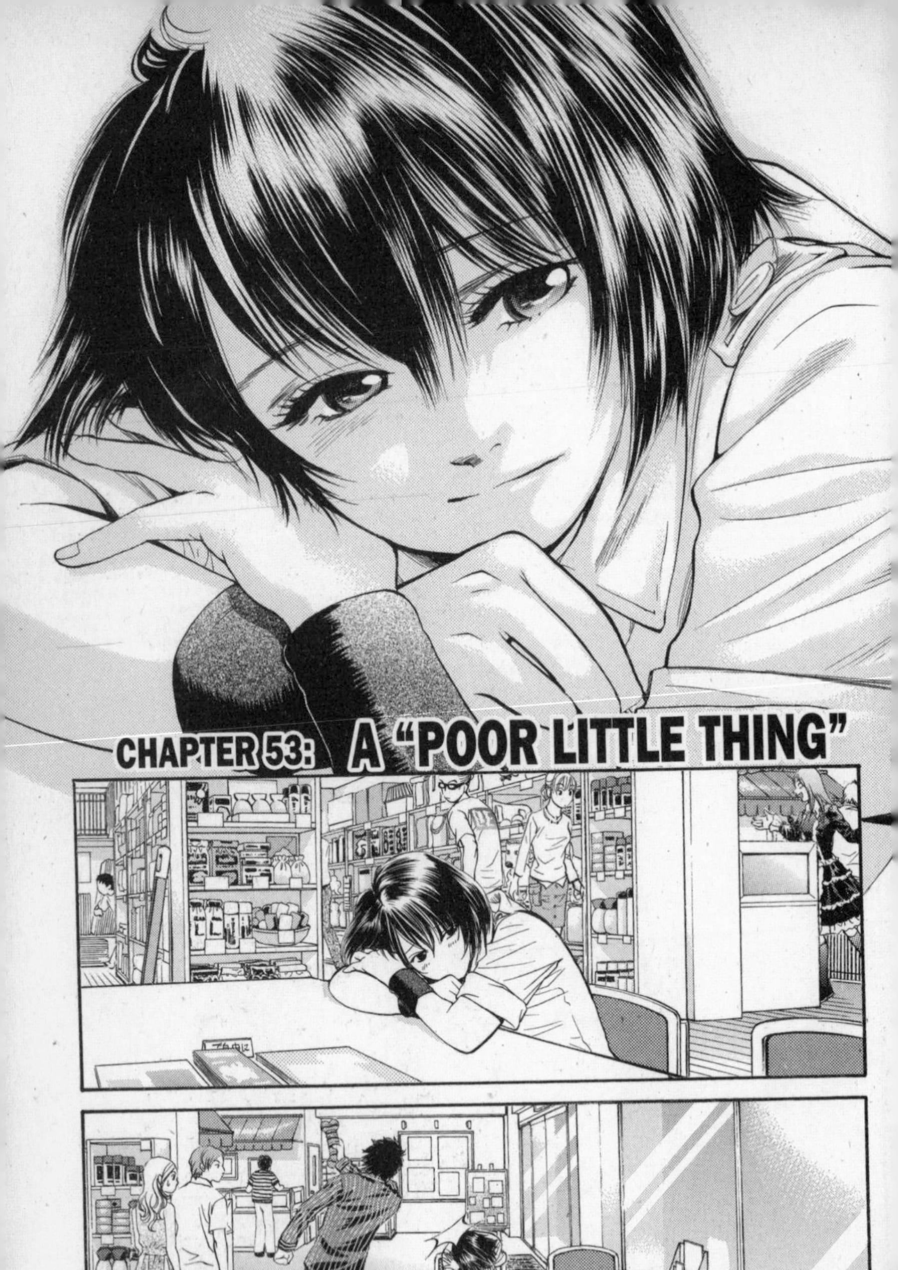

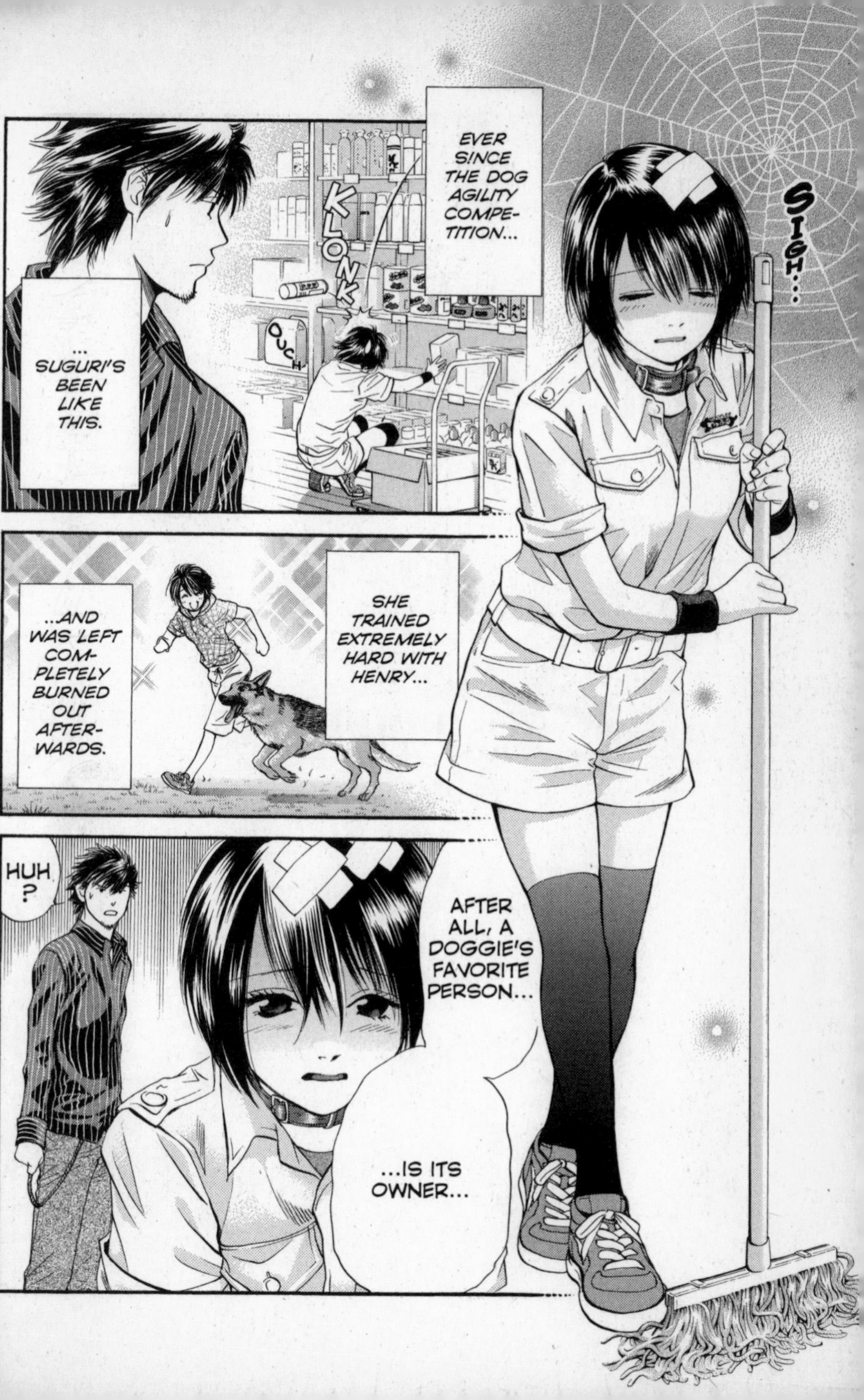
SIGH...
EVER SINCE THE DOG AGILITY COMPETITION...
KLONK
OUCH
...SUGURI'S BEEN LIKE THIS.
SHE TRAINED EXTREMELY HARD WITH HENRY...
...AND WAS LEFT COMPLETELY BURNED OUT AFTERWARDS.
HUH?
AFTER ALL, A DOGGIE'S FAVORITE PERSON...
...IS ITS OWNER...

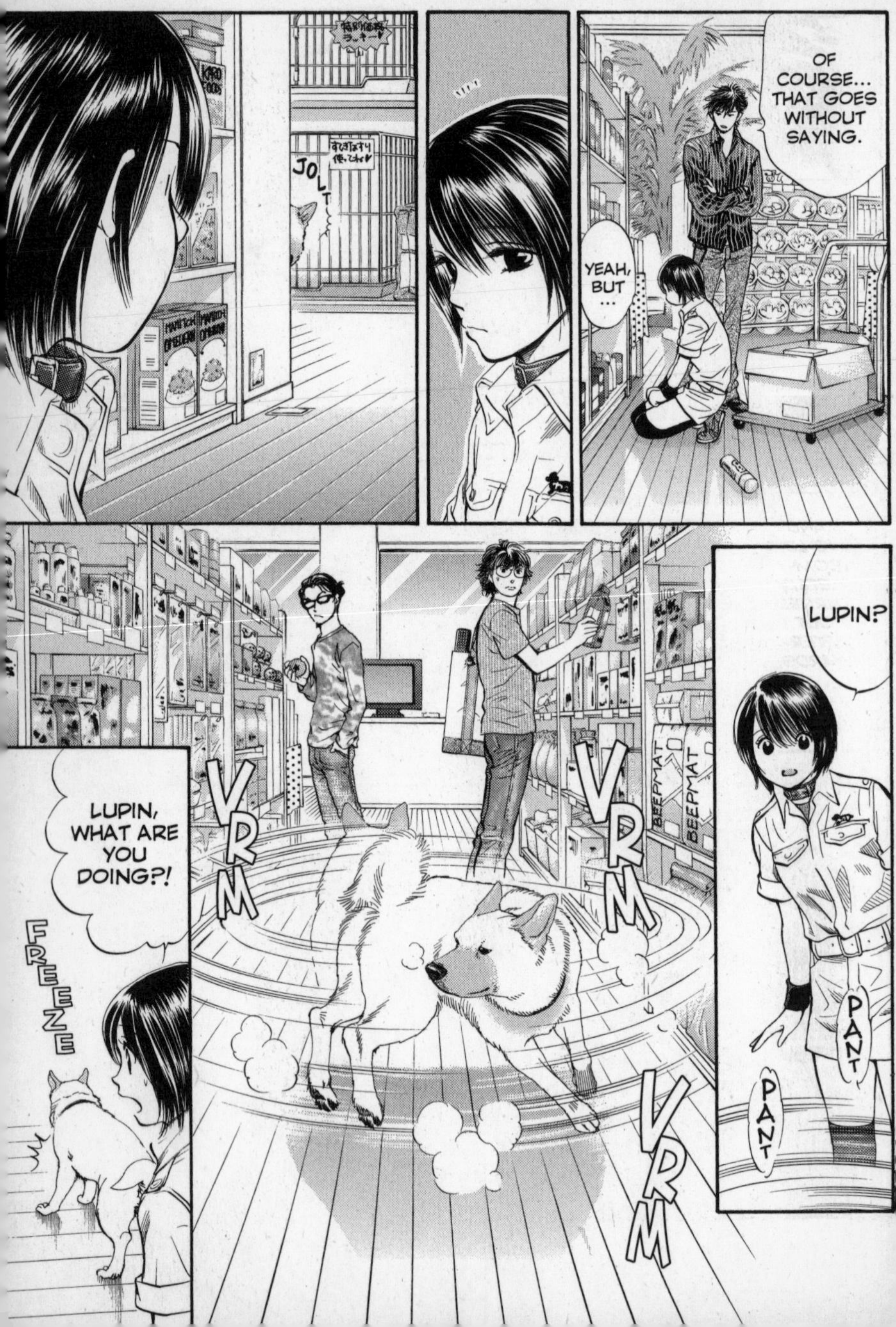
OF COURSE... THAT GOES WITHOUT SAYING.
YEAH, BUT ...
JOLT
LUPIN?
PANT
PANT
VRM
VRM
VRM
BEEPMAT
BEEPMAT
LUPIN, WHAT ARE YOU DOING?!
FREEZE

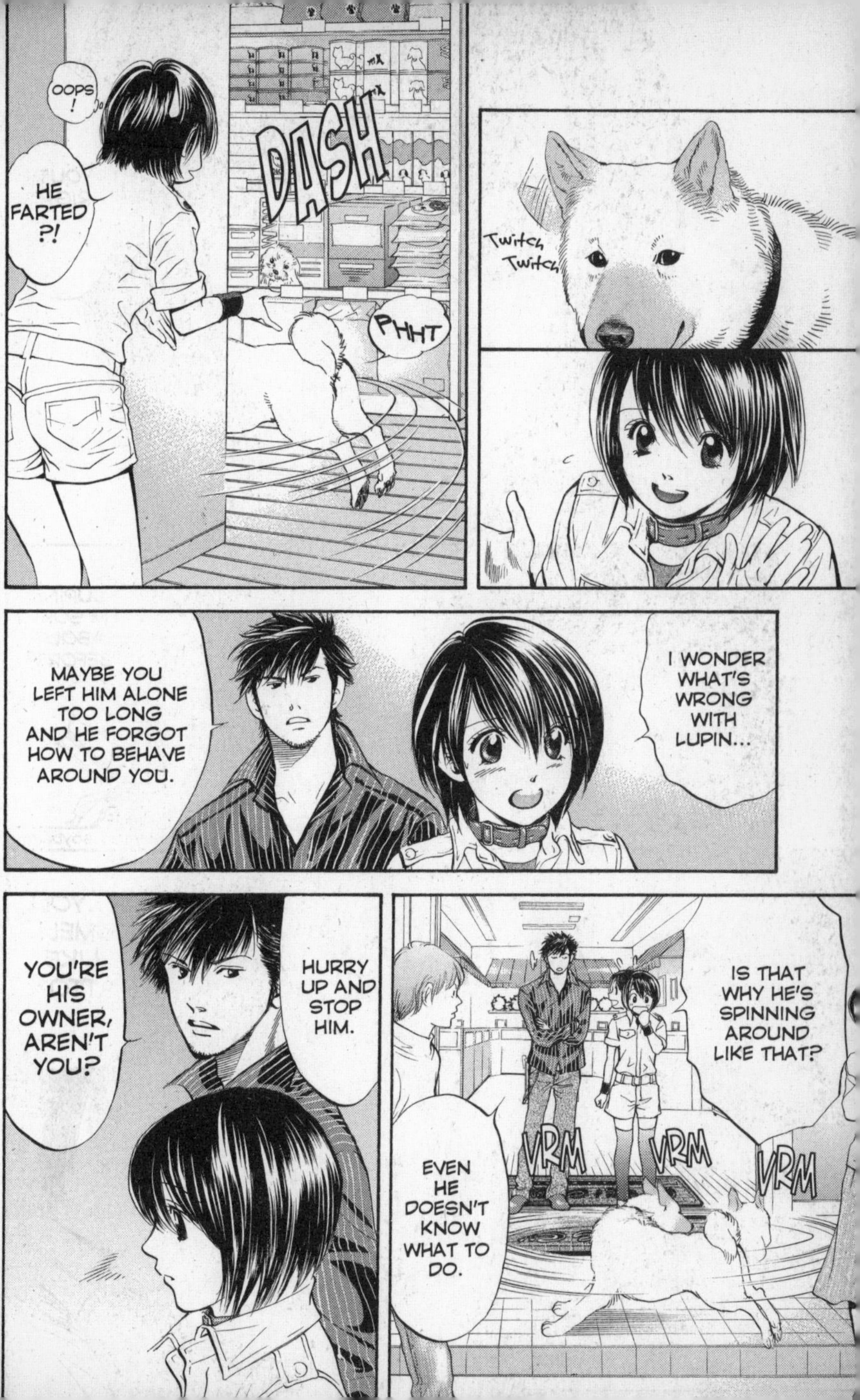
Twitch
Twitch
DASH
PHHT
OOPS!
HE FARTED?!
I WONDER WHAT'S WRONG WITH LUPIN...
MAYBE YOU LEFT HIM ALONE TOO LONG AND HE FORGOT HOW TO BEHAVE AROUND YOU.
IS THAT WHY HE'S SPINNING AROUND LIKE THAT?
VRM
VRM
VRM
EVEN HE DOESN'T KNOW WHAT TO DO.
HURRY UP AND STOP HIM.
YOU'RE HIS OWNER, AREN'T YOU?

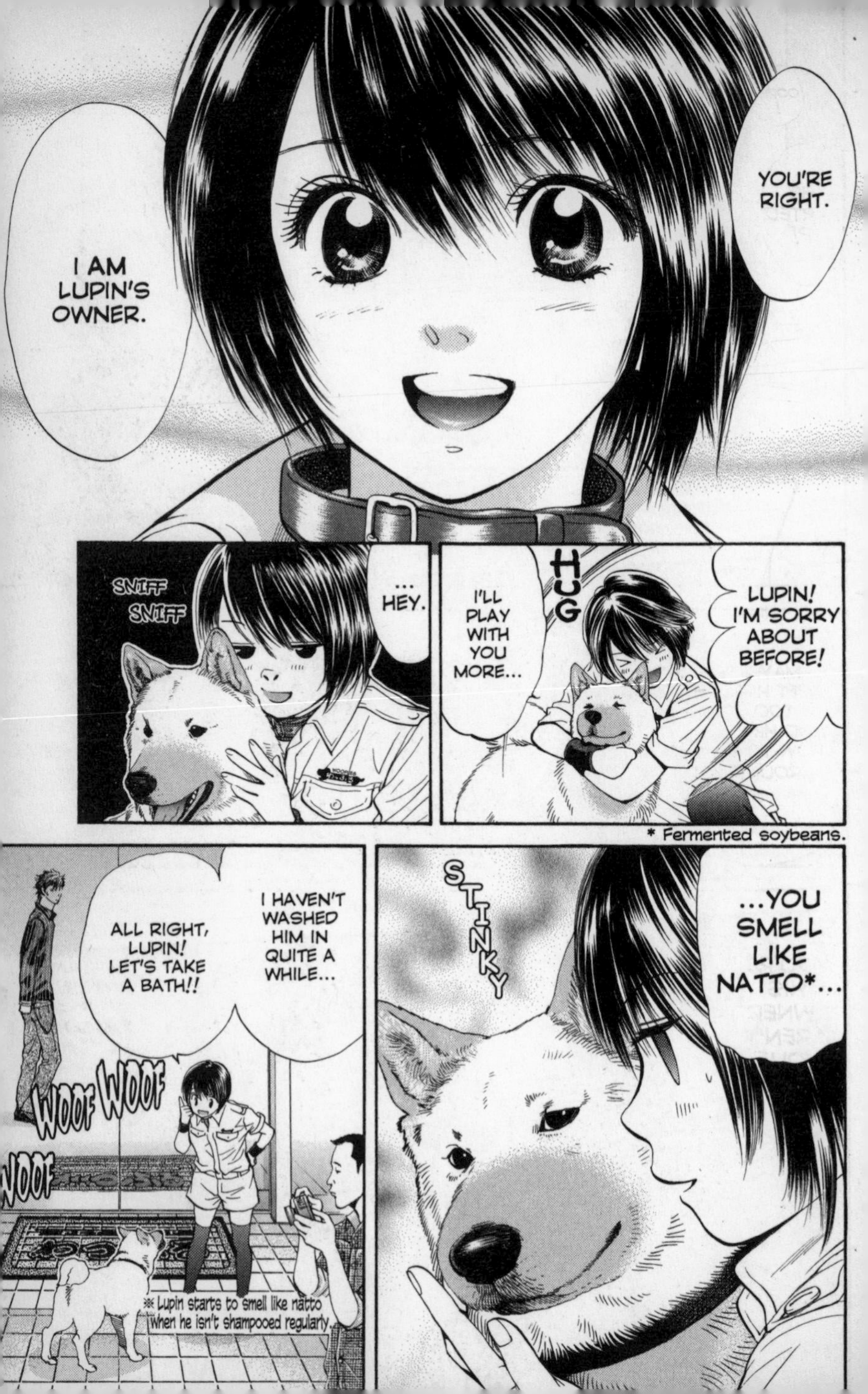
YOU'RE RIGHT.
I AM LUPIN'S OWNER.
LUPIN! I'M SORRY ABOUT BEFORE!
HUG
I'LL PLAY WITH YOU MORE...
...HEY.
SNIFF SNIFF
* Fermented soybeans.
...YOU SMELL LIKE NATTO*...
STINKY
I HAVEN'T WASHED HIM IN QUITE A WHILE...
ALL RIGHT, LUPIN! LET'S TAKE A BATH!!
WOOF WOOF
WOOF
※ Lupin starts to smell like natto when he isn't shampooed regularly.

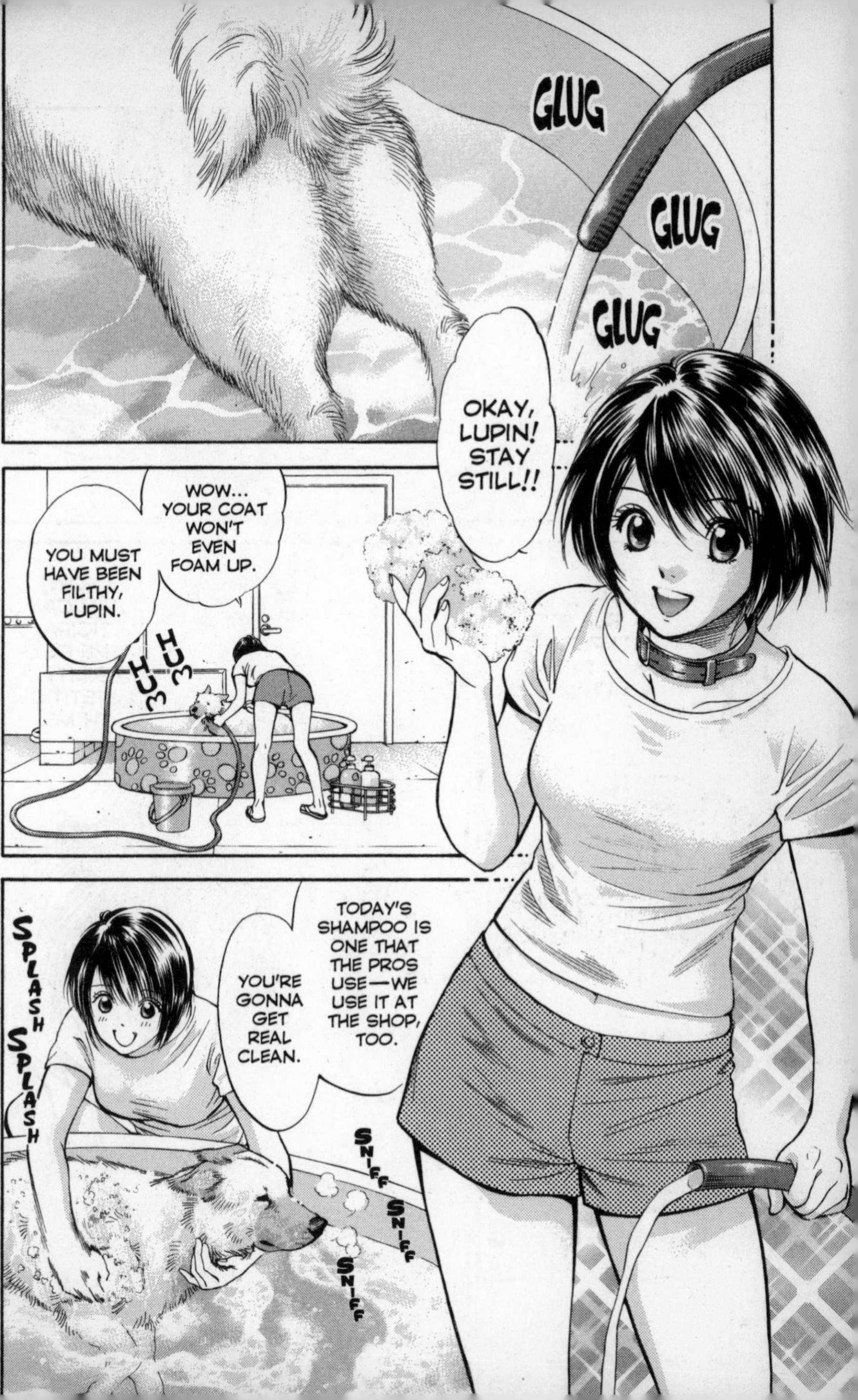
GLUG
GLUG
GLUG
OKAY, LUPIN! STAY STILL!!
WOW... YOUR COAT WON'T EVEN FOAM UP.
YOU MUST HAVE BEEN FILTHY, LUPIN.
HU3
HU3
TODAY'S SHAMPOO IS ONE THAT THE PROS USE—WE USE IT AT THE SHOP, TOO.
YOU'RE GONNA GET REAL CLEAN.
SPLASH
SPLASH
SNIFF
SNIFF
SNIFF

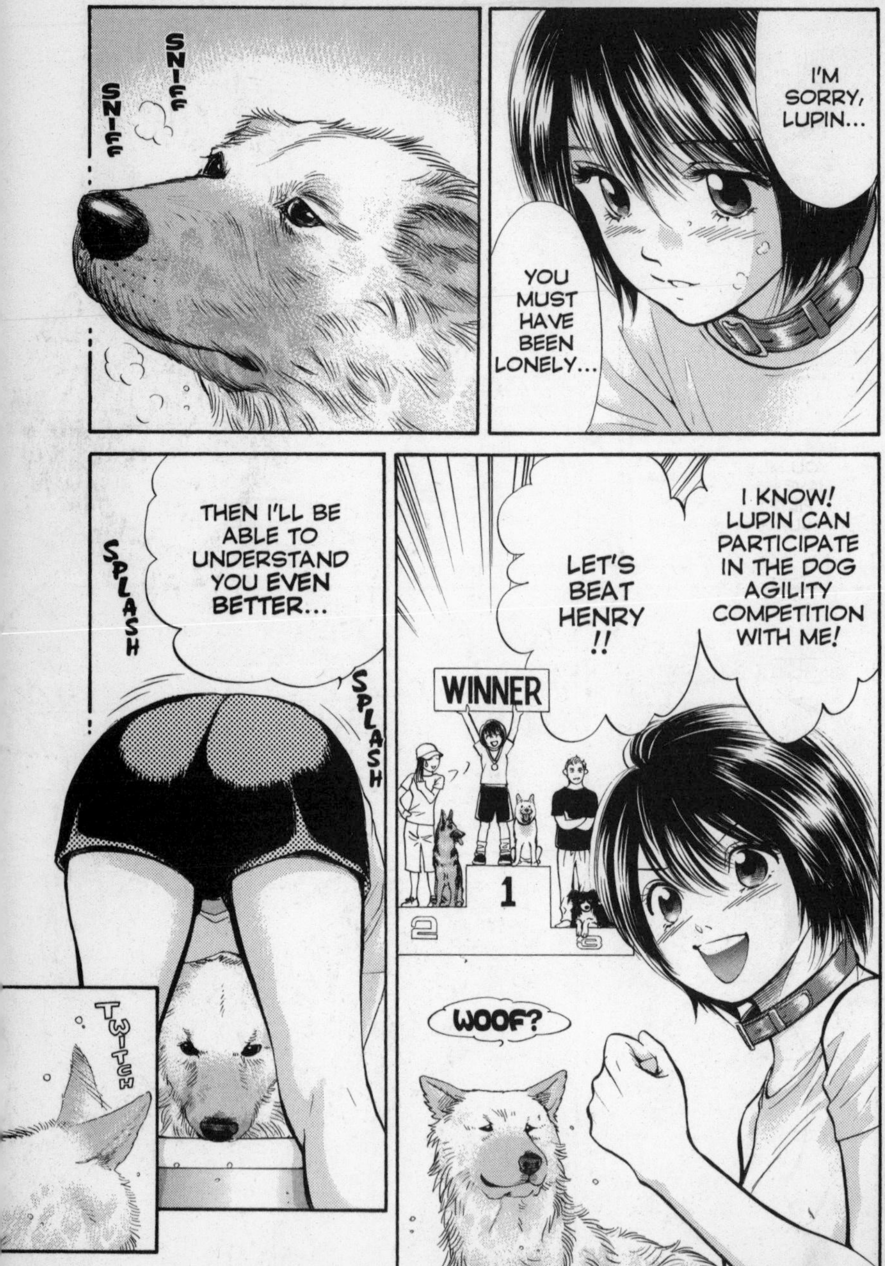
I'M SORRY, LUPIN...
YOU MUST HAVE BEEN LONELY...
SNIFF
SNIFF
I KNOW! LUPIN CAN PARTICIPATE IN THE DOG AGILITY COMPETITION WITH ME!
LET'S BEAT HENRY!!
WINNER
1
2
3
WOOF?
THEN I'LL BE ABLE TO UNDERSTAND YOU EVEN BETTER...
SPLASH
SPLASH
TWITCH

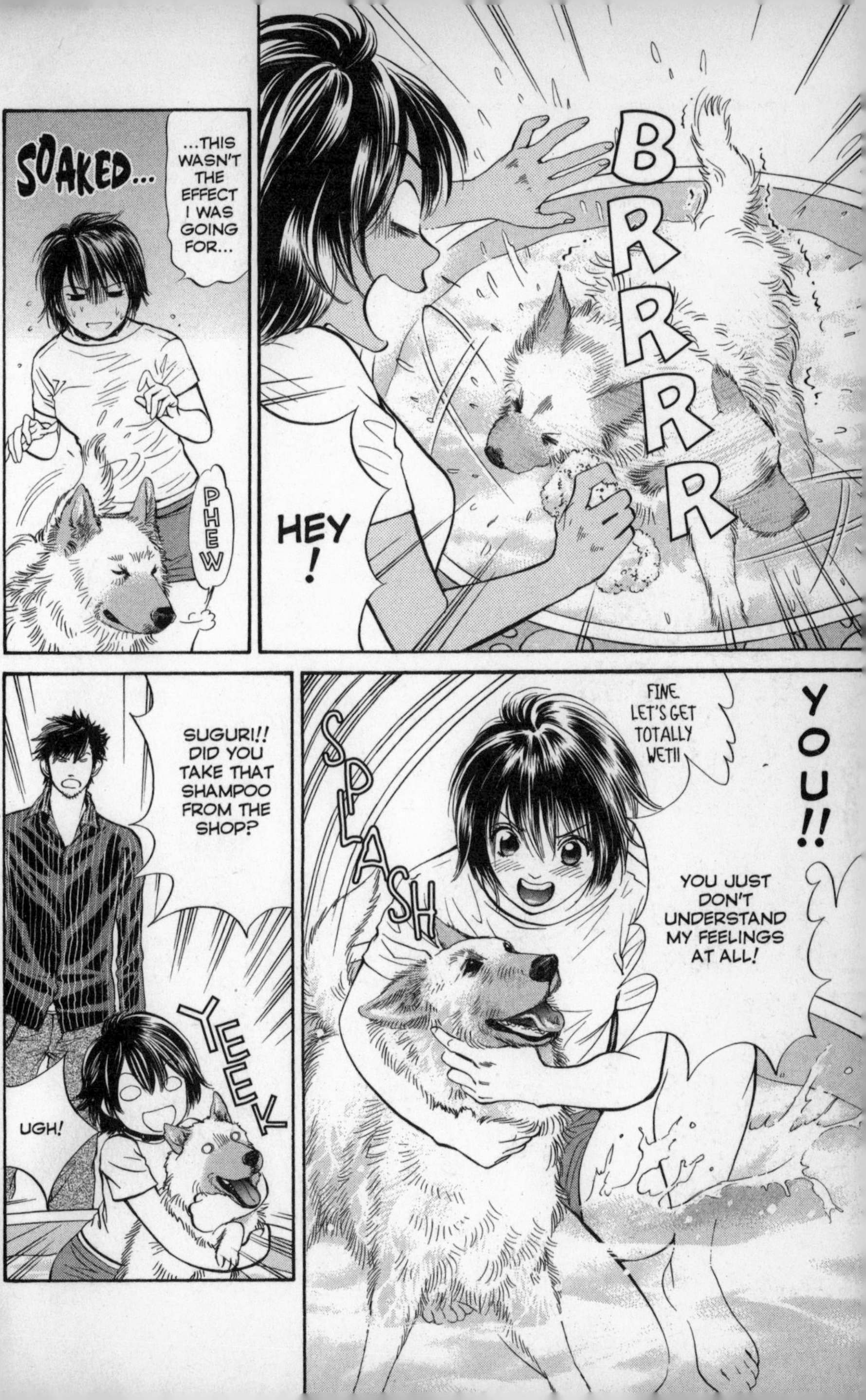
BRRRR
HEY!
SOAKED...
...THIS WASN'T THE EFFECT I WAS GOING FOR...
PHEW
YOU!!
FINE LET'S GET TOTALLY WET!!
SPLASH
YOU JUST DON'T UNDERSTAND MY FEELINGS AT ALL!
SUGURI!! DID YOU TAKE THAT SHAMPOO FROM THE SHOP?
YEEEK
UGH!

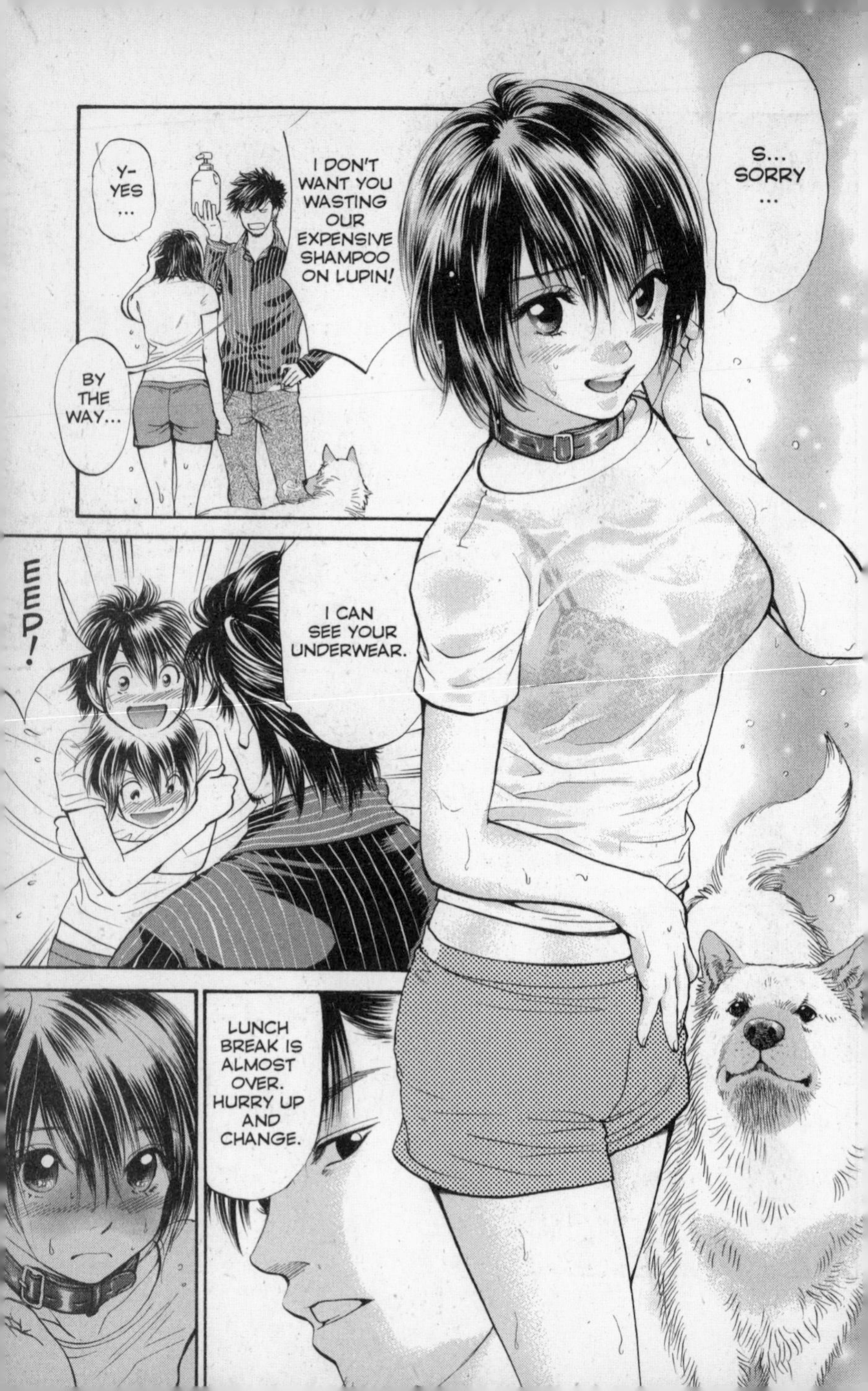
S... SORRY...
I DON'T WANT YOU WASTING OUR EXPENSIVE SHAMPOO ON LUPIN!
Y-YES...
BY THE WAY...
I CAN SEE YOUR UNDERWEAR.
EEP!
LUNCH BREAK IS ALMOST OVER. HURRY UP AND CHANGE.

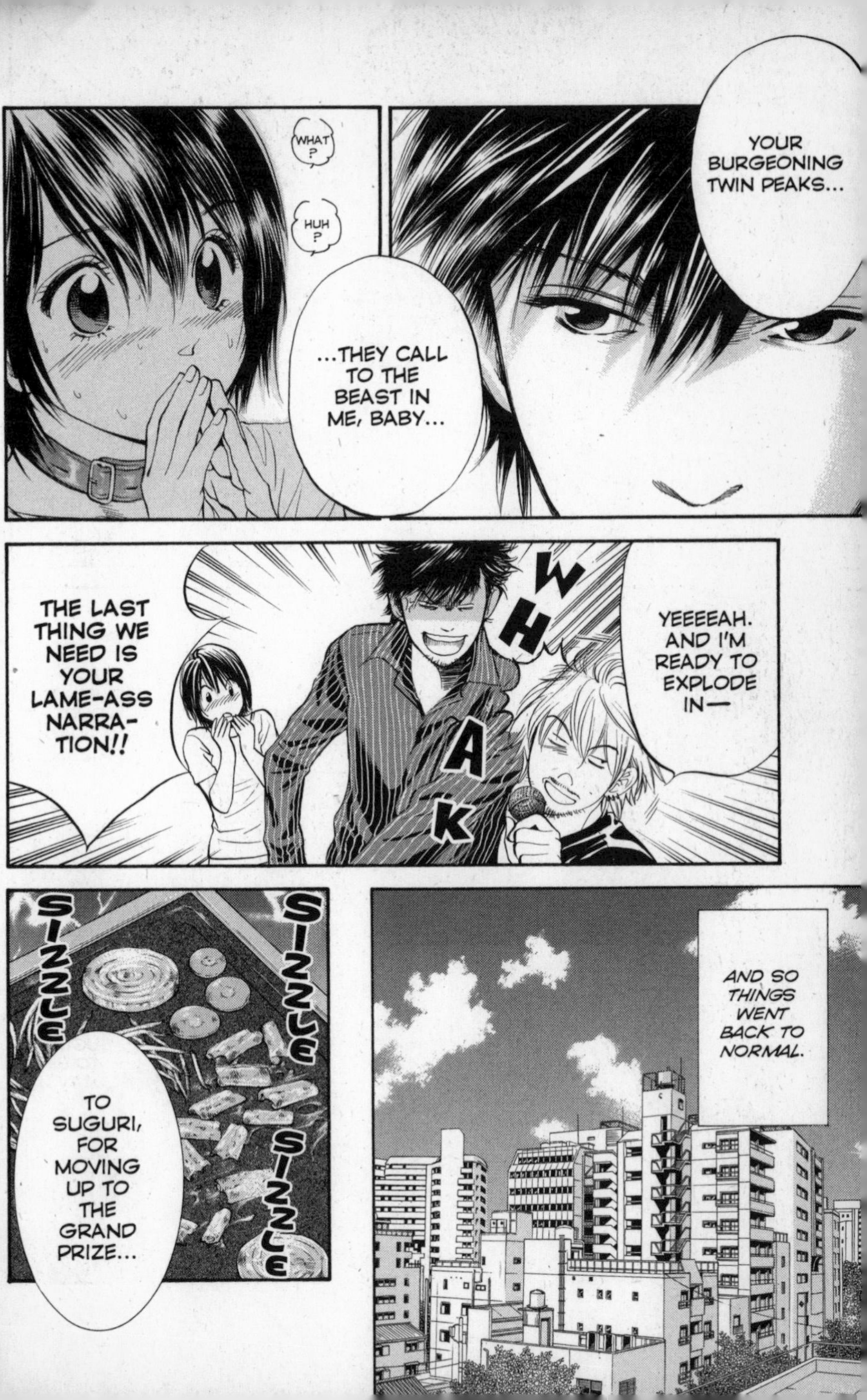
YOUR BURGEONING TWIN PEAKS...
...THEY CALL TO THE BEAST IN ME, BABY...
WHAT?
HUH?
YEEEEAH. AND I'M READY TO EXPLODE IN—
WHAK
THE LAST THING WE NEED IS YOUR LAME-ASS NARRATION!!
AND SO THINGS WENT BACK TO NORMAL.
SIZZLE
SIZZLE
TO SUGURI, FOR MOVING UP TO THE GRAND PRIZE...
SIZZLE

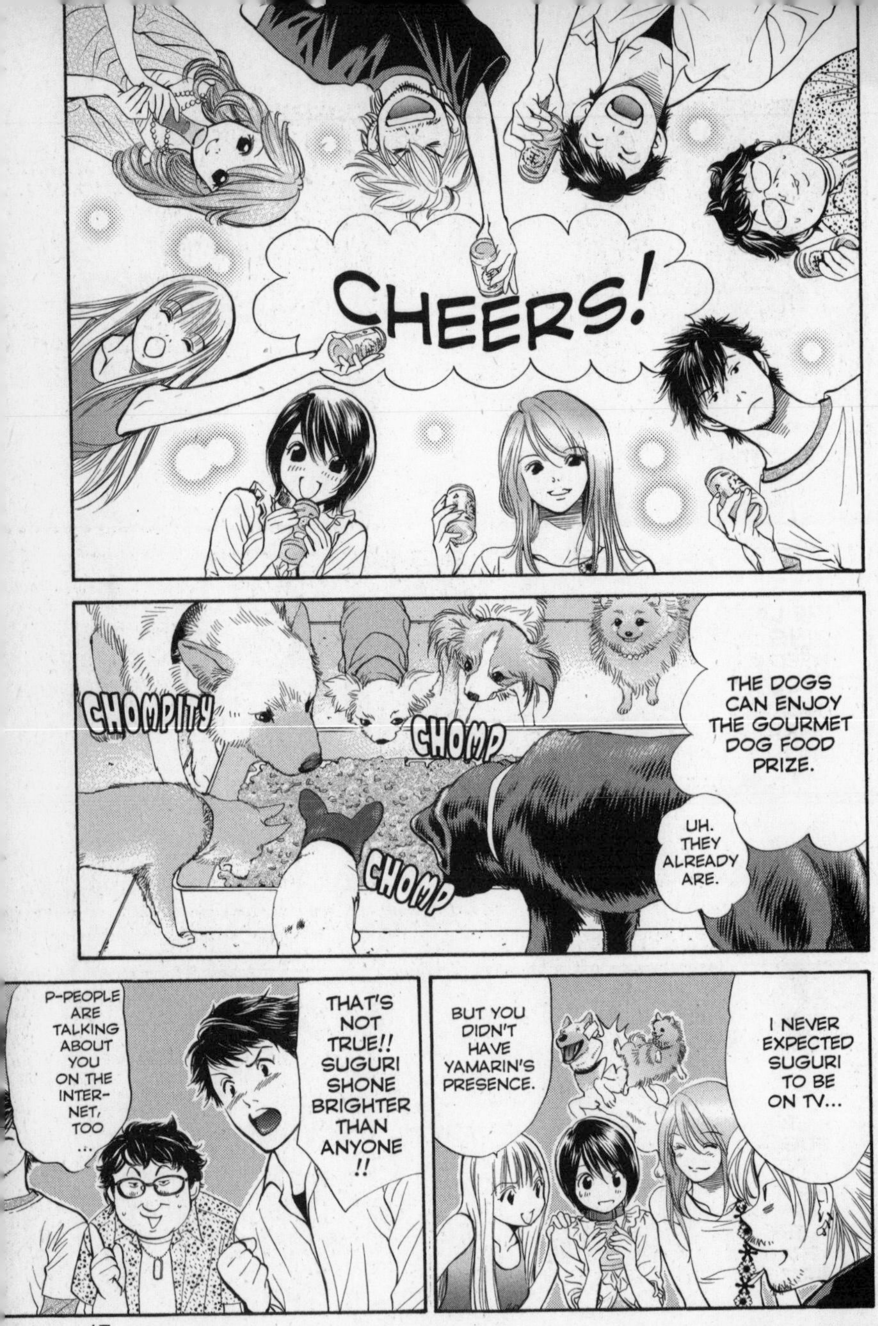
CHEERS!
THE DOGS CAN ENJOY THE GOURMET DOG FOOD PRIZE.
UH. THEY ALREADY ARE.
CHOMP
CHOMPITY
CHOMP
I NEVER EXPECTED SUGURI TO BE ON TV...
BUT YOU DIDN'T HAVE YAMARIN'S PRESENCE.
THAT'S NOT TRUE!! SUGURI SHONE BRIGHTER THAN ANYONE!!
P-PEOPLE ARE TALKING ABOUT YOU ON THE INTERNET, TOO...

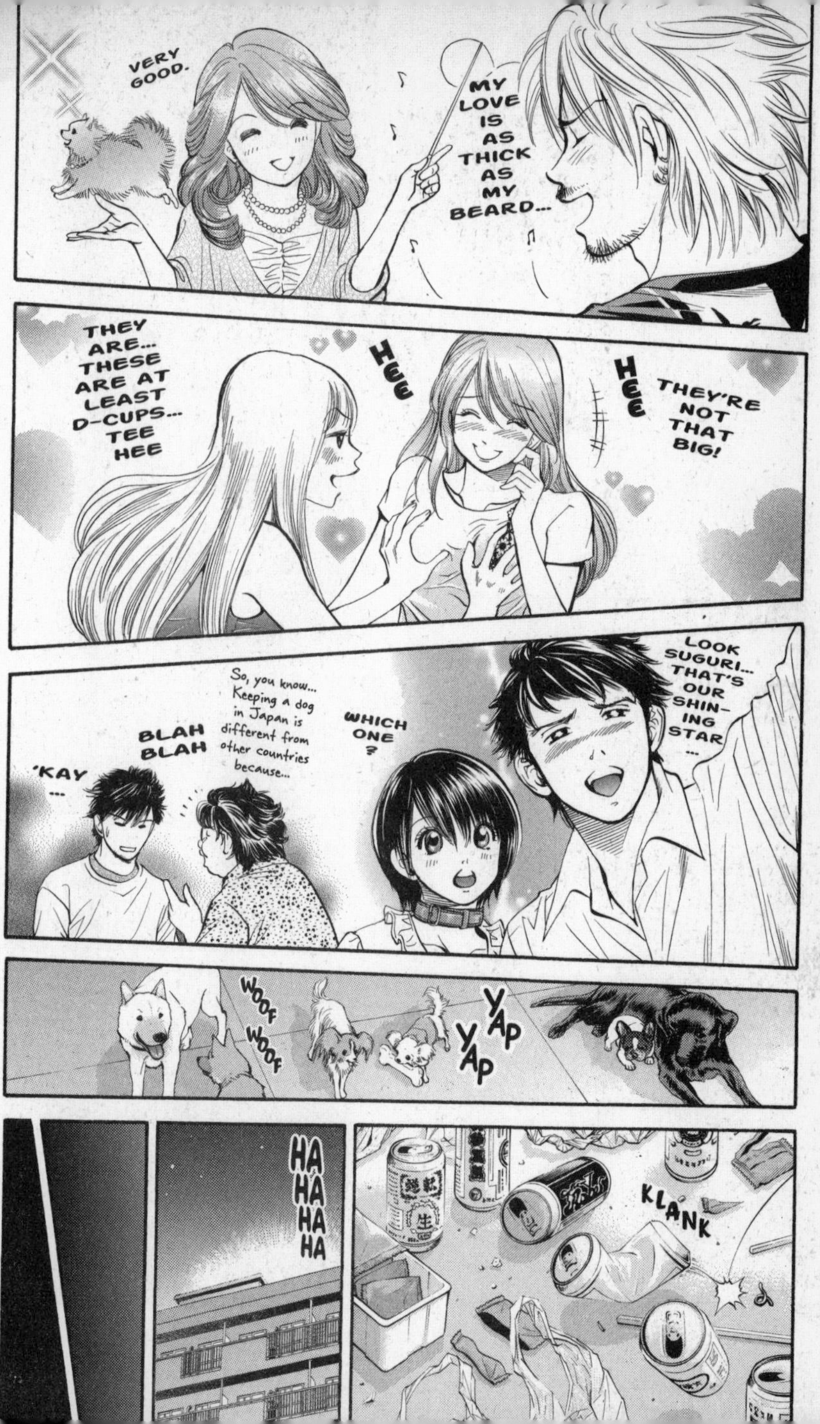
MY LOVE IS AS THICK AS MY BEARD...
VERY GOOD.
THEY'RE NOT THAT BIG!
HEE HEE
THEY ARE... THESE ARE AT LEAST D-CUPS... TEE HEE
LOOK SUGURI... THAT'S OUR SHINING STAR...
WHICH ONE?
So, you know... Keeping a dog in Japan is different from other countries because...
BLAH BLAH
'KAY...
YAP YAP
WOOF WOOF
KLANK
HA HA HA HA HA

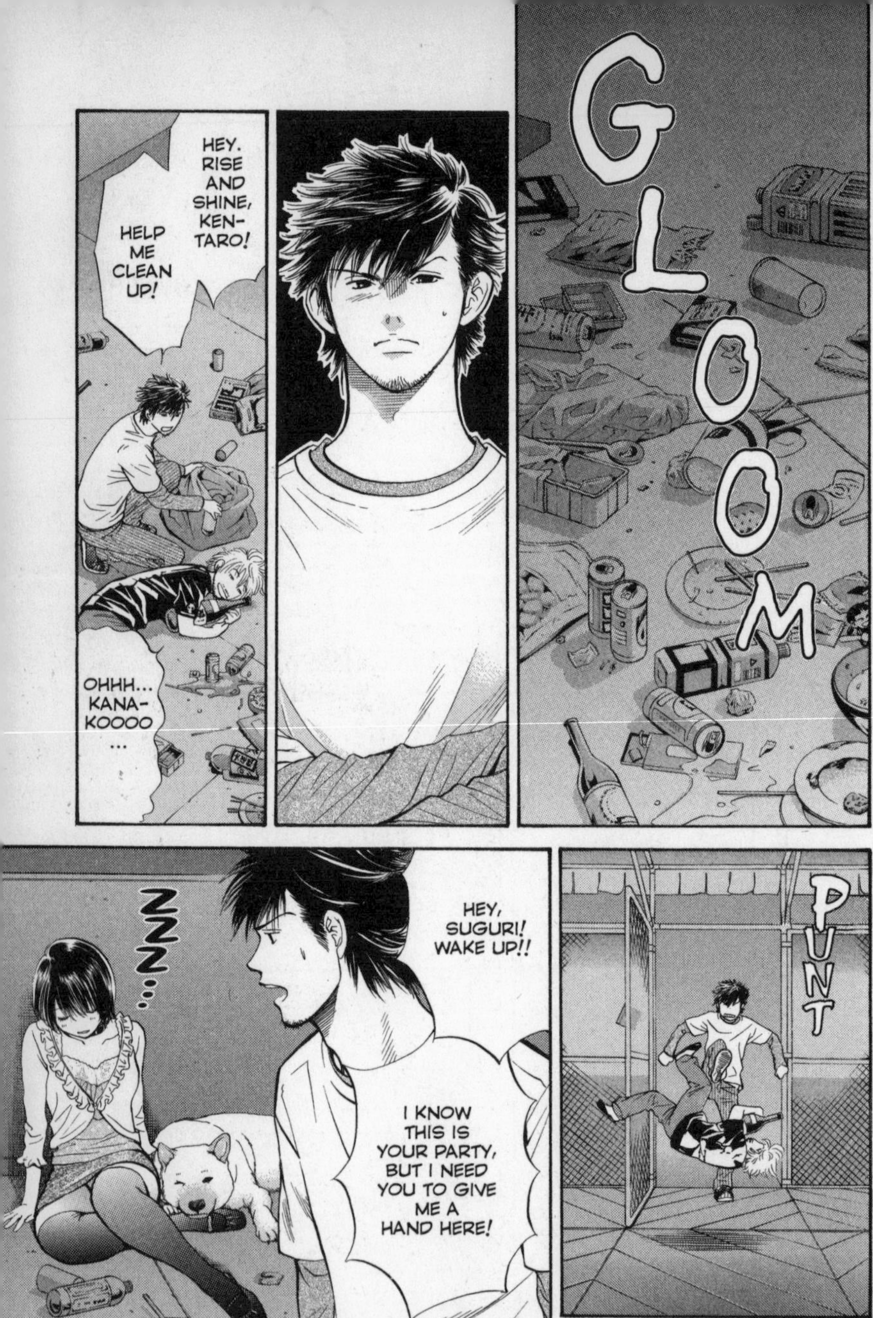
GLOOM
HEY. RISE AND SHINE, KEN-TARO!
HELP ME CLEAN UP!
OHHH... KANA-KOOOO...
PUNT
HEY, SUGURI! WAKE UP!!
ZZZ...
I KNOW THIS IS YOUR PARTY, BUT I NEED YOU TO GIVE ME A HAND HERE!

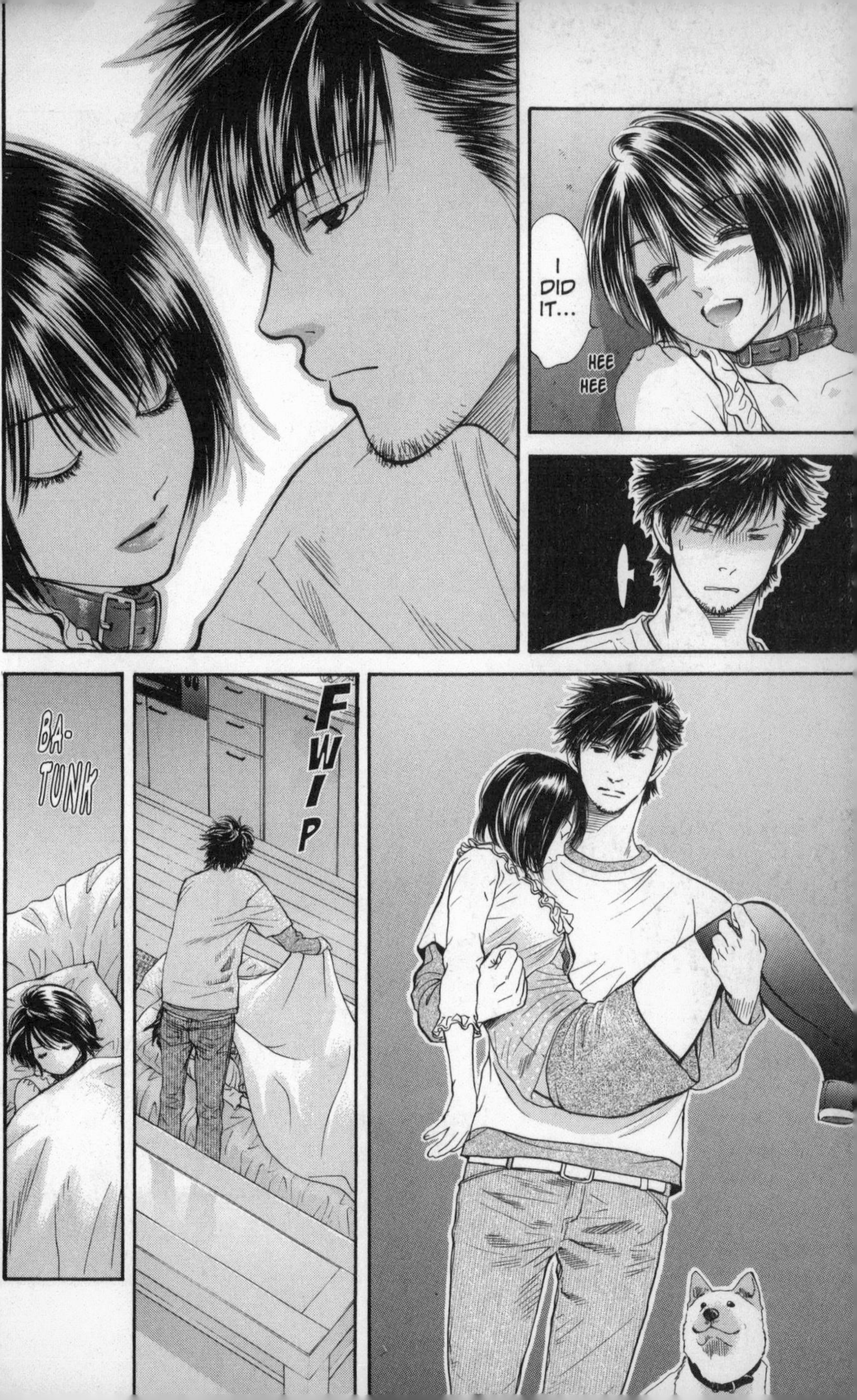
I DID IT...
HEE HEE
FWIP
BA-TUNK

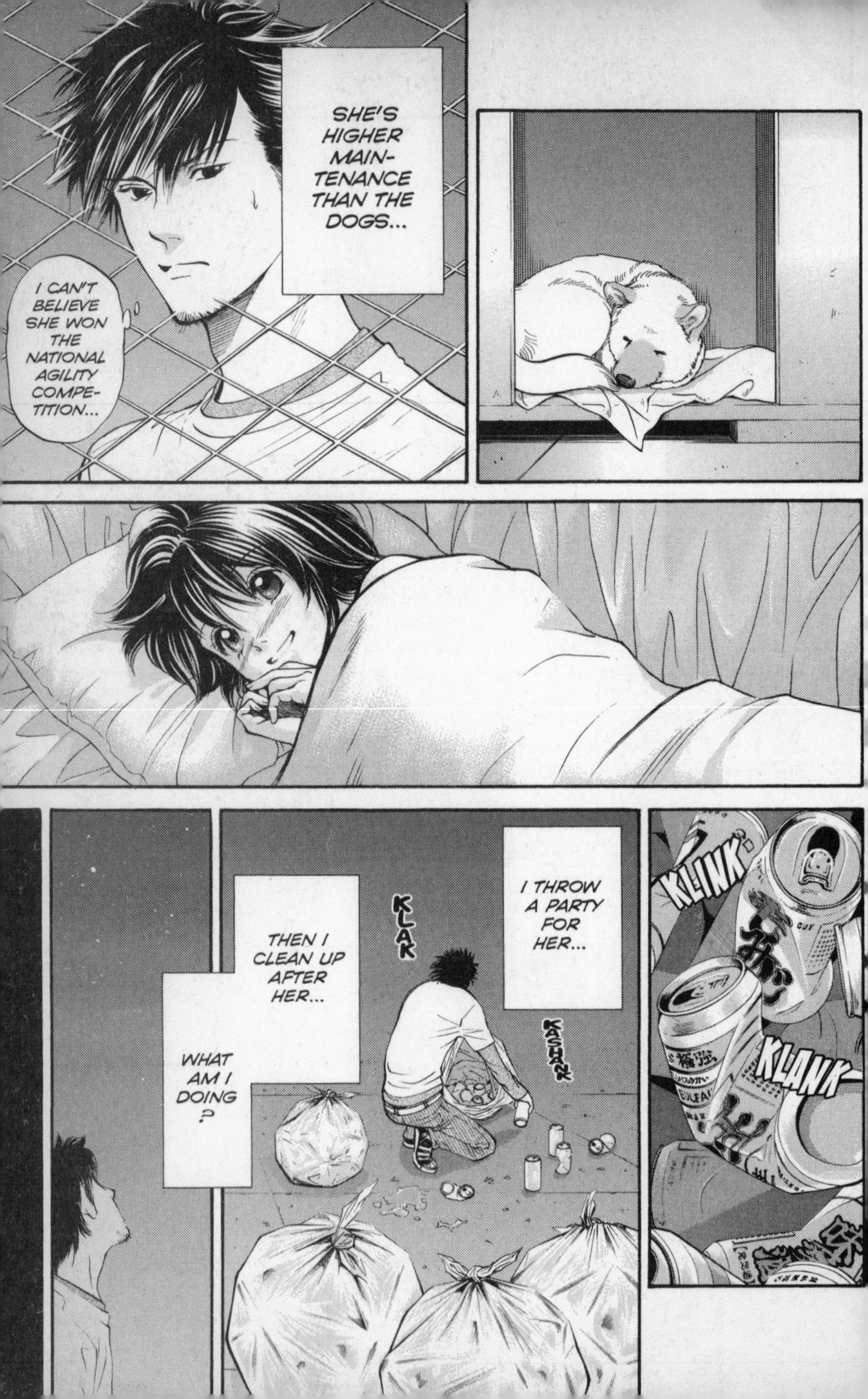
SHE'S HIGHER MAIN-TENANCE THAN THE DOGS...
I CAN'T BELIEVE SHE WON THE NATIONAL AGILITY COMPE-TITION...
KLINK
KLANK
I THROW A PARTY FOR HER...
KLAK
THEN I CLEAN UP AFTER HER...
KASHANK
WHAT AM I DOING?

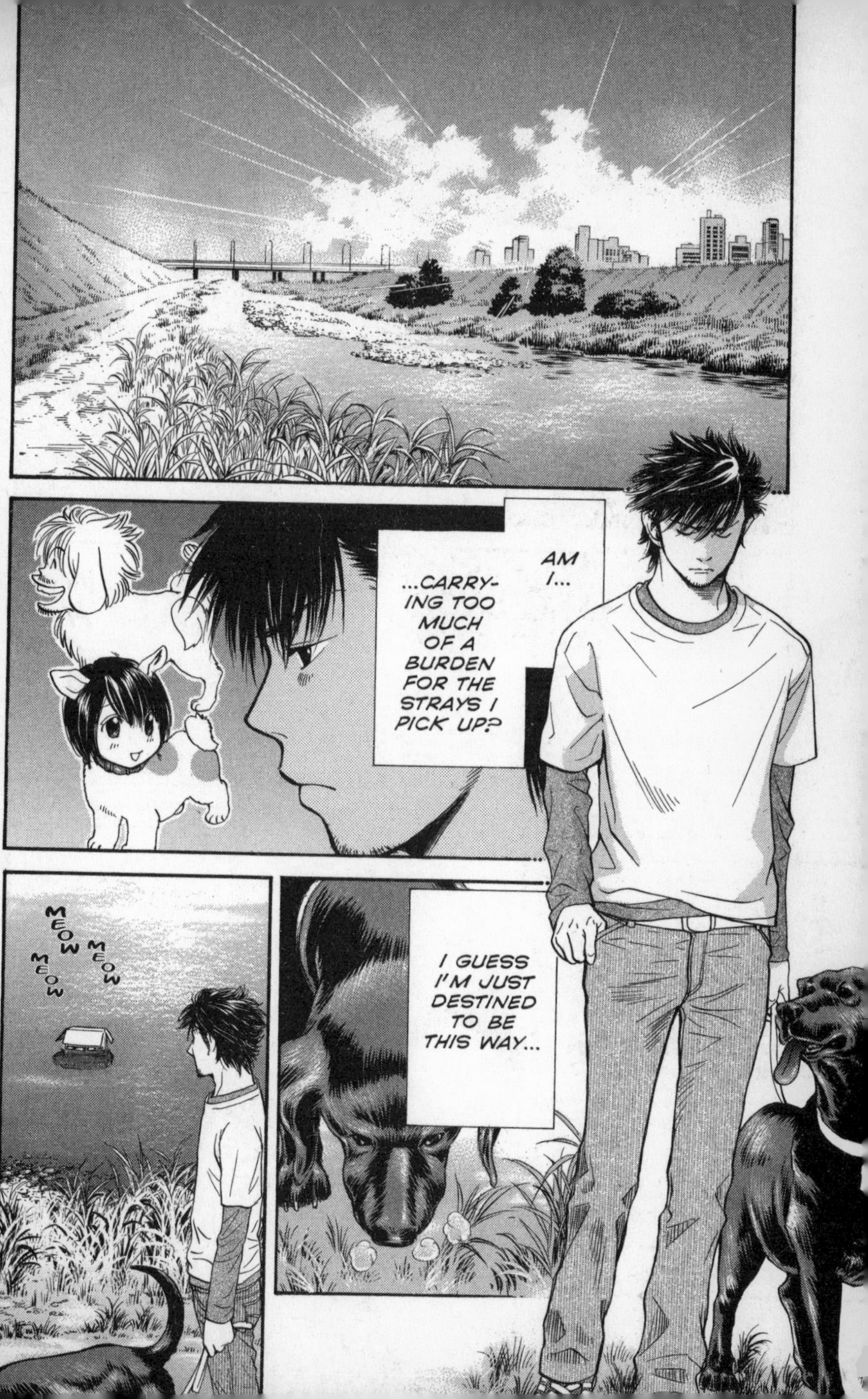
AM I...
...CARRY-ING TOO MUCH OF A BURDEN FOR THE STRAYS I PICK UP?
I GUESS I'M JUST DESTINED TO BE THIS WAY...
MEOW MEOW MEOW

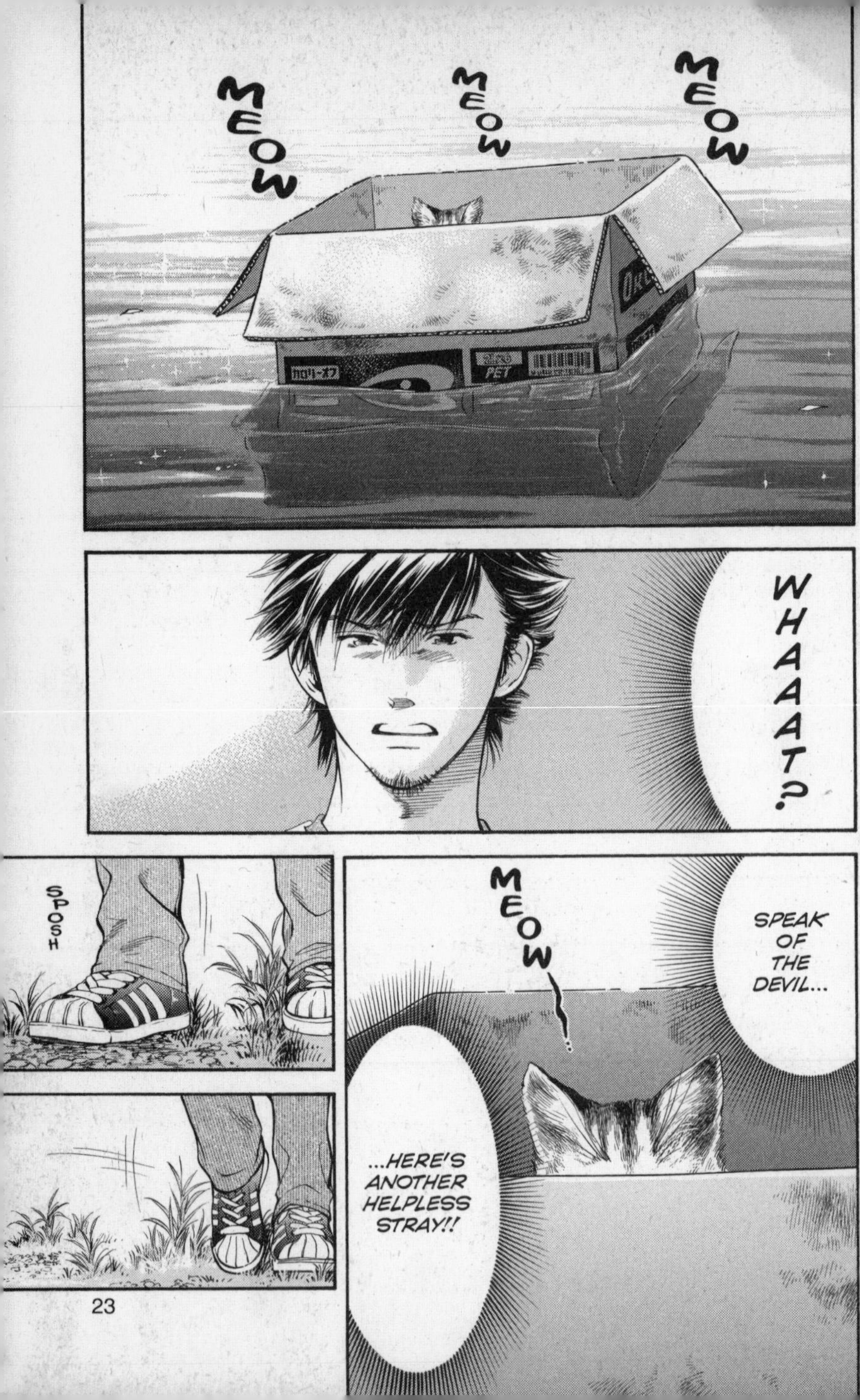
MEOW
MEOW
MEOW
WHAAAT?
MEOW
SPEAK OF THE DEVIL...
...HERE'S ANOTHER HELPLESS STRAY!!
SPOSH

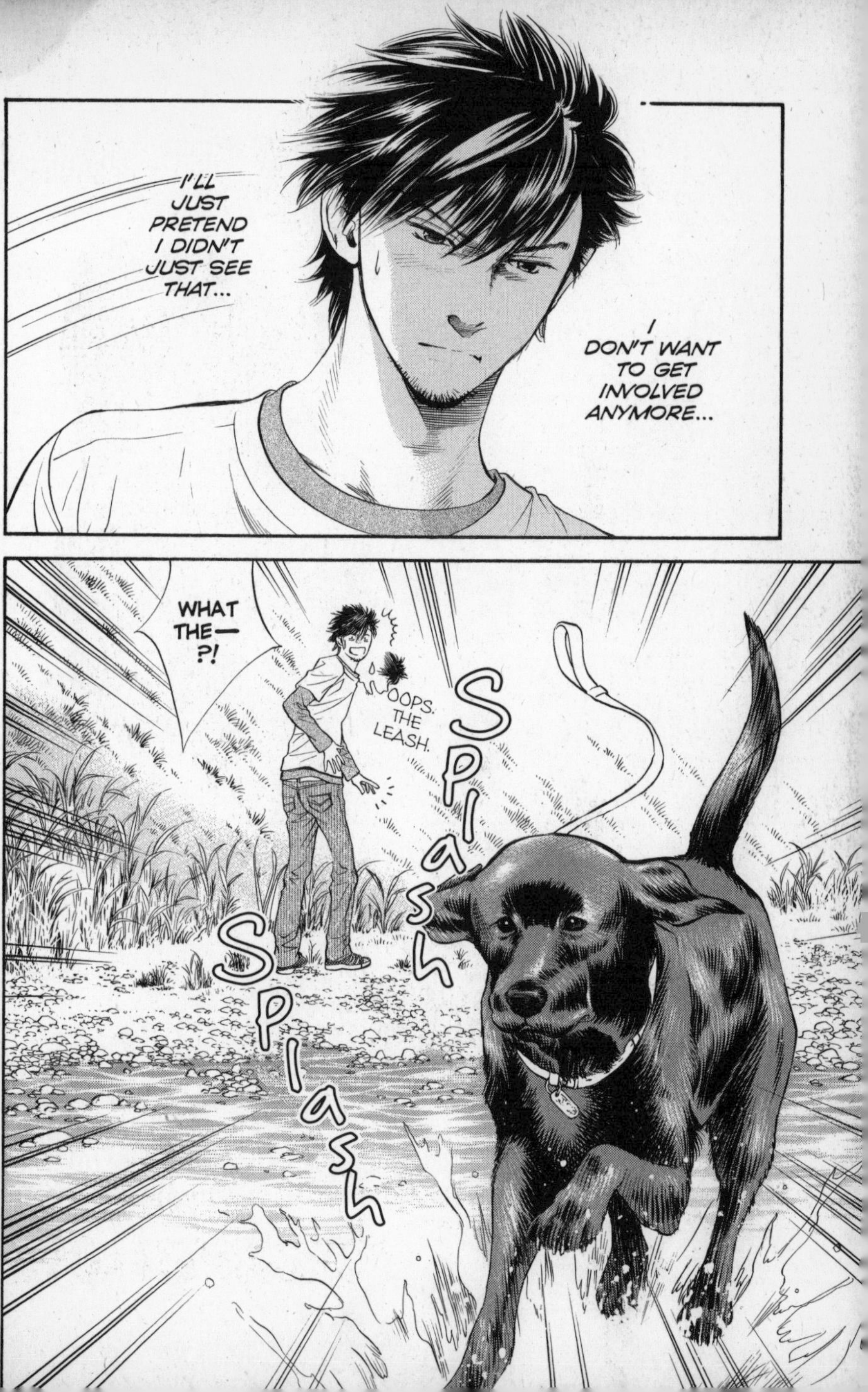
I DON'T WANT TO GET INVOLVED ANYMORE...
I'LL JUST PRETEND I DIDN'T JUST SEE THAT...
Splash
Splash
OOPS. THE LEASH.
WHAT THE—?!

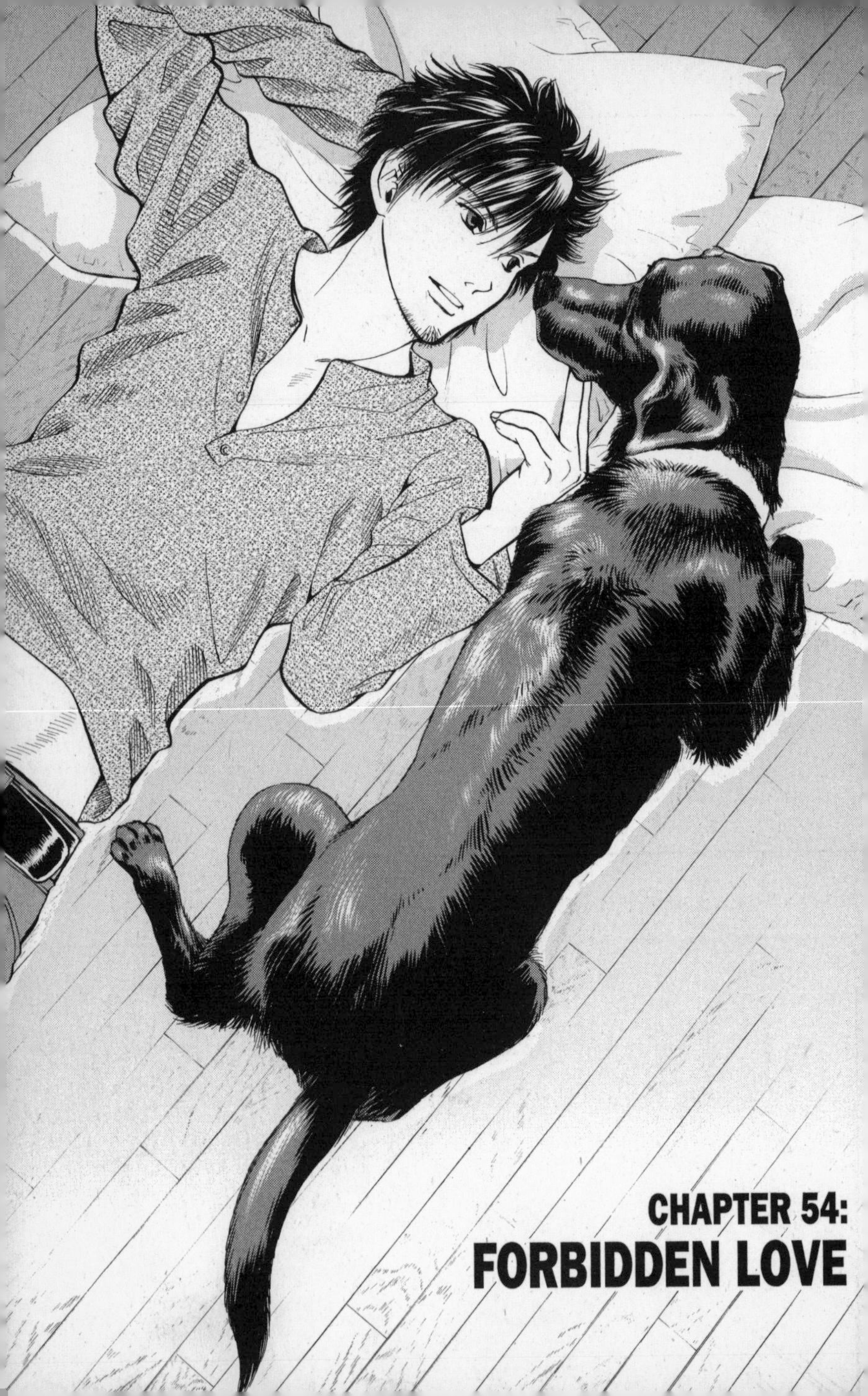

CHAPTER 54:
FORBIDDEN LOVE

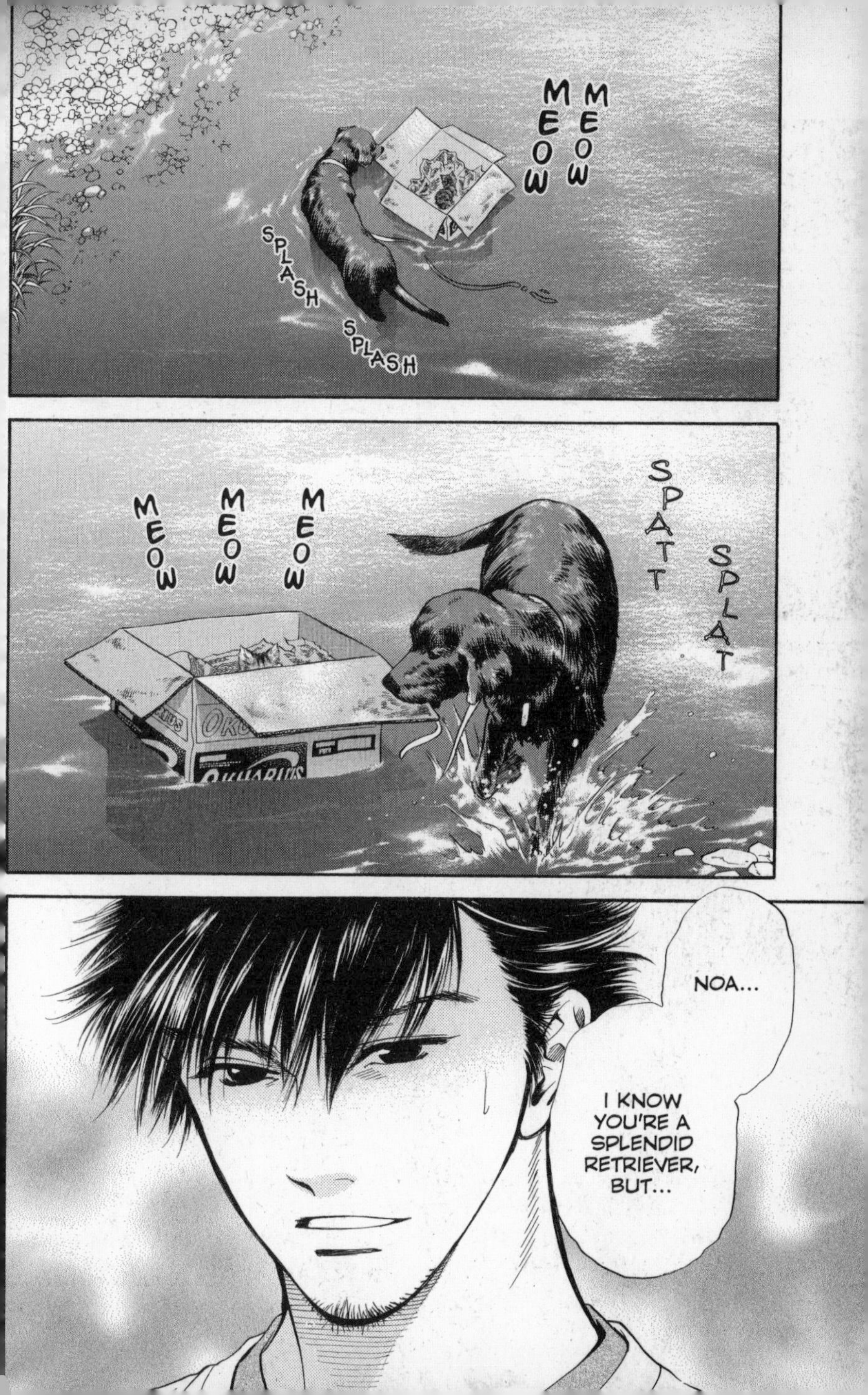
MEOW MEOW
MEOW MEOW
SPLASH
SPLASH
SPATT
SPLAT
MEOW
MEOW
MEOW
NOA...
I KNOW YOU'RE A SPLENDID RETRIEVER, BUT...

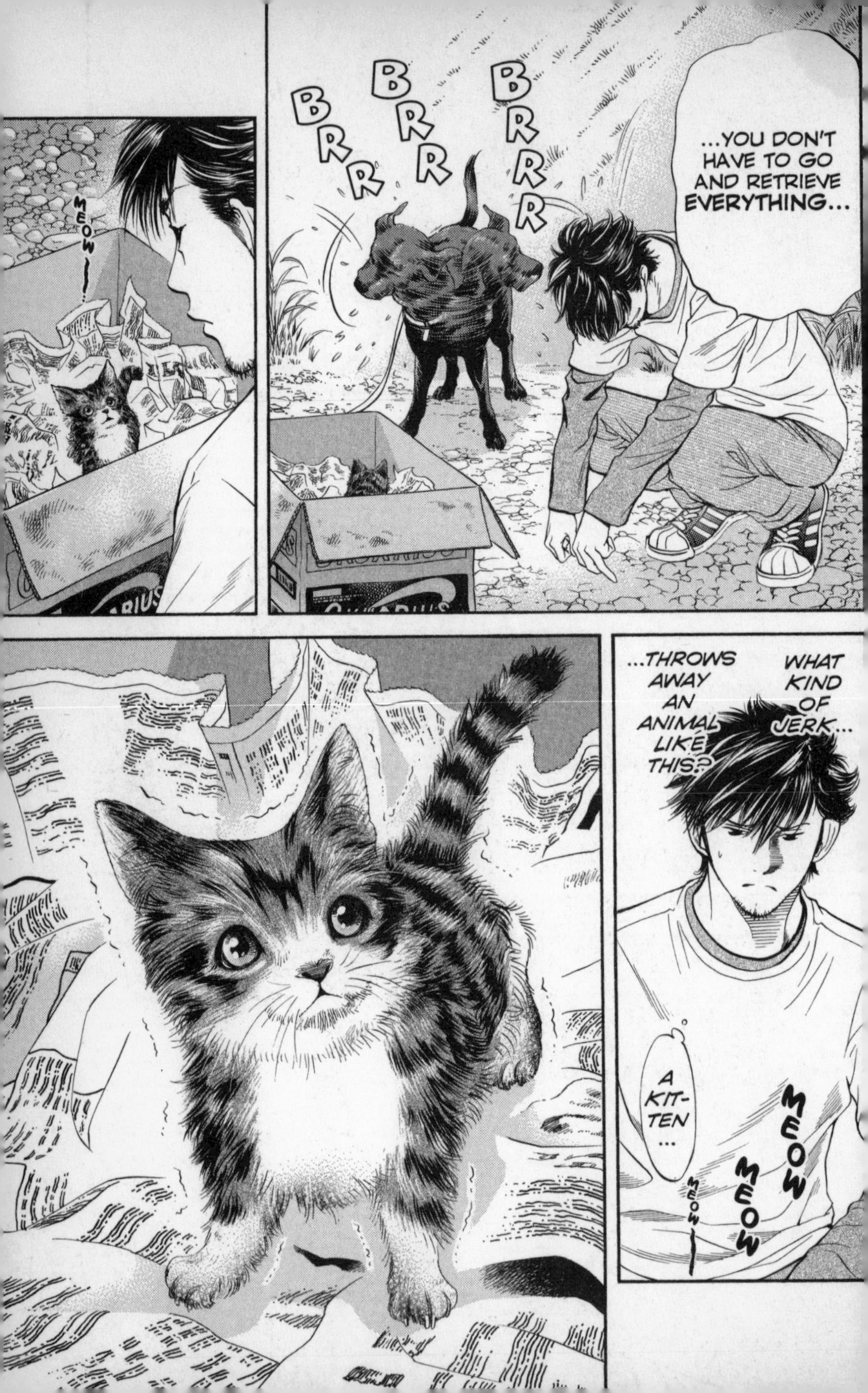
...YOU DON'T HAVE TO GO AND RETRIEVE EVERYTHING...
BRRR
BRRR
BRRR
MEOW!
WHAT KIND OF JERK...
...THROWS AWAY AN ANIMAL LIKE THIS?
A KIT-TEN...
MEOW
MEOW
MEOW!

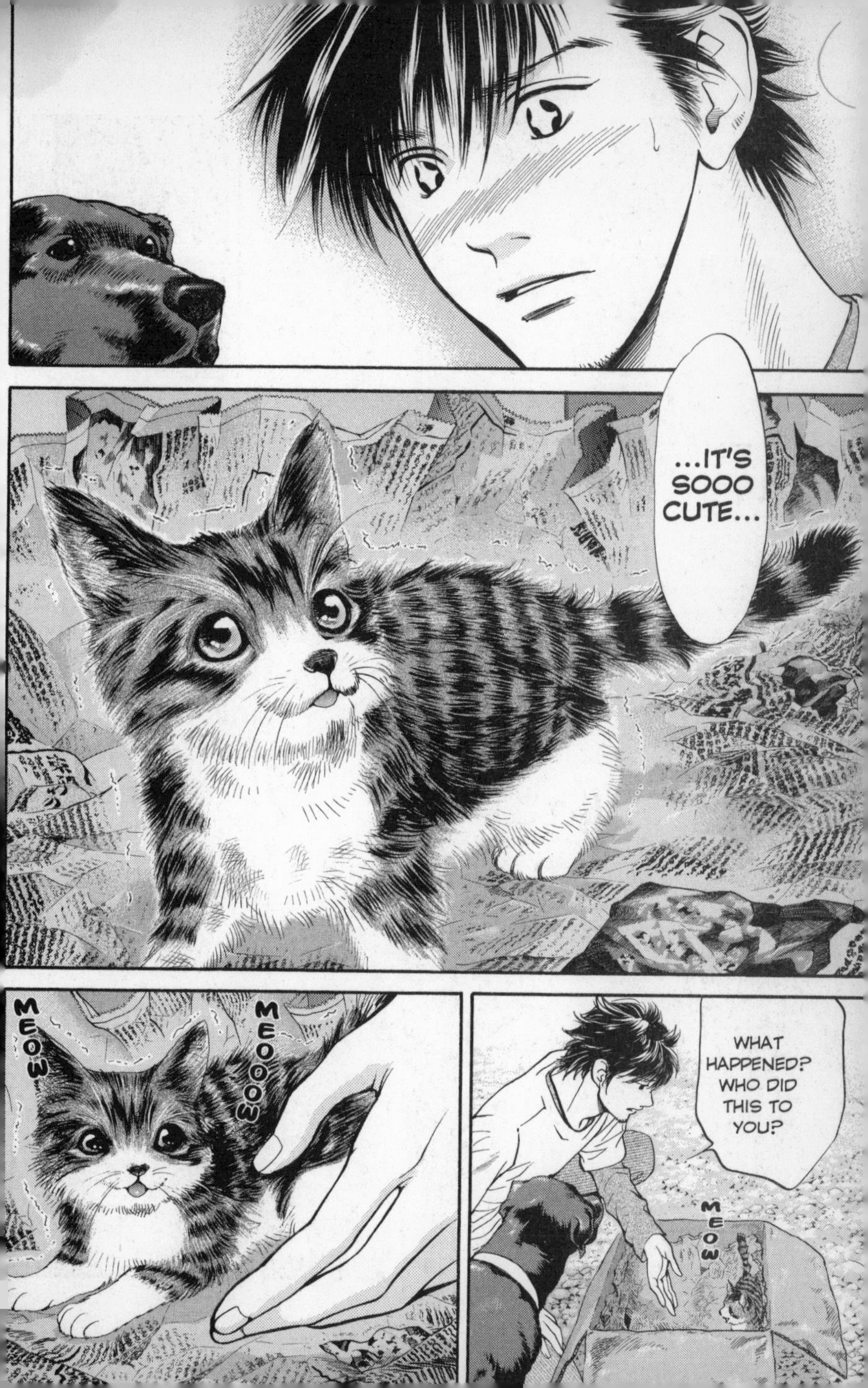
...IT'S SOOO CUTE...
MEOOOOW
MEOW
WHAT HAPPENED? WHO DID THIS TO YOU?
MEOW

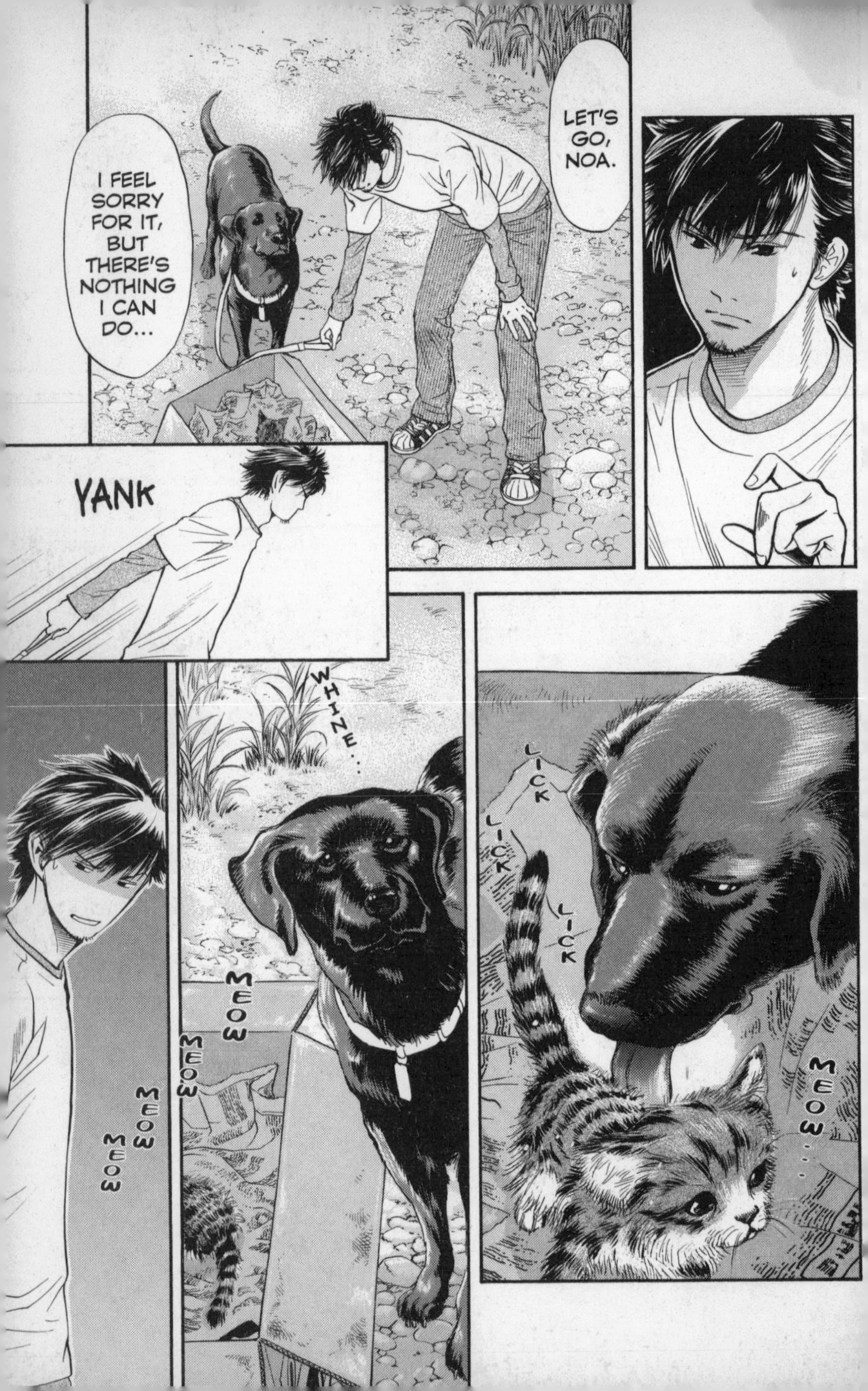
LET'S GO, NOA.
I FEEL SORRY FOR IT, BUT THERE'S NOTHING I CAN DO...
YANK
LICK
LICK
LICK
MEOW...
WHINE...
MEOW
MEOW
MEOW
MEOW

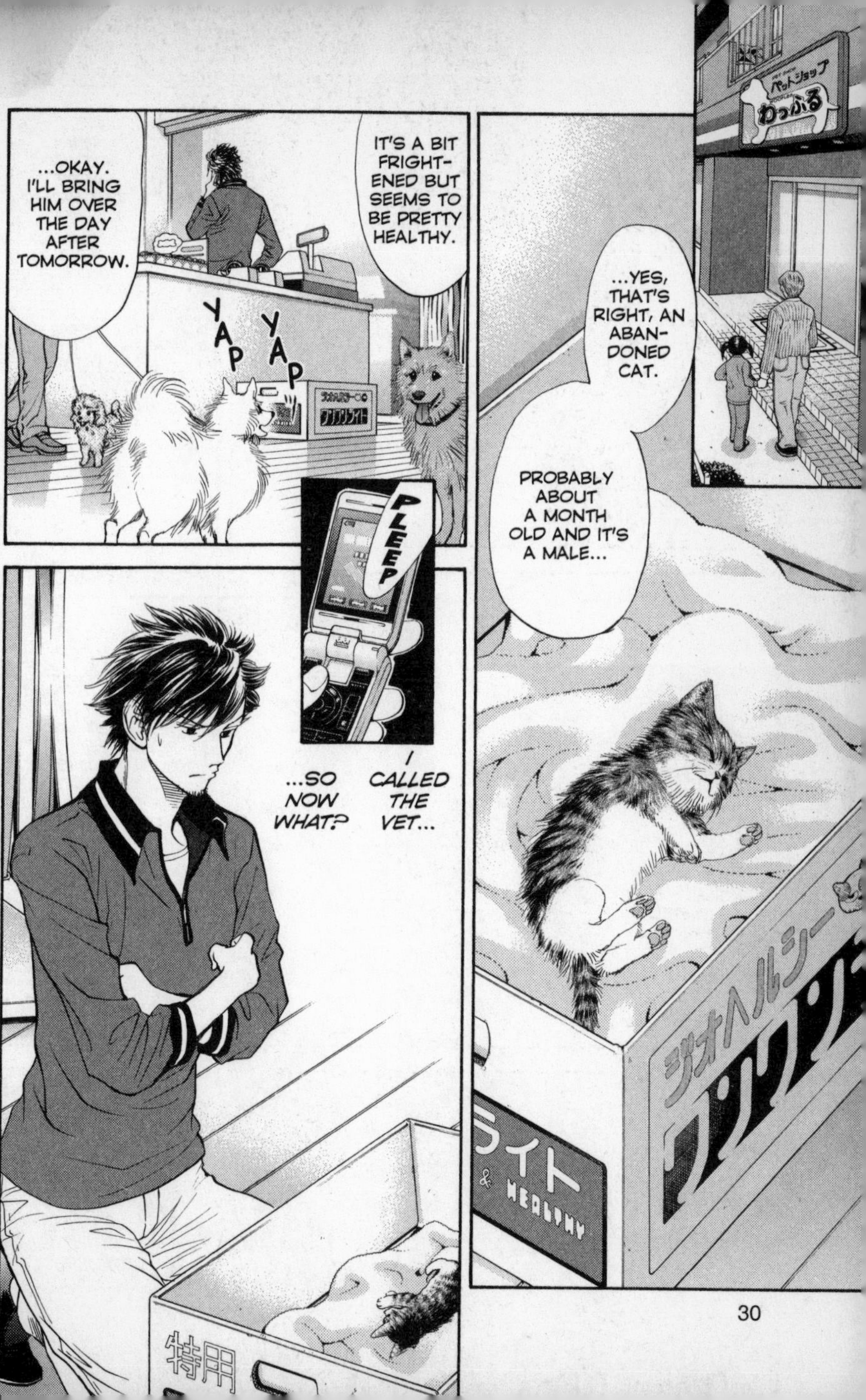
ペットショップ
わっぷる
...YES, THAT'S RIGHT, AN ABAN-DONED CAT.
PROBABLY ABOUT A MONTH OLD AND IT'S A MALE...
ライト
& HEALTHY
IT'S A BIT FRIGHT-ENED BUT SEEMS TO BE PRETTY HEALTHY.
YAP YAP
...OKAY. I'LL BRING HIM OVER THE DAY AFTER TOMORROW.
PLEEEP
I CALLED THE VET...
...SO NOW WHAT?
特用

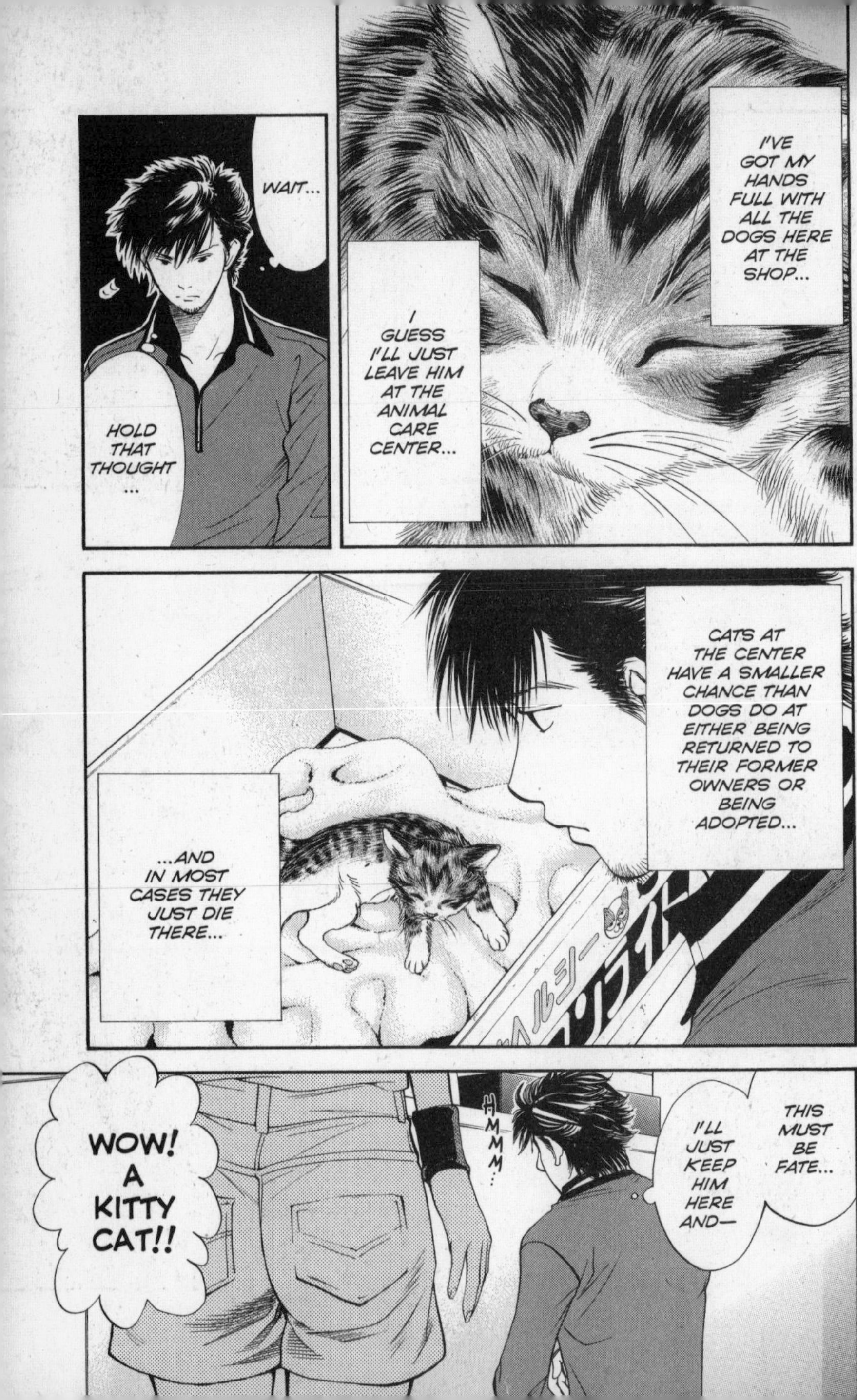
I'VE GOT MY HANDS FULL WITH ALL THE DOGS HERE AT THE SHOP...
I GUESS I'LL JUST LEAVE HIM AT THE ANIMAL CARE CENTER...
WAIT...
HOLD THAT THOUGHT...
CATS AT THE CENTER HAVE A SMALLER CHANCE THAN DOGS DO AT EITHER BEING RETURNED TO THEIR FORMER OWNERS OR BEING ADOPTED...
...AND IN MOST CASES THEY JUST DIE THERE...
THIS MUST BE FATE...
I'LL JUST KEEP HIM HERE AND—
HMMM...
WOW! A KITTY CAT!!

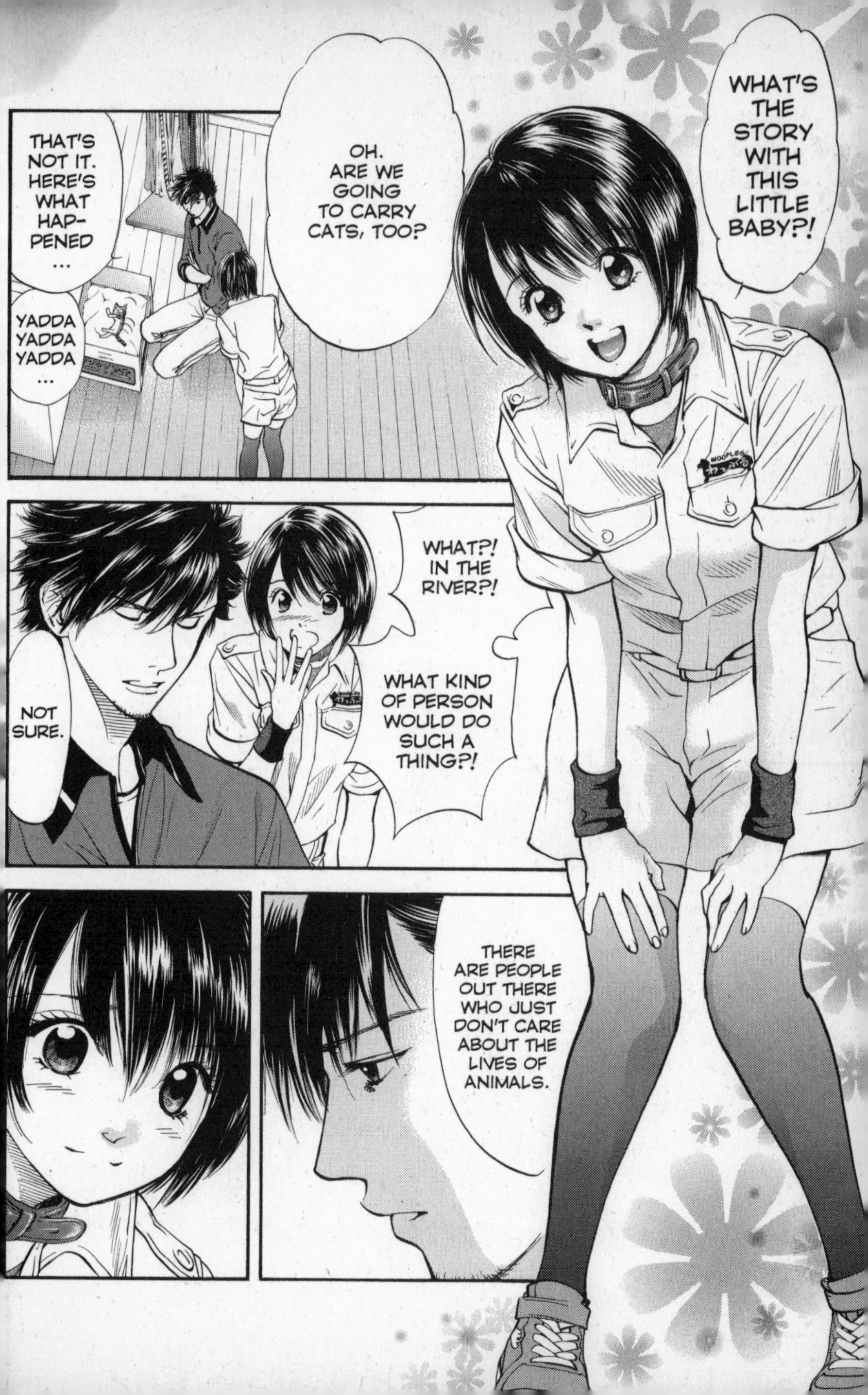

WHAT'S THE STORY WITH THIS LITTLE BABY?!
OH. ARE WE GOING TO CARRY CATS, TOO?
THAT'S NOT IT. HERE'S WHAT HAP-PENED ...
YADDA YADDA YADDA ...
WHAT?! IN THE RIVER?!
WHAT KIND OF PERSON WOULD DO SUCH A THING?!
NOT SURE.
THERE ARE PEOPLE OUT THERE WHO JUST DON'T CARE ABOUT THE LIVES OF ANIMALS.

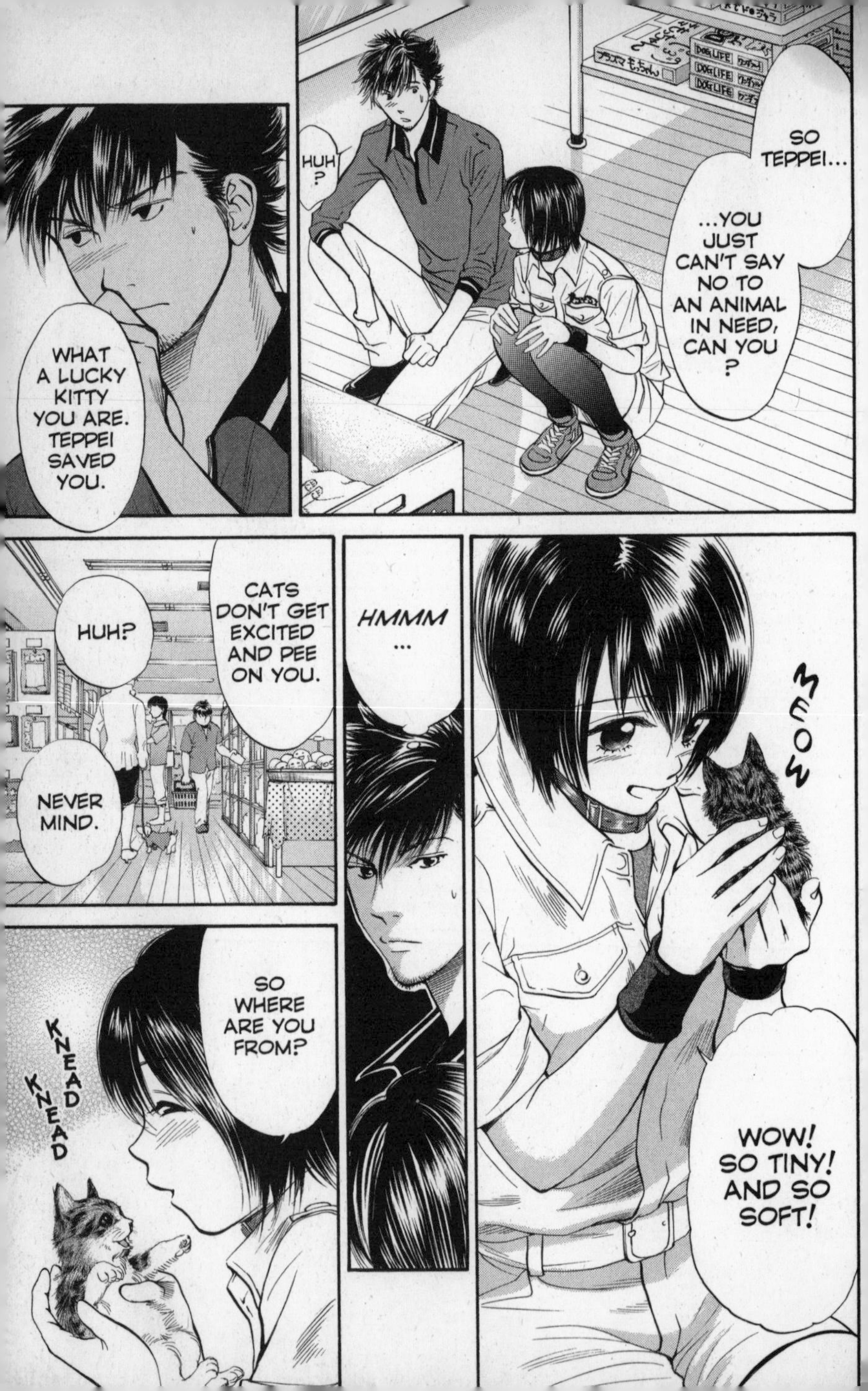
SO TEPPEI...
...YOU JUST CAN'T SAY NO TO AN ANIMAL IN NEED, CAN YOU?
HUH?
WHAT A LUCKY KITTY YOU ARE. TEPPEI SAVED YOU.
MEOW
WOW! SO TINY! AND SO SOFT!
HMMM...
CATS DON'T GET EXCITED AND PEE ON YOU.
HUH?
NEVER MIND.
SO WHERE ARE YOU FROM?
KNEAD KNEAD

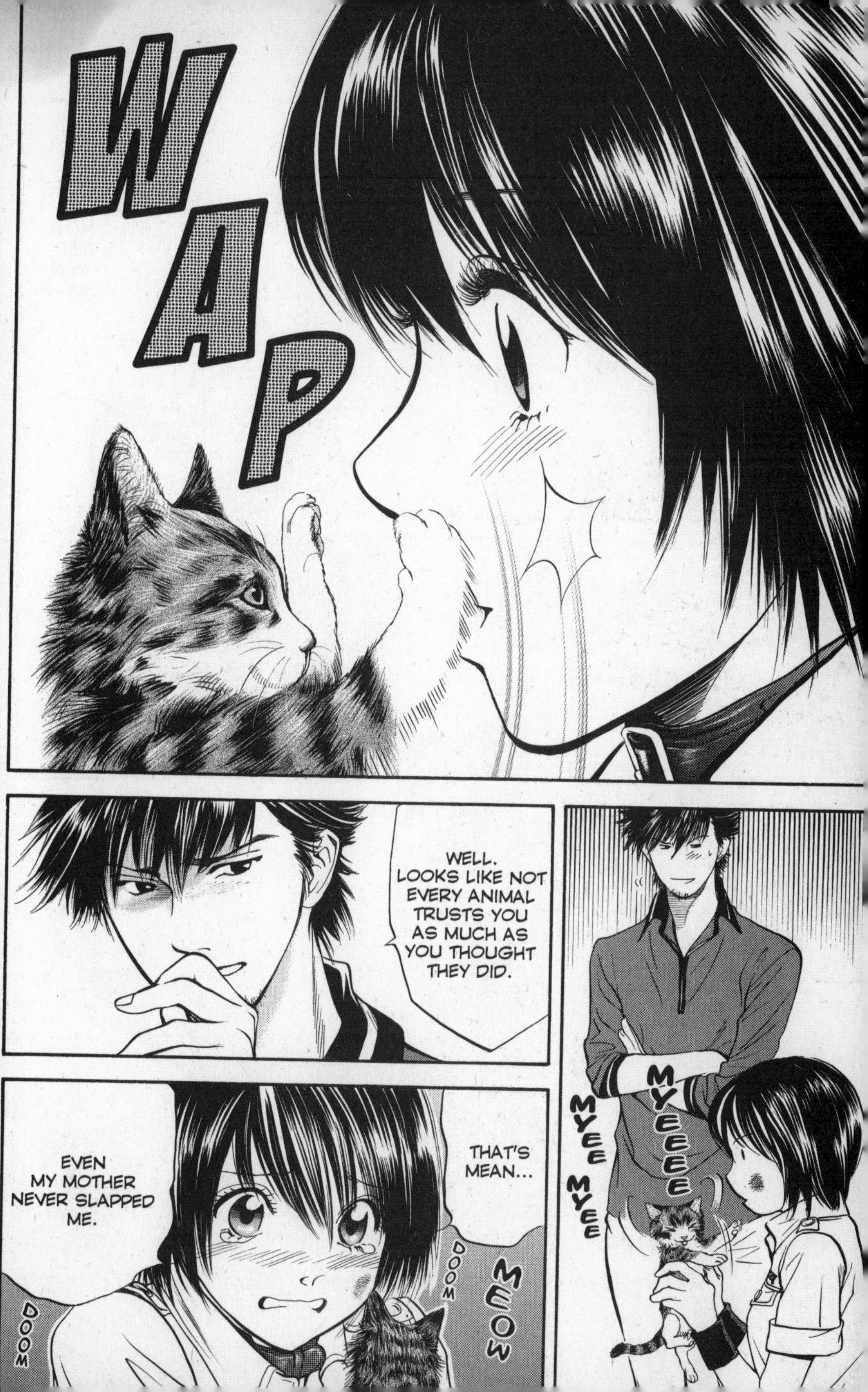
WAP
MYEEEE
MYEE MYEE
WELL. LOOKS LIKE NOT EVERY ANIMAL TRUSTS YOU AS MUCH AS YOU THOUGHT THEY DID.
THAT'S MEAN...
EVEN MY MOTHER NEVER SLAPPED ME.
MEOW
DOOM DOOM
DOOM

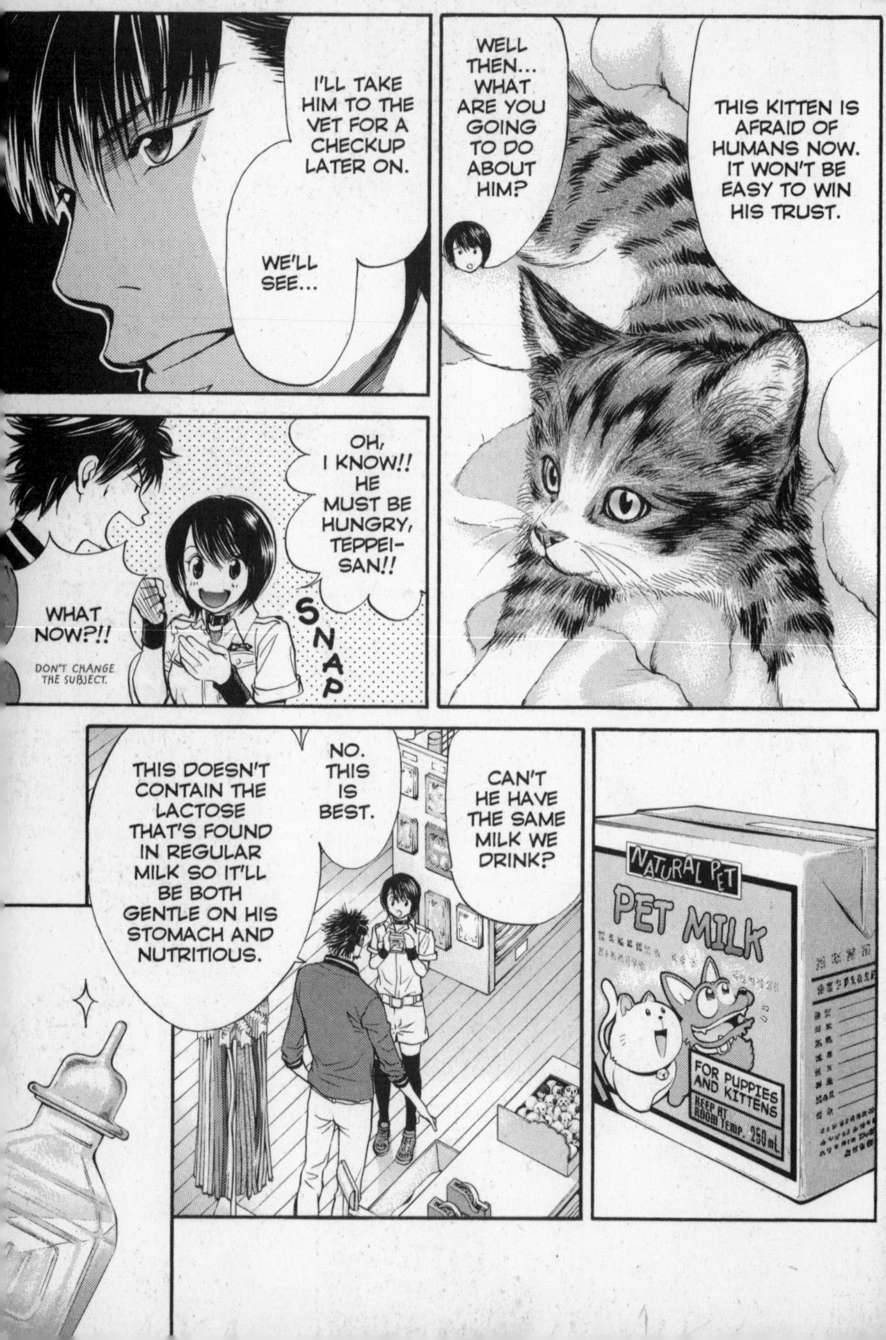
THIS KITTEN IS AFRAID OF HUMANS NOW. IT WON'T BE EASY TO WIN HIS TRUST.
WELL THEN... WHAT ARE YOU GOING TO DO ABOUT HIM?
I'LL TAKE HIM TO THE VET FOR A CHECKUP LATER ON.
WE'LL SEE...
OH, I KNOW!! HE MUST BE HUNGRY, TEPPEI-SAN!!
SNAP
WHAT NOW?!!
DON'T CHANGE THE SUBJECT.
NATURAL PET
PET MILK
FOR PUPPIES AND KITTENS
KEEP AT ROOM Temp. 250mL
CAN'T HE HAVE THE SAME MILK WE DRINK?
NO. THIS IS BEST.
THIS DOESN'T CONTAIN THE LACTOSE THAT'S FOUND IN REGULAR MILK SO IT'LL BE BOTH GENTLE ON HIS STOMACH AND NUTRITIOUS.

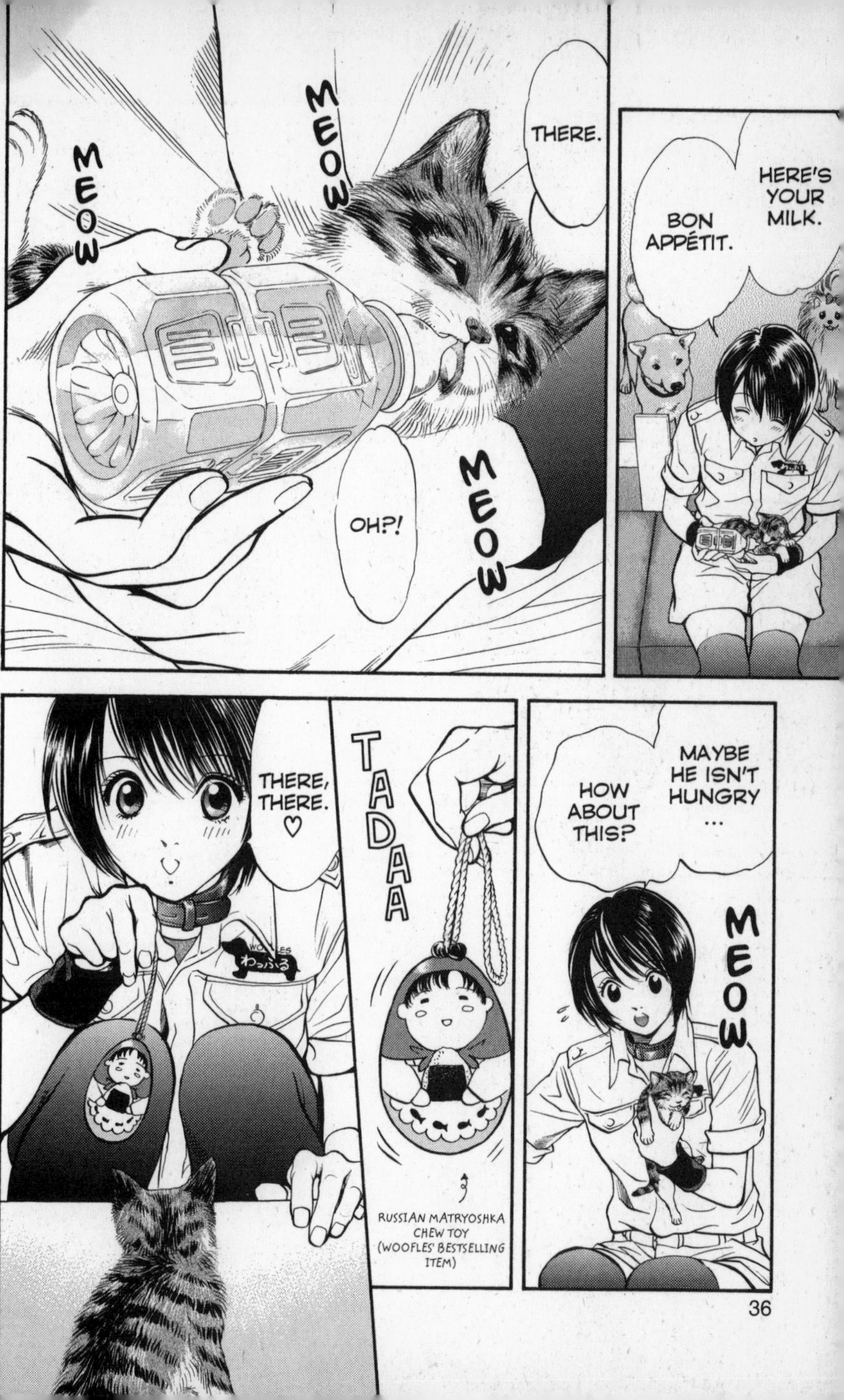
HERE'S YOUR MILK.
BON APPÉTIT.
THERE.
MEOW
MEOW
MEOW
OH?!
MAYBE HE ISN'T HUNGRY ...
HOW ABOUT THIS?
MEOW
TADAA
RUSSIAN MATRYOSHKA CHEW TOY (WOOFLES' BESTSELLING ITEM)
THERE, THERE. ♡
WOOFLES
わっふる

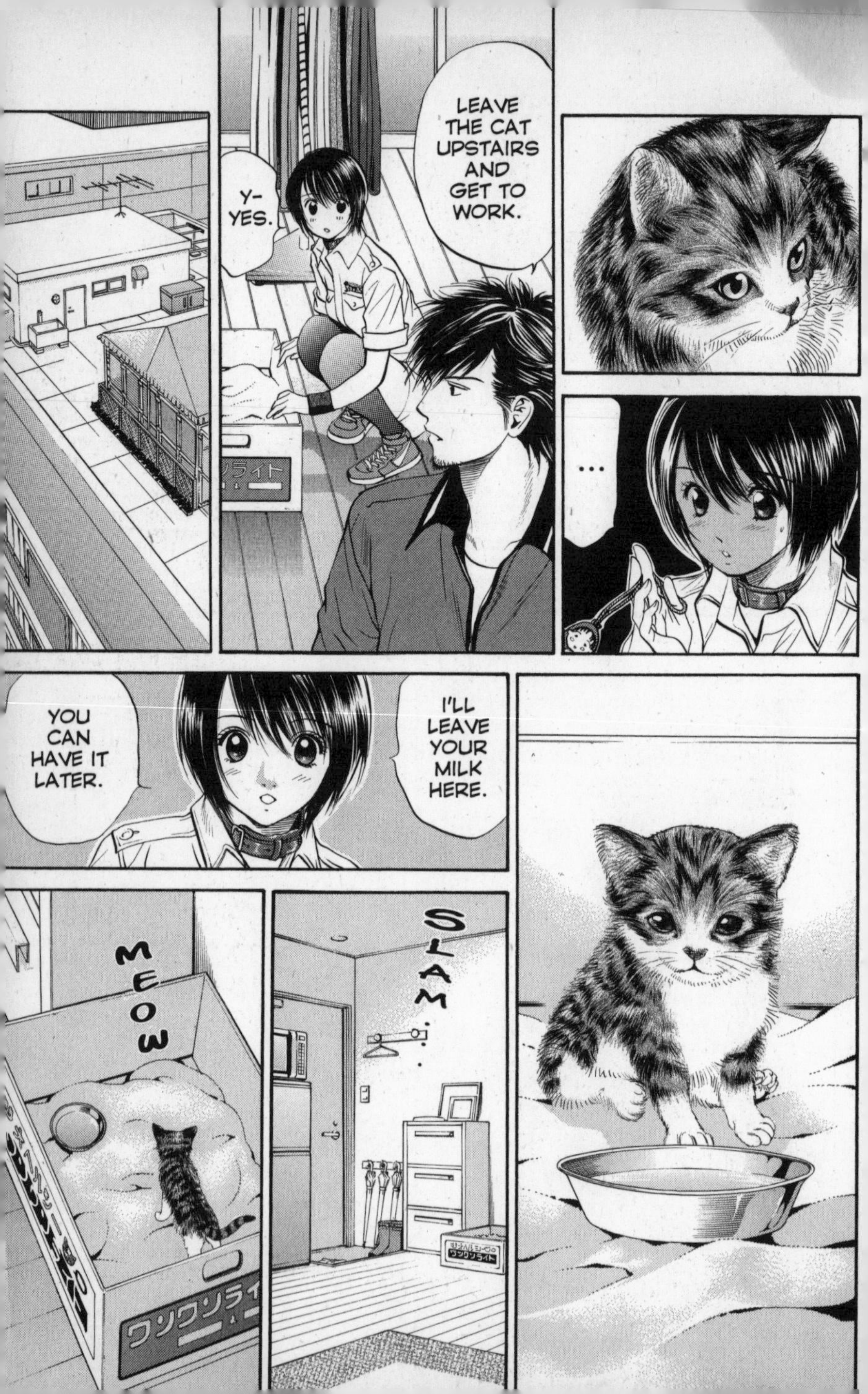
...
LEAVE THE CAT UPSTAIRS AND GET TO WORK.
Y-YES.
I'LL LEAVE YOUR MILK HERE.
YOU CAN HAVE IT LATER.
SLAM
MEOW

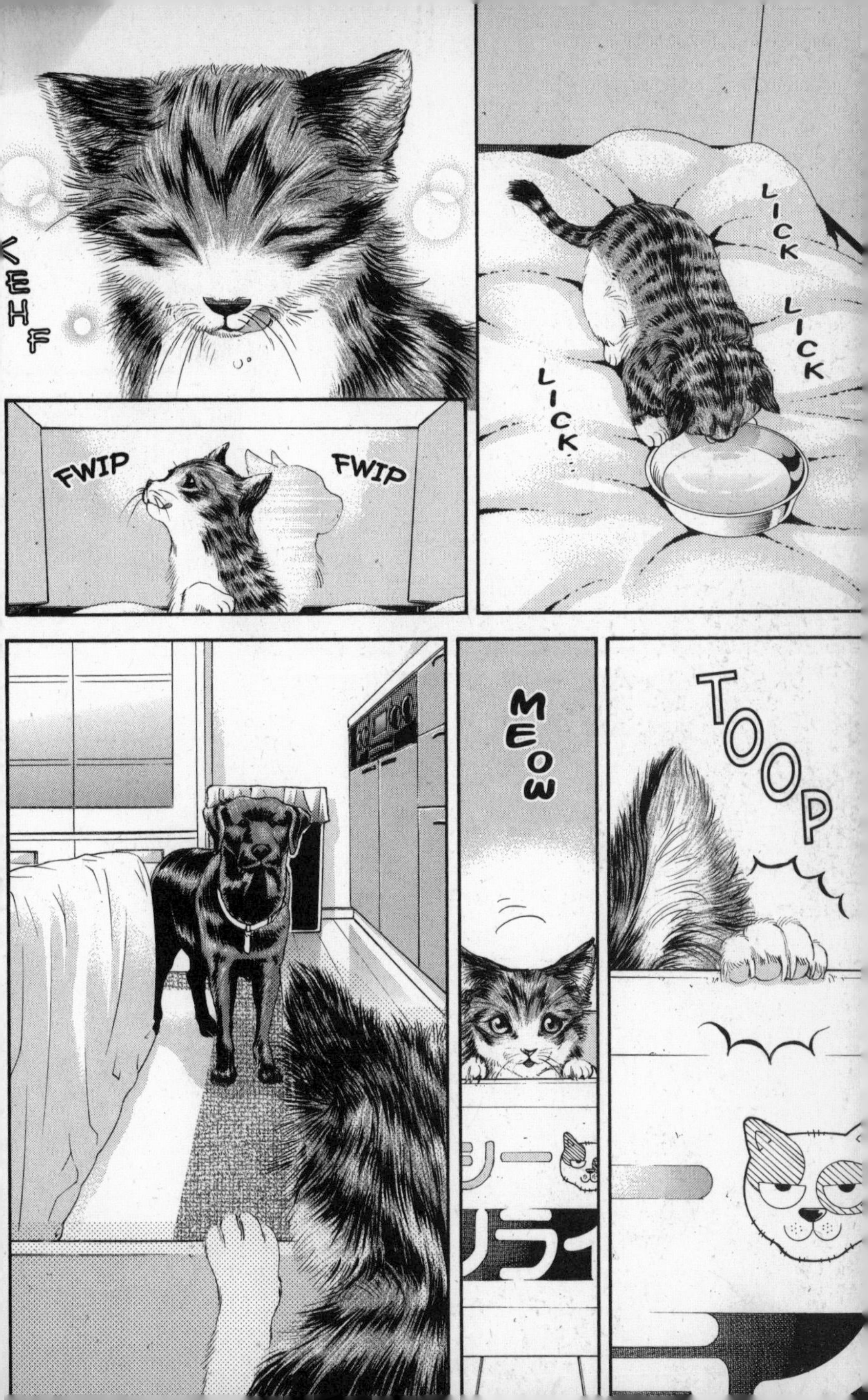
LICK LICK
LICK...
KEHF
FWIP
FWIP
TOOP
MEOW

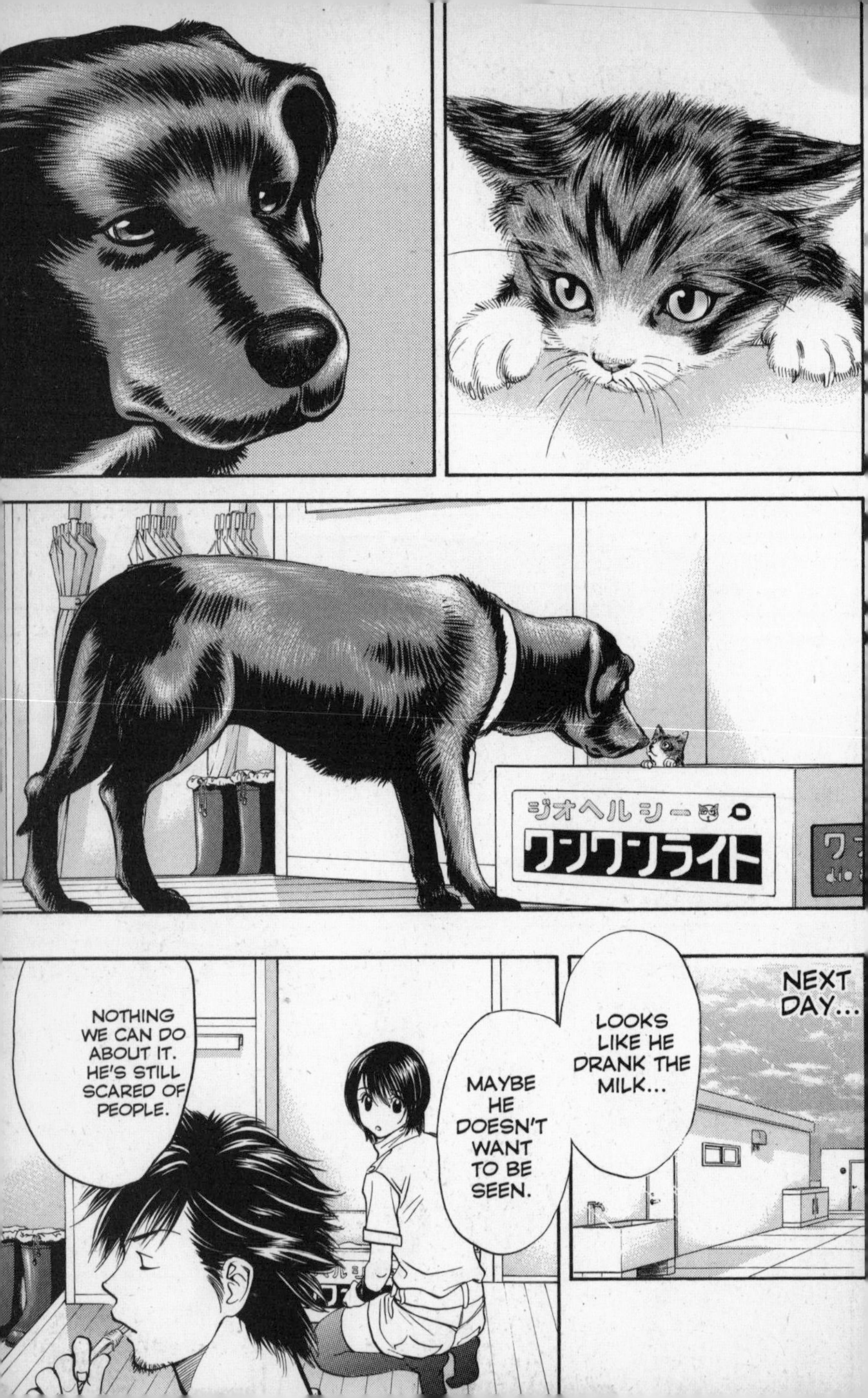
ジオヘルシー
ワンワンライト
NEXT DAY...
LOOKS LIKE HE DRANK THE MILK...
MAYBE HE DOESN'T WANT TO BE SEEN.
NOTHING WE CAN DO ABOUT IT. HE'S STILL SCARED OF PEOPLE.

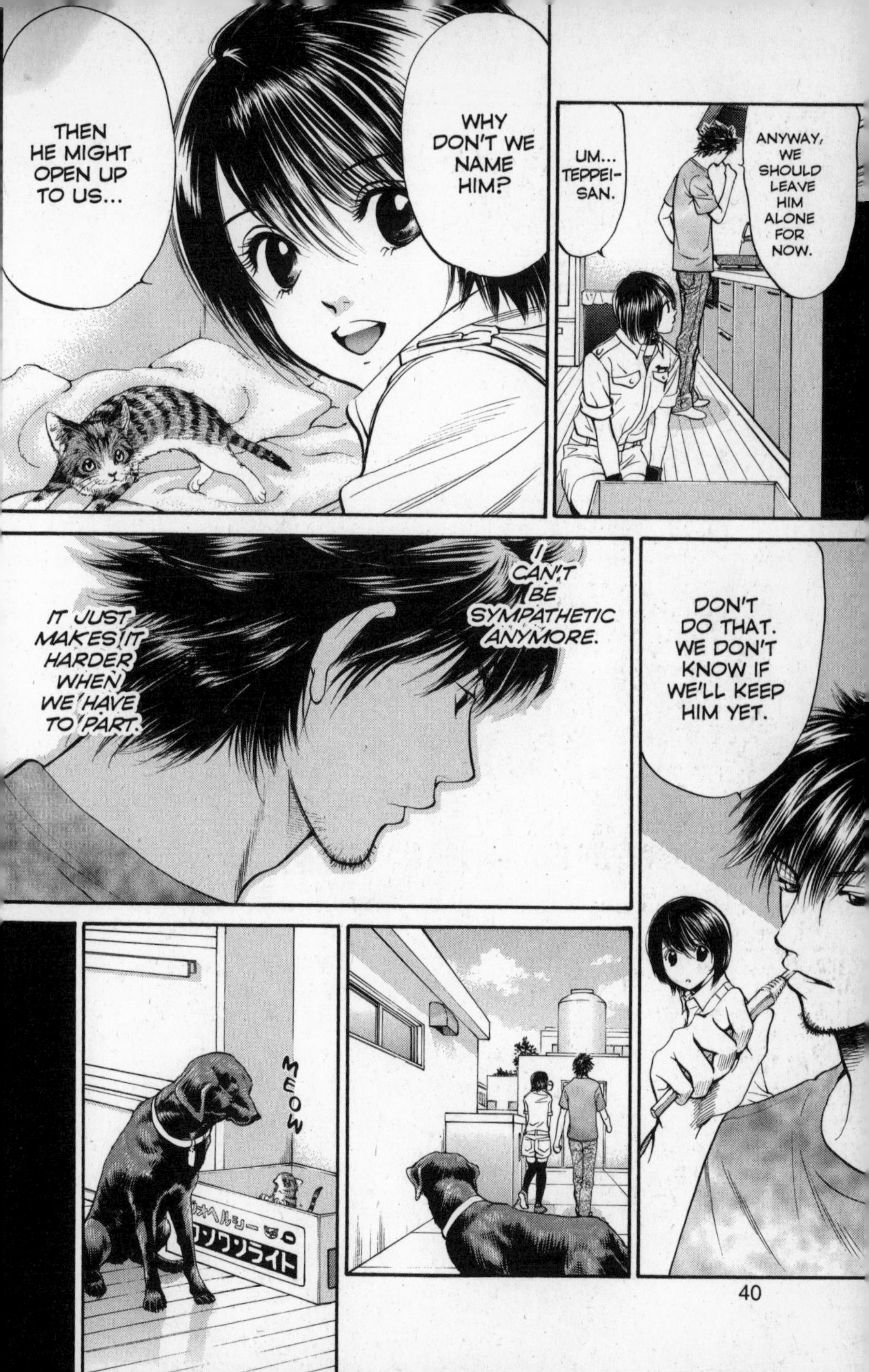
ANYWAY, WE SHOULD LEAVE HIM ALONE FOR NOW.
UM... TEPPEI-SAN.
WHY DON'T WE NAME HIM?
THEN HE MIGHT OPEN UP TO US...
DON'T DO THAT. WE DON'T KNOW IF WE'LL KEEP HIM YET.
I CAN'T BE SYMPATHETIC ANYMORE.
IT JUST MAKES IT HARDER WHEN WE HAVE TO PART.
MEOW

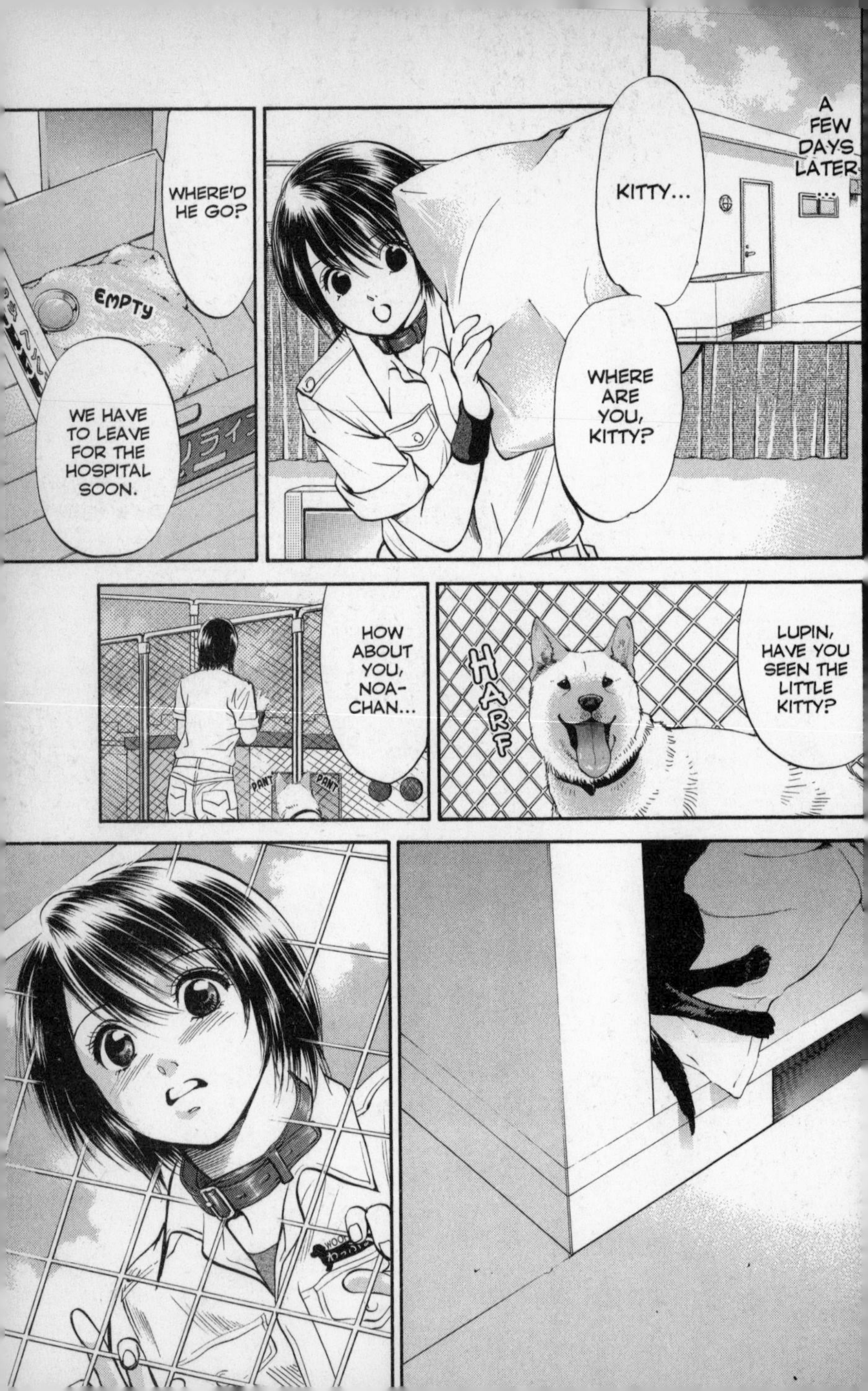
A FEW DAYS LATER...
KITTY...
WHERE ARE YOU, KITTY?
WHERE'D HE GO?
EMPTY
WE HAVE TO LEAVE FOR THE HOSPITAL SOON.
LUPIN, HAVE YOU SEEN THE LITTLE KITTY?
HARF
HOW ABOUT YOU, NOA-CHAN...
PANT
PANT
WOOF

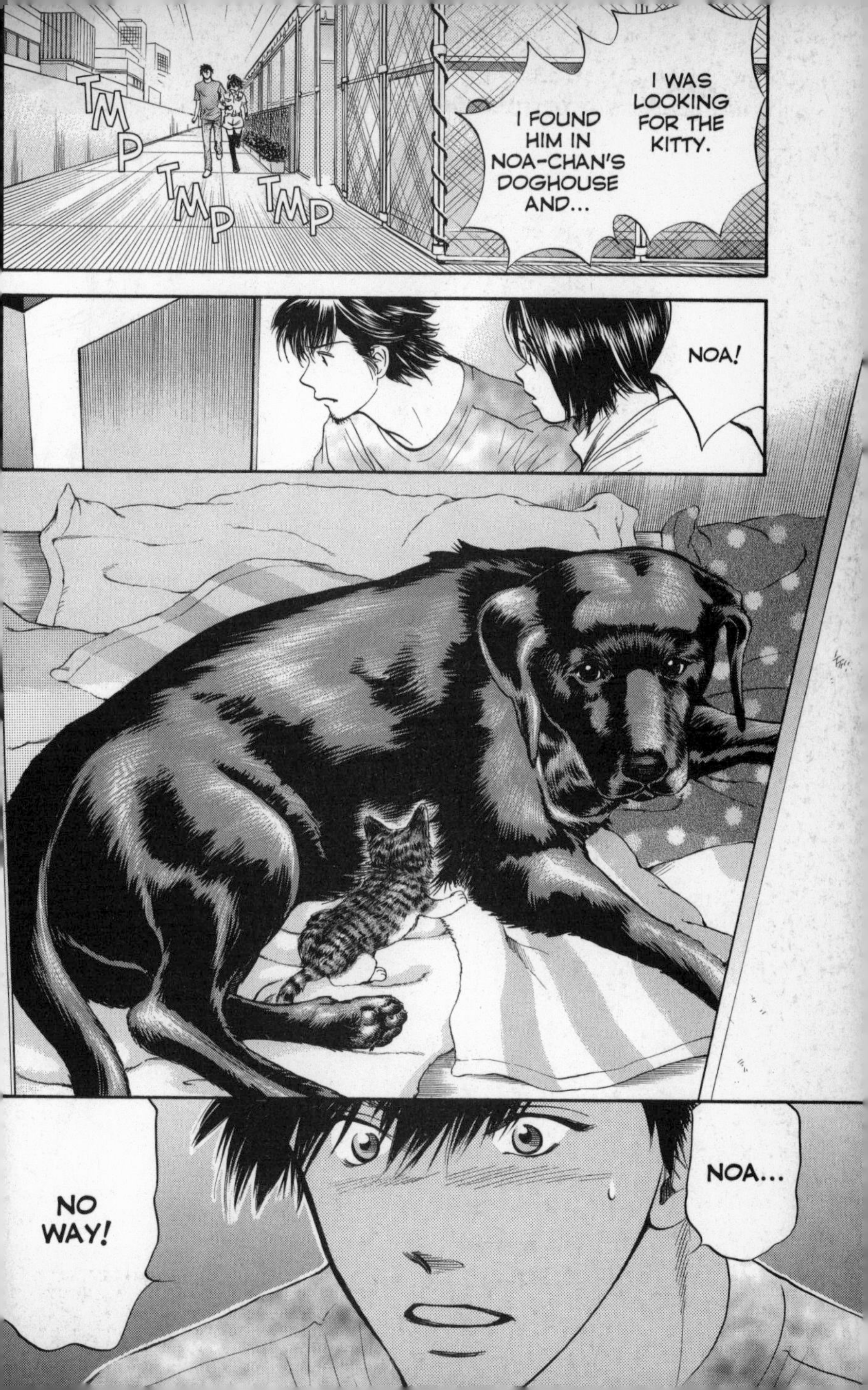
I WAS LOOKING FOR THE KITTY.
I FOUND HIM IN NOA-CHAN'S DOGHOUSE AND...
TMP
TMP
TMP
NOA!
NOA...
NO WAY!

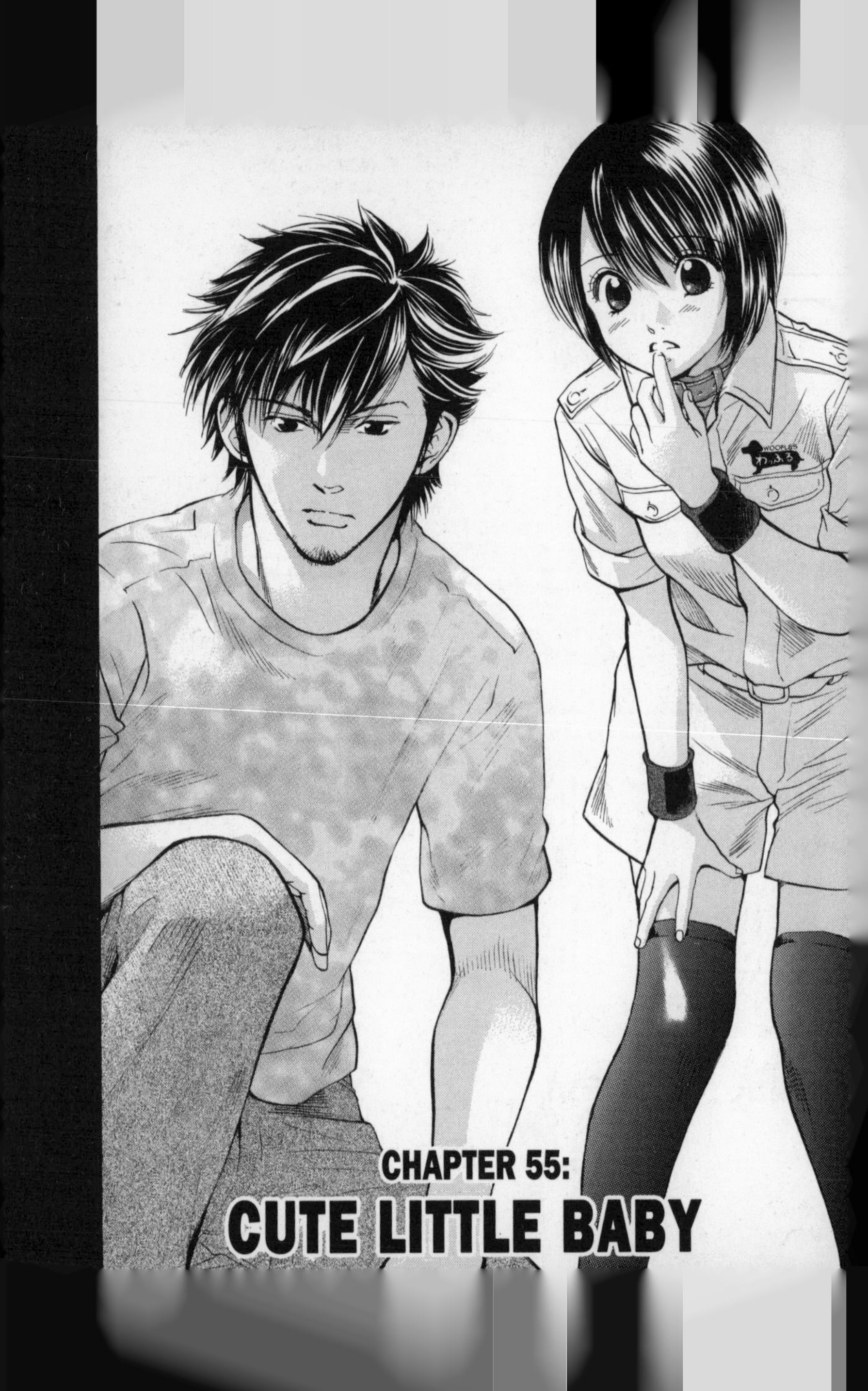
WOOFLES
わっふる
CHAPTER 55:
CUTE LITTLE BABY

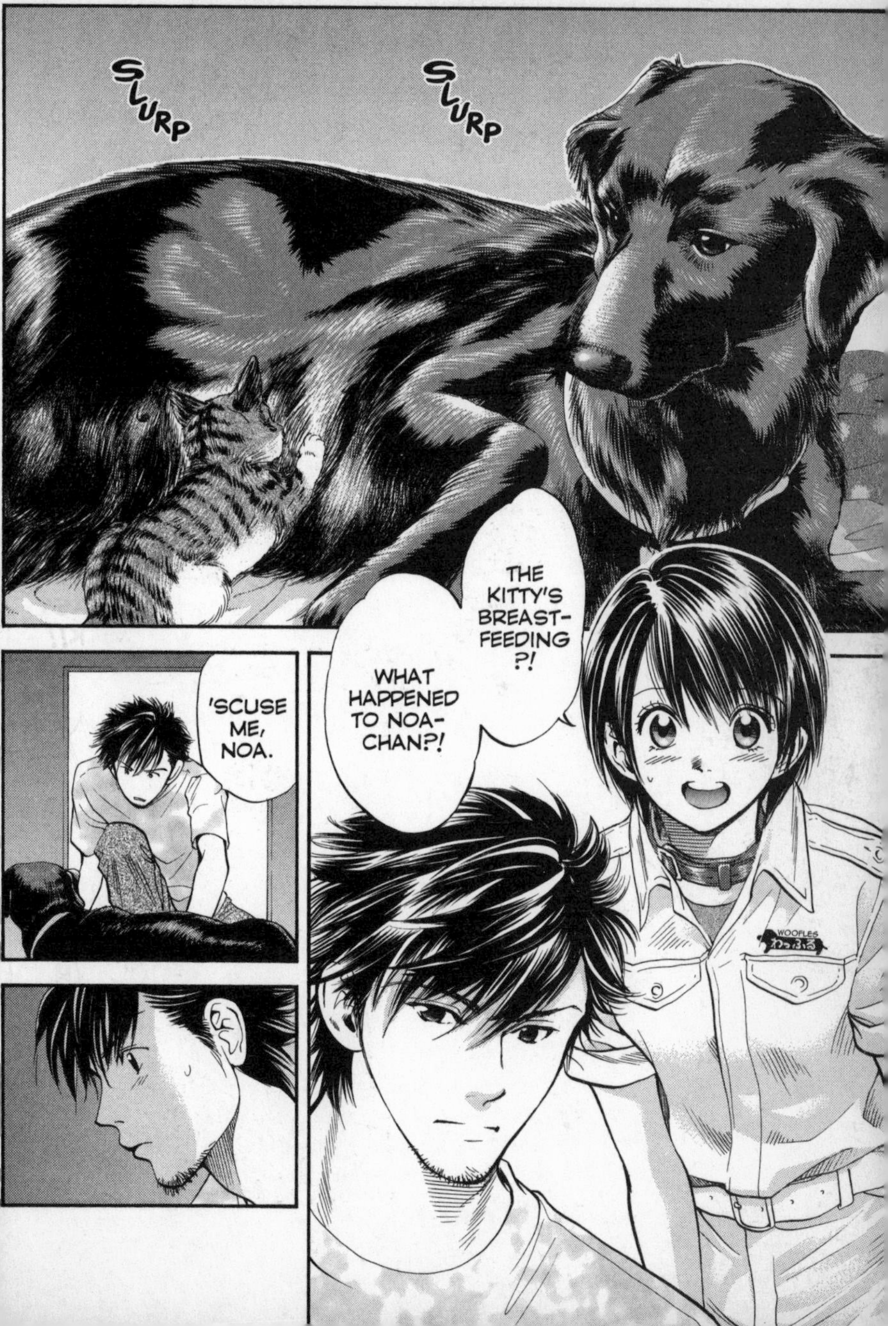
SLURP
SLURP
THE KITTY'S BREAST-FEEDING?!
WHAT HAPPENED TO NOA-CHAN?!
WOOFLES
'SCUSE ME, NOA.

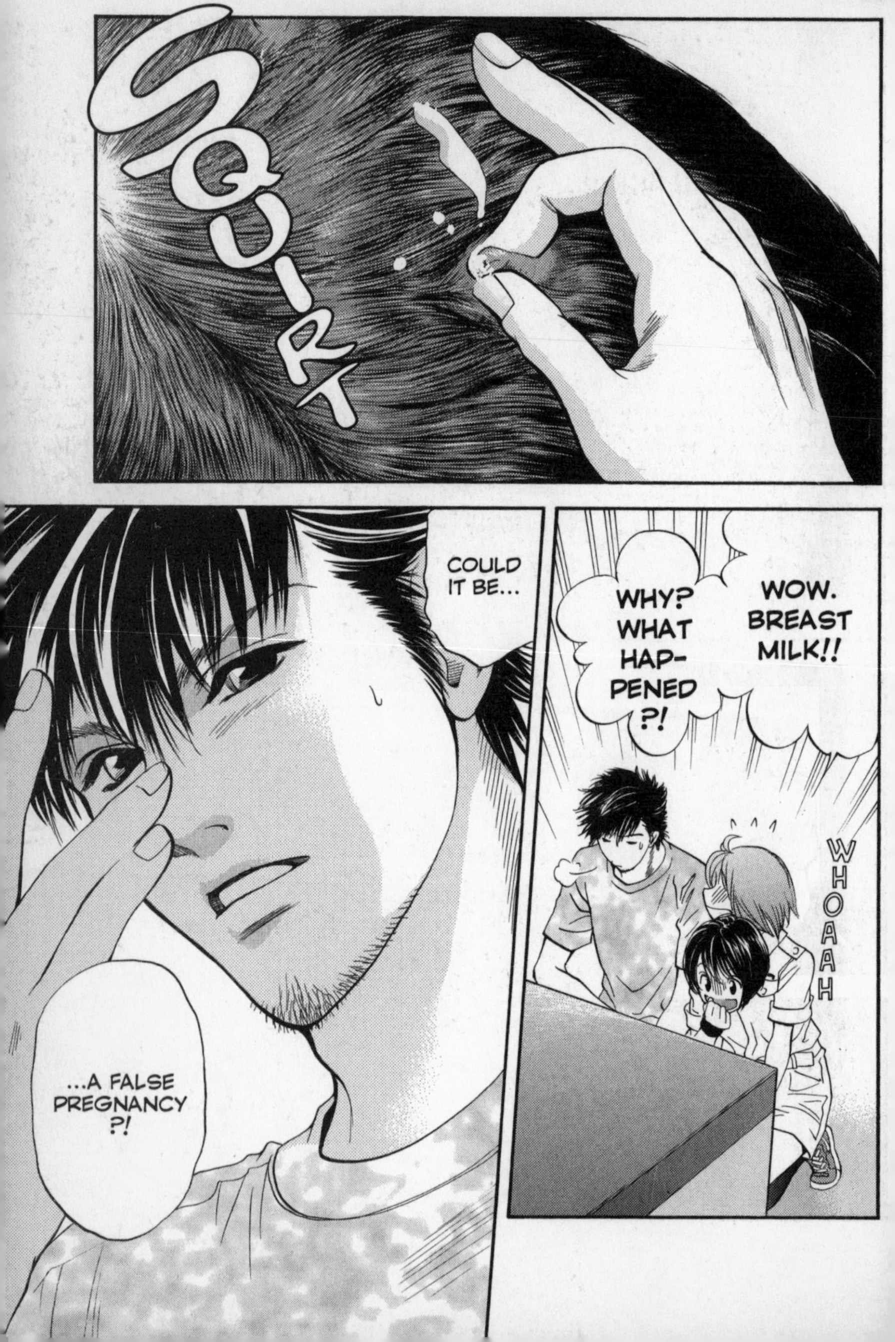
SQUIRT
WOW. BREAST MILK!!
WHY? WHAT HAP-PENED?!
WHOAAH
COULD IT BE...
...A FALSE PREGNANCY?!

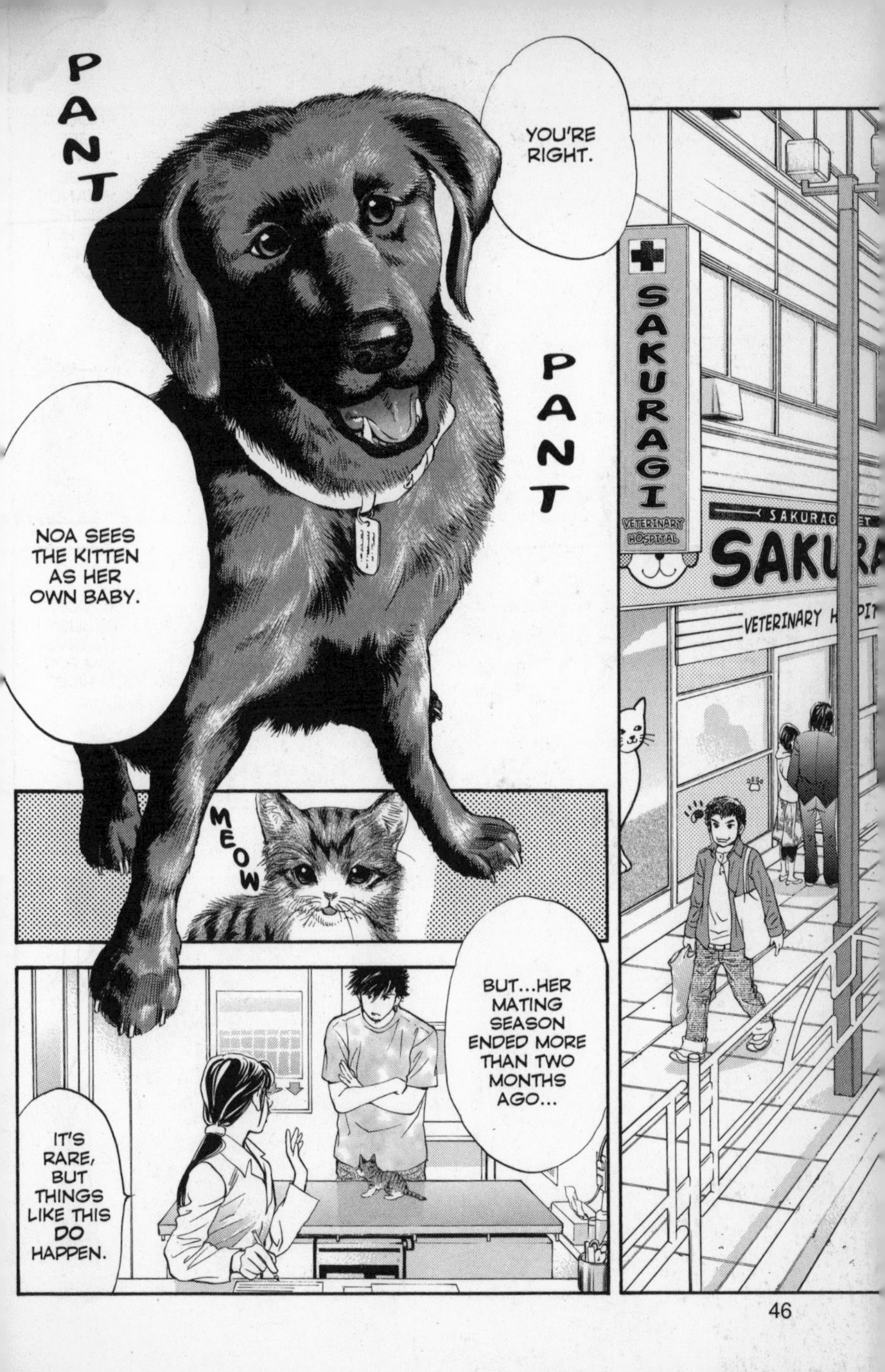
SAKURAGI
VETERINARY HOSPITAL
PANT
PANT
YOU'RE RIGHT.
NOA SEES THE KITTEN AS HER OWN BABY.
MEOW
BUT...HER MATING SEASON ENDED MORE THAN TWO MONTHS AGO...
IT'S RARE, BUT THINGS LIKE THIS DO HAPPEN.

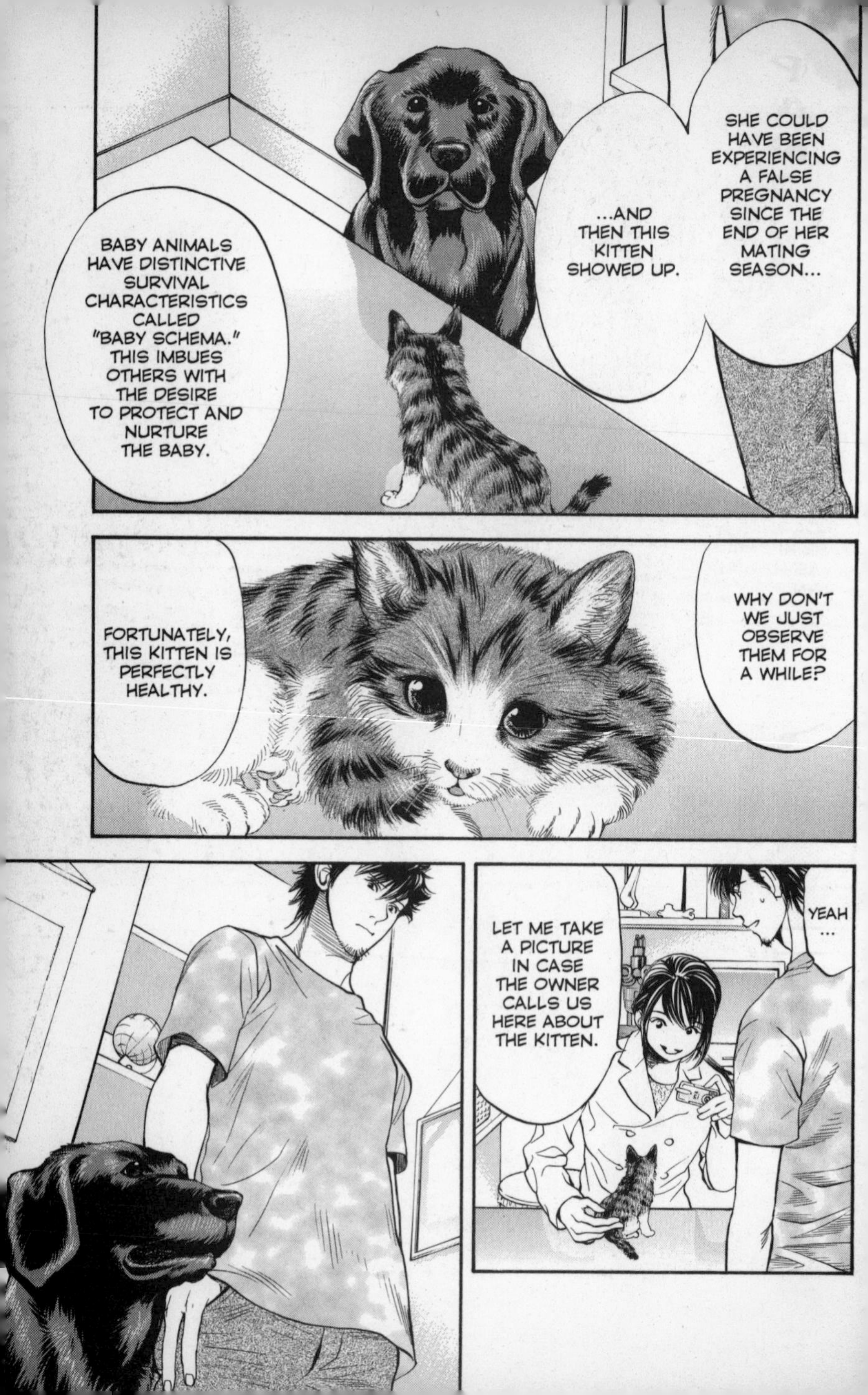
SHE COULD HAVE BEEN EXPERIENCING A FALSE PREGNANCY SINCE THE END OF HER MATING SEASON...
...AND THEN THIS KITTEN SHOWED UP.
BABY ANIMALS HAVE DISTINCTIVE SURVIVAL CHARACTERISTICS CALLED "BABY SCHEMA." THIS IMBUES OTHERS WITH THE DESIRE TO PROTECT AND NURTURE THE BABY.
WHY DON'T WE JUST OBSERVE THEM FOR A WHILE?
FORTUNATELY, THIS KITTEN IS PERFECTLY HEALTHY.
YEAH ...
LET ME TAKE A PICTURE IN CASE THE OWNER CALLS US HERE ABOUT THE KITTEN.

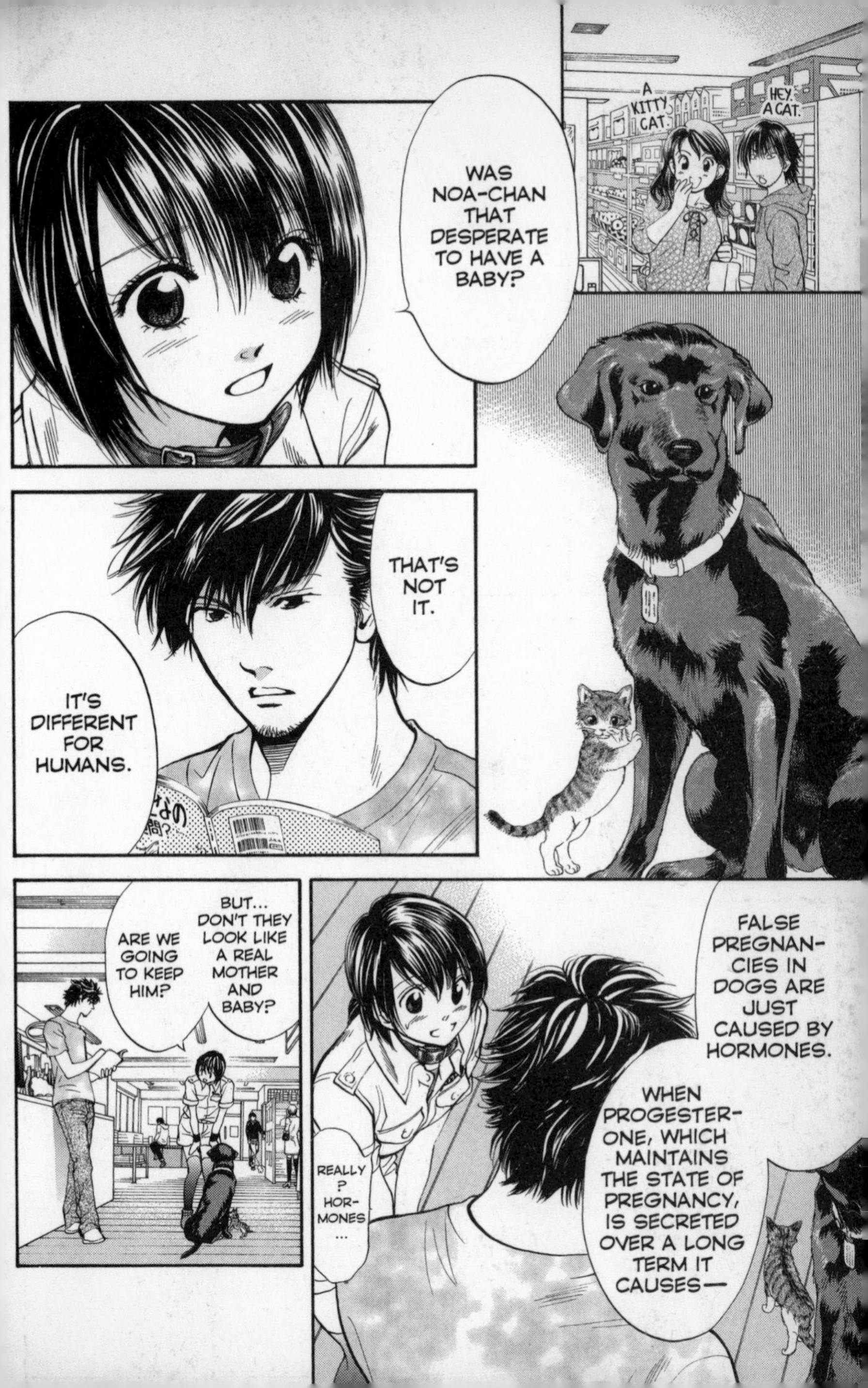
HEY. A CAT.
A KITTY CAT.
WAS NOA-CHAN THAT DESPERATE TO HAVE A BABY?
THAT'S NOT IT.
IT'S DIFFERENT FOR HUMANS.
FALSE PREGNANCIES IN DOGS ARE JUST CAUSED BY HORMONES.
WHEN PROGESTERONE, WHICH MAINTAINS THE STATE OF PREGNANCY, IS SECRETED OVER A LONG TERM IT CAUSES—
REALLY? HORMONES...
BUT... DON'T THEY LOOK LIKE A REAL MOTHER AND BABY?
ARE WE GOING TO KEEP HIM?

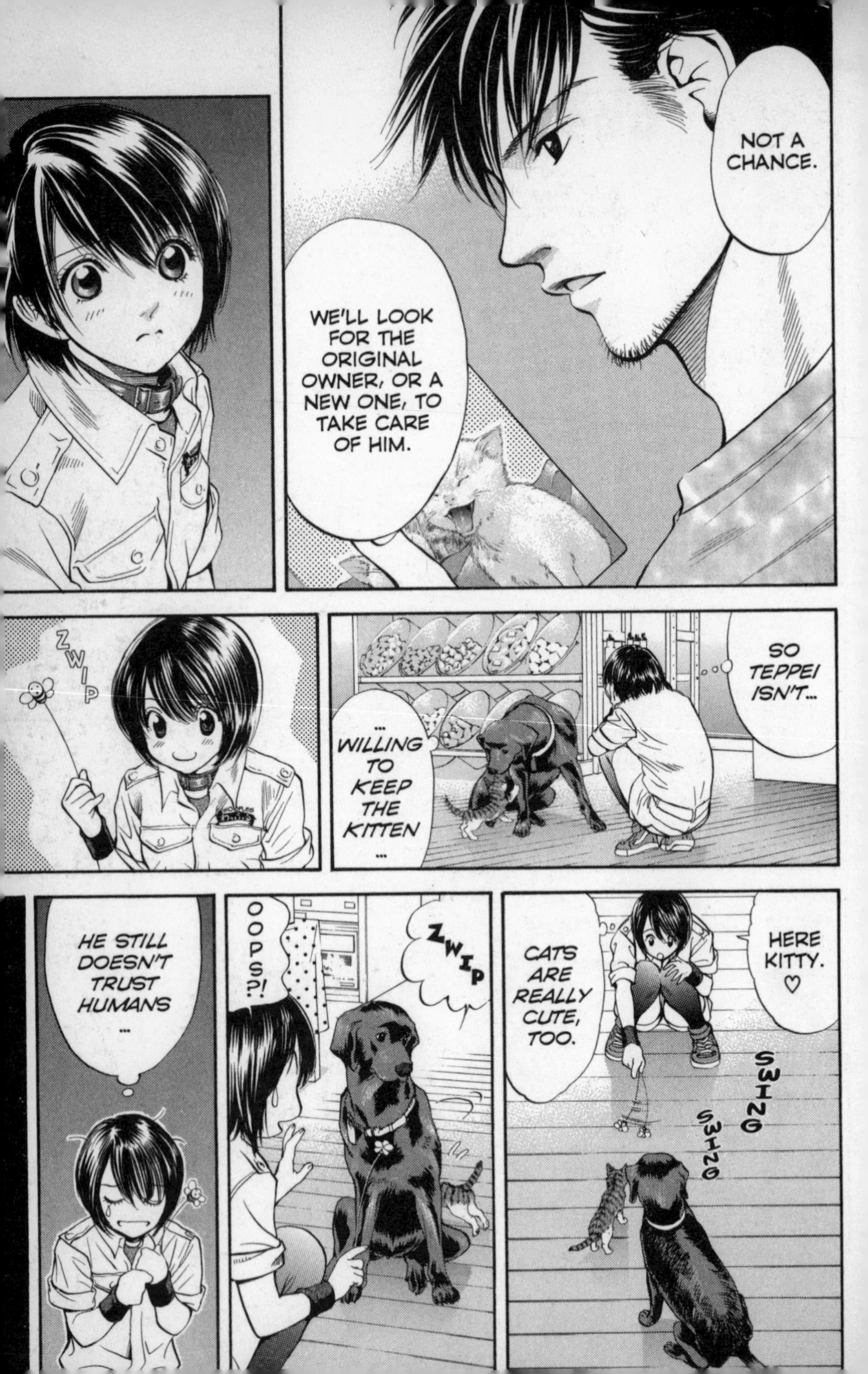
NOT A CHANCE.
WE'LL LOOK FOR THE ORIGINAL OWNER, OR A NEW ONE, TO TAKE CARE OF HIM.
SO TEPPEI ISN'T...
... WILLING TO KEEP THE KITTEN ...
ZWIP
HERE KITTY. ♡
CATS ARE REALLY CUTE, TOO.
SWING
SWING
ZWIP
OOPS?!
HE STILL DOESN'T TRUST HUMANS ...

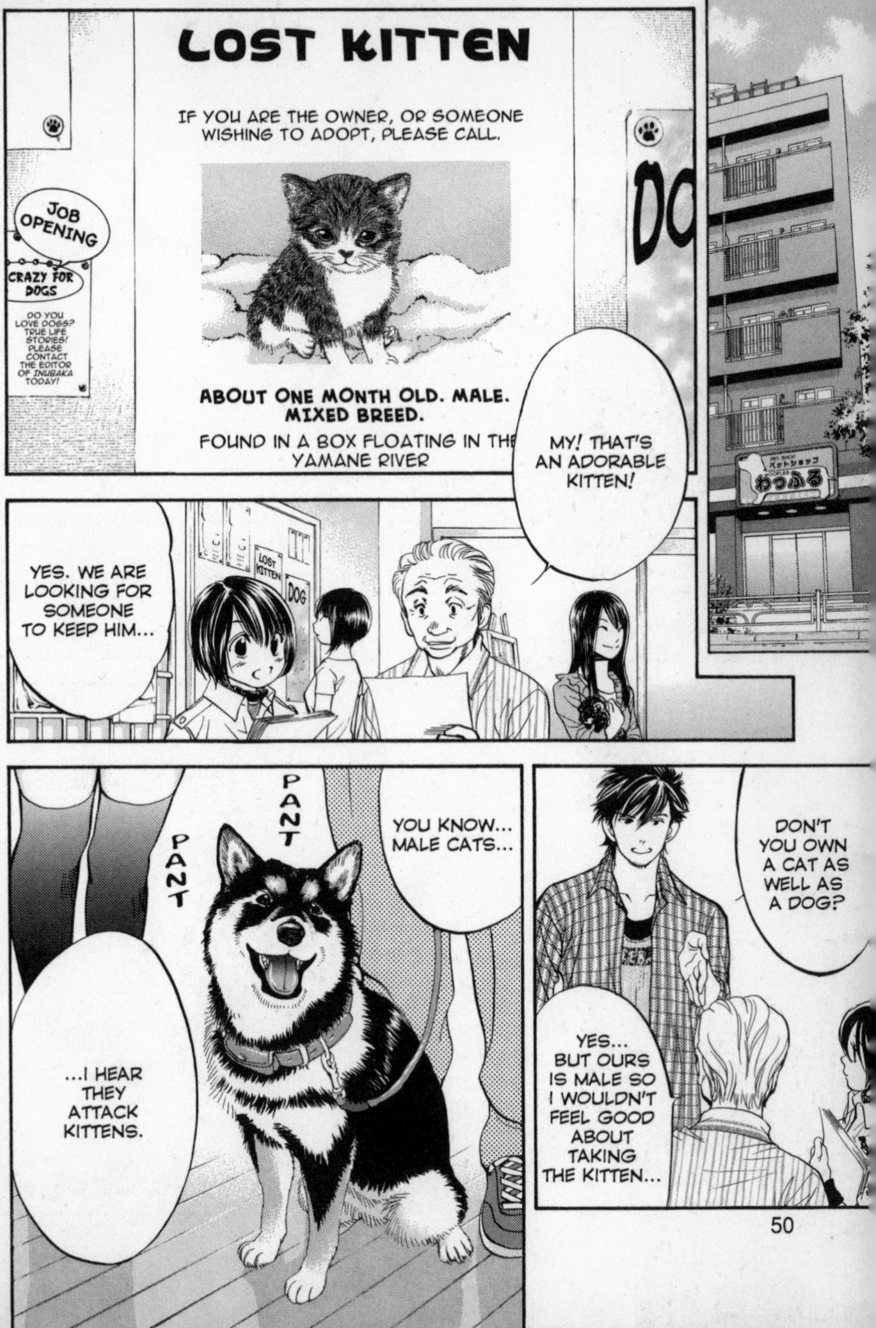
わっふる
LOST KITTEN
IF YOU ARE THE OWNER, OR SOMEONE WISHING TO ADOPT, PLEASE CALL.
ABOUT ONE MONTH OLD. MALE. MIXED BREED.
FOUND IN A BOX FLOATING IN THE YAMANE RIVER
JOB OPENING
CRAZY FOR DOGS
DO YOU LOVE DOGS? TRUE LIFE STORIES! PLEASE CONTACT THE EDITOR OF INUBAKA TODAY!
DO
MY! THAT'S AN ADORABLE KITTEN!
LOST KITTEN
DOG
YES. WE ARE LOOKING FOR SOMEONE TO KEEP HIM...
DON'T YOU OWN A CAT AS WELL AS A DOG?
YES... BUT OURS IS MALE SO I WOULDN'T FEEL GOOD ABOUT TAKING THE KITTEN...
PANT
PANT
YOU KNOW... MALE CATS...
...I HEAR THEY ATTACK KITTENS.

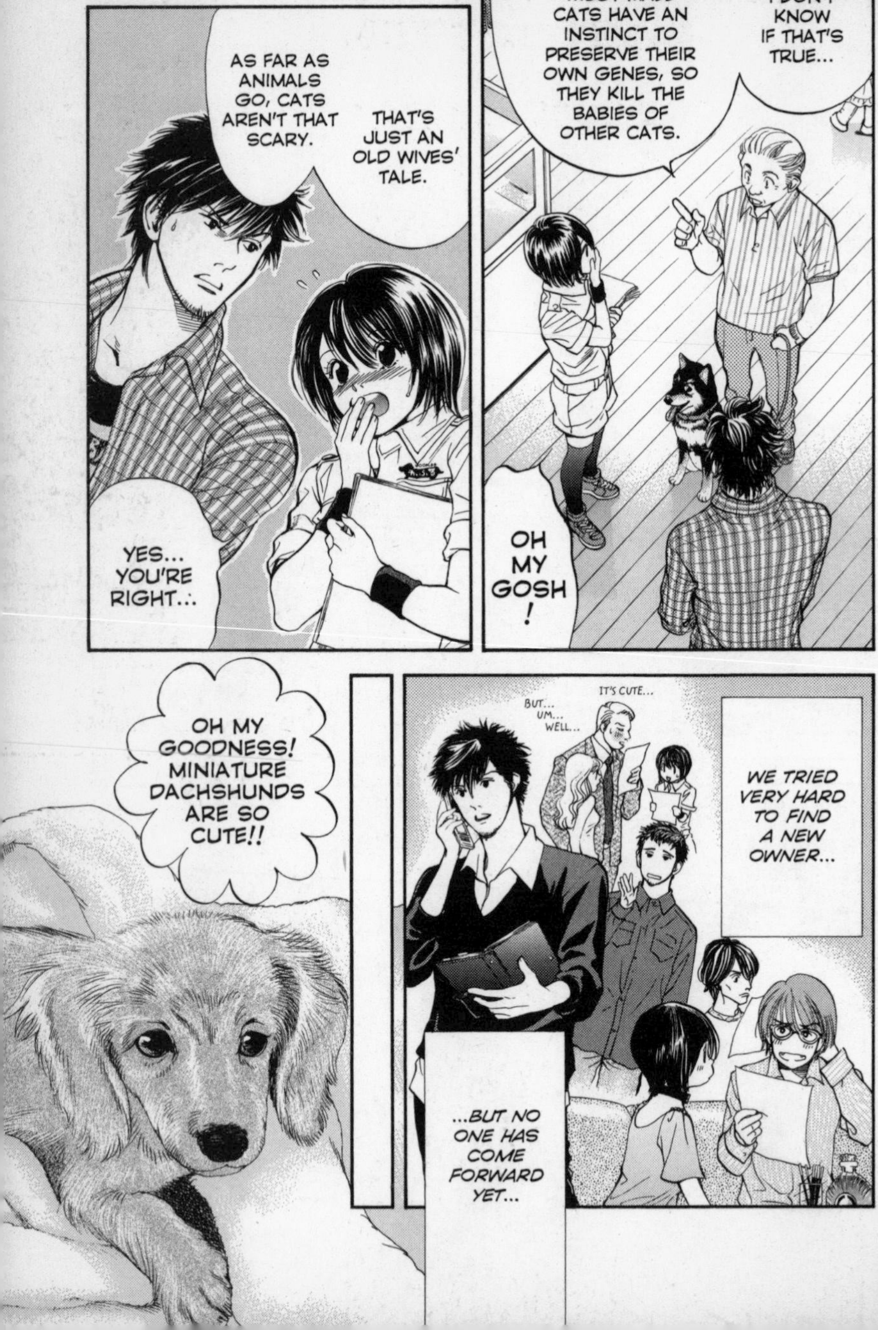
I DON'T KNOW IF THAT'S TRUE...
...BUT MALE CATS HAVE AN INSTINCT TO PRESERVE THEIR OWN GENES, SO THEY KILL THE BABIES OF OTHER CATS.
OH MY GOSH!
AS FAR AS ANIMALS GO, CATS AREN'T THAT SCARY.
THAT'S JUST AN OLD WIVES' TALE.
YES... YOU'RE RIGHT...
WE TRIED VERY HARD TO FIND A NEW OWNER...
IT'S CUTE...
BUT... UM... WELL...
...BUT NO ONE HAS COME FORWARD YET...
OH MY GOODNESS! MINIATURE DACHSHUNDS ARE SO CUTE!!

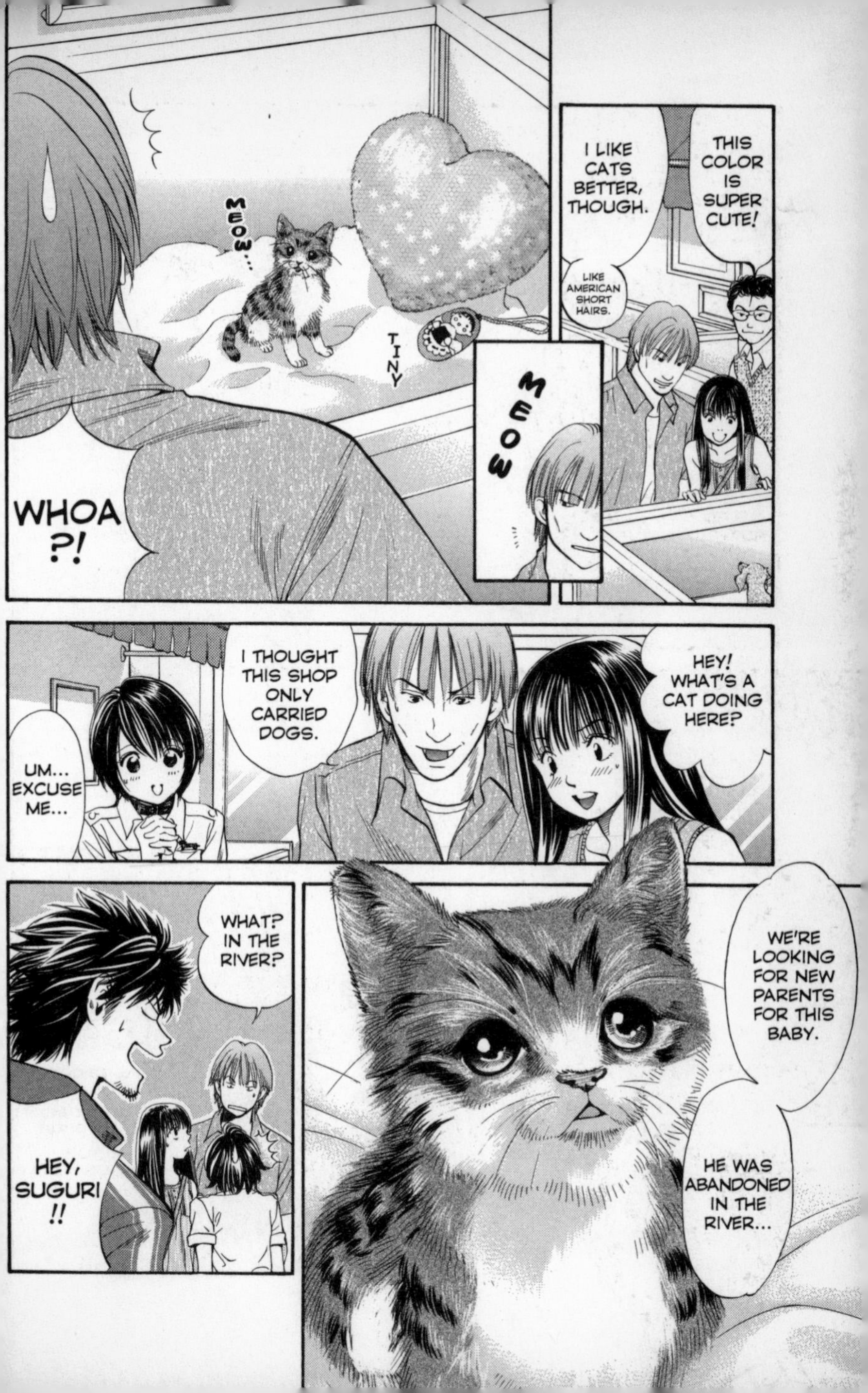
THIS COLOR IS SUPER CUTE!
I LIKE CATS BETTER, THOUGH.
LIKE AMERICAN SHORT HAIRS.
MEOW MEOW
MEOW...
TINY
WHOA?!
HEY! WHAT'S A CAT DOING HERE?
I THOUGHT THIS SHOP ONLY CARRIED DOGS.
UM... EXCUSE ME...
WE'RE LOOKING FOR NEW PARENTS FOR THIS BABY.
HE WAS ABANDONED IN THE RIVER...
WHAT? IN THE RIVER?
HEY, SUGURI!!

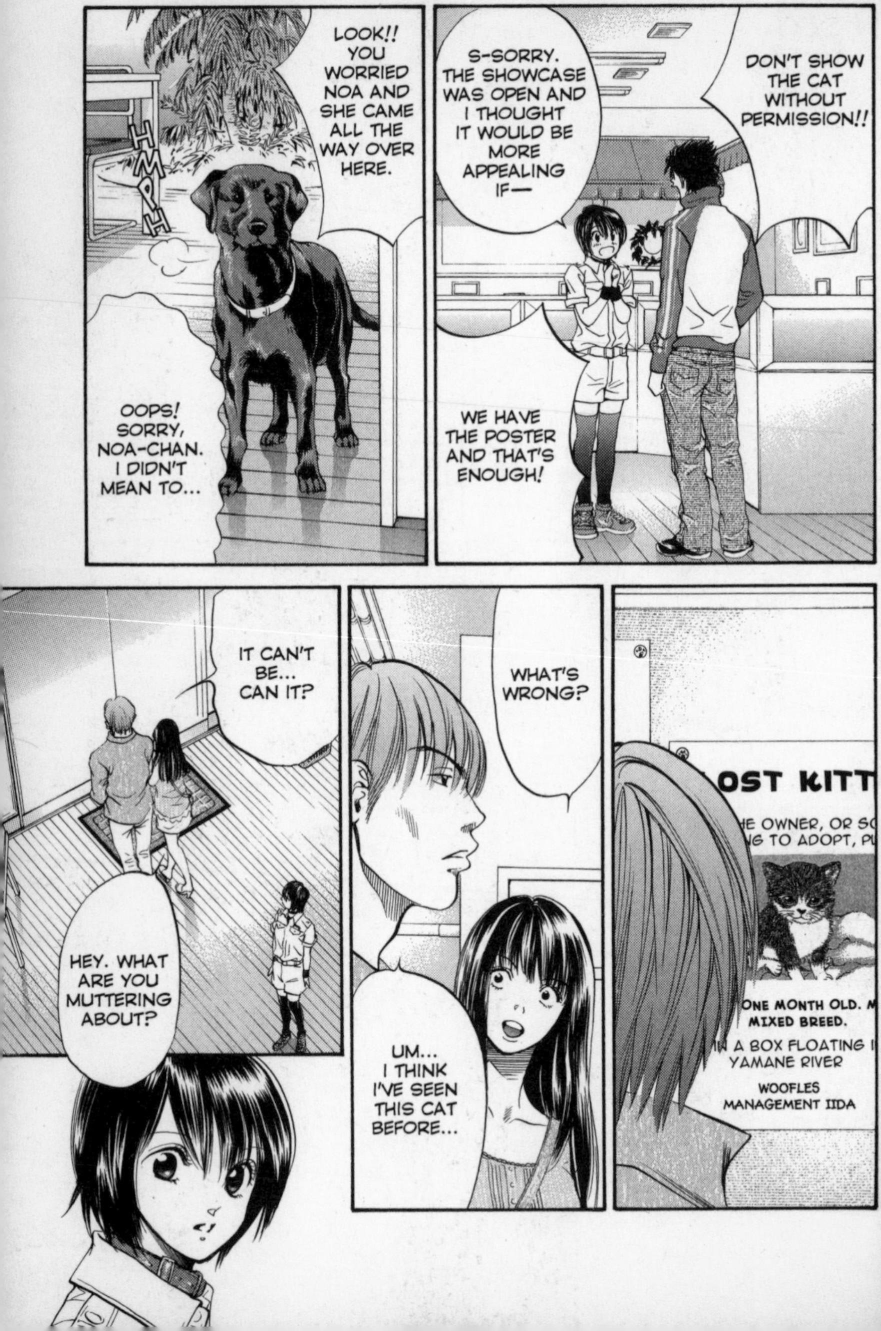
DON'T SHOW THE CAT WITHOUT PERMISSION!!
S-SORRY. THE SHOWCASE WAS OPEN AND I THOUGHT IT WOULD BE MORE APPEALING IF—
WE HAVE THE POSTER AND THAT'S ENOUGH!
LOOK!! YOU WORRIED NOA AND SHE CAME ALL THE WAY OVER HERE.
HMPH
OOPS! SORRY, NOA-CHAN. I DIDN'T MEAN TO...
OST KITT
HE OWNER, OR SO
NG TO ADOPT, PL
ONE MONTH OLD. M
MIXED BREED.
IN A BOX FLOATING I
YAMANE RIVER
WOOFLES
MANAGEMENT IIDA
WHAT'S WRONG?
UM... I THINK I'VE SEEN THIS CAT BEFORE...
IT CAN'T BE... CAN IT?
HEY. WHAT ARE YOU MUTTERING ABOUT?

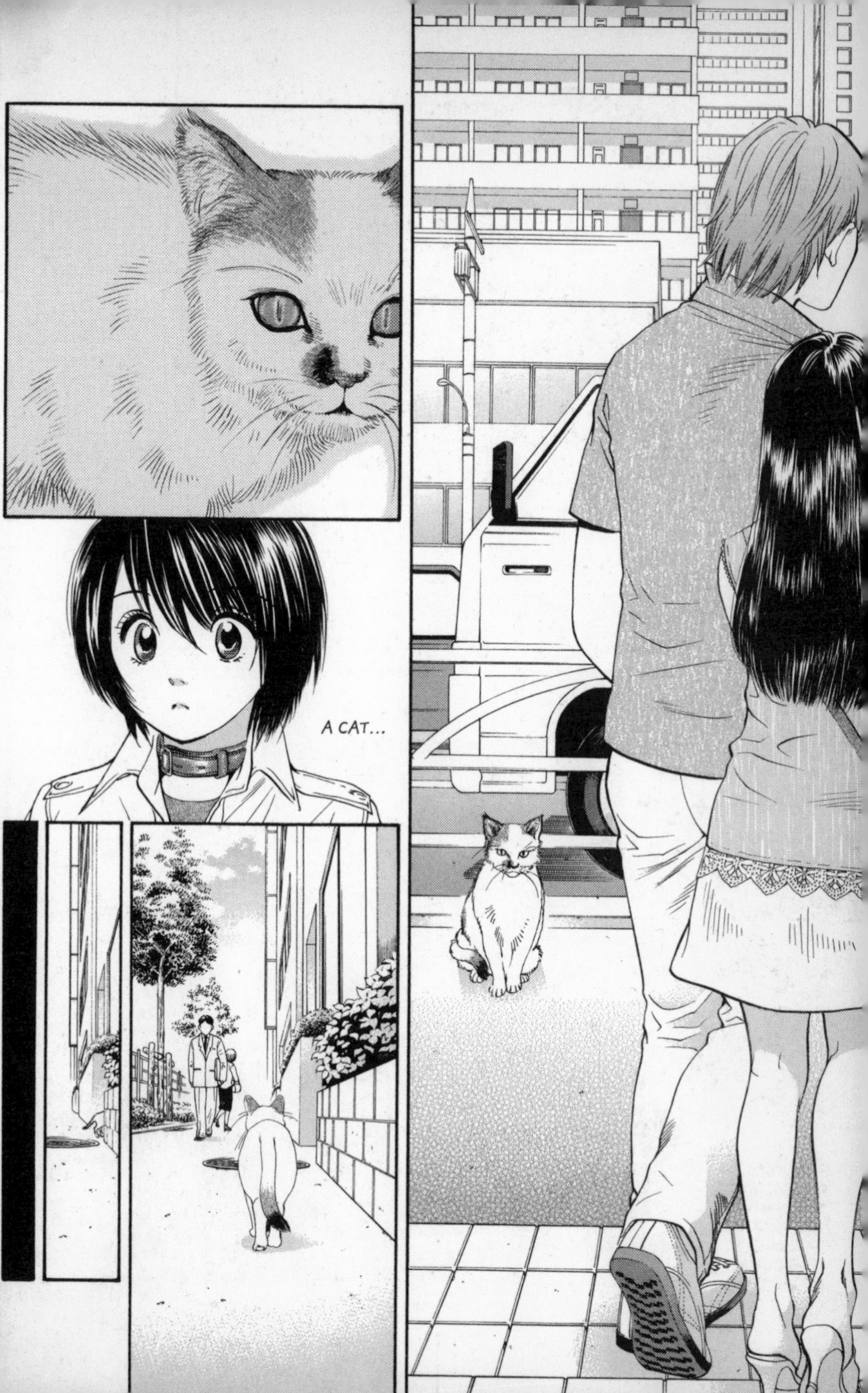
A CAT...

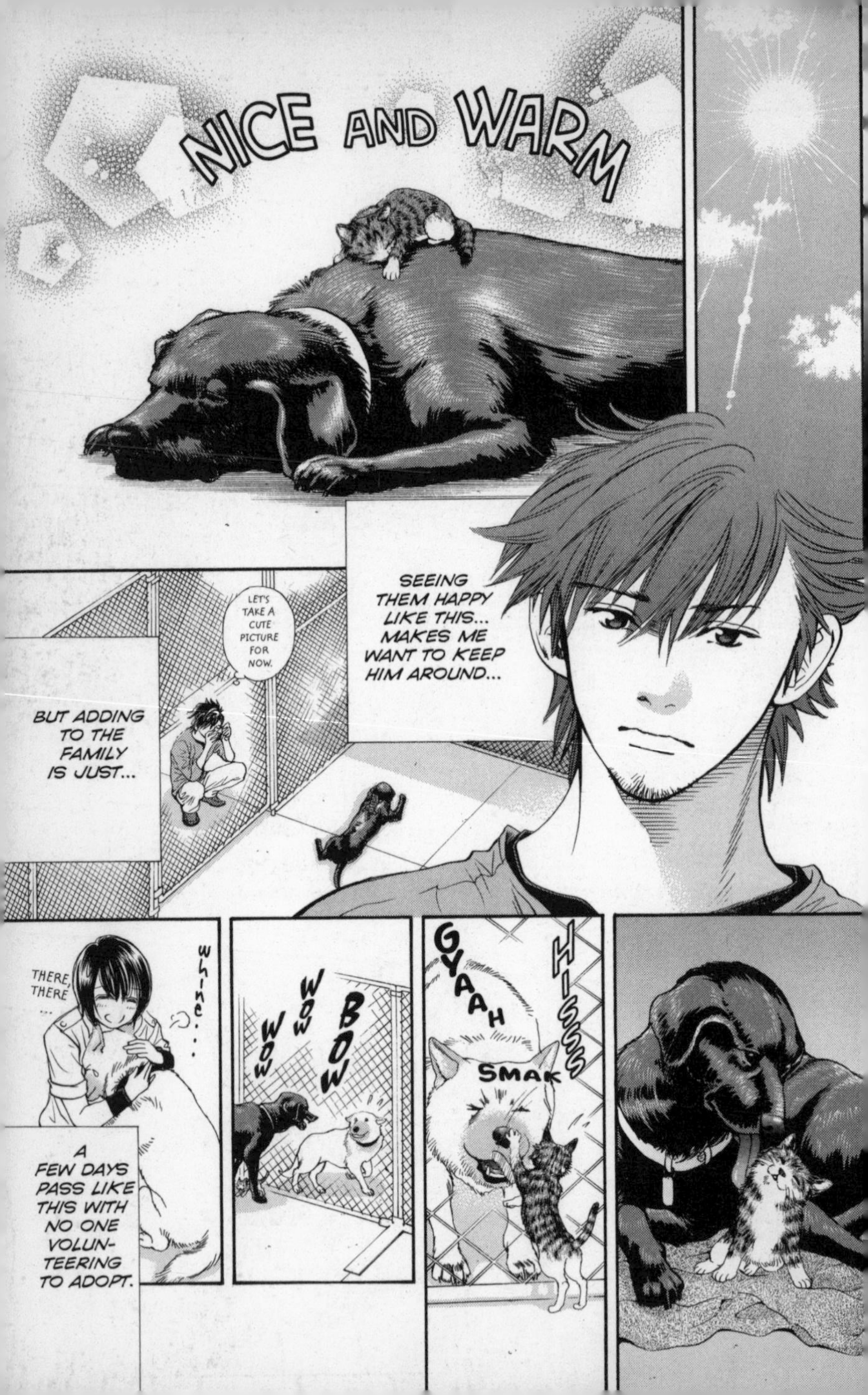
NICE AND WARM
SEEING THEM HAPPY LIKE THIS... MAKES ME WANT TO KEEP HIM AROUND...
LET'S TAKE A CUTE PICTURE FOR NOW.
BUT ADDING TO THE FAMILY IS JUST...
HISSS
GYAAH
SMAK
BOW
WOW
WOW
WOW
whine...
THERE, THERE...
A FEW DAYS PASS LIKE THIS WITH NO ONE VOLUN-TEERING TO ADOPT.

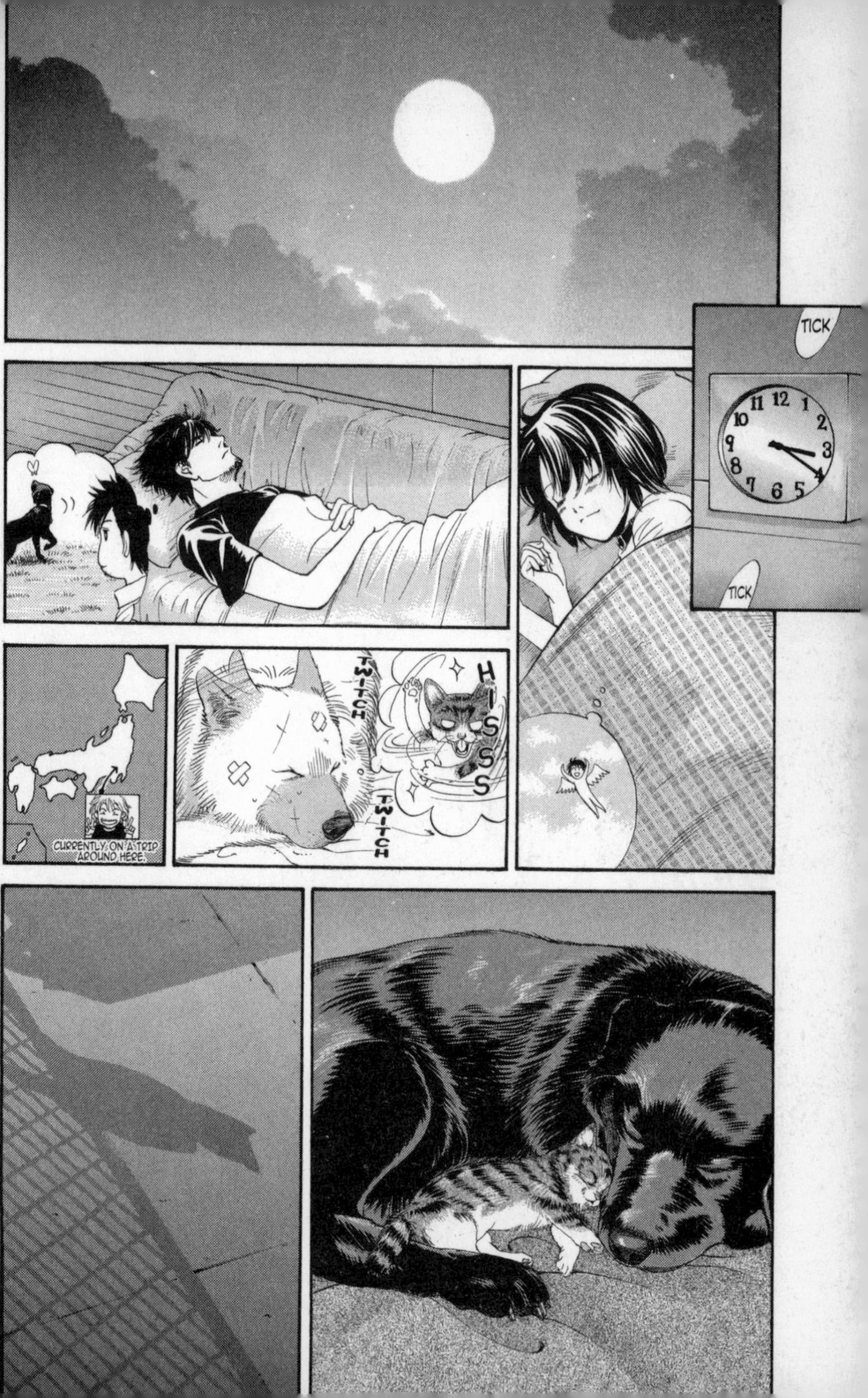
TICK
TICK
HISSS
TWITCH
TWITCH
CURRENTLY ON A TRIP AROUND HERE.

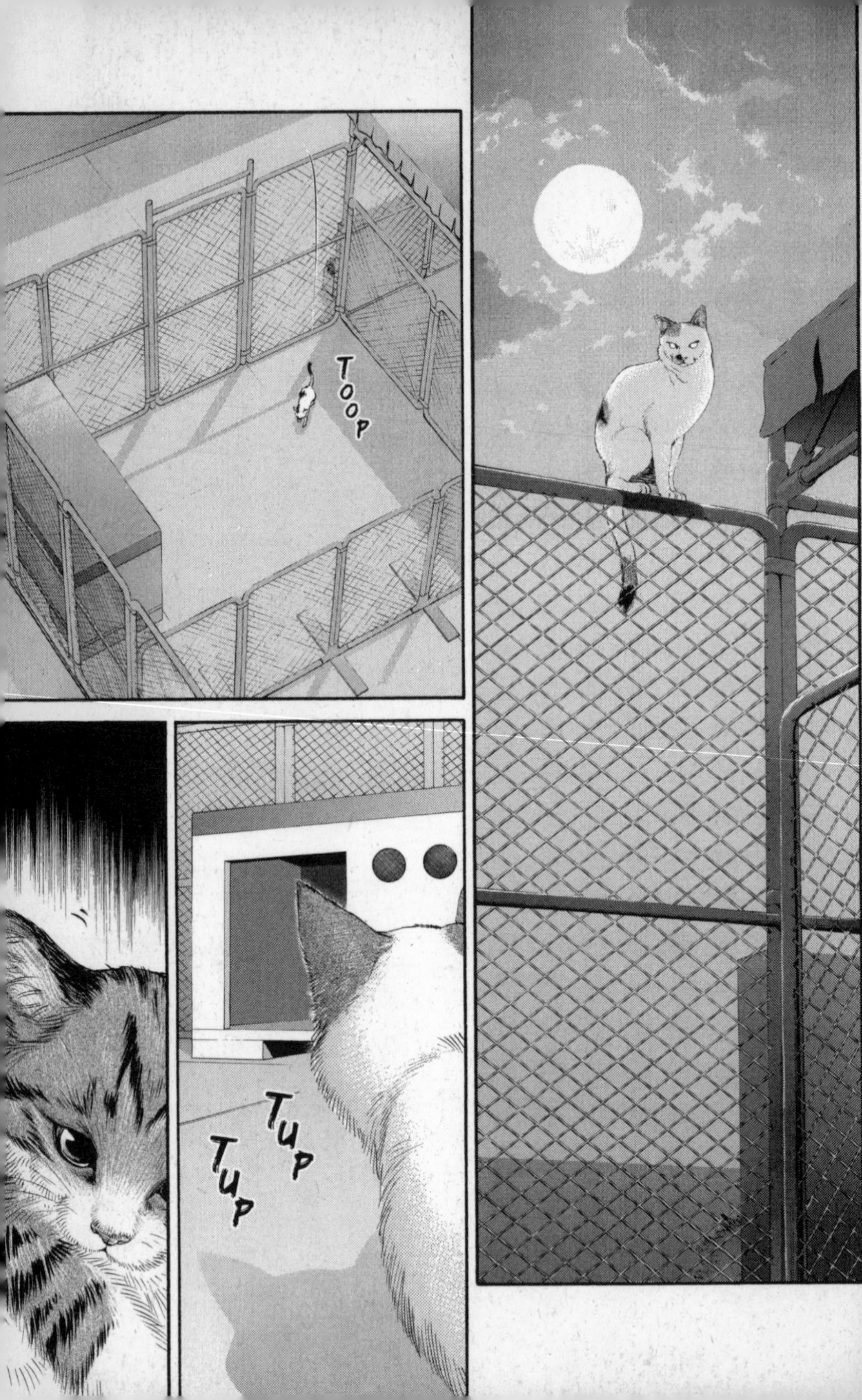
TOOP
TUP
TUP

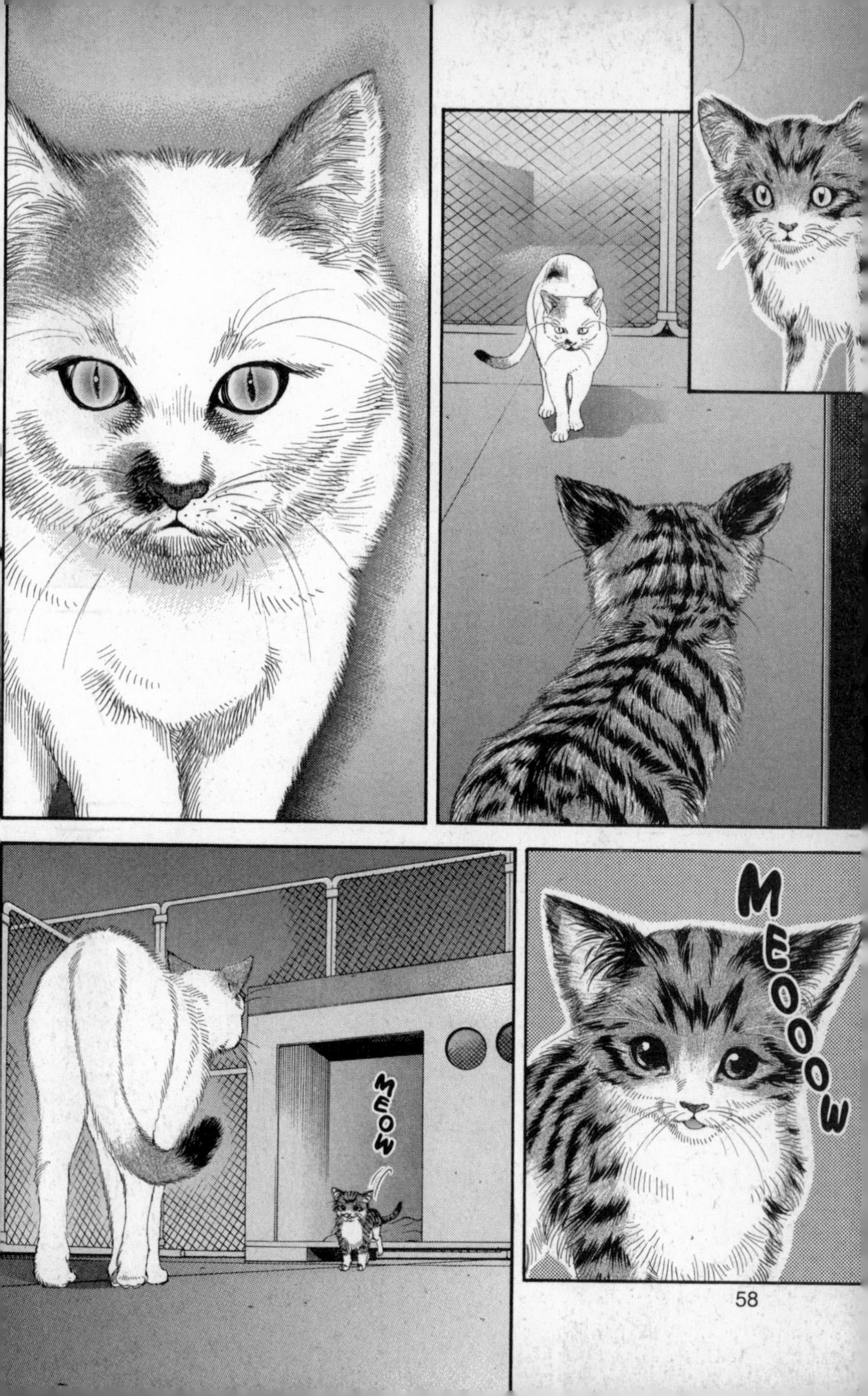
MEOOOOW
MEOW

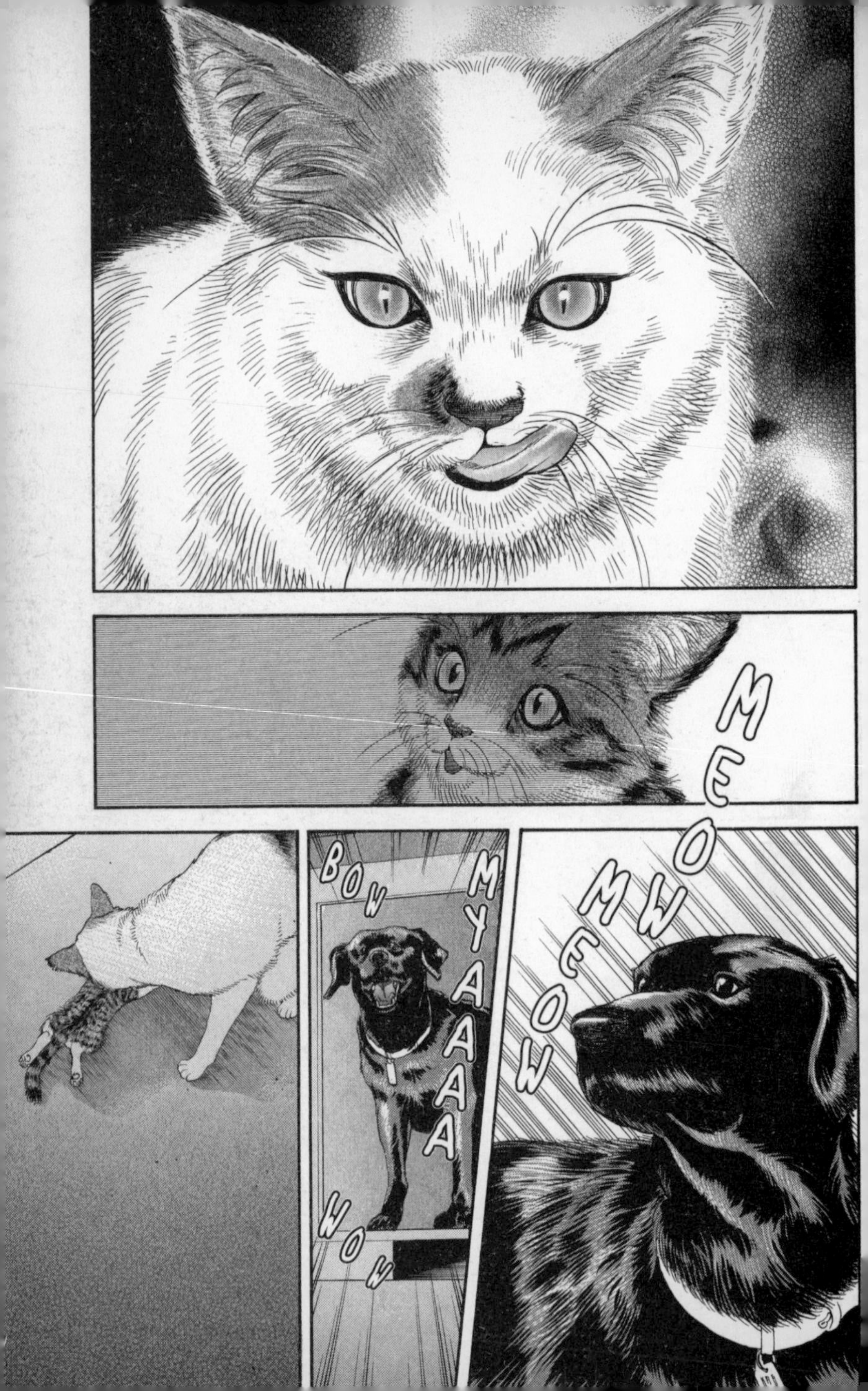
MEOW
MEOW
MYAAAAA
BOW
WOW

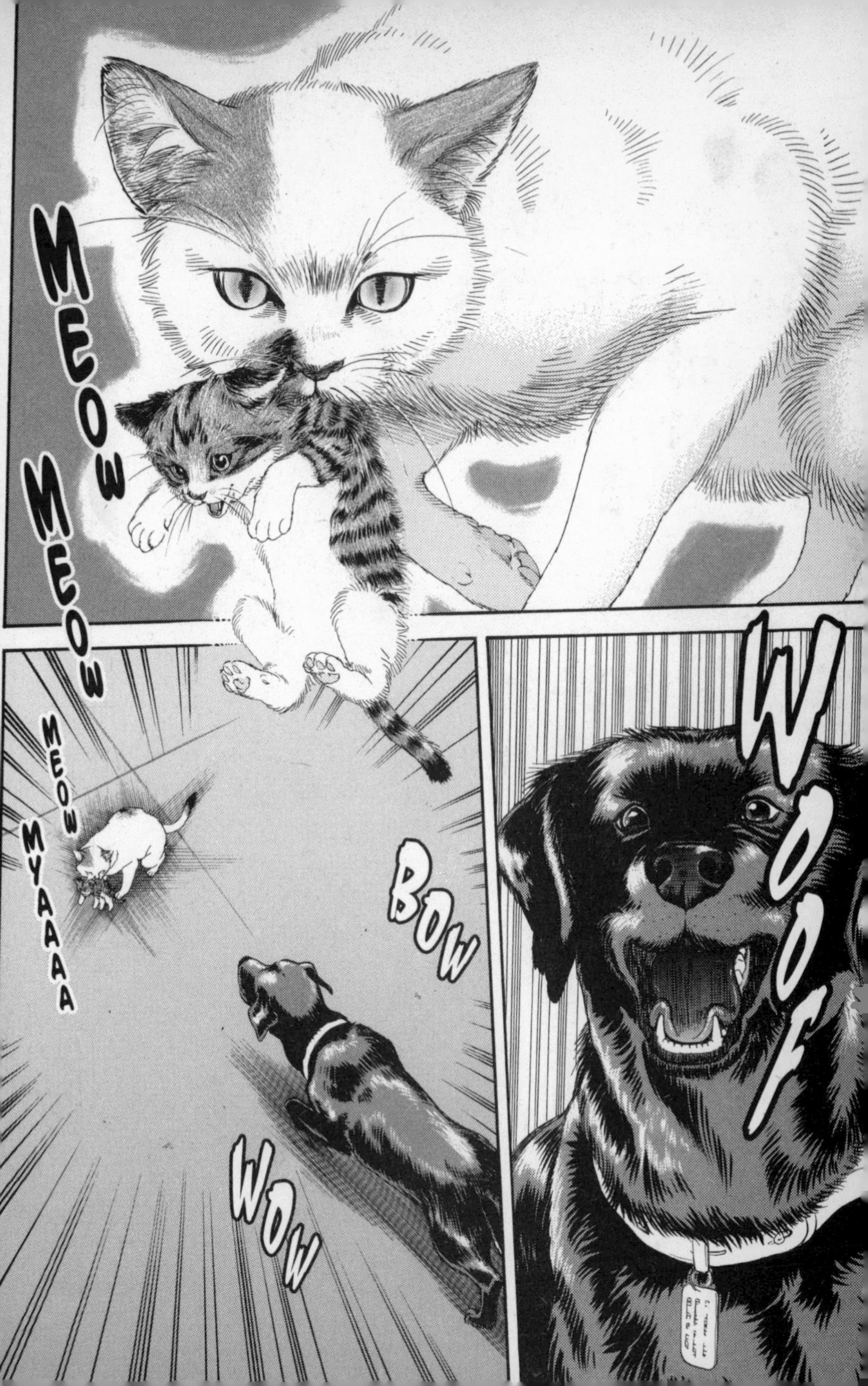
MEOW
MEOW
WOOF
MEOW
MYAAAA
BOW
WOW

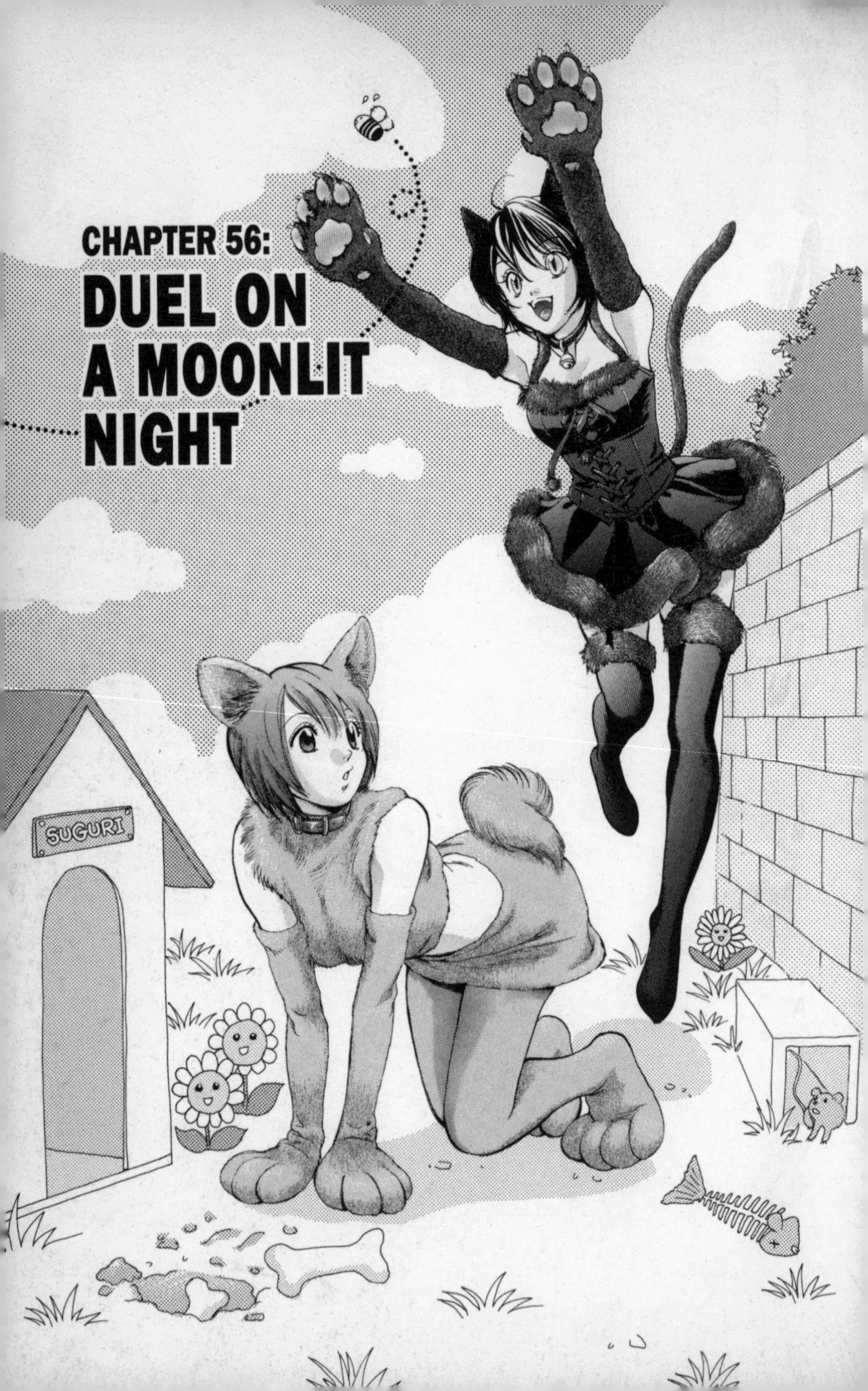
CHAPTER 56:
DUEL ON A MOONLIT NIGHT
SUGURI

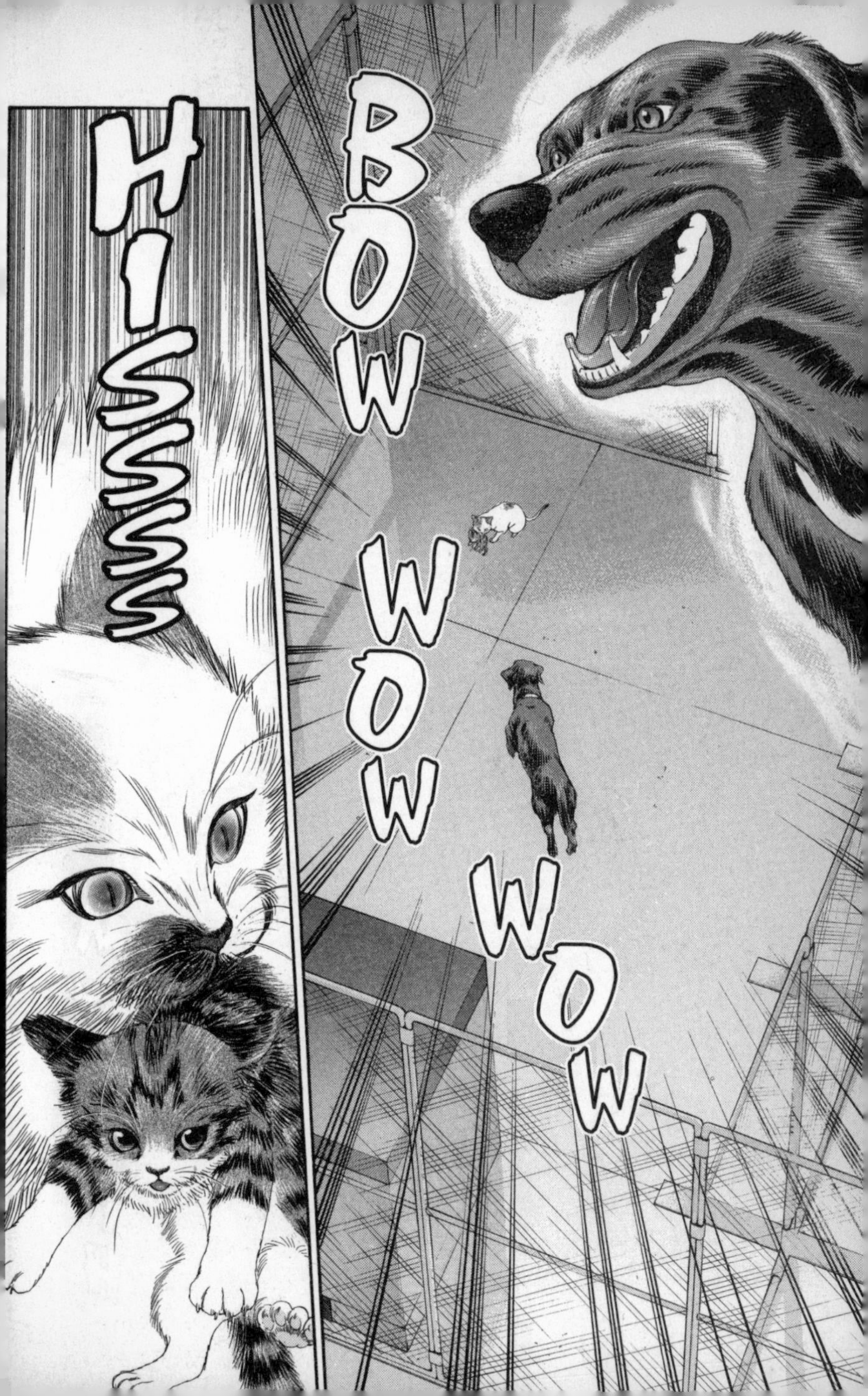
BOW WOW WOW WOW
HISSSS

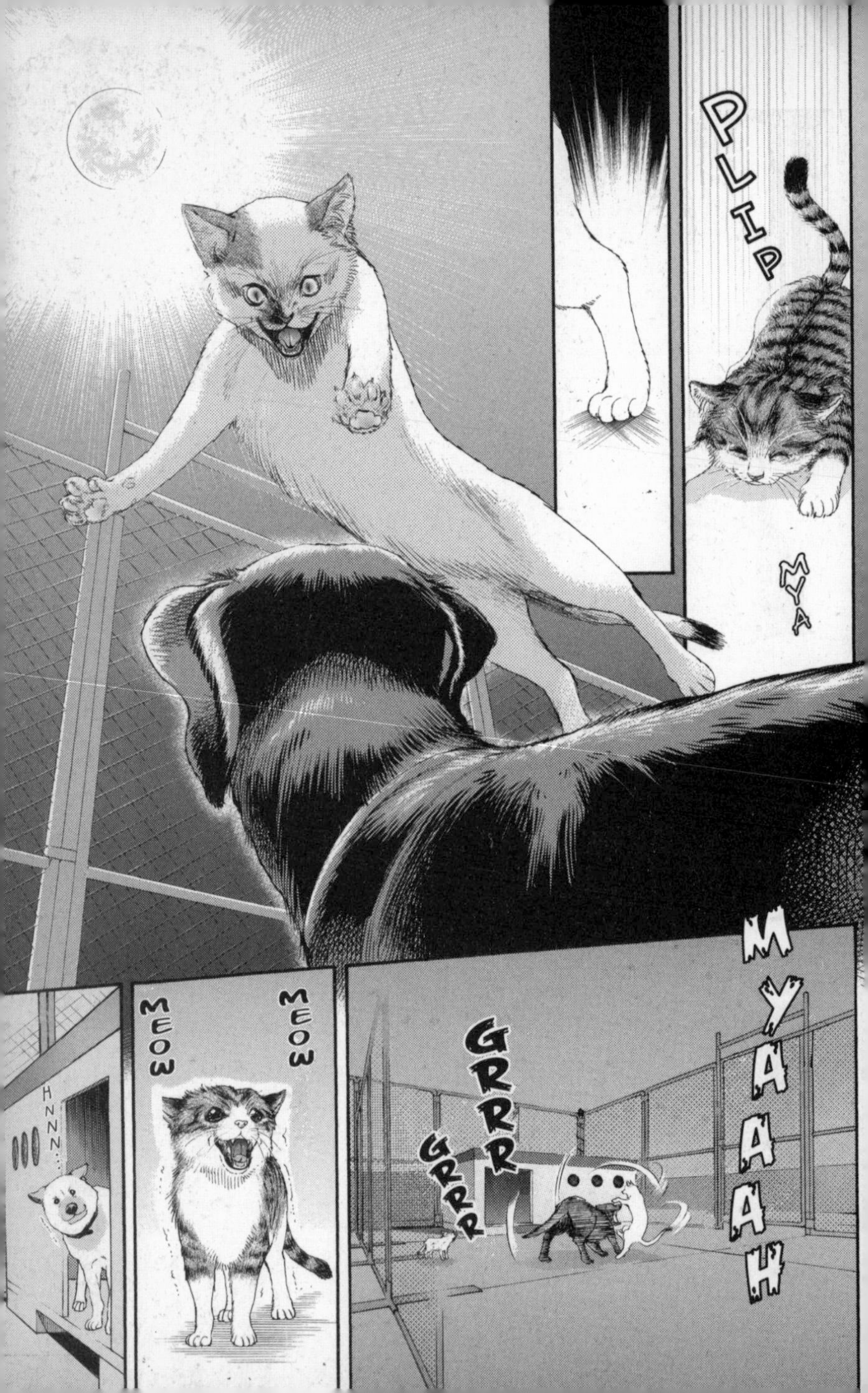
PLIP
MYA
MYAAAAH
GRRR
GRRR
MEOW
MEOW
HNNN...

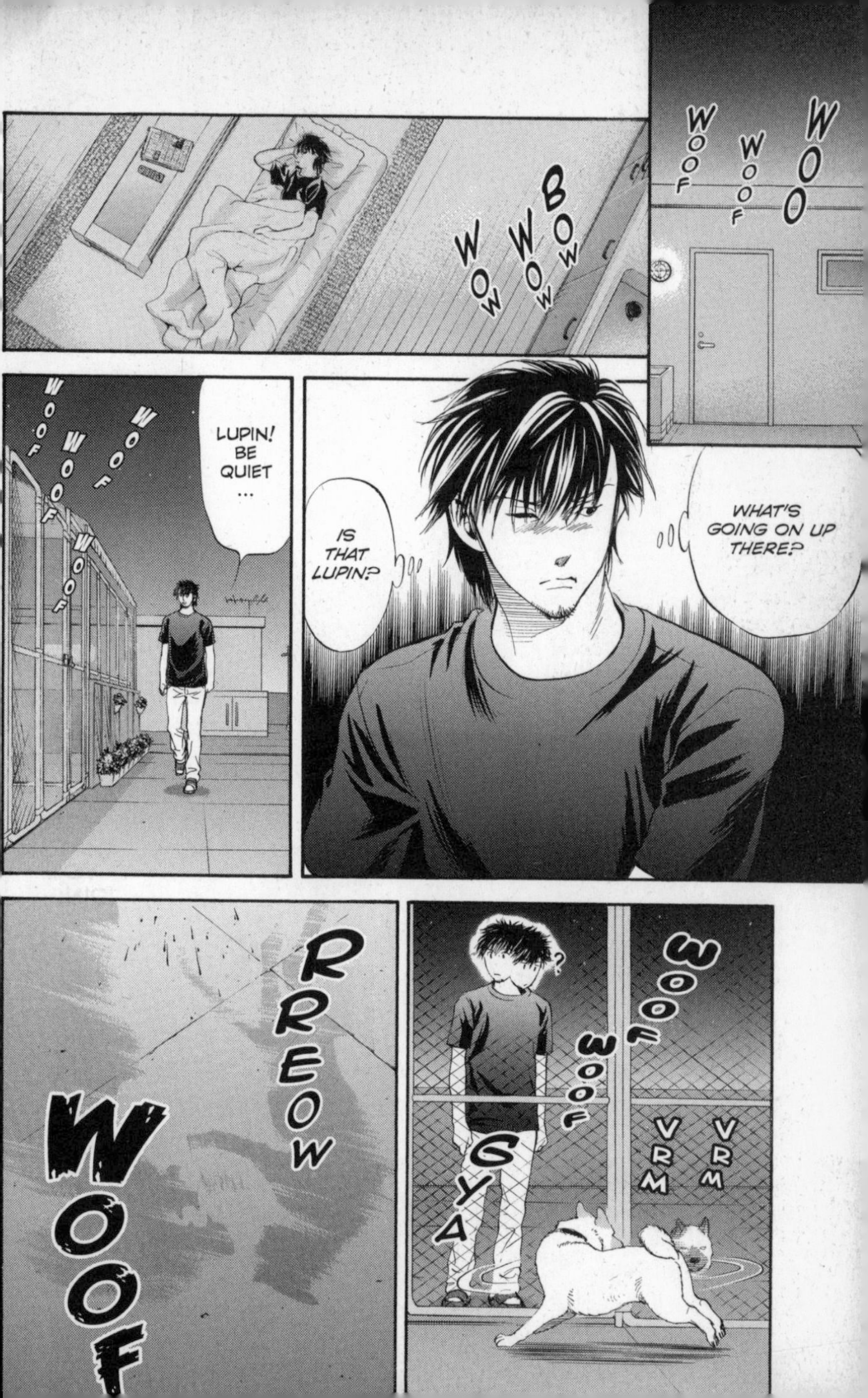
WOO
WOOF
WOOF
BOW
WOW
WOW
WHAT'S GOING ON UP THERE?
IS THAT LUPIN?
WOOF
WOOF
WOOF
WOOF
LUPIN! BE QUIET ...
WOOF
WOOF
GYA
VRM
VRM
RREOW
WOOF

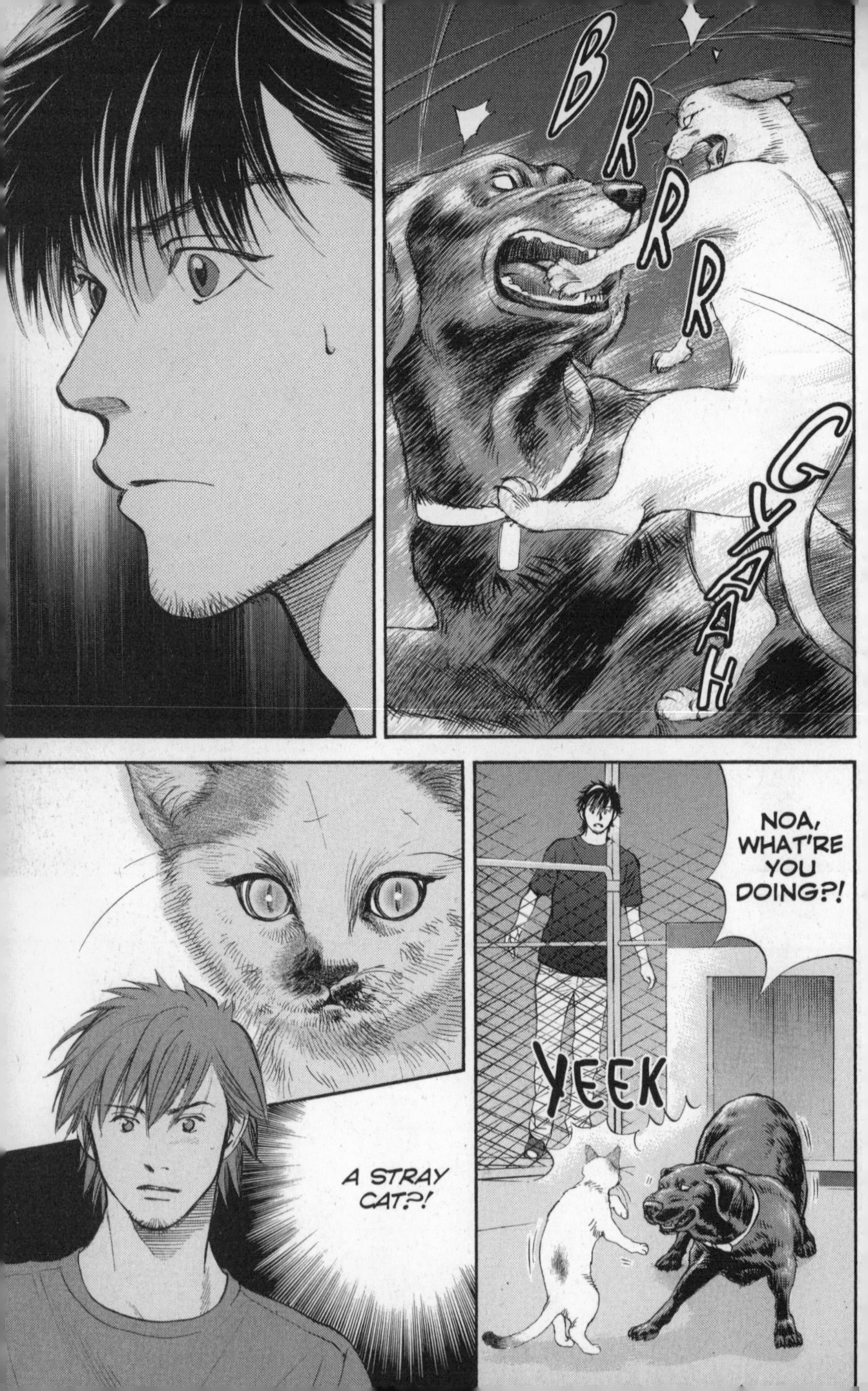
BRRRR
GYAAAH
NOA, WHAT'RE YOU DOING?!
YEEK
A STRAY CAT?!

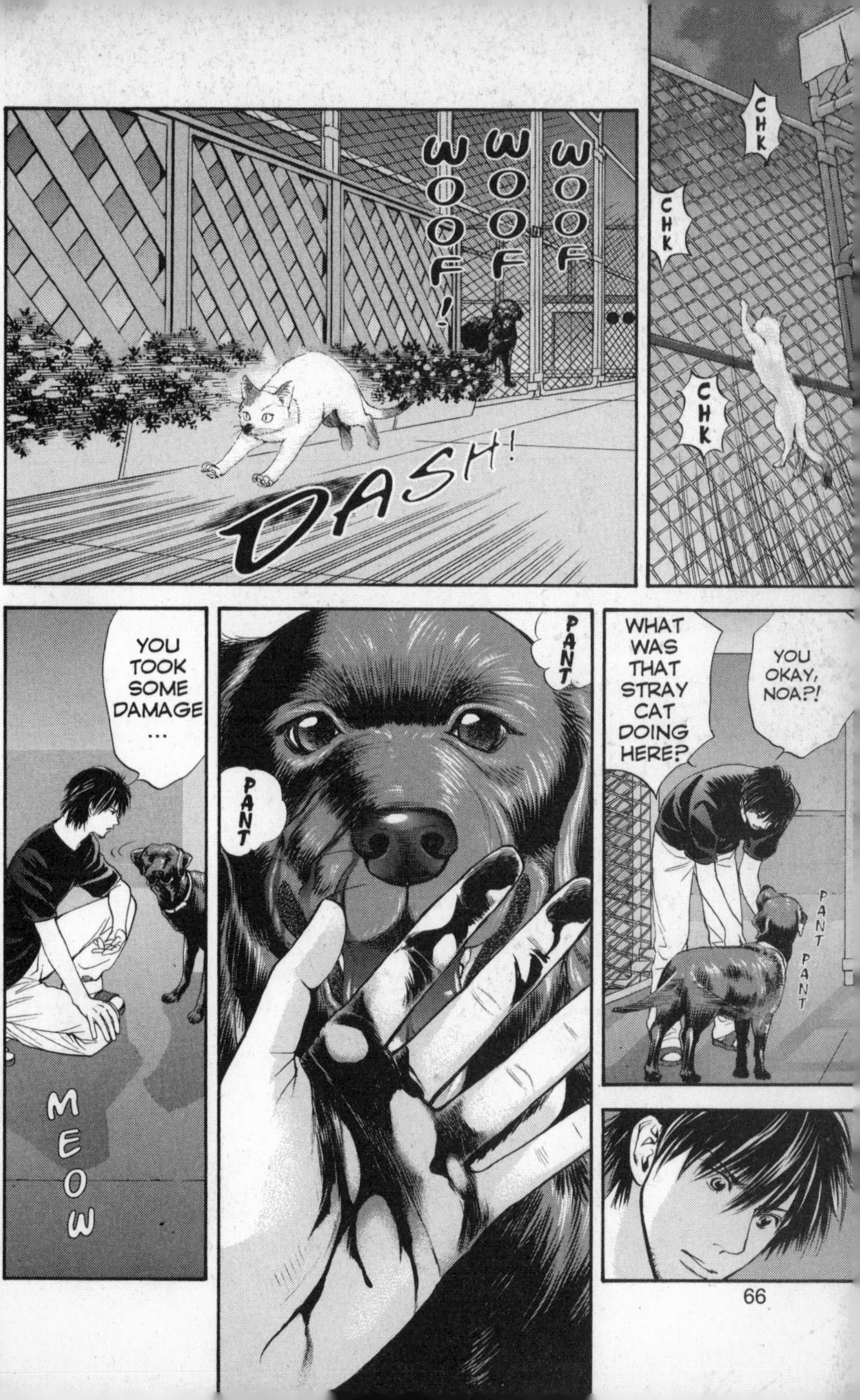
CHK
CHK
CHK
WOOF
WOOF
WOOF!
DASH!
YOU OKAY, NOA?!
WHAT WAS THAT STRAY CAT DOING HERE?
PANT PANT PANT
PANT
PANT
YOU TOOK SOME DAMAGE...
MEOW

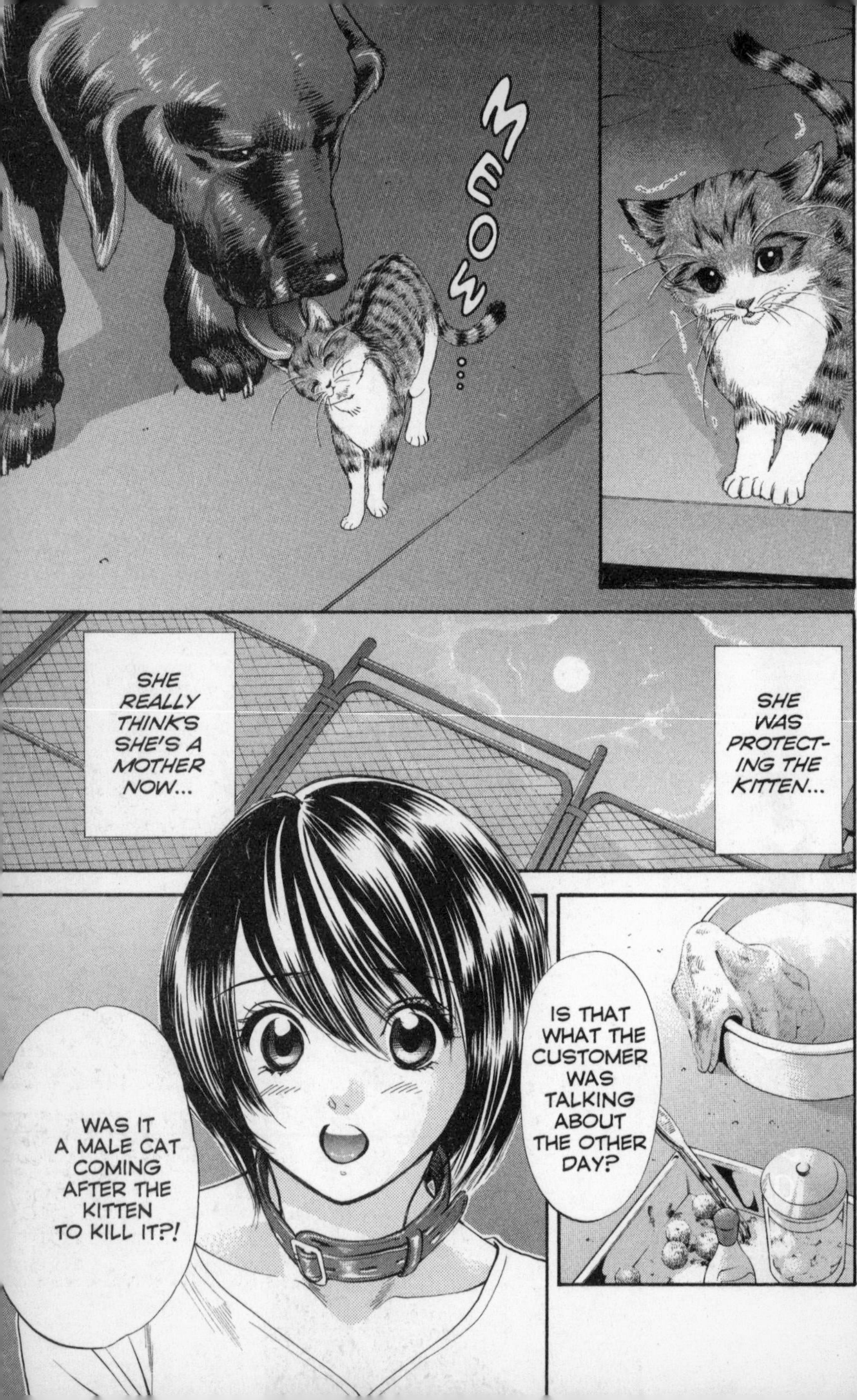
MEOW...
SHE WAS PROTECTING THE KITTEN...
SHE REALLY THINKS SHE'S A MOTHER NOW...
IS THAT WHAT THE CUSTOMER WAS TALKING ABOUT THE OTHER DAY?
WAS IT A MALE CAT COMING AFTER THE KITTEN TO KILL IT?!

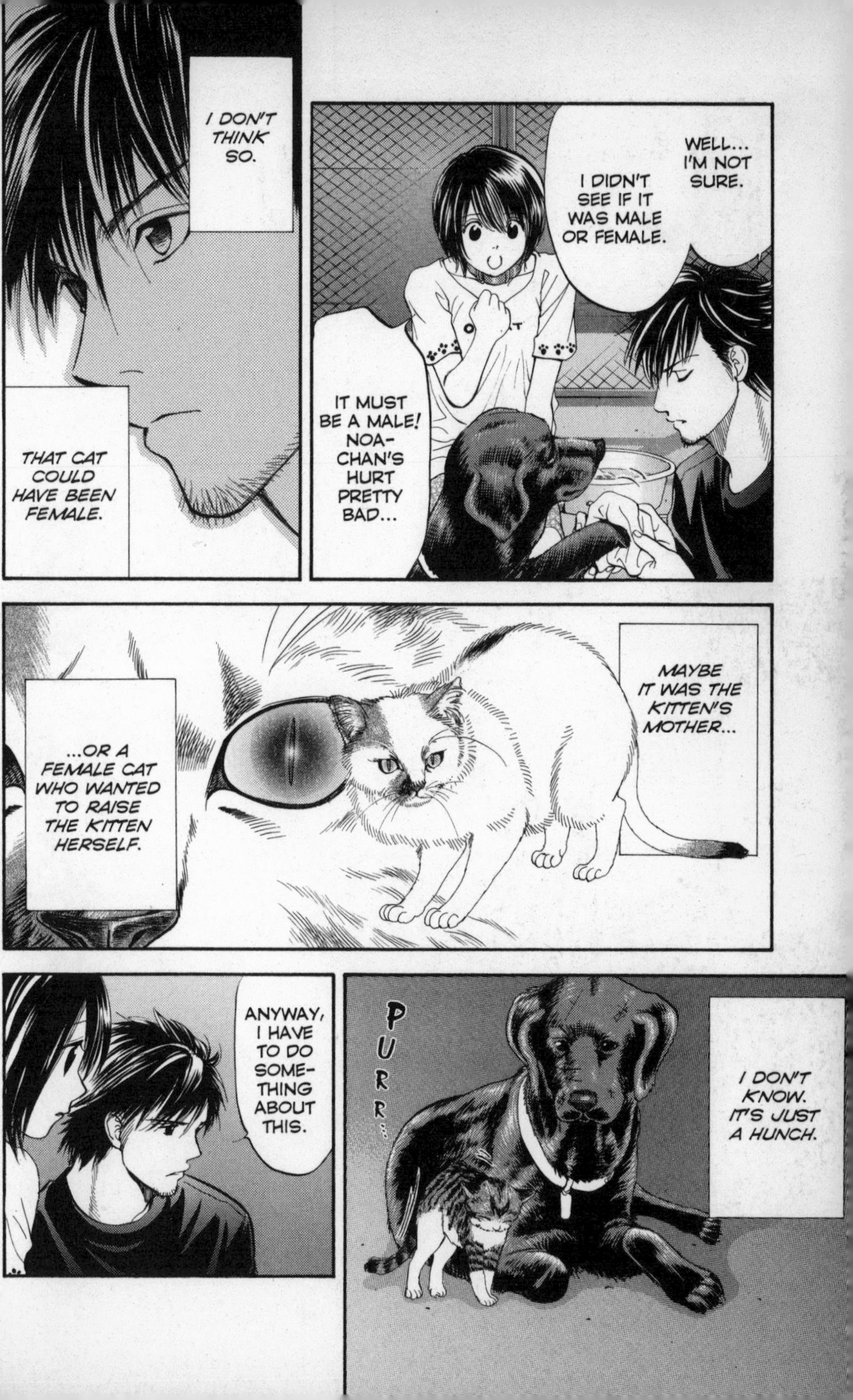
WELL... I'M NOT SURE.
I DIDN'T SEE IF IT WAS MALE OR FEMALE.
IT MUST BE A MALE! NOA-CHAN'S HURT PRETTY BAD...
I DON'T THINK SO.
THAT CAT COULD HAVE BEEN FEMALE.
MAYBE IT WAS THE KITTEN'S MOTHER...
...OR A FEMALE CAT WHO WANTED TO RAISE THE KITTEN HERSELF.
I DON'T KNOW. IT'S JUST A HUNCH.
PURR...
ANYWAY, I HAVE TO DO SOMETHING ABOUT THIS.

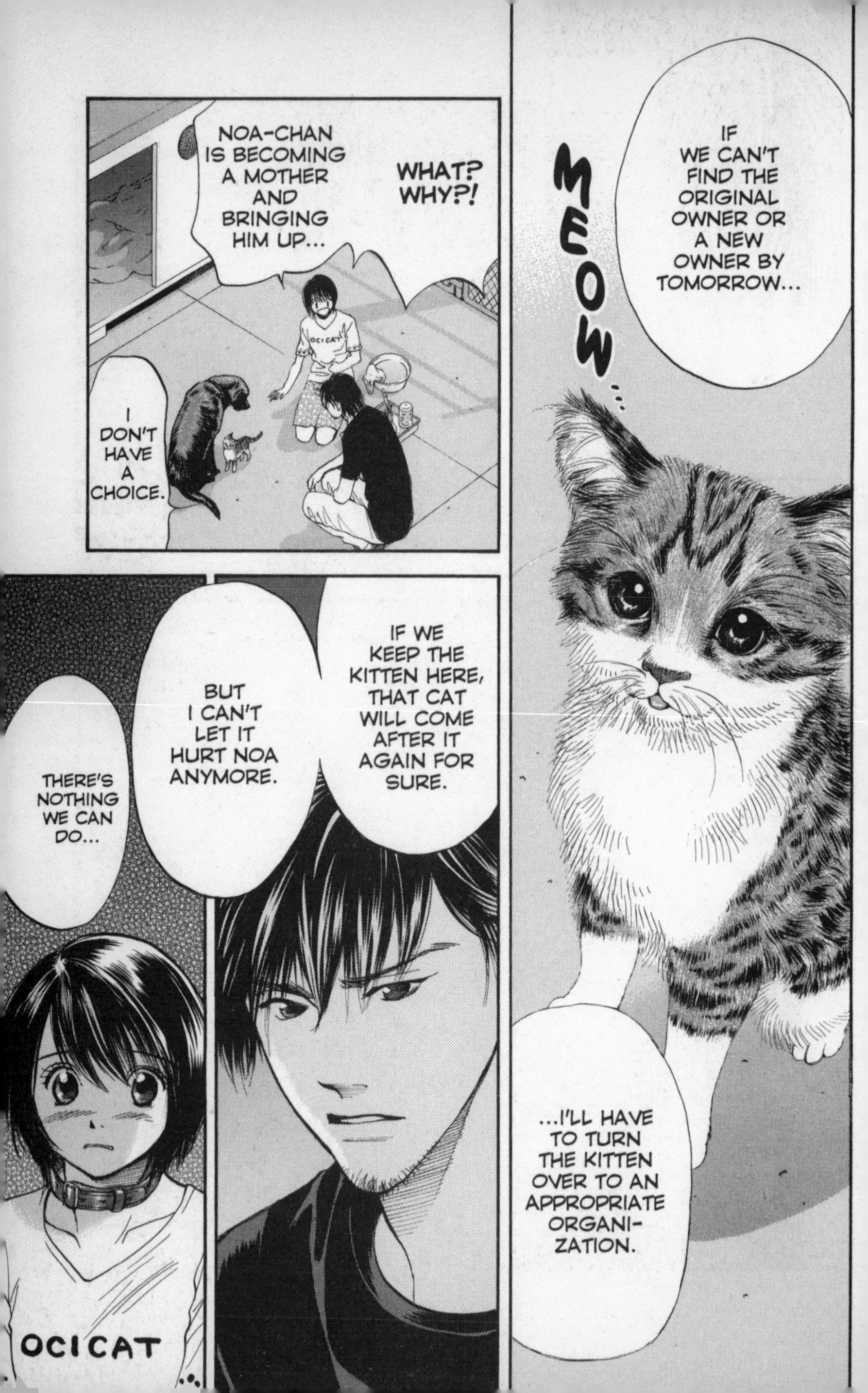
IF WE CAN'T FIND THE ORIGINAL OWNER OR A NEW OWNER BY TOMORROW...
MEOW...
...I'LL HAVE TO TURN THE KITTEN OVER TO AN APPROPRIATE ORGANI-ZATION.
WHAT? WHY?!
NOA-CHAN IS BECOMING A MOTHER AND BRINGING HIM UP...
OCICAT
I DON'T HAVE A CHOICE.
IF WE KEEP THE KITTEN HERE, THAT CAT WILL COME AFTER IT AGAIN FOR SURE.
BUT I CAN'T LET IT HURT NOA ANYMORE.
THERE'S NOTHING WE CAN DO...
OCICAT

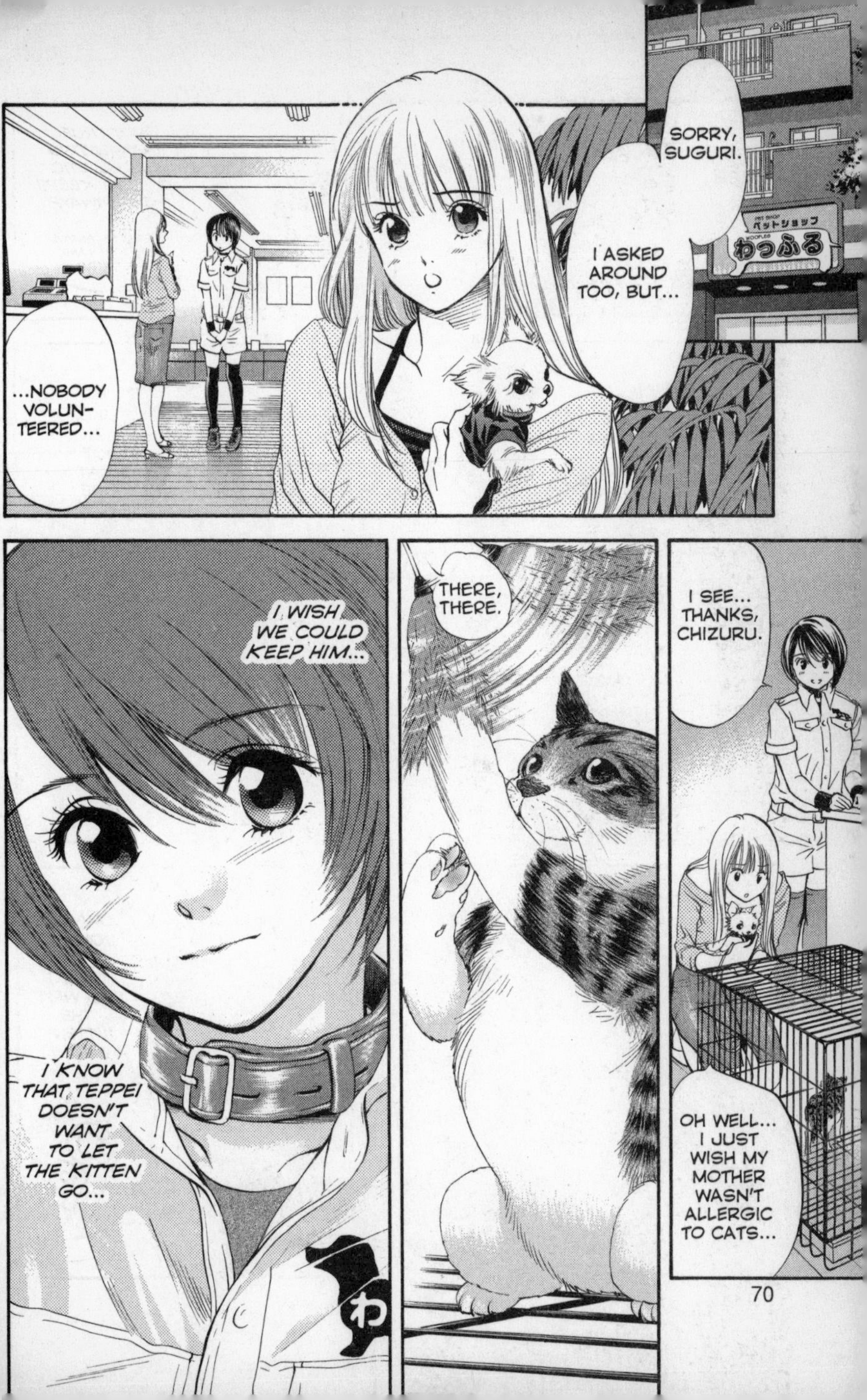
ペットショップ
わっふる
SORRY, SUGURI.
I ASKED AROUND TOO, BUT...
...NOBODY VOLUN-TEERED...
I SEE... THANKS, CHIZURU.
OH WELL... I JUST WISH MY MOTHER WASN'T ALLERGIC TO CATS...
THERE, THERE.
I WISH WE COULD KEEP HIM...
I KNOW THAT TEPPEI DOESN'T WANT TO LET THE KITTEN GO...
わ

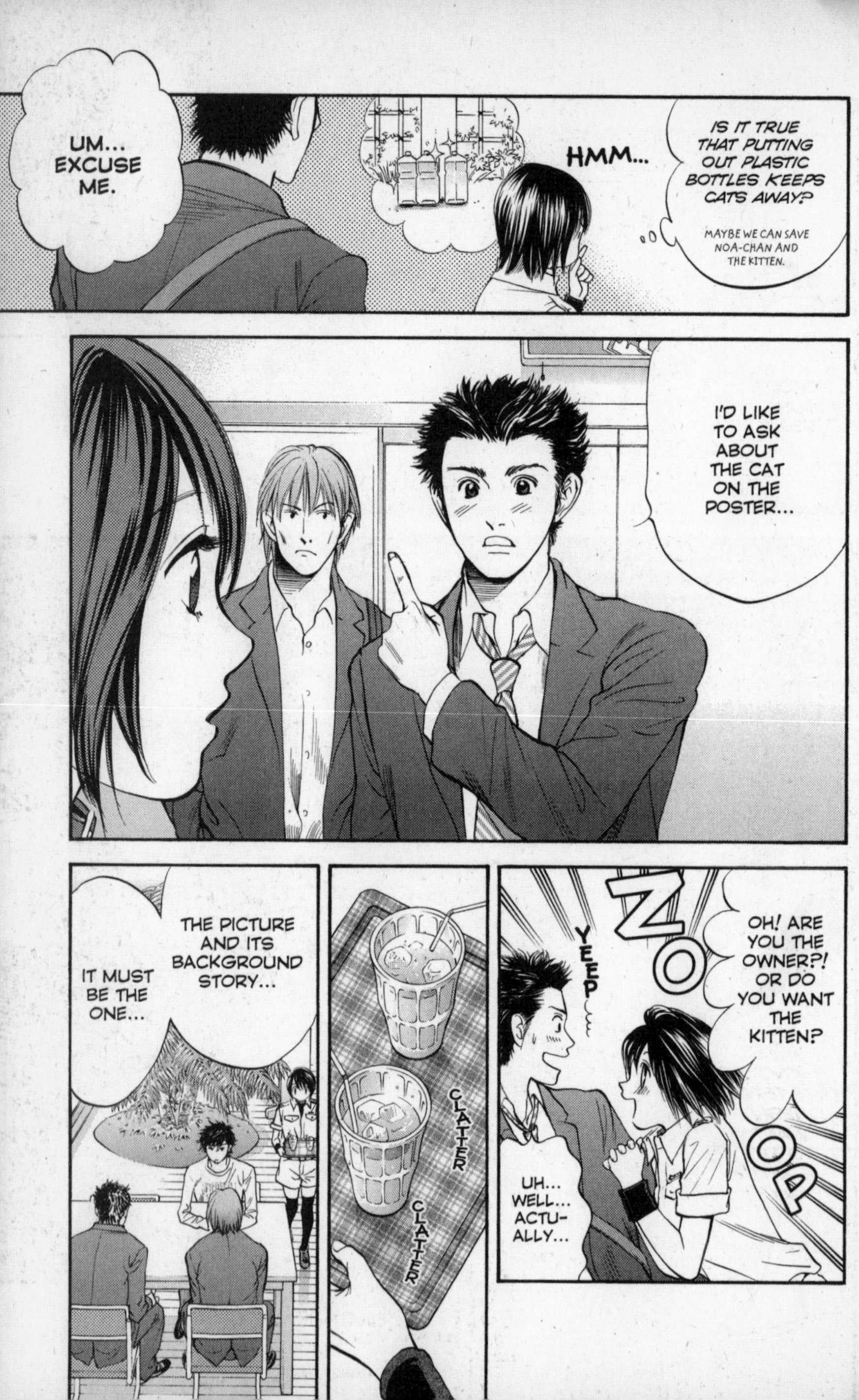
IS IT TRUE THAT PUTTING OUT PLASTIC BOTTLES KEEPS CATS AWAY?
MAYBE WE CAN SAVE NOA-CHAN AND THE KITTEN.
HMM...
UM... EXCUSE ME.
I'D LIKE TO ASK ABOUT THE CAT ON THE POSTER...
OH! ARE YOU THE OWNER?! OR DO YOU WANT THE KITTEN?
ZOOOP
YEEP
UH... WELL... ACTU-ALLY...
CLATTER
CLATTER
THE PICTURE AND ITS BACKGROUND STORY...
IT MUST BE THE ONE...

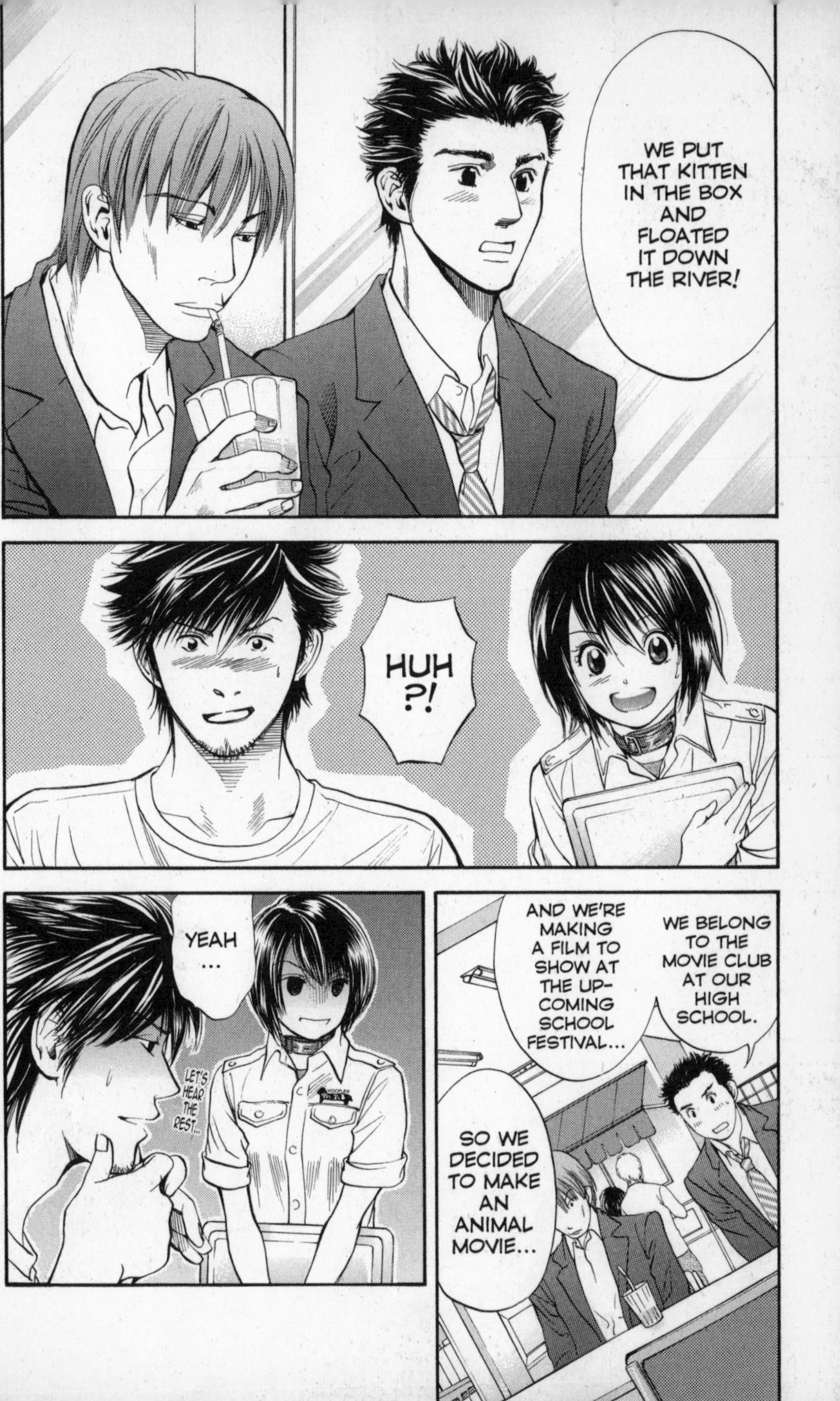
WE PUT THAT KITTEN IN THE BOX AND FLOATED IT DOWN THE RIVER!
HUH ?!
WE BELONG TO THE MOVIE CLUB AT OUR HIGH SCHOOL.
AND WE'RE MAKING A FILM TO SHOW AT THE UP-COMING SCHOOL FESTIVAL...
SO WE DECIDED TO MAKE AN ANIMAL MOVIE...
YEAH ...
LET'S HEAR THE REST...

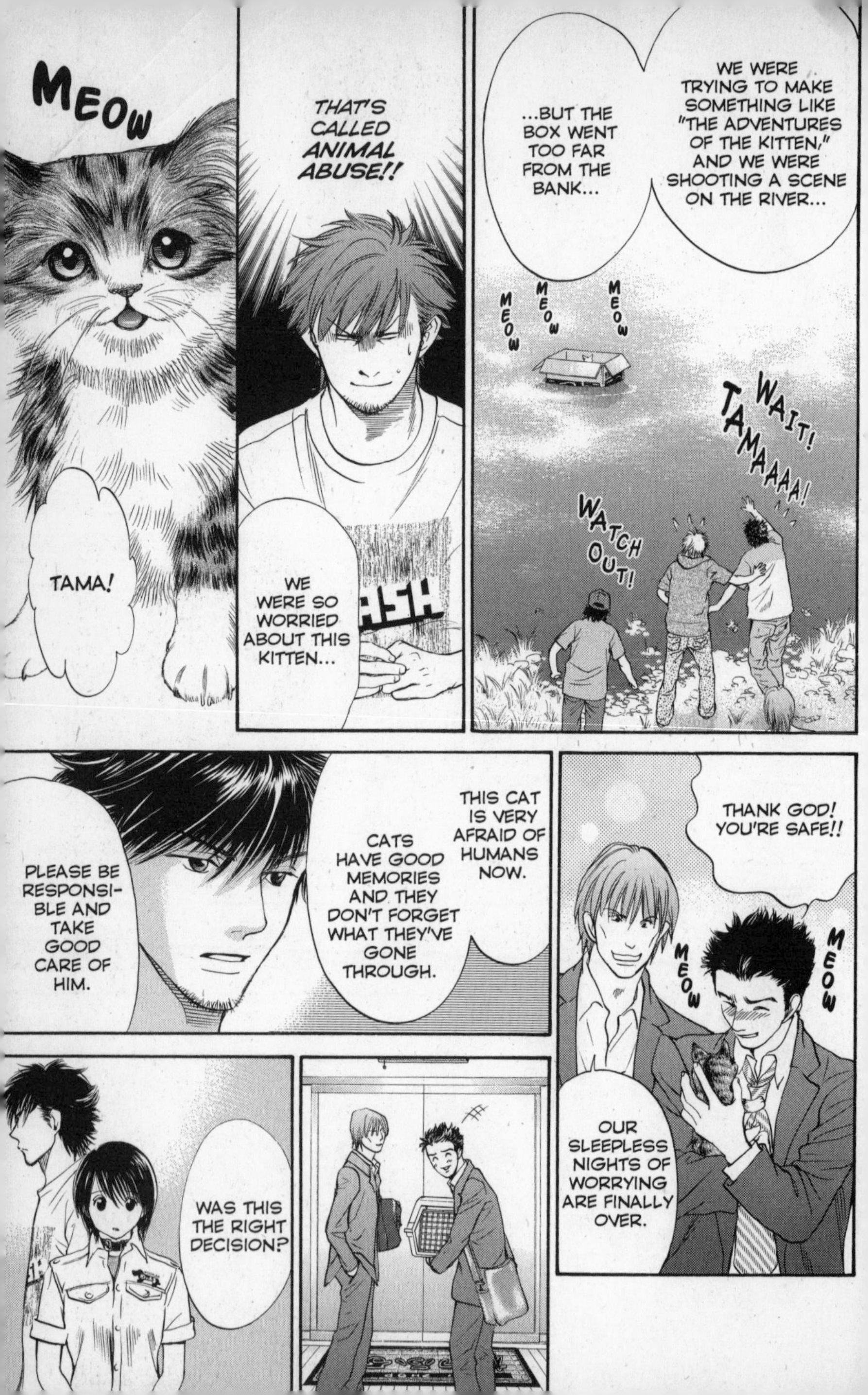
WE WERE TRYING TO MAKE SOMETHING LIKE "THE ADVENTURES OF THE KITTEN," AND WE WERE SHOOTING A SCENE ON THE RIVER...
...BUT THE BOX WENT TOO FAR FROM THE BANK...
MEOW
MEOW
MEOW
WAIT! TAMAAAAA!
WATCH OUT!
THAT'S CALLED ANIMAL ABUSE!!
WE WERE SO WORRIED ABOUT THIS KITTEN...
MEOW
TAMA!
THANK GOD! YOU'RE SAFE!!
MEOW
MEOW
OUR SLEEPLESS NIGHTS OF WORRYING ARE FINALLY OVER.
THIS CAT IS VERY AFRAID OF HUMANS NOW.
CATS HAVE GOOD MEMORIES AND THEY DON'T FORGET WHAT THEY'VE GONE THROUGH.
PLEASE BE RESPONSI-BLE AND TAKE GOOD CARE OF HIM.
WAS THIS THE RIGHT DECISION?

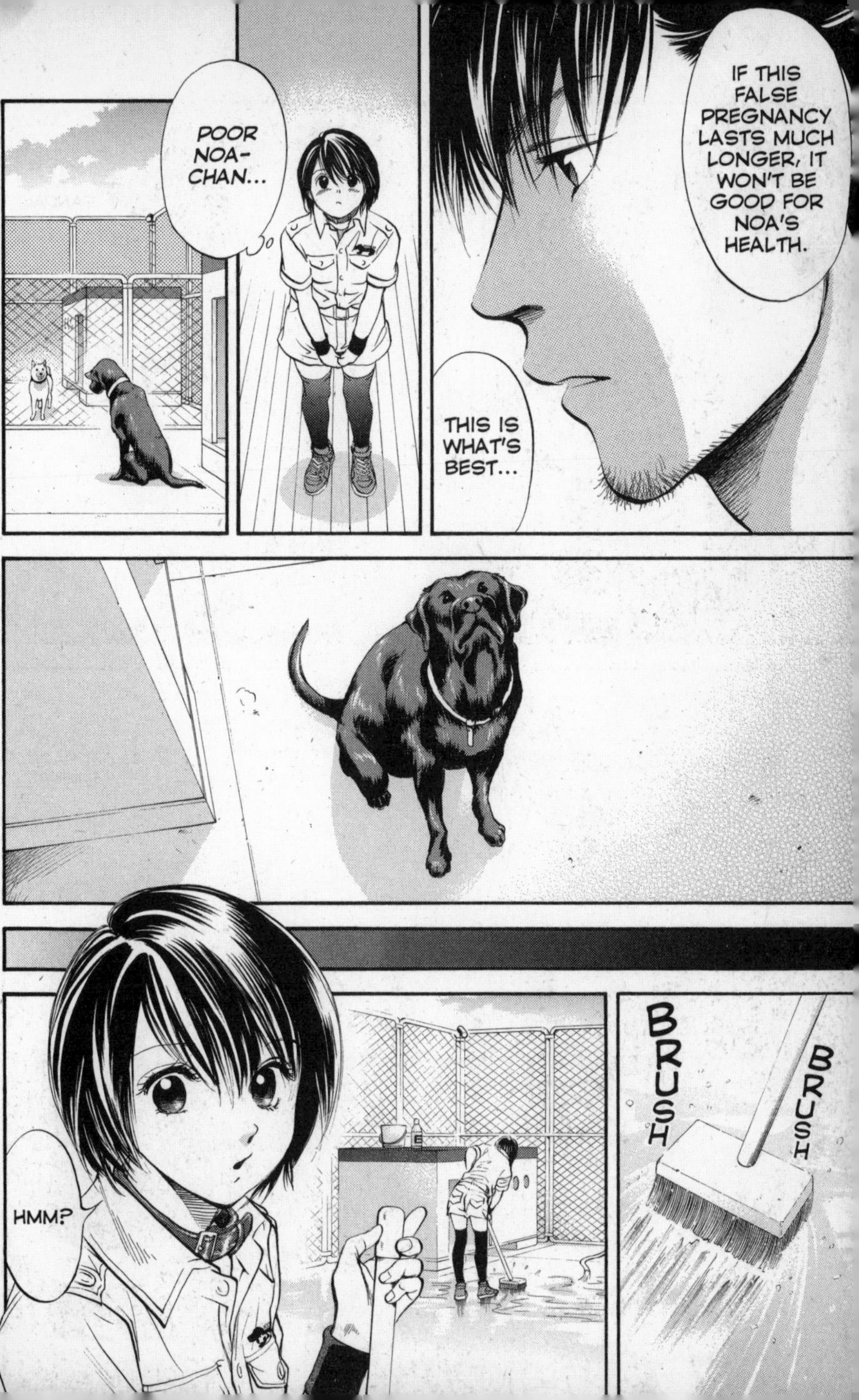
IF THIS FALSE PREGNANCY LASTS MUCH LONGER, IT WON'T BE GOOD FOR NOA'S HEALTH.
THIS IS WHAT'S BEST...
POOR NOA-CHAN...
BRUSH
BRUSH
HMM?

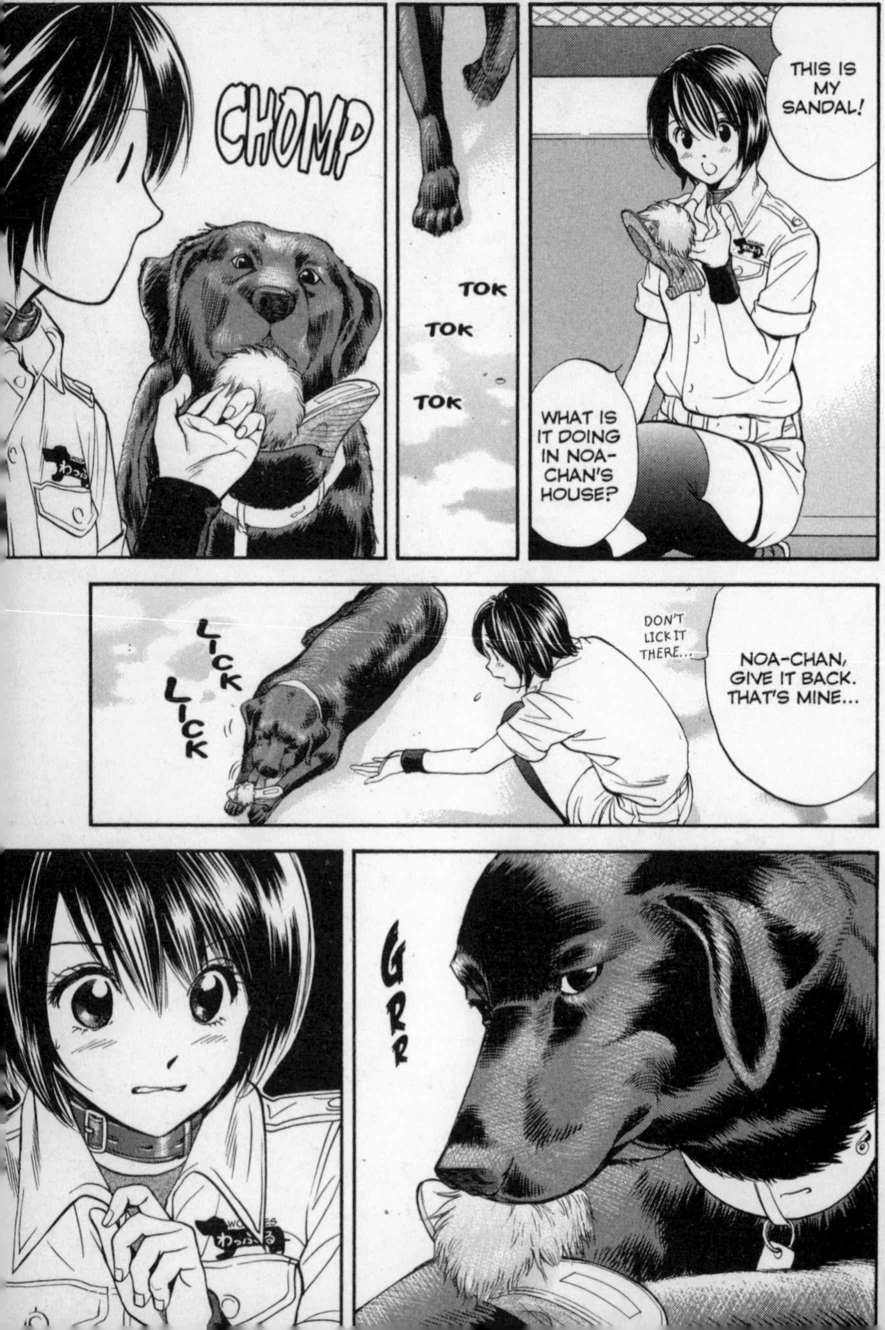
THIS IS MY SANDAL!
WHAT IS IT DOING IN NOA-CHAN'S HOUSE?
TOK
TOK
TOK
CHOMP
NOA-CHAN, GIVE IT BACK. THAT'S MINE...
DON'T LICK IT THERE...
LICK
LICK
GRR

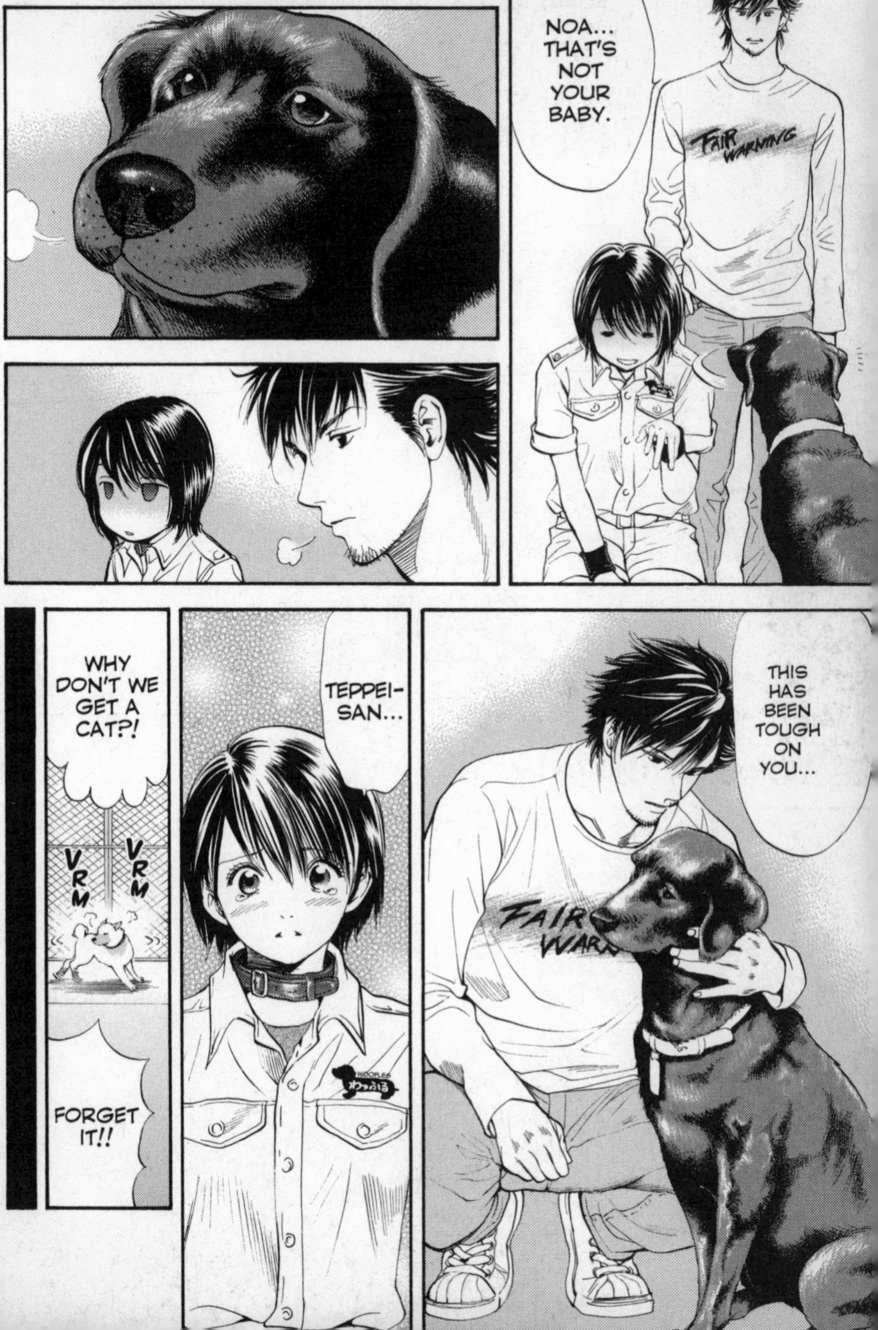

NOA... THAT'S NOT YOUR BABY.
FAIR WARNING
THIS HAS BEEN TOUGH ON YOU...
FAIR WARN
TEPPEI-SAN...
WOOFLES
わっふる
WHY DON'T WE GET A CAT?!
VRM
VRM
FORGET IT!!

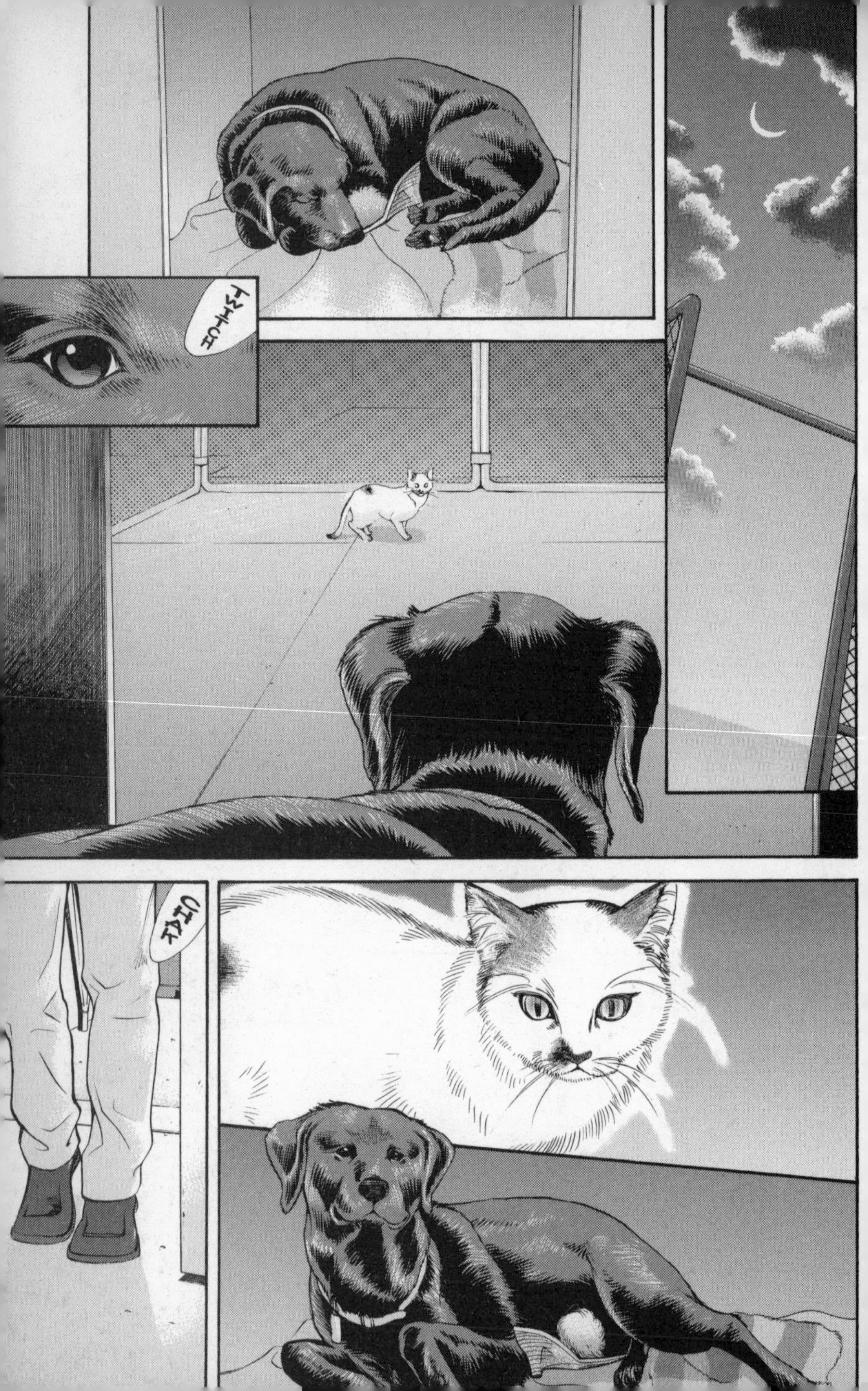
TWITCH
CHAK

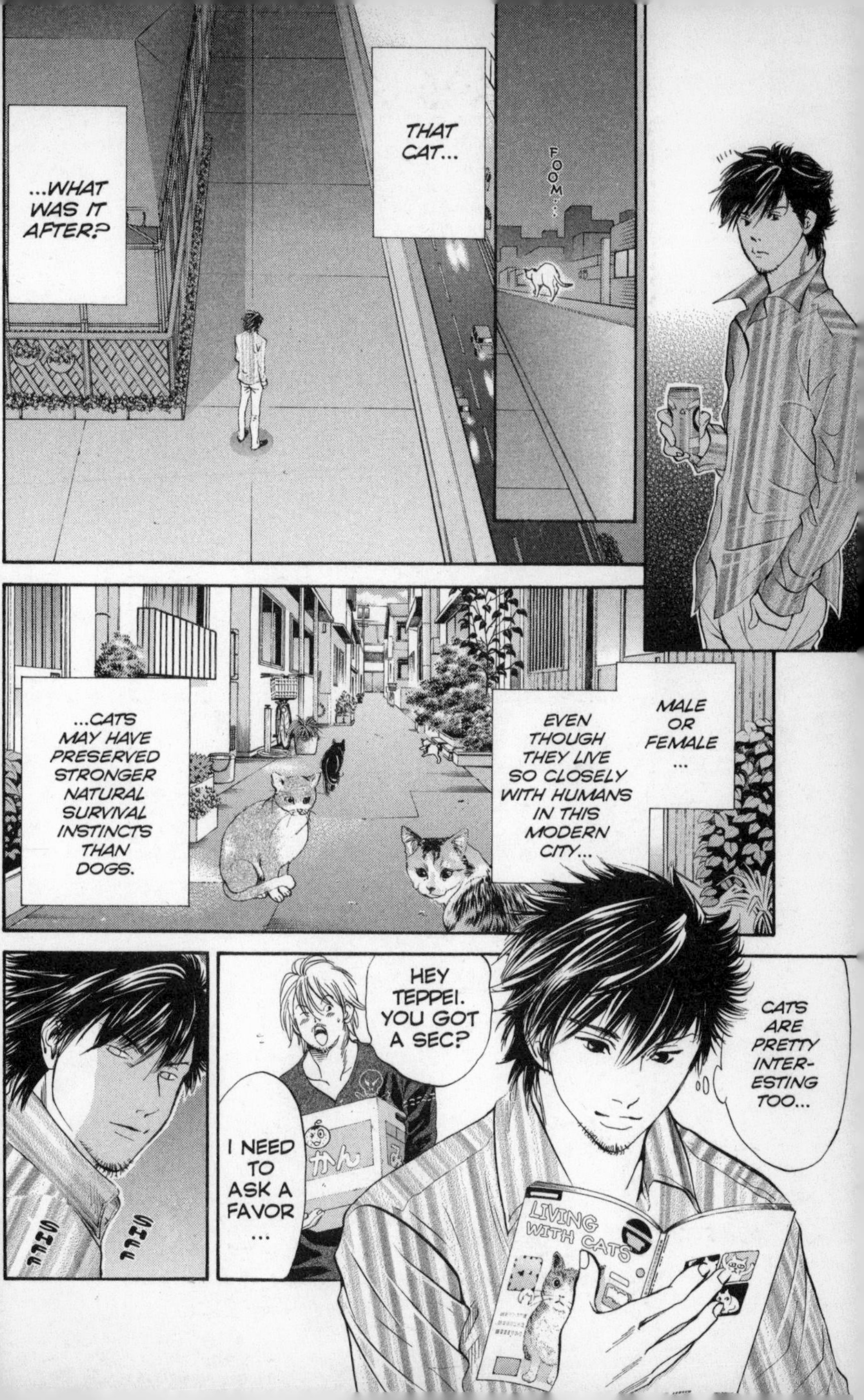
FOOM...
THAT CAT...
...WHAT WAS IT AFTER?
MALE OR FEMALE ...
EVEN THOUGH THEY LIVE SO CLOSELY WITH HUMANS IN THIS MODERN CITY...
...CATS MAY HAVE PRESERVED STRONGER NATURAL SURVIVAL INSTINCTS THAN DOGS.
CATS ARE PRETTY INTER-ESTING TOO...
LIVING WITH CATS
HEY TEPPEI. YOU GOT A SEC?
I NEED TO ASK A FAVOR ...
かん
STILL
STILL

SUGURI HUSTLES

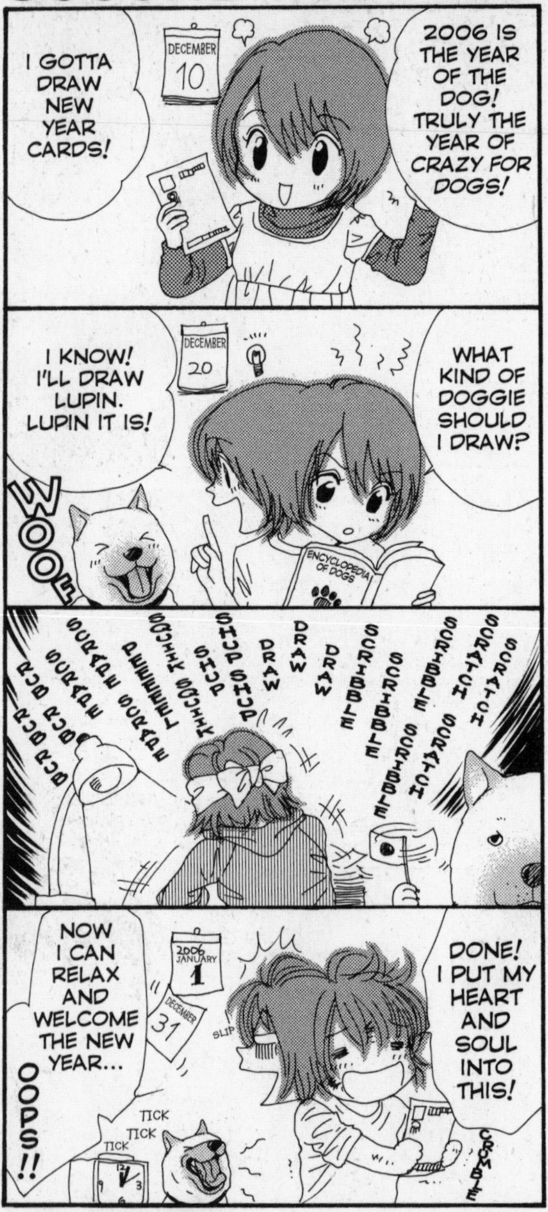
2006 IS THE YEAR OF THE DOG! TRULY THE YEAR OF CRAZY FOR DOGS!
DECEMBER 10
I GOTTA DRAW NEW YEAR CARDS!
WHAT KIND OF DOGGIE SHOULD I DRAW?
DECEMBER 20
I KNOW! I'LL DRAW LUPIN. LUPIN IT IS!
ENCYCLOPEDIA OF DOGS
WOOF
SCRATCH
SCRATCH
SCRIBBLE SCRATCH
SCRIBBLE SCRIBBLE
SCRIBBLE
DRAW
DRAW
DRAW
SHUP SHUP
SHUP
SQUIK SQUIK
PEEEEEL
SCRAPE SCRAPE
SCRAPE
RCB RCB
RCB RCB RCB
DONE! I PUT MY HEART AND SOUL INTO THIS!
CRUMBLE
2006 JANUARY 1
DECEMBER 31
SLIP
NOW I CAN RELAX AND WELCOME THE NEW YEAR...
TICK
TICK
TICK
OOPS!!

THE FINISHED DRAWING IS ON PAGE 171 !!

TYPICAL PUNCH LINE...

CHAPTER 57:
RUFF RUFF! DIG HERE!

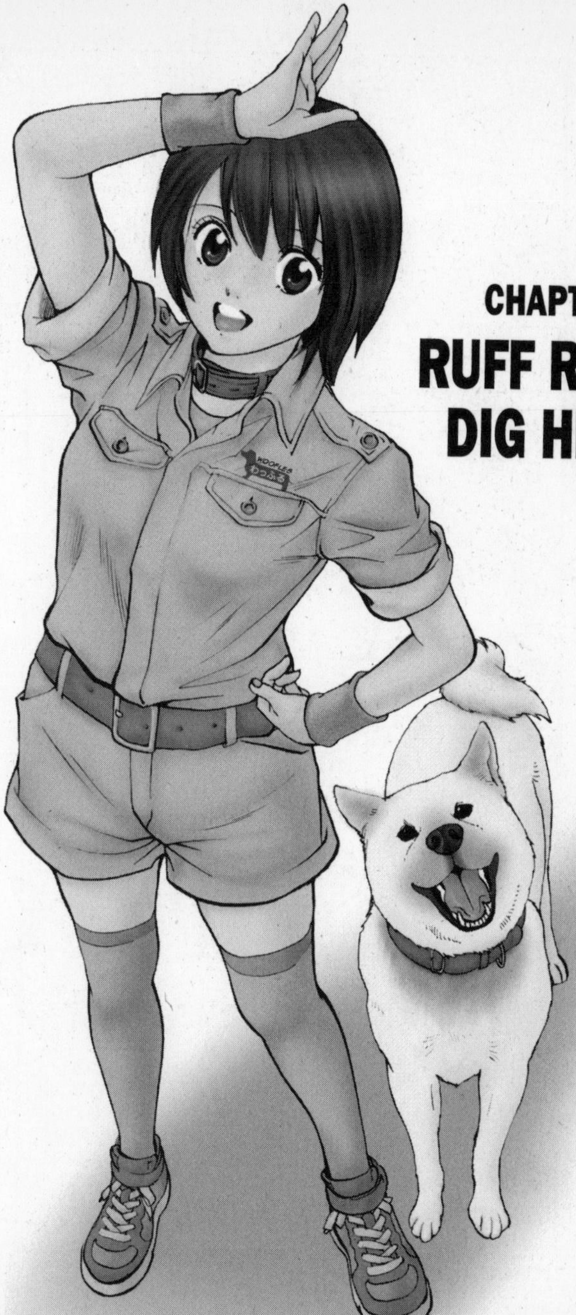

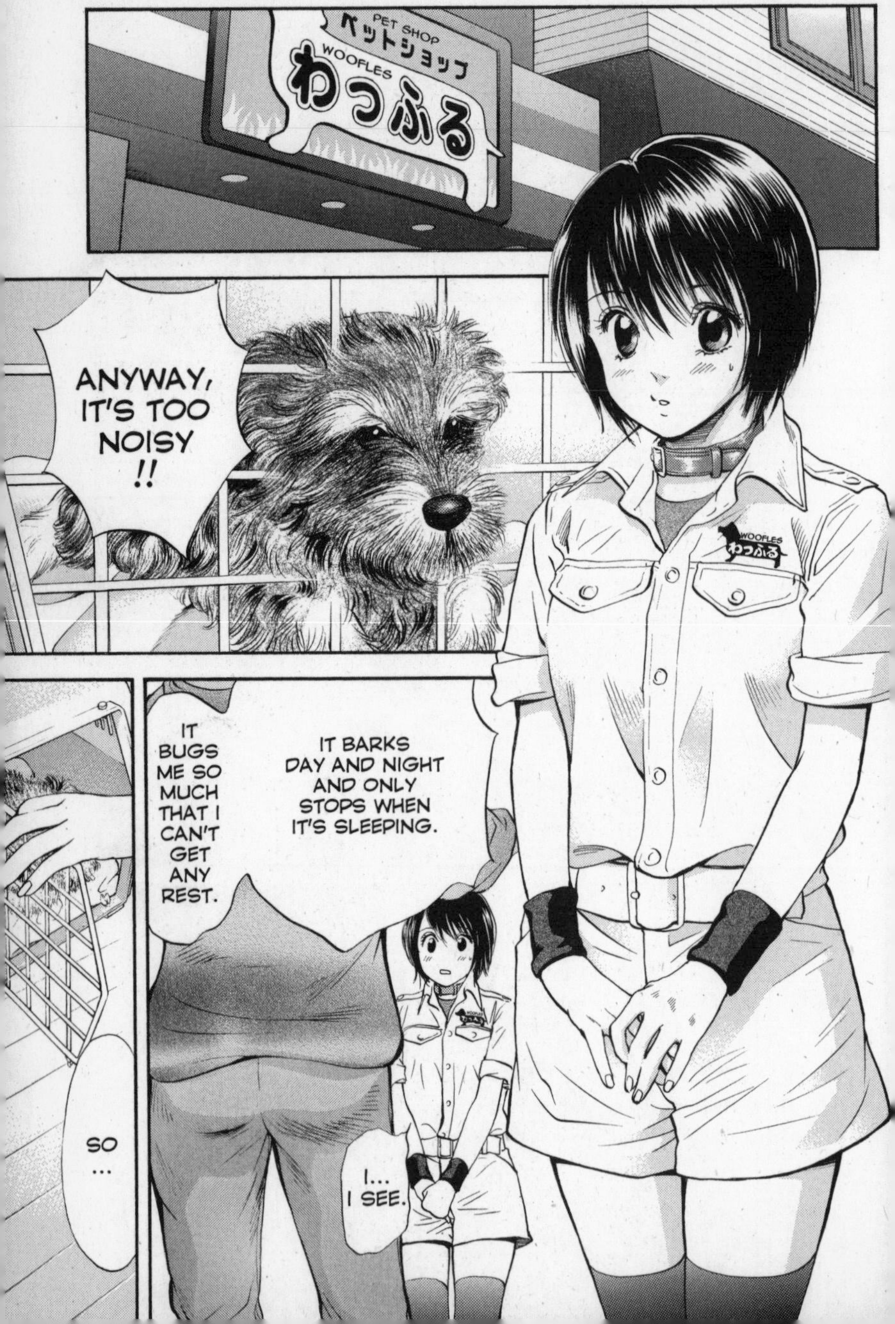
PET SHOP
ペットショップ
WOOFLES
わっふる
ANYWAY, IT'S TOO NOISY !!
WOOFLES
わっふる
IT BARKS DAY AND NIGHT AND ONLY STOPS WHEN IT'S SLEEPING.
IT BUGS ME SO MUCH THAT I CAN'T GET ANY REST.
I... I SEE.
SO ...

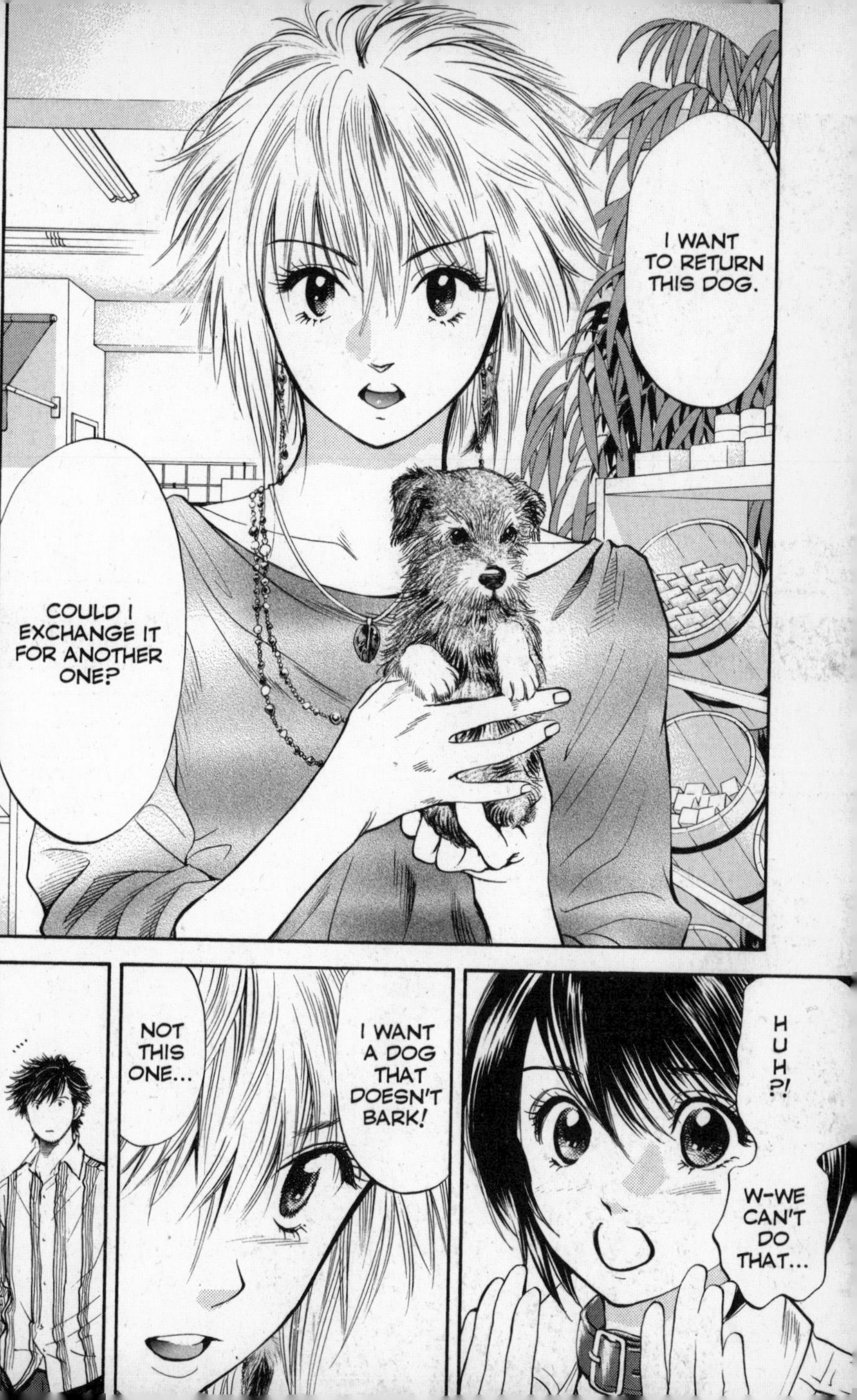
I WANT TO RETURN THIS DOG.
COULD I EXCHANGE IT FOR ANOTHER ONE?
HUH?!
W-WE CAN'T DO THAT...
I WANT A DOG THAT DOESN'T BARK!
NOT THIS ONE...
...

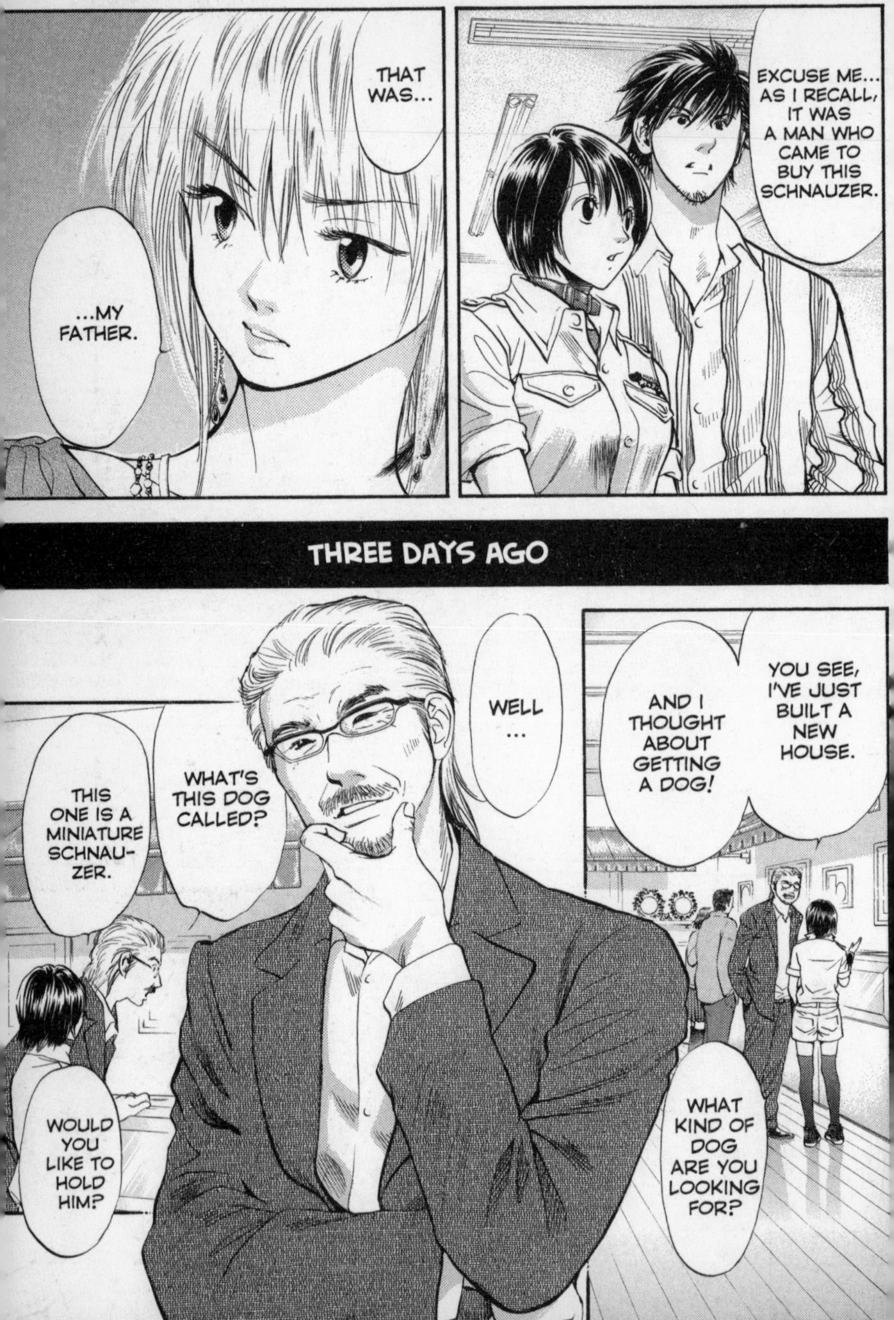
EXCUSE ME... AS I RECALL, IT WAS A MAN WHO CAME TO BUY THIS SCHNAUZER.
THAT WAS...
...MY FATHER.
THREE DAYS AGO
YOU SEE, I'VE JUST BUILT A NEW HOUSE.
AND I THOUGHT ABOUT GETTING A DOG!
WHAT KIND OF DOG ARE YOU LOOKING FOR?
WELL ...
WHAT'S THIS DOG CALLED?
THIS ONE IS A MINIATURE SCHNAU-ZER.
WOULD YOU LIKE TO HOLD HIM?

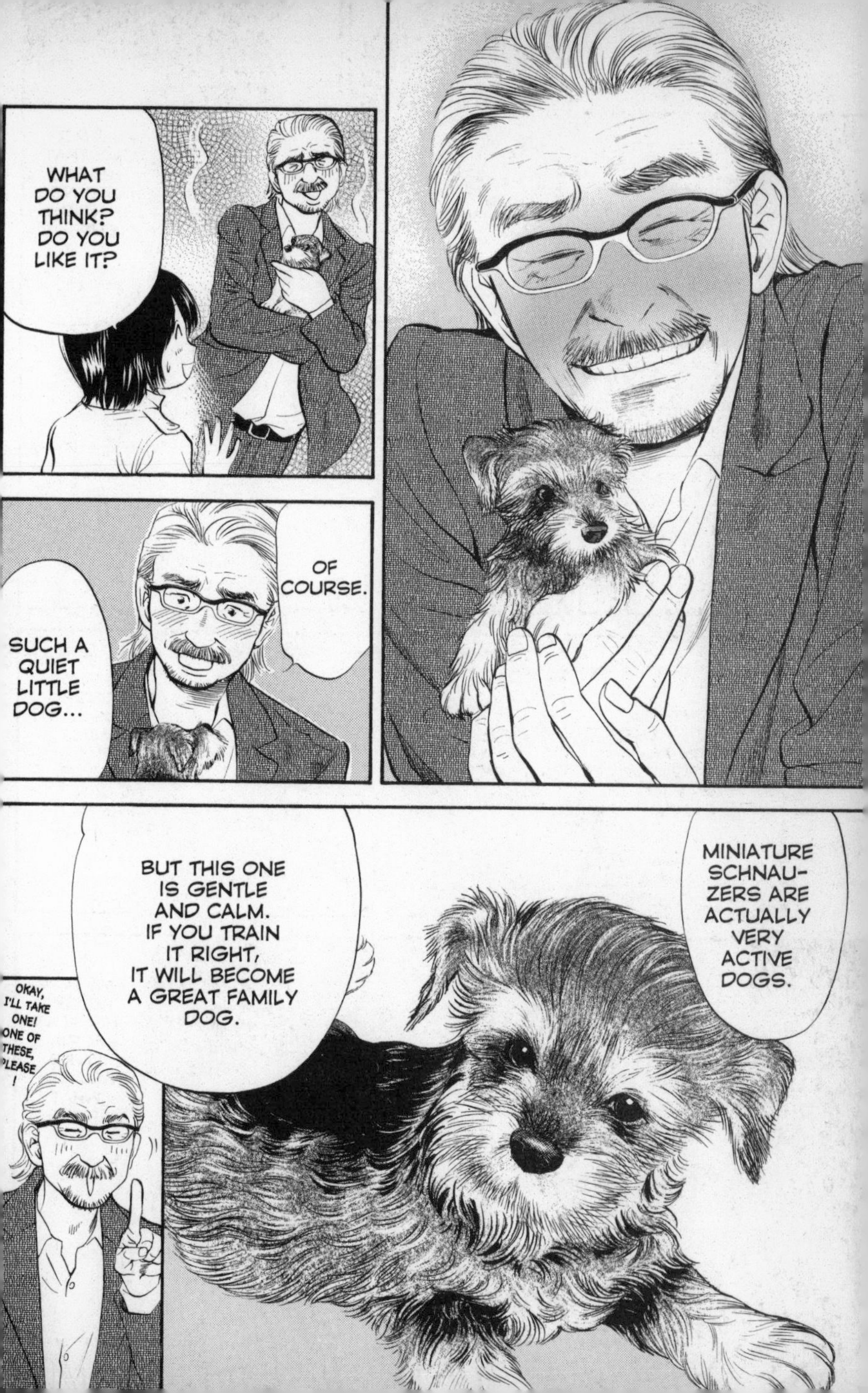
WHAT DO YOU THINK? DO YOU LIKE IT?
OF COURSE.
SUCH A QUIET LITTLE DOG...
MINIATURE SCHNAUZERS ARE ACTUALLY VERY ACTIVE DOGS.
BUT THIS ONE IS GENTLE AND CALM. IF YOU TRAIN IT RIGHT, IT WILL BECOME A GREAT FAMILY DOG.
OKAY, I'LL TAKE ONE! ONE OF THESE, PLEASE!

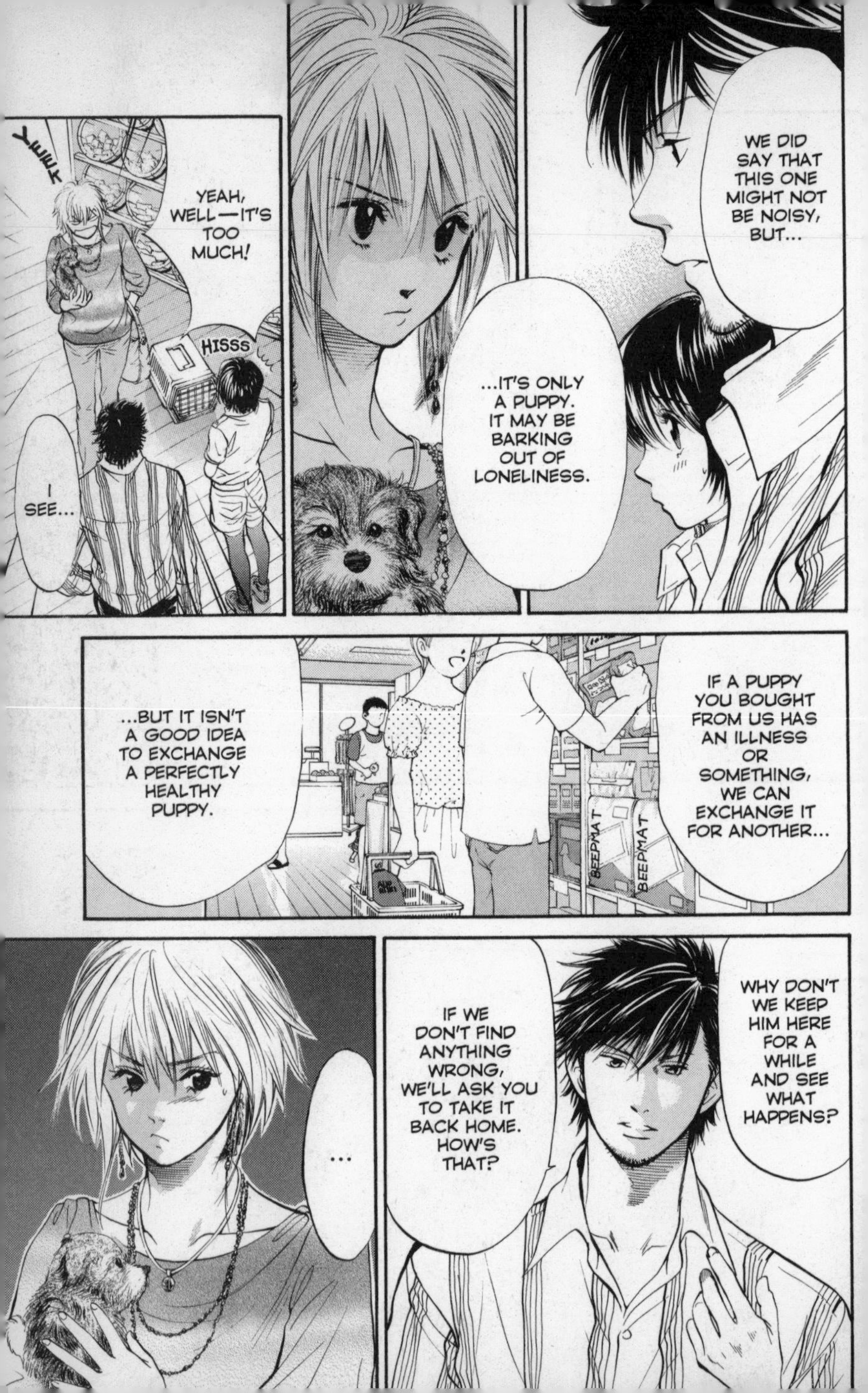
WE DID SAY THAT THIS ONE MIGHT NOT BE NOISY, BUT...
...IT'S ONLY A PUPPY. IT MAY BE BARKING OUT OF LONELINESS.
YEEK
YEAH, WELL—IT'S TOO MUCH!
HISSS
I SEE...
IF A PUPPY YOU BOUGHT FROM US HAS AN ILLNESS OR SOMETHING, WE CAN EXCHANGE IT FOR ANOTHER...
BEEPMAT
BEEPMAT
...BUT IT ISN'T A GOOD IDEA TO EXCHANGE A PERFECTLY HEALTHY PUPPY.
WHY DON'T WE KEEP HIM HERE FOR A WHILE AND SEE WHAT HAPPENS?
IF WE DON'T FIND ANYTHING WRONG, WE'LL ASK YOU TO TAKE IT BACK HOME. HOW'S THAT?
...

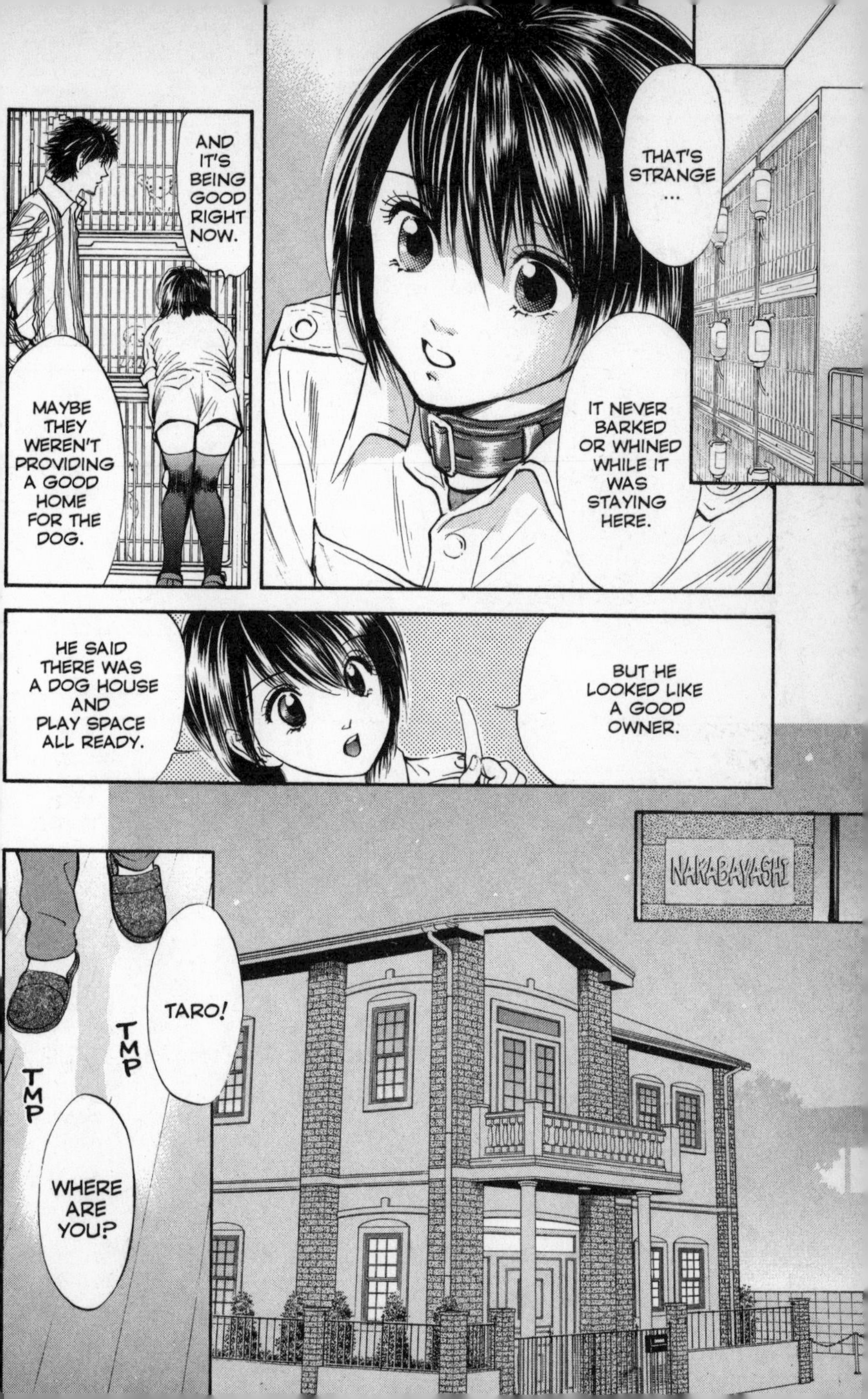
THAT'S STRANGE...
IT NEVER BARKED OR WHINED WHILE IT WAS STAYING HERE.
AND IT'S BEING GOOD RIGHT NOW.
MAYBE THEY WEREN'T PROVIDING A GOOD HOME FOR THE DOG.
BUT HE LOOKED LIKE A GOOD OWNER.
HE SAID THERE WAS A DOG HOUSE AND PLAY SPACE ALL READY.
NAKABAYASHI
TARO!
TMP
TMP
WHERE ARE YOU?

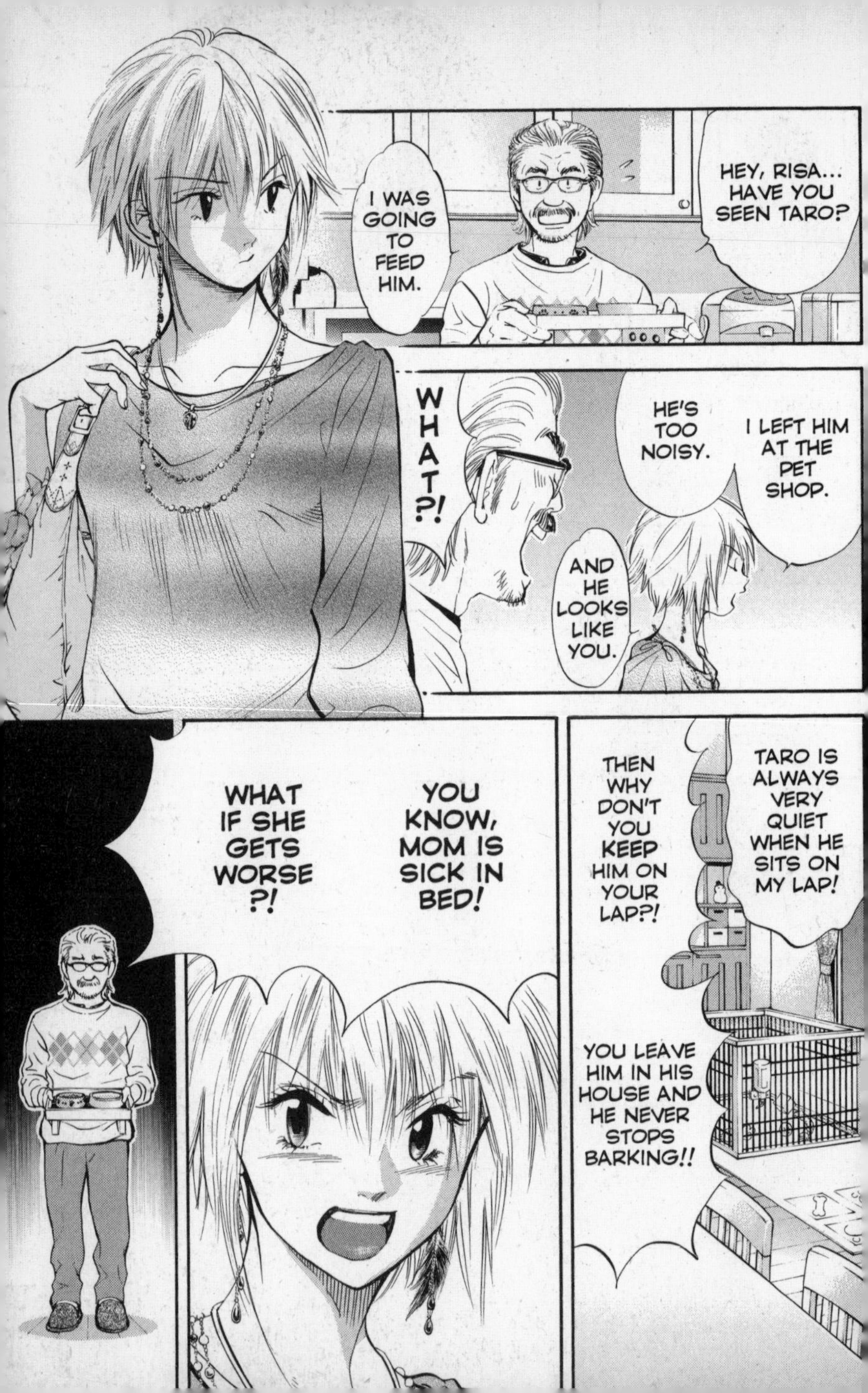
HEY, RISA... HAVE YOU SEEN TARO?
I WAS GOING TO FEED HIM.
I LEFT HIM AT THE PET SHOP.
HE'S TOO NOISY.
WHAT?!
AND HE LOOKS LIKE YOU.
TARO IS ALWAYS VERY QUIET WHEN HE SITS ON MY LAP!
THEN WHY DON'T YOU KEEP HIM ON YOUR LAP?!
YOU LEAVE HIM IN HIS HOUSE AND HE NEVER STOPS BARKING!!
YOU KNOW, MOM IS SICK IN BED!
WHAT IF SHE GETS WORSE?!

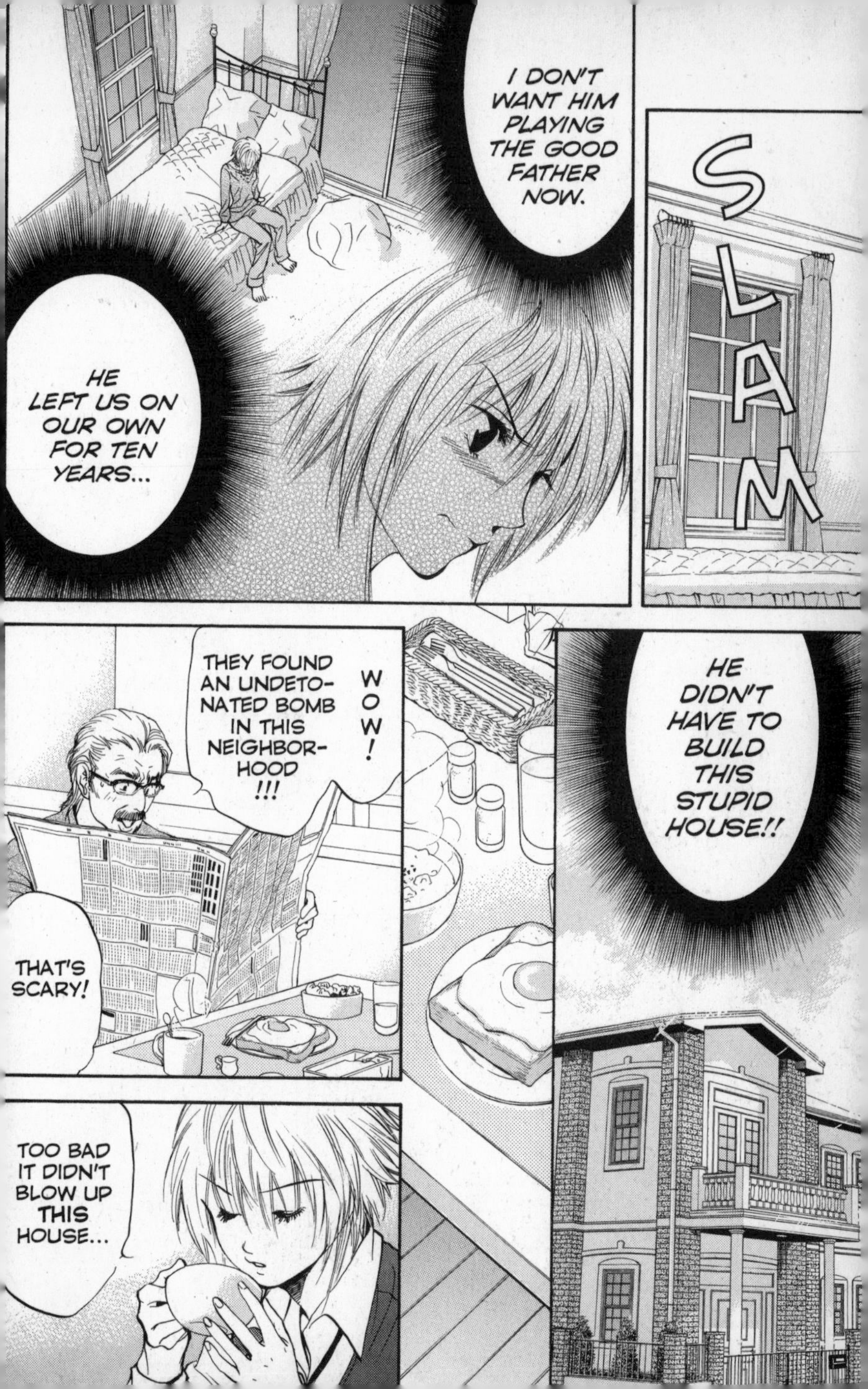
SLAM
I DON'T WANT HIM PLAYING THE GOOD FATHER NOW.
HE LEFT US ON OUR OWN FOR TEN YEARS...
HE DIDN'T HAVE TO BUILD THIS STUPID HOUSE!!
WOW!
THEY FOUND AN UNDETO-NATED BOMB IN THIS NEIGHBOR-HOOD !!!
THAT'S SCARY!
TOO BAD IT DIDN'T BLOW UP THIS HOUSE...

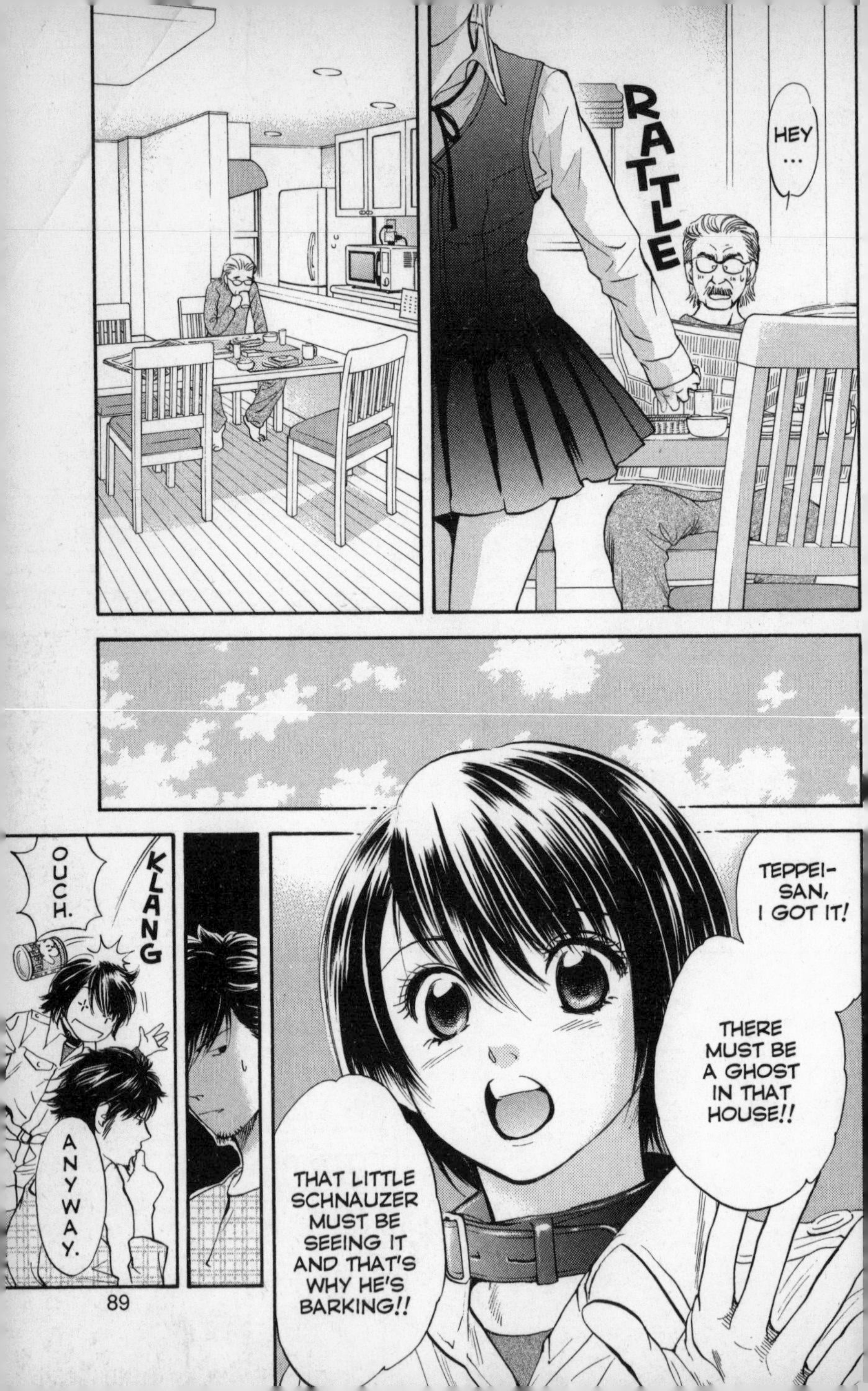

RATTLE
HEY ...
TEPPEI-SAN, I GOT IT!
THERE MUST BE A GHOST IN THAT HOUSE!!
THAT LITTLE SCHNAUZER MUST BE SEEING IT AND THAT'S WHY HE'S BARKING!!
KLANG
OUCH.
ANYWAY.

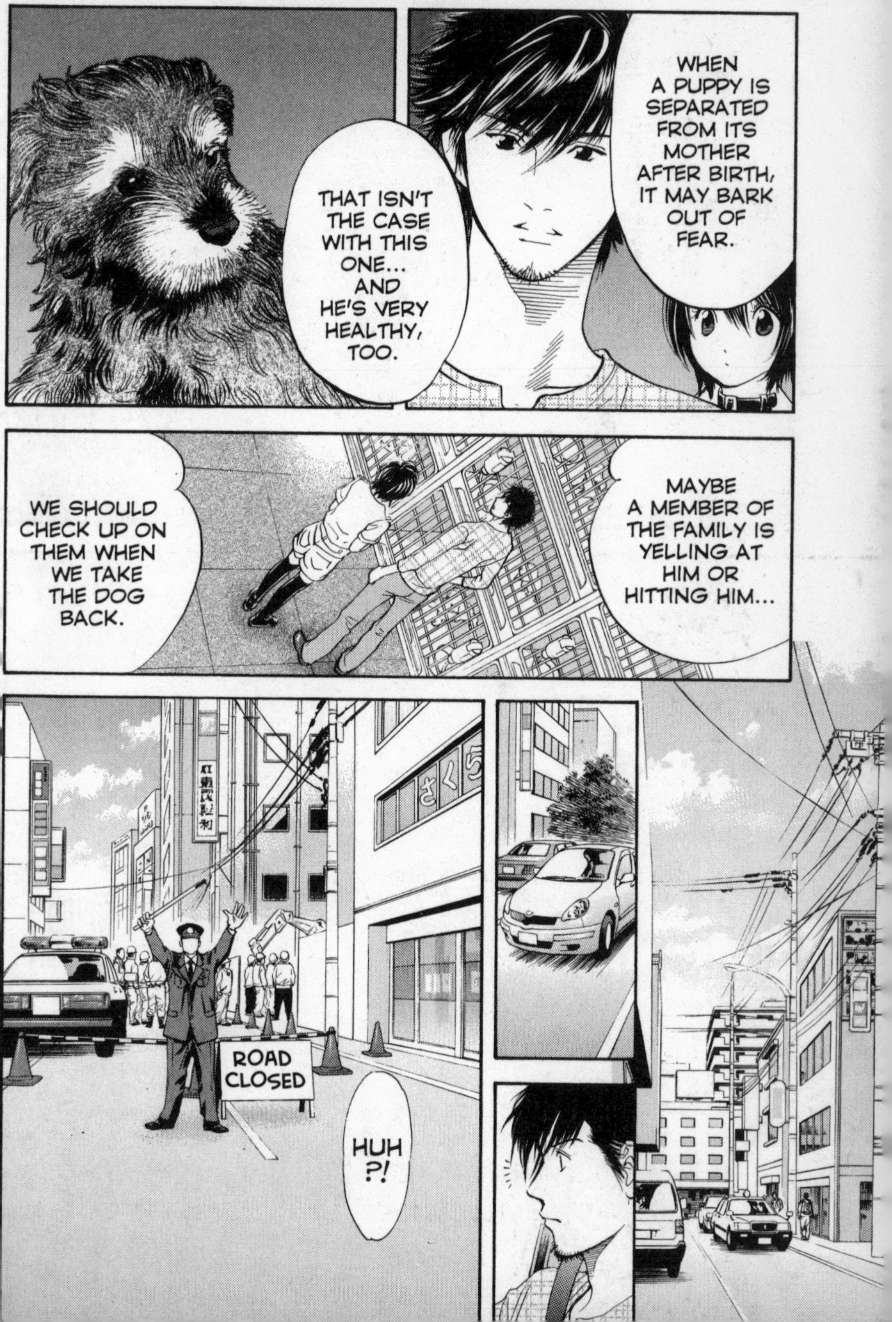
WHEN A PUPPY IS SEPARATED FROM ITS MOTHER AFTER BIRTH, IT MAY BARK OUT OF FEAR.
THAT ISN'T THE CASE WITH THIS ONE... AND HE'S VERY HEALTHY, TOO.
MAYBE A MEMBER OF THE FAMILY IS YELLING AT HIM OR HITTING HIM...
WE SHOULD CHECK UP ON THEM WHEN WE TAKE THE DOG BACK.
ROAD CLOSED
HUH ?!

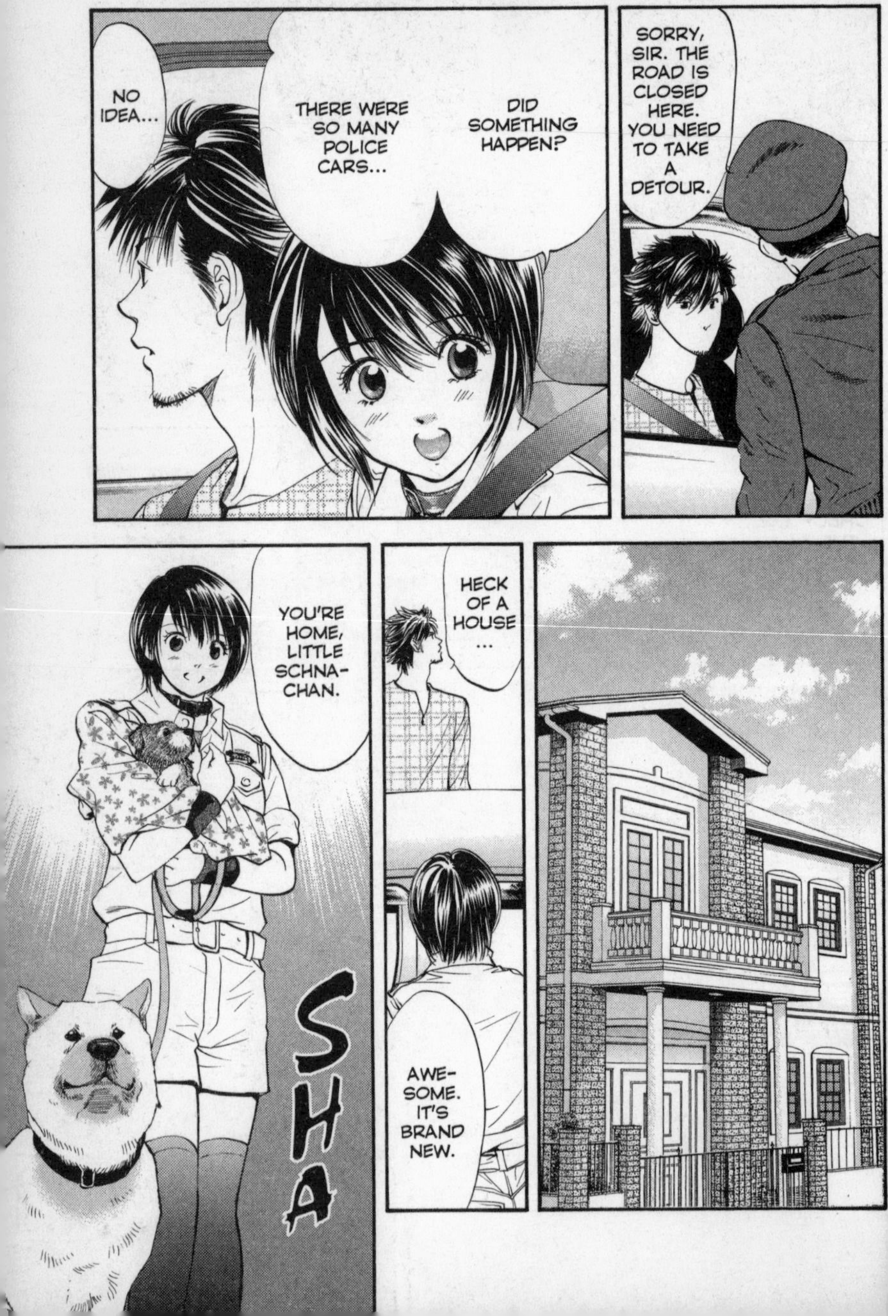
SORRY, SIR. THE ROAD IS CLOSED HERE. YOU NEED TO TAKE A DETOUR.
DID SOMETHING HAPPEN?
THERE WERE SO MANY POLICE CARS...
NO IDEA...
HECK OF A HOUSE ...
AWE-SOME. IT'S BRAND NEW.
YOU'RE HOME, LITTLE SCHNA-CHAN.
SHA

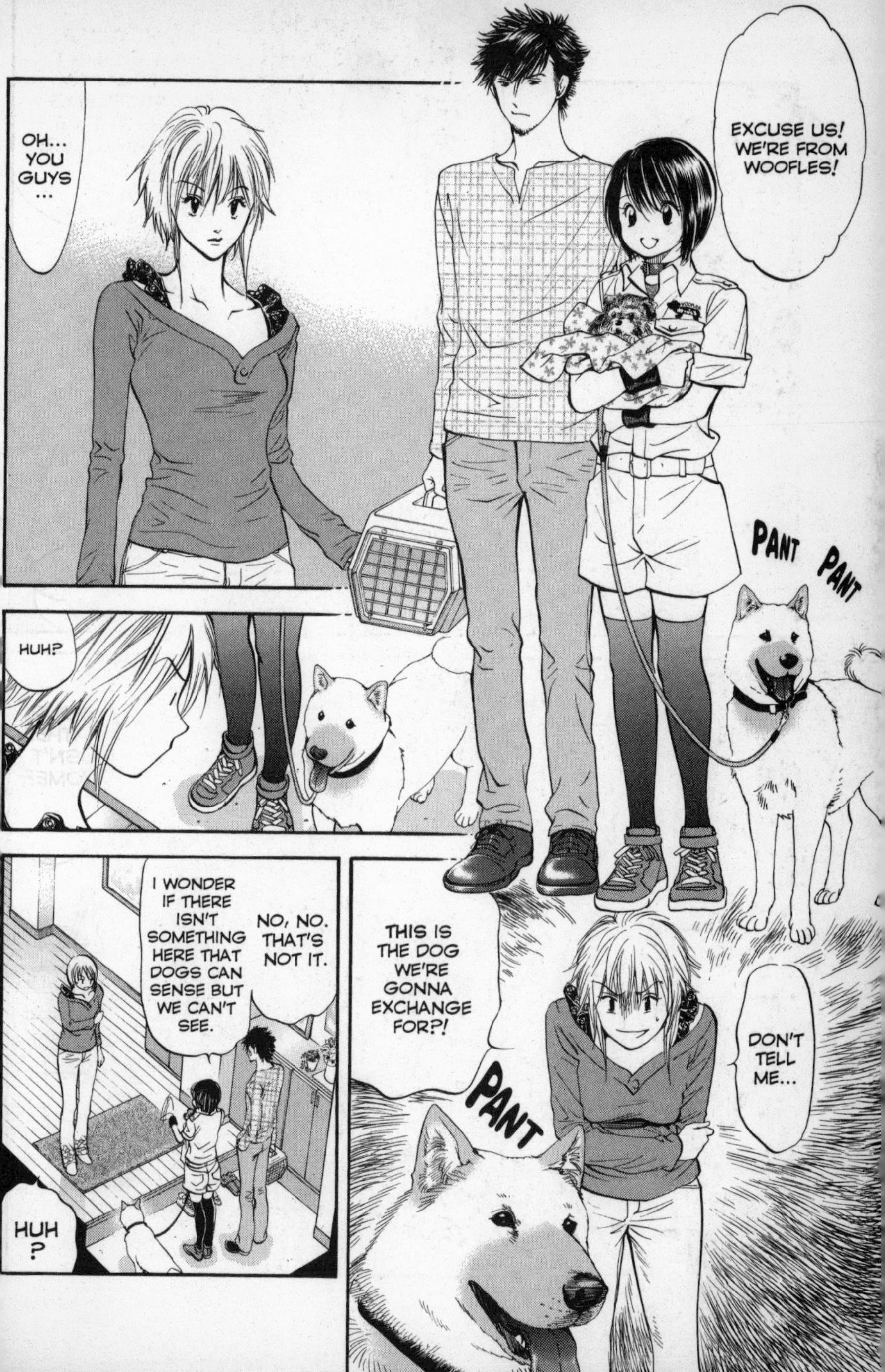
EXCUSE US! WE'RE FROM WOOFLES!
OH... YOU GUYS ...
PANT PANT
HUH?
DON'T TELL ME...
THIS IS THE DOG WE'RE GONNA EXCHANGE FOR?!
PANT
I WONDER IF THERE ISN'T SOMETHING HERE THAT DOGS CAN SENSE BUT WE CAN'T SEE.
NO, NO. THAT'S NOT IT.
HUH ?

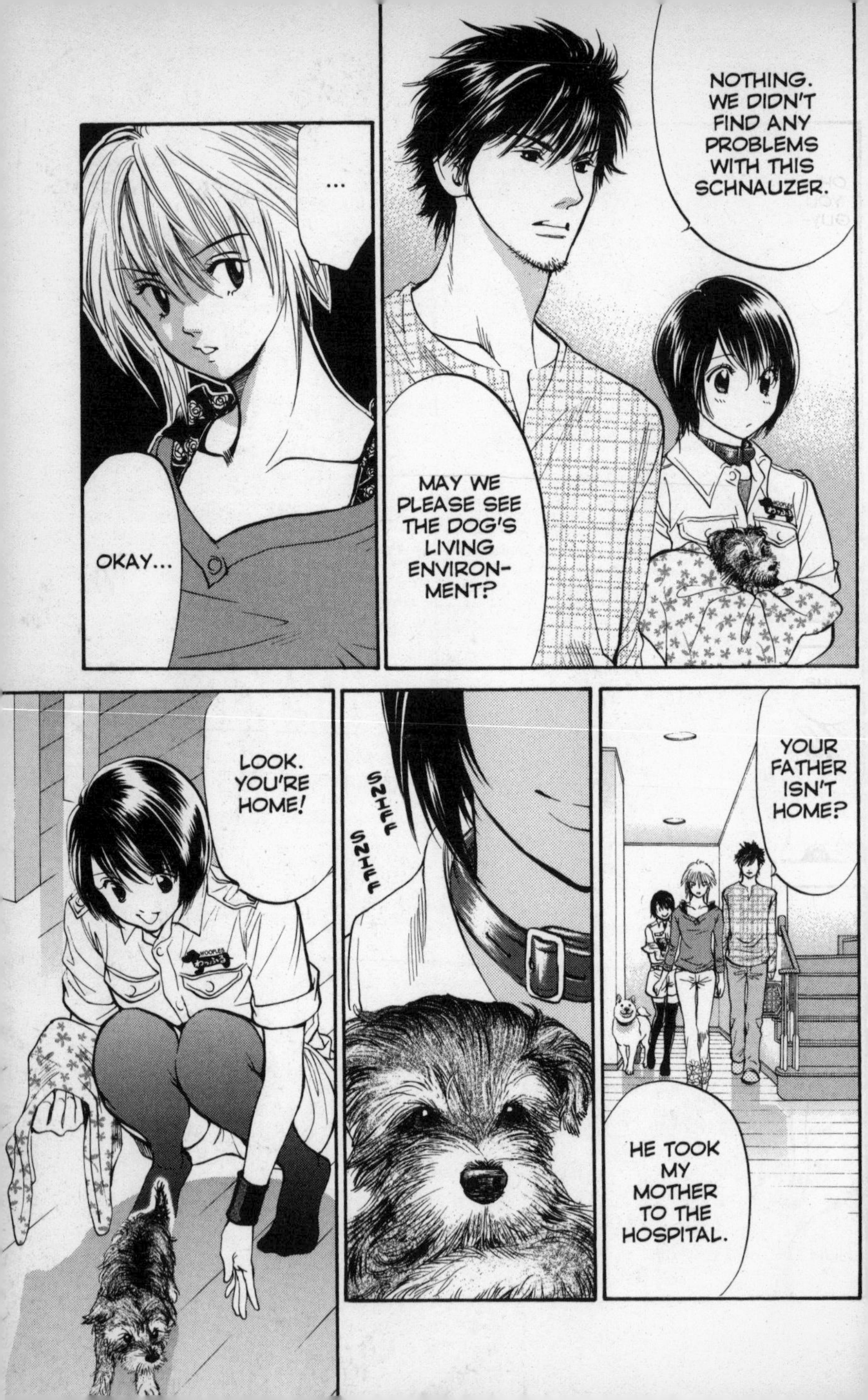
NOTHING. WE DIDN'T FIND ANY PROBLEMS WITH THIS SCHNAUZER.
MAY WE PLEASE SEE THE DOG'S LIVING ENVIRON-MENT?
...
OKAY...
YOUR FATHER ISN'T HOME?
HE TOOK MY MOTHER TO THE HOSPITAL.
SNIFF
SNIFF
LOOK. YOU'RE HOME!

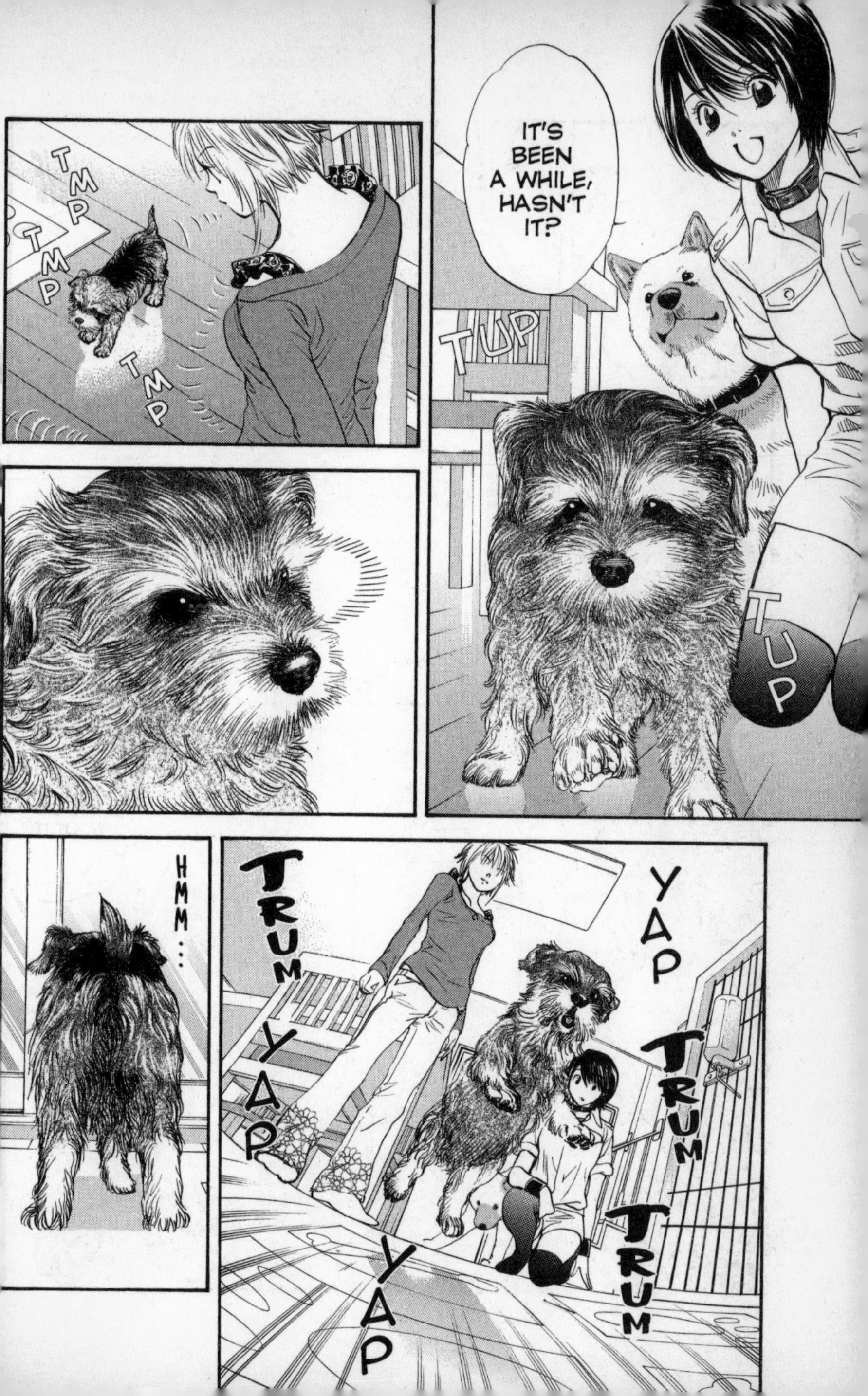
IT'S BEEN A WHILE, HASN'T IT?
TUP
TUP
TMP TMP TMP
TMP
YAP
TRUM
TRUM
TRUM
YAP YAP
YAP YAP
HMM...

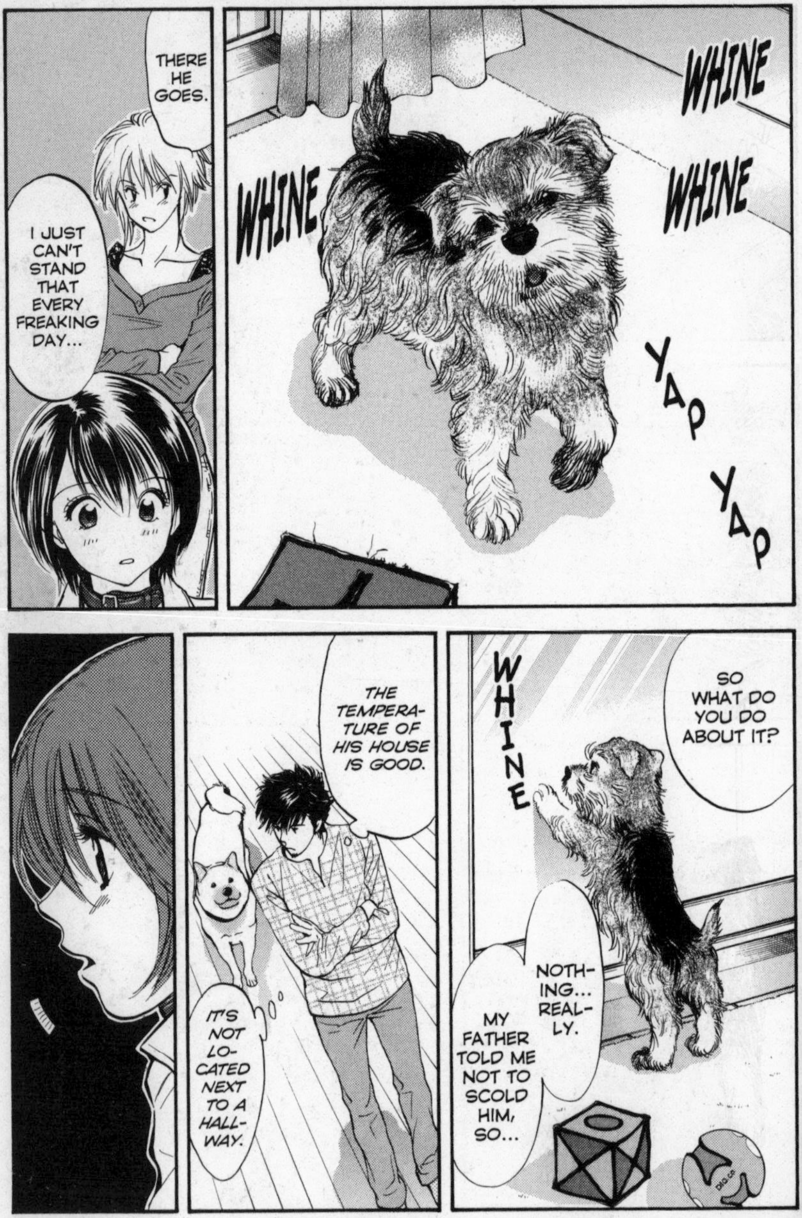
WHINE
WHINE
WHINE
YAP
YAP
THERE HE GOES.
I JUST CAN'T STAND THAT EVERY FREAKING DAY...
SO WHAT DO YOU DO ABOUT IT?
WHINE
NOTHING... REALLY.
MY FATHER TOLD ME NOT TO SCOLD HIM, SO...
THE TEMPERATURE OF HIS HOUSE IS GOOD.
IT'S NOT LOCATED NEXT TO A HALLWAY.

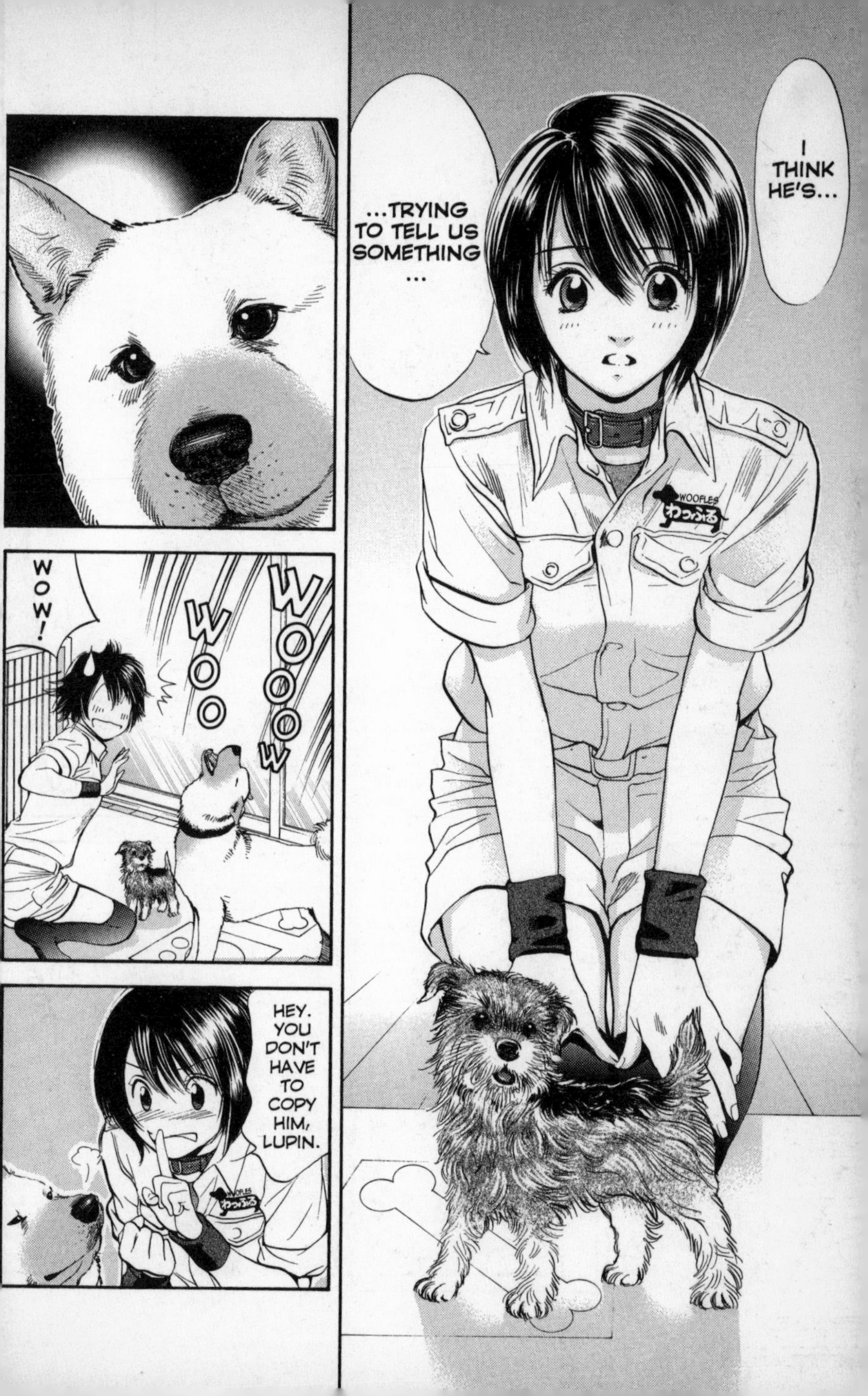
I THINK HE'S...
...TRYING TO TELL US SOMETHING ...
WOOFLES わっふる
WOOOOW
WOOO
WOW!
HEY. YOU DON'T HAVE TO COPY HIM, LUPIN.

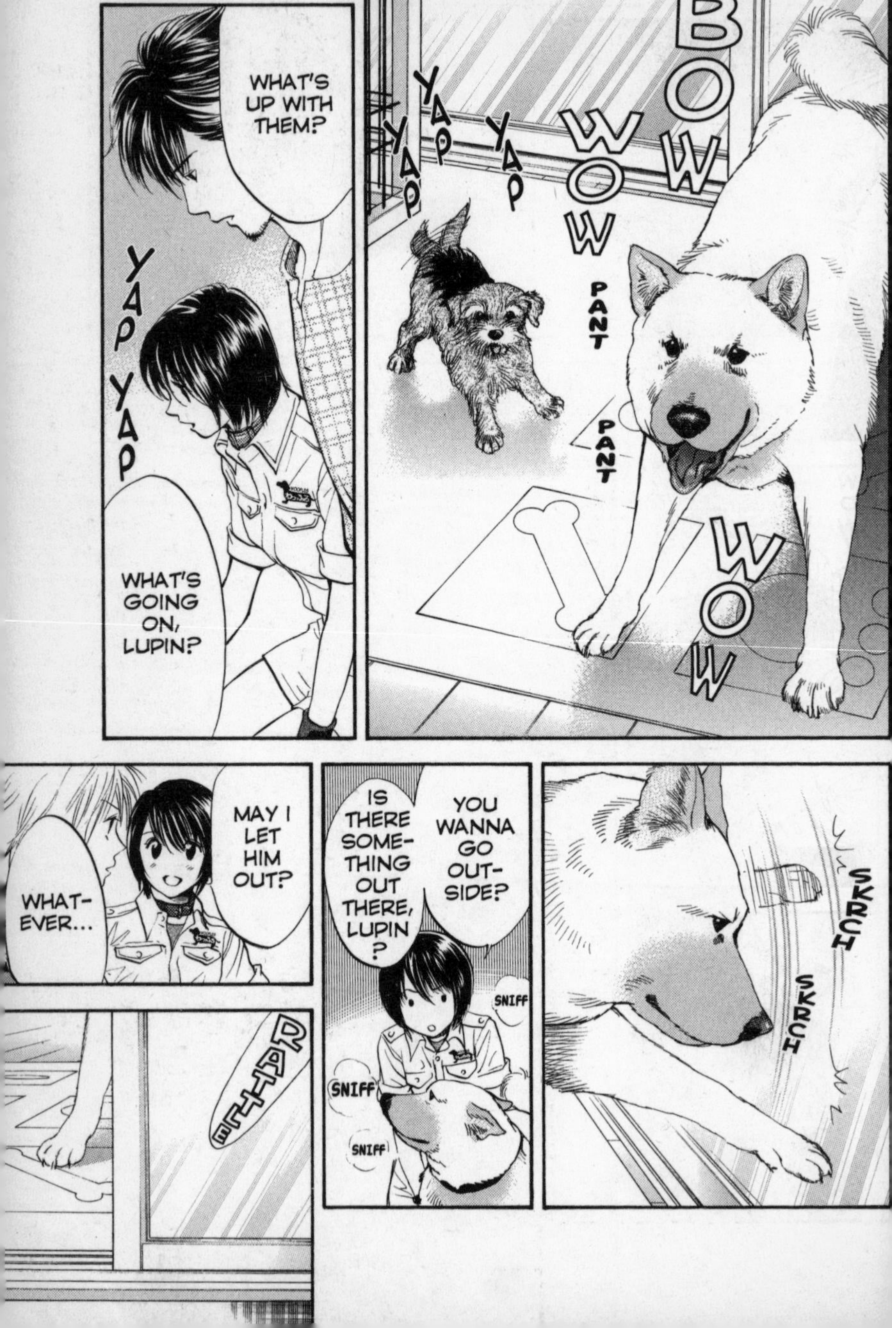
YAP YAP
YAP YAP
BOWWOW
WOWWOW
PANT
PANT
WOW WOW
WHAT'S UP WITH THEM?
YAP YAP YAP
WHAT'S GOING ON, LUPIN?
SKRCH
SKRCH
YOU WANNA GO OUT-SIDE?
IS THERE SOME-THING OUT THERE, LUPIN?
SNIFF
SNIFF
SNIFF
MAY I LET HIM OUT?
WHAT-EVER...
RATTLE

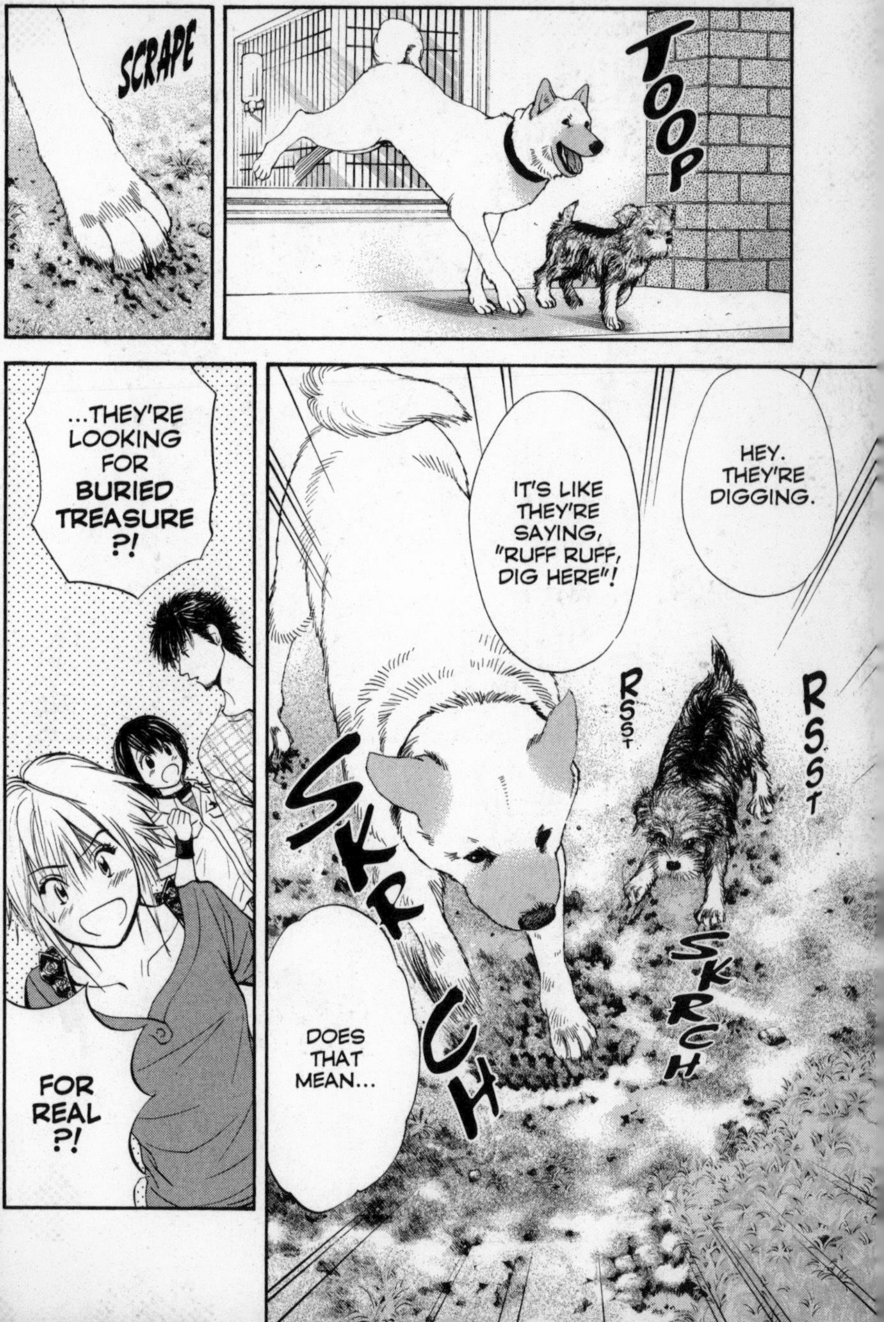
TOOP
SCRAPE
HEY. THEY'RE DIGGING.
IT'S LIKE THEY'RE SAYING, "RUFF RUFF, DIG HERE"!
RSST
RSST
SKRCH
SKRUH
DOES THAT MEAN...
...THEY'RE LOOKING FOR BURIED TREASURE ?!
FOR REAL ?!

CHAPTER 58: DANGER IS DANGEROUS!

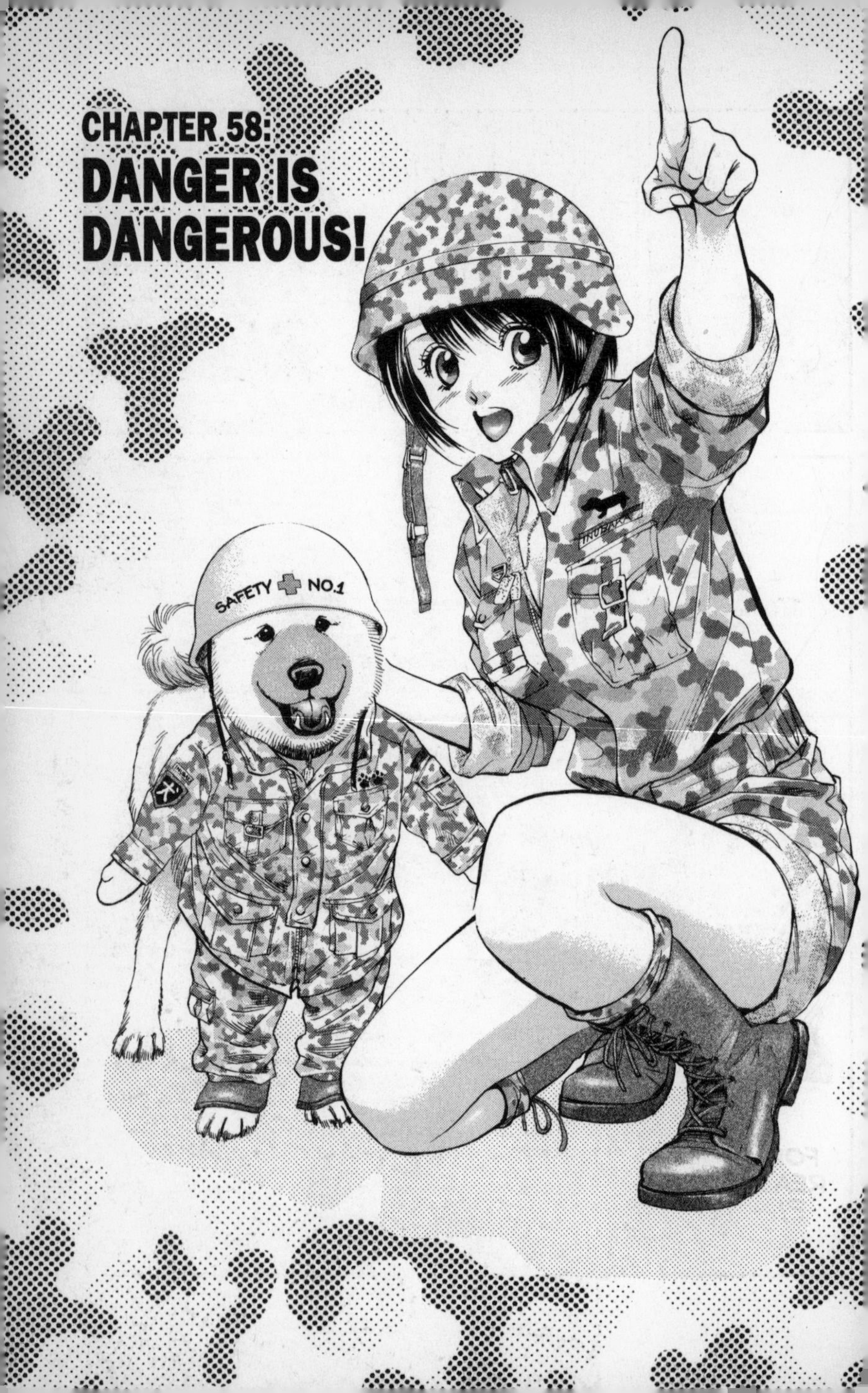
SAFETY NO.1

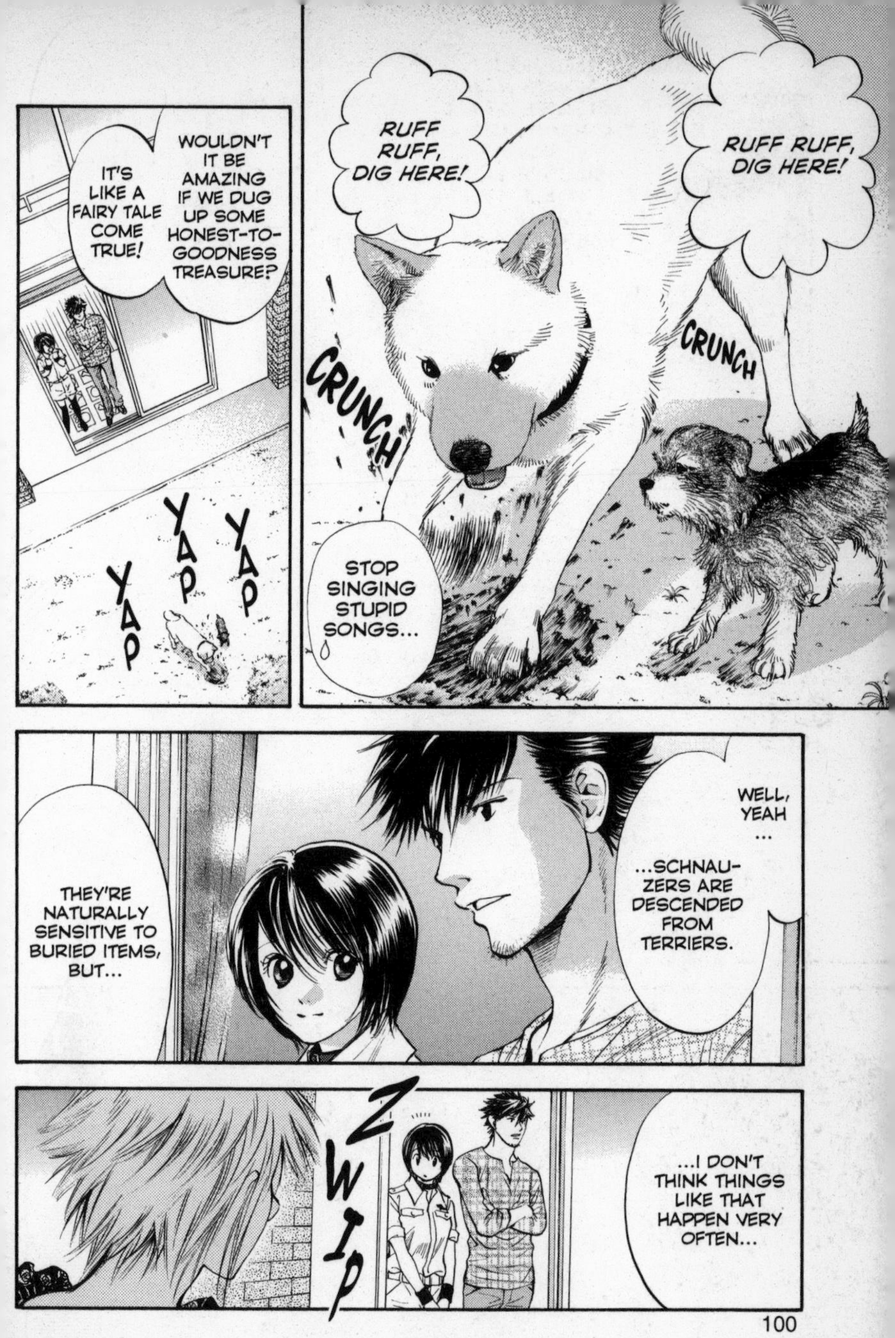
RUFF RUFF, DIG HERE!
RUFF RUFF, DIG HERE!
CRUNCH
CRUNCH
STOP SINGING STUPID SONGS...
WOULDN'T IT BE AMAZING IF WE DUG UP SOME HONEST-TO-GOODNESS TREASURE?
IT'S LIKE A FAIRY TALE COME TRUE!
YAP YAP YAP
WELL, YEAH...
...SCHNAUZERS ARE DESCENDED FROM TERRIERS.
THEY'RE NATURALLY SENSITIVE TO BURIED ITEMS, BUT...
...I DON'T THINK THINGS LIKE THAT HAPPEN VERY OFTEN...
ZWIP

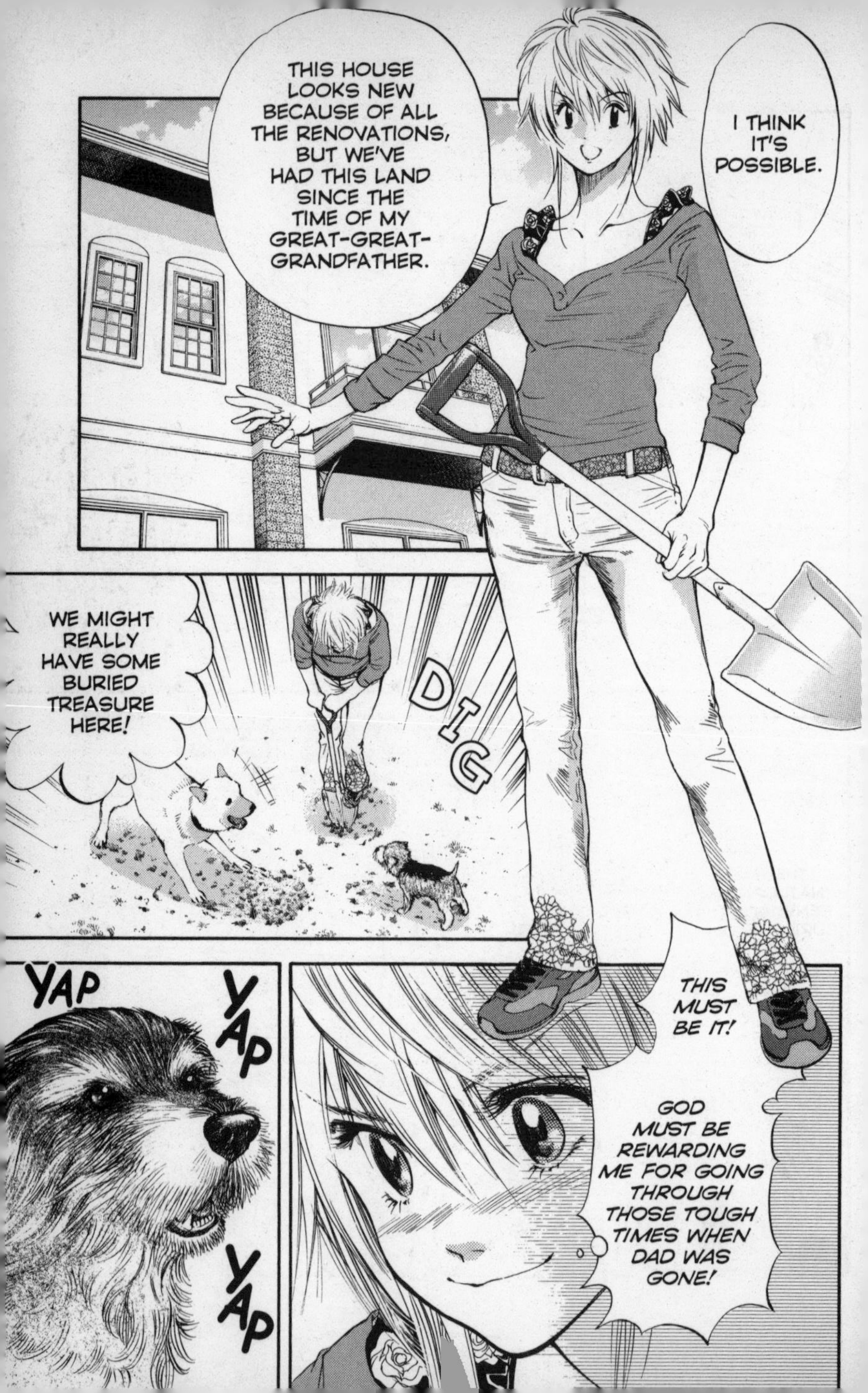
I THINK IT'S POSSIBLE.
THIS HOUSE LOOKS NEW BECAUSE OF ALL THE RENOVATIONS, BUT WE'VE HAD THIS LAND SINCE THE TIME OF MY GREAT-GREAT-GRANDFATHER.
DIG
WE MIGHT REALLY HAVE SOME BURIED TREASURE HERE!
THIS MUST BE IT!
GOD MUST BE REWARDING ME FOR GOING THROUGH THOSE TOUGH TIMES WHEN DAD WAS GONE!
YAP
YAP
YAP
YAP

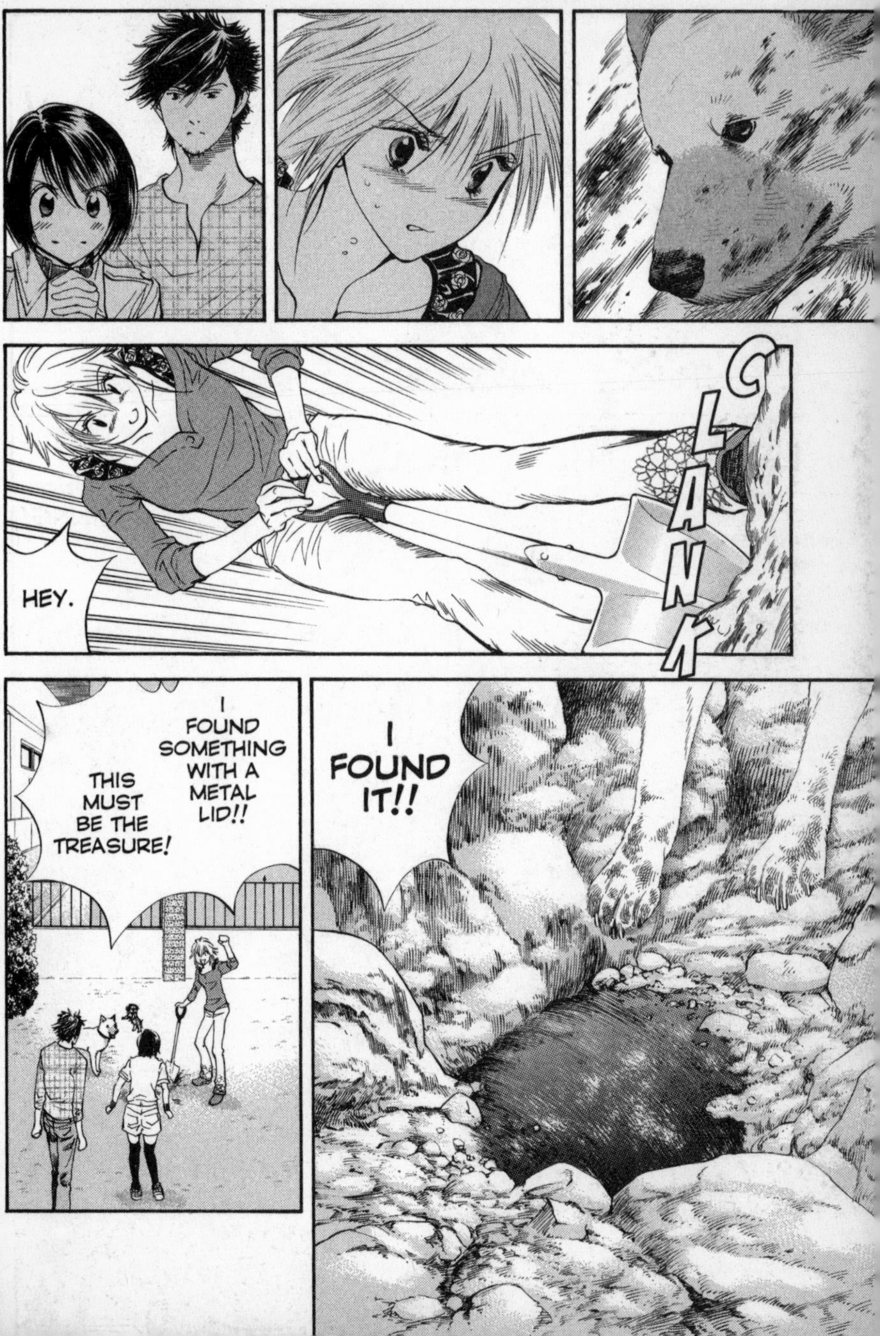
CLANK
HEY.
I FOUND IT!!
I FOUND SOMETHING WITH A METAL LID!!
THIS MUST BE THE TREASURE!

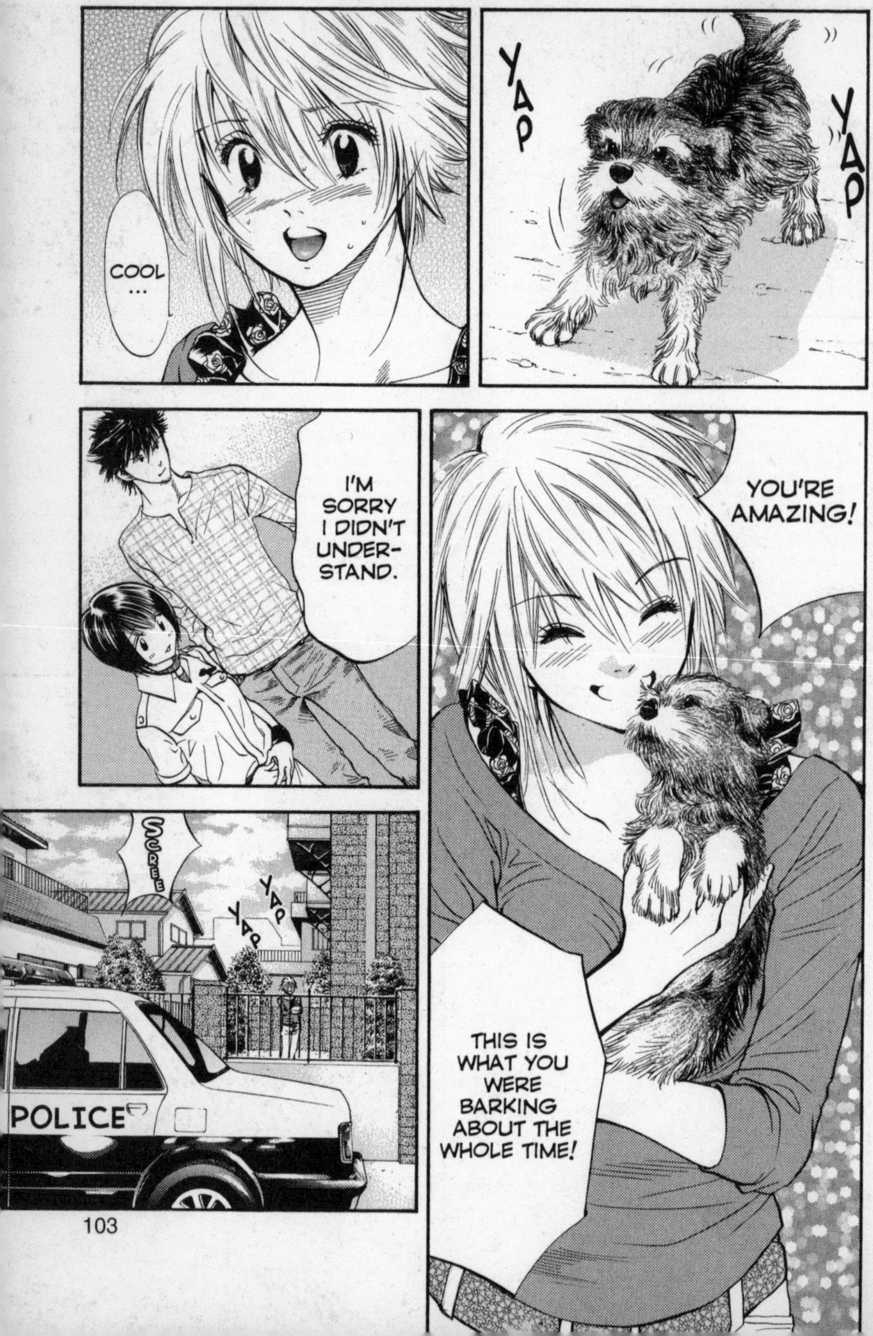
YAP
YAP
COOL ...
YOU'RE AMAZING!
THIS IS WHAT YOU WERE BARKING ABOUT THE WHOLE TIME!
I'M SORRY I DIDN'T UNDER-STAND.
SCREEE
YAP
YAP
POLICE

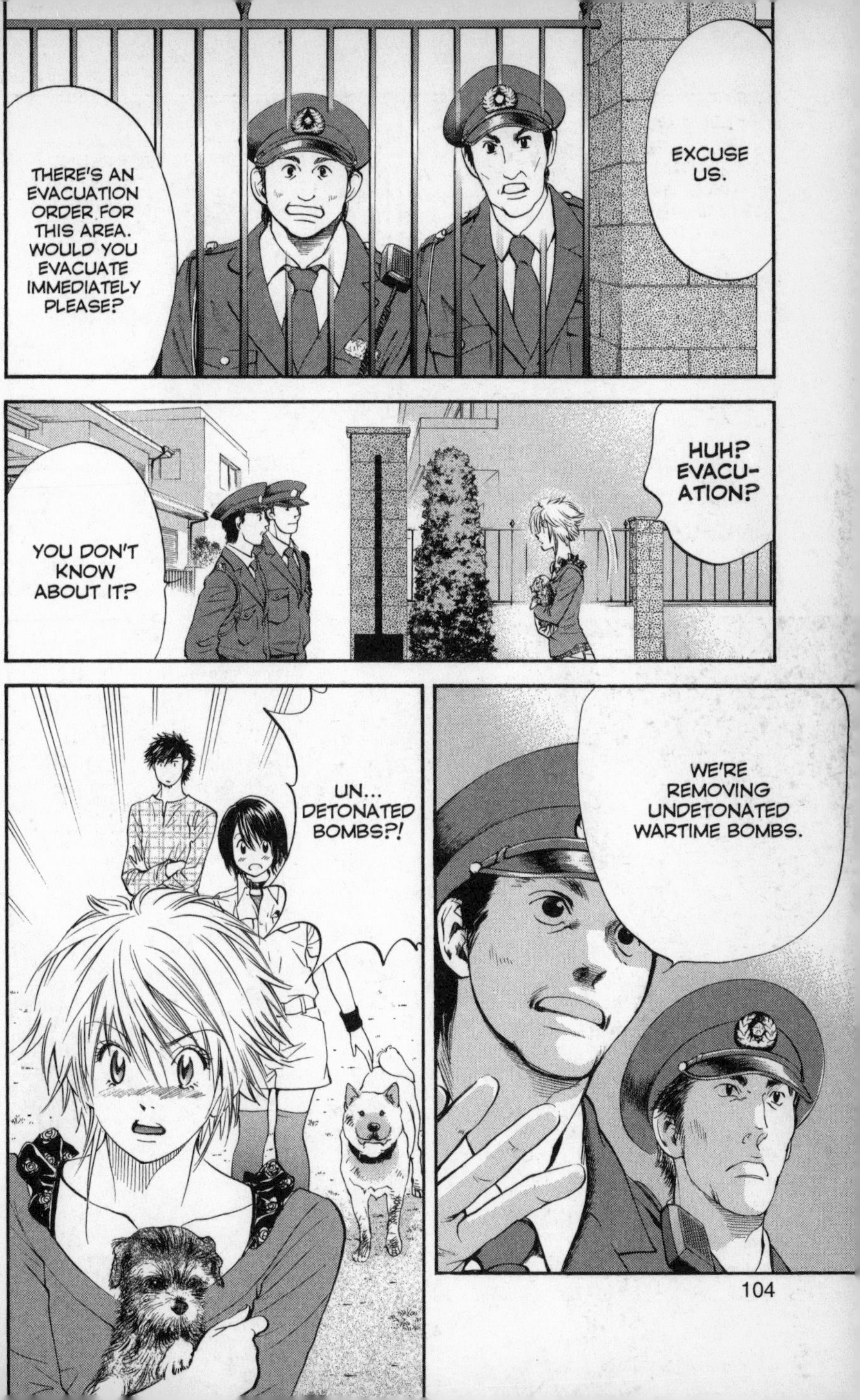
EXCUSE US.
THERE'S AN EVACUATION ORDER FOR THIS AREA. WOULD YOU EVACUATE IMMEDIATELY PLEASE?
HUH? EVACU-ATION?
YOU DON'T KNOW ABOUT IT?
WE'RE REMOVING UNDETONATED WARTIME BOMBS.
UN... DETONATED BOMBS?!

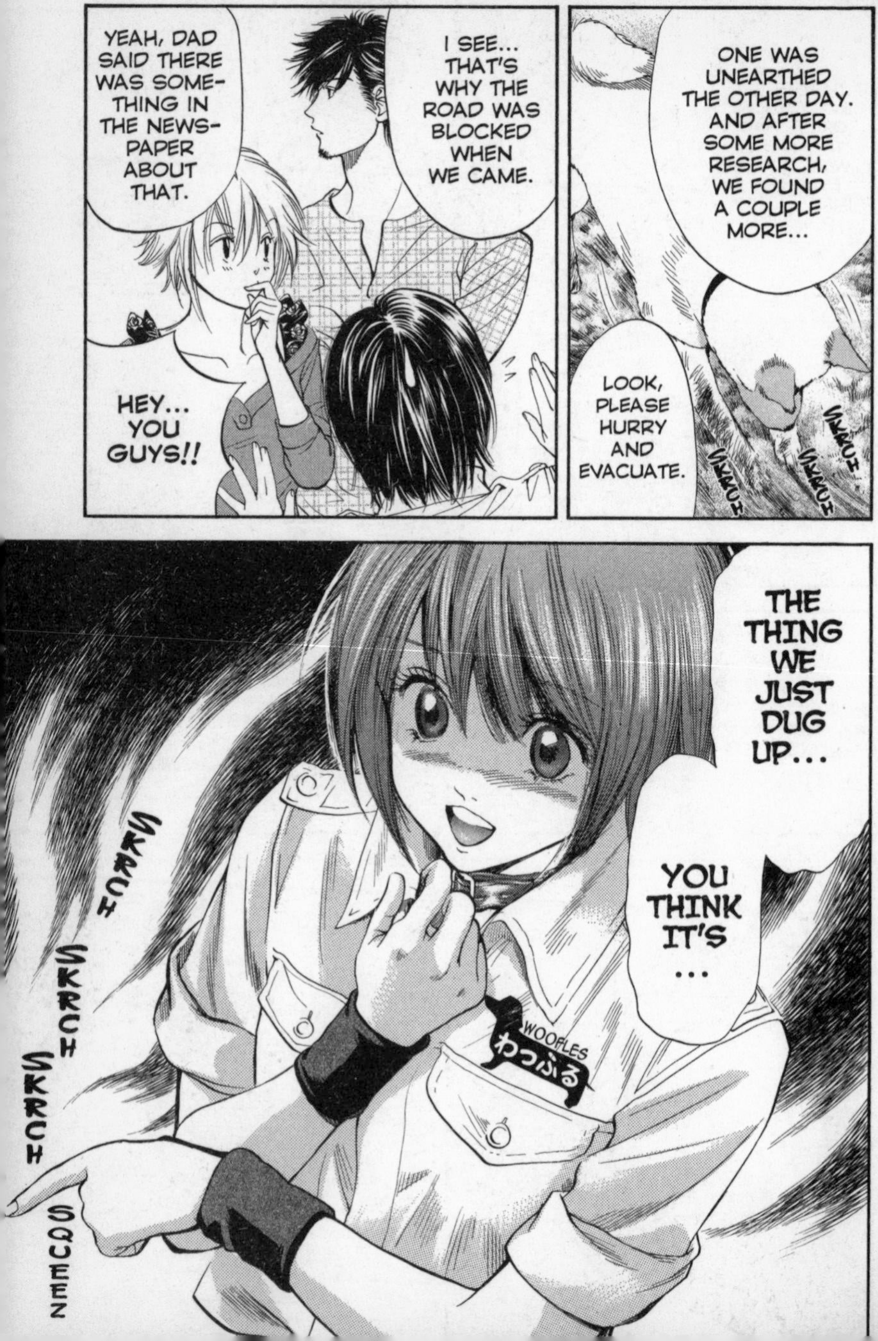
ONE WAS UNEARTHED THE OTHER DAY. AND AFTER SOME MORE RESEARCH, WE FOUND A COUPLE MORE...
LOOK, PLEASE HURRY AND EVACUATE.
SKRCH
SKRCH
SKRCH
I SEE... THAT'S WHY THE ROAD WAS BLOCKED WHEN WE CAME.
YEAH, DAD SAID THERE WAS SOME-THING IN THE NEWS-PAPER ABOUT THAT.
HEY... YOU GUYS!!
THE THING WE JUST DUG UP...
YOU THINK IT'S...
WOOFLES
わっふる
SKRCH
SKRCH
SKRCH
SQUEEN

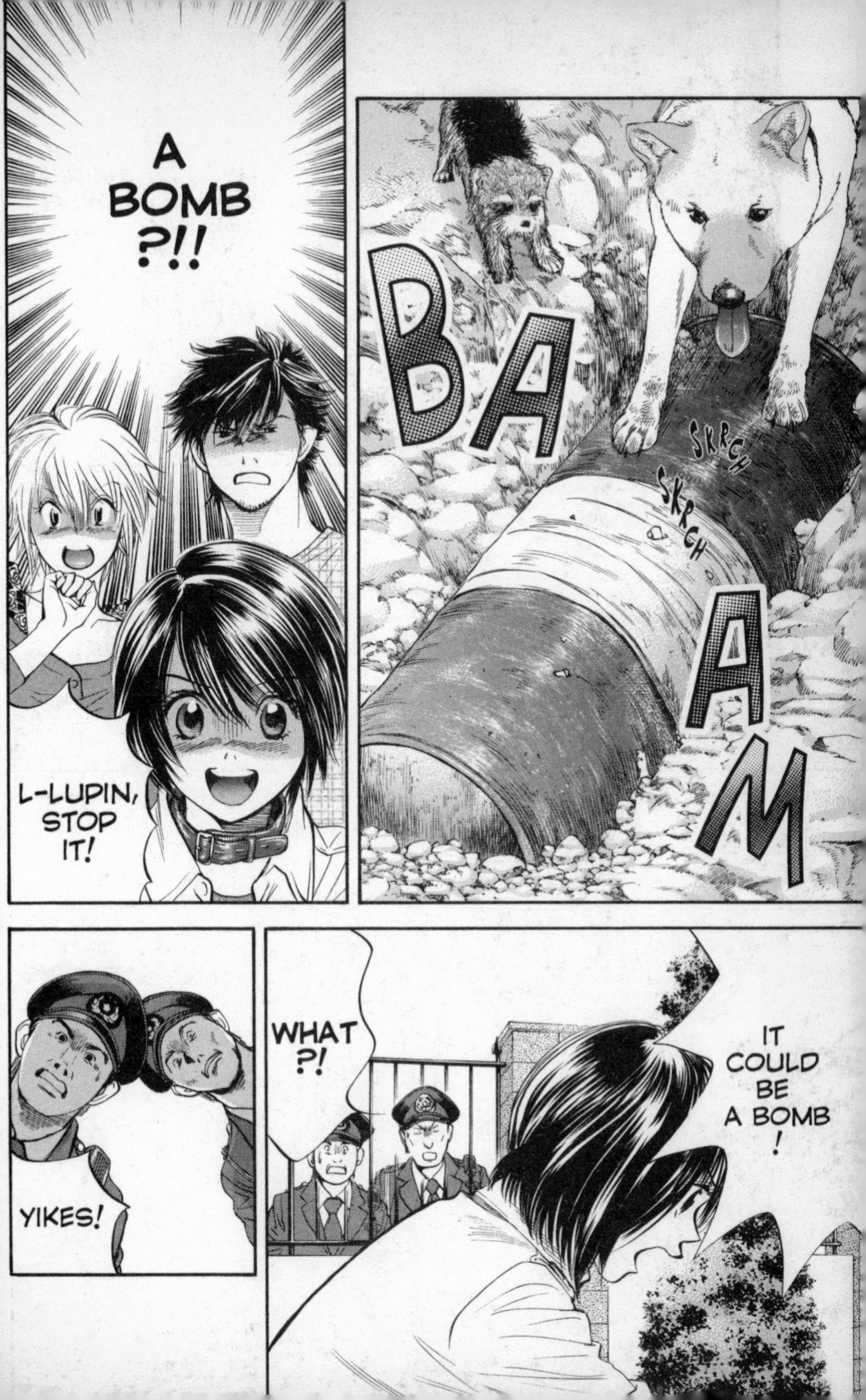
BAAM
SKRCH
SKRCH
A BOMB?!!
L-LUPIN, STOP IT!
IT COULD BE A BOMB!
WHAT?!
YIKES!

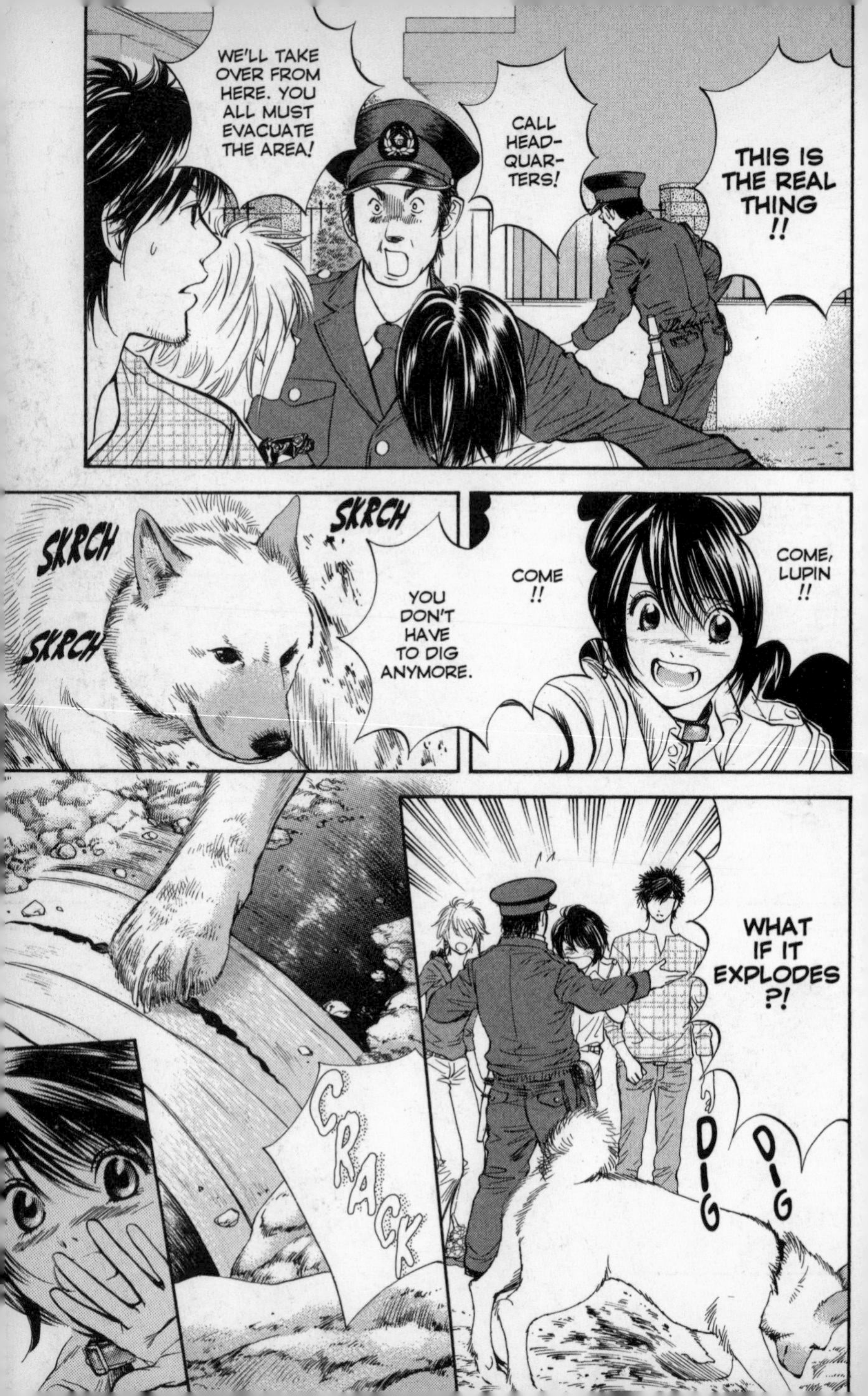
THIS IS THE REAL THING!!
CALL HEAD-QUARTERS!
WE'LL TAKE OVER FROM HERE. YOU ALL MUST EVACUATE THE AREA!
COME, LUPIN!!
COME!!
SKRCH
YOU DON'T HAVE TO DIG ANYMORE.
SKRCH
SKRCH
WHAT IF IT EXPLODES?!
DIG
DIG
CRACK

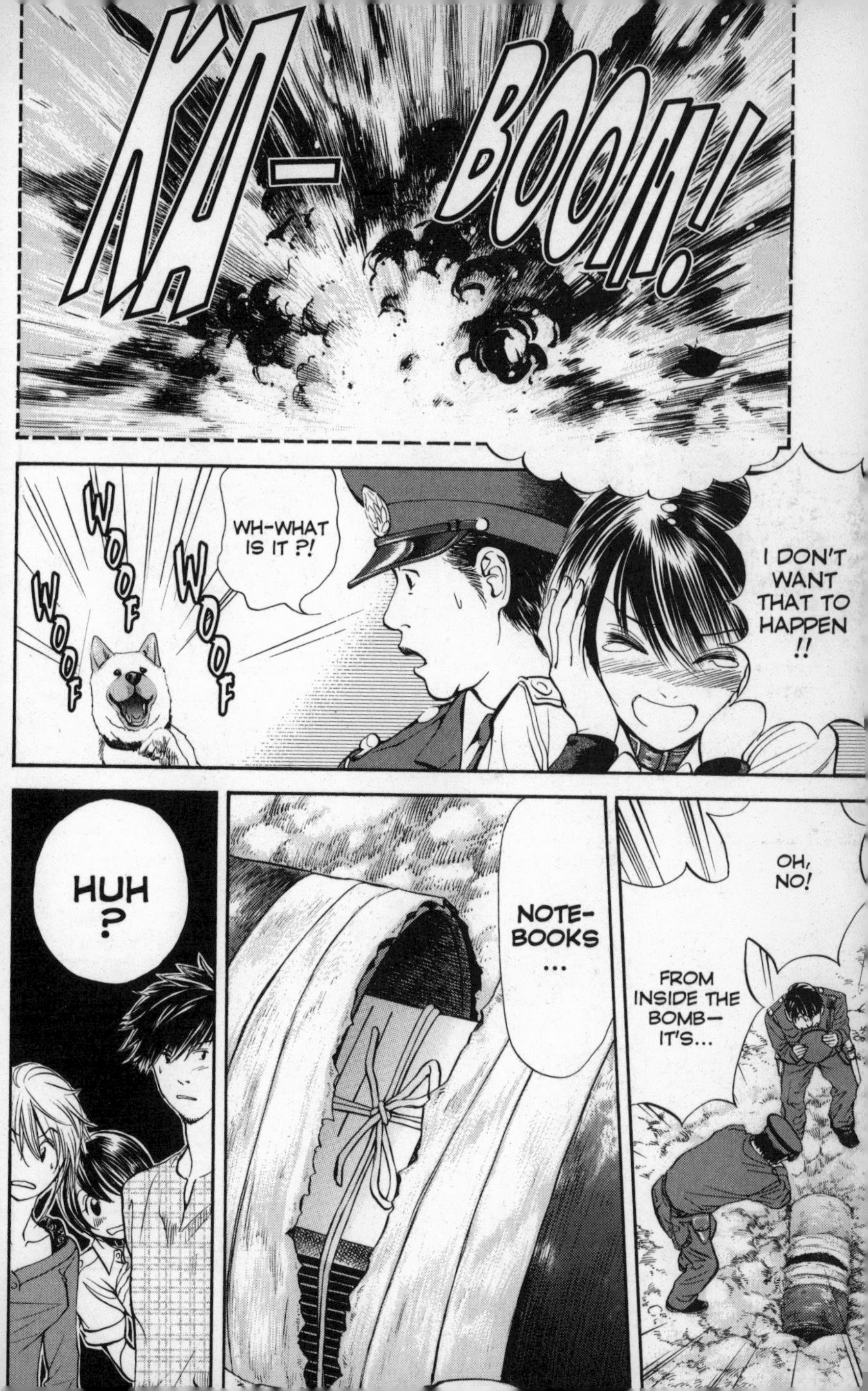
KA- BOOM!
I DON'T WANT THAT TO HAPPEN!!
WH-WHAT IS IT?!
WOOF WOOF
WOOF WOOF
OH, NO!
FROM INSIDE THE BOMB— IT'S...
NOTE-BOOKS...
HUH?

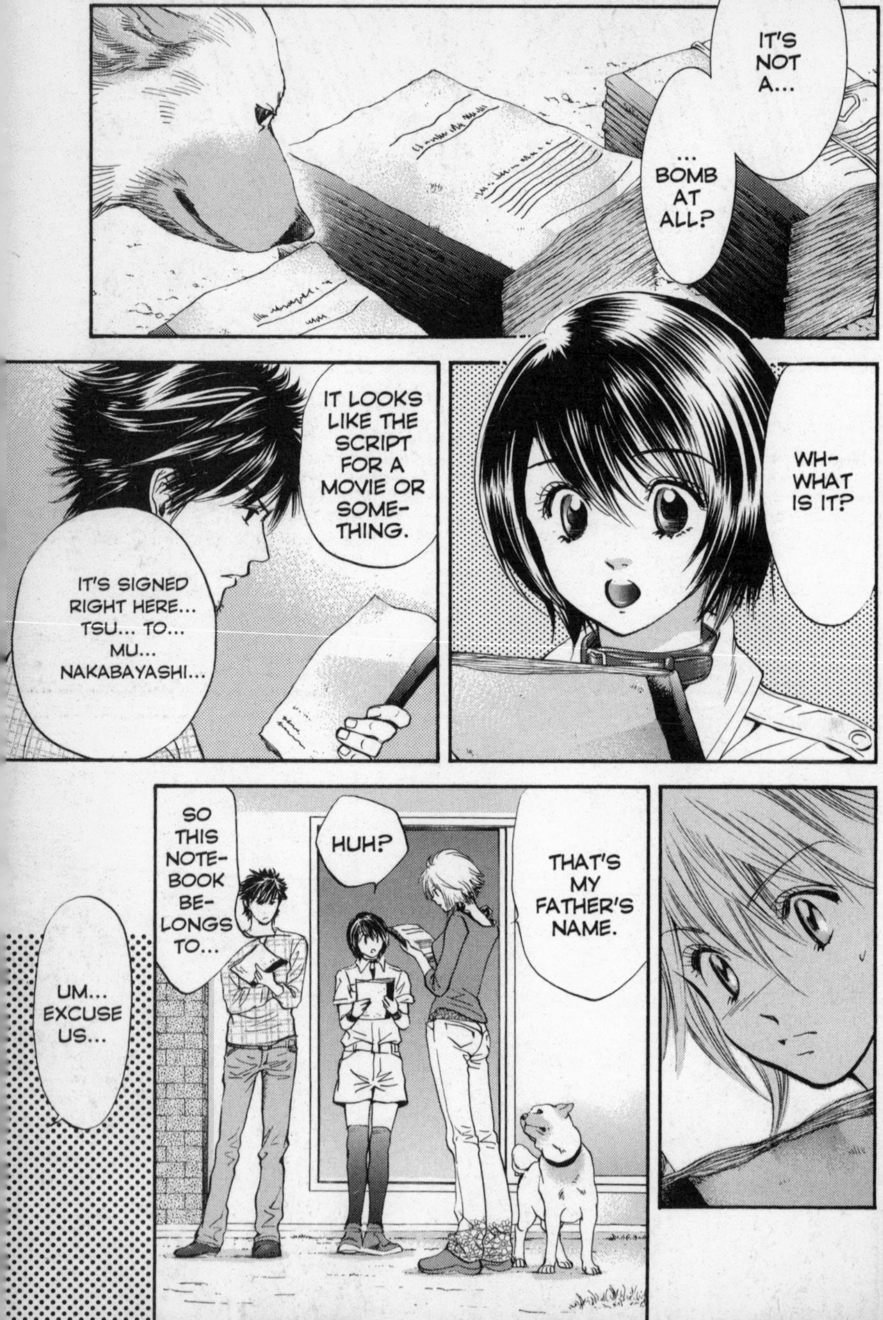
IT'S NOT A...
... BOMB AT ALL?
WH-WHAT IS IT?
IT LOOKS LIKE THE SCRIPT FOR A MOVIE OR SOME-THING.
IT'S SIGNED RIGHT HERE... TSU... TO... MU... NAKABAYASHI...
THAT'S MY FATHER'S NAME.
HUH?
SO THIS NOTE-BOOK BE-LONGS TO...
UM... EXCUSE US...

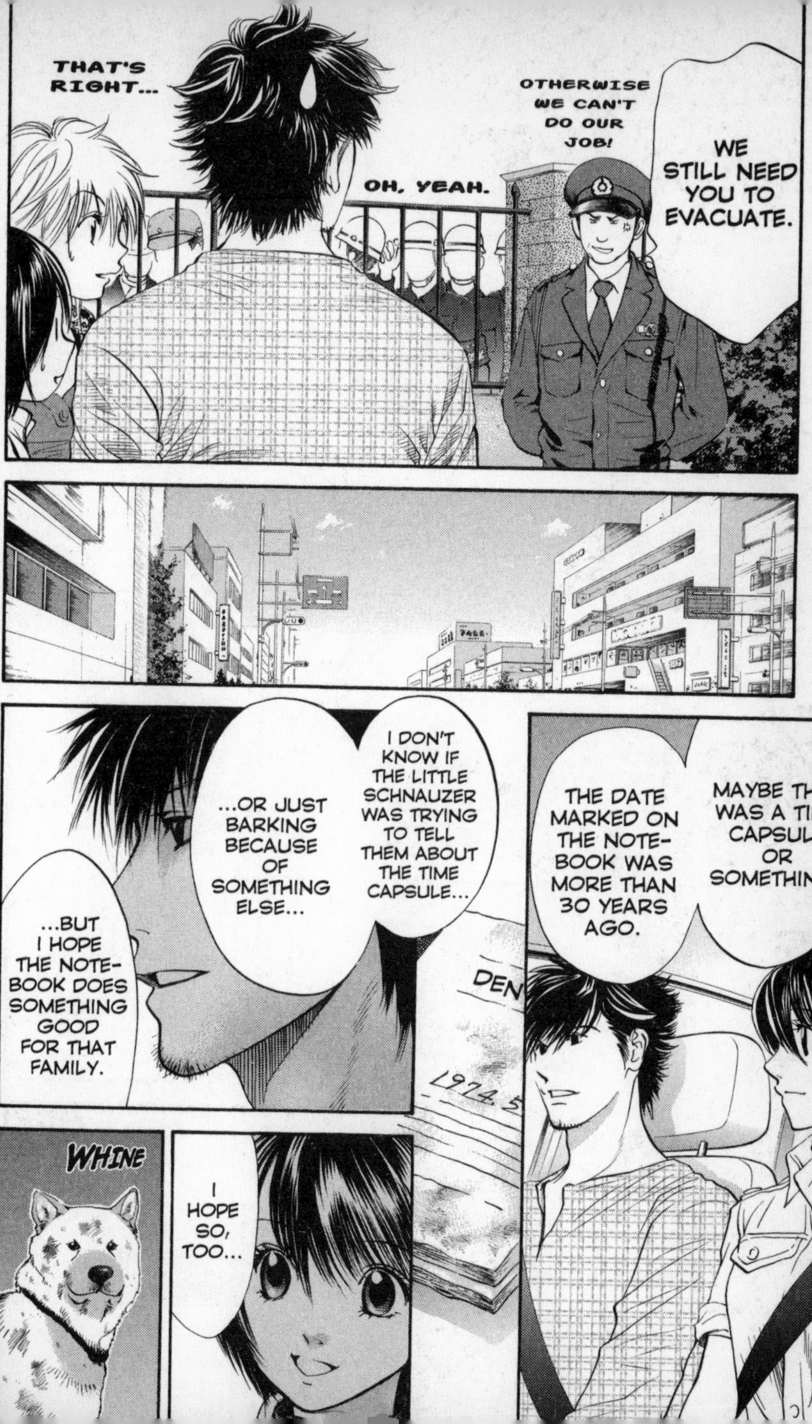
WE STILL NEED YOU TO EVACUATE.
OTHERWISE WE CAN'T DO OUR JOB!
OH, YEAH.
THAT'S RIGHT...
MAYBE THAT WAS A TIME CAPSULE OR SOMETHING.
THE DATE MARKED ON THE NOTE-BOOK WAS MORE THAN 30 YEARS AGO.
I DON'T KNOW IF THE LITTLE SCHNAUZER WAS TRYING TO TELL THEM ABOUT THE TIME CAPSULE...
...OR JUST BARKING BECAUSE OF SOMETHING ELSE...
...BUT I HOPE THE NOTE-BOOK DOES SOMETHING GOOD FOR THAT FAMILY.
DEN
1974 5
I HOPE SO, TOO...
WHINE

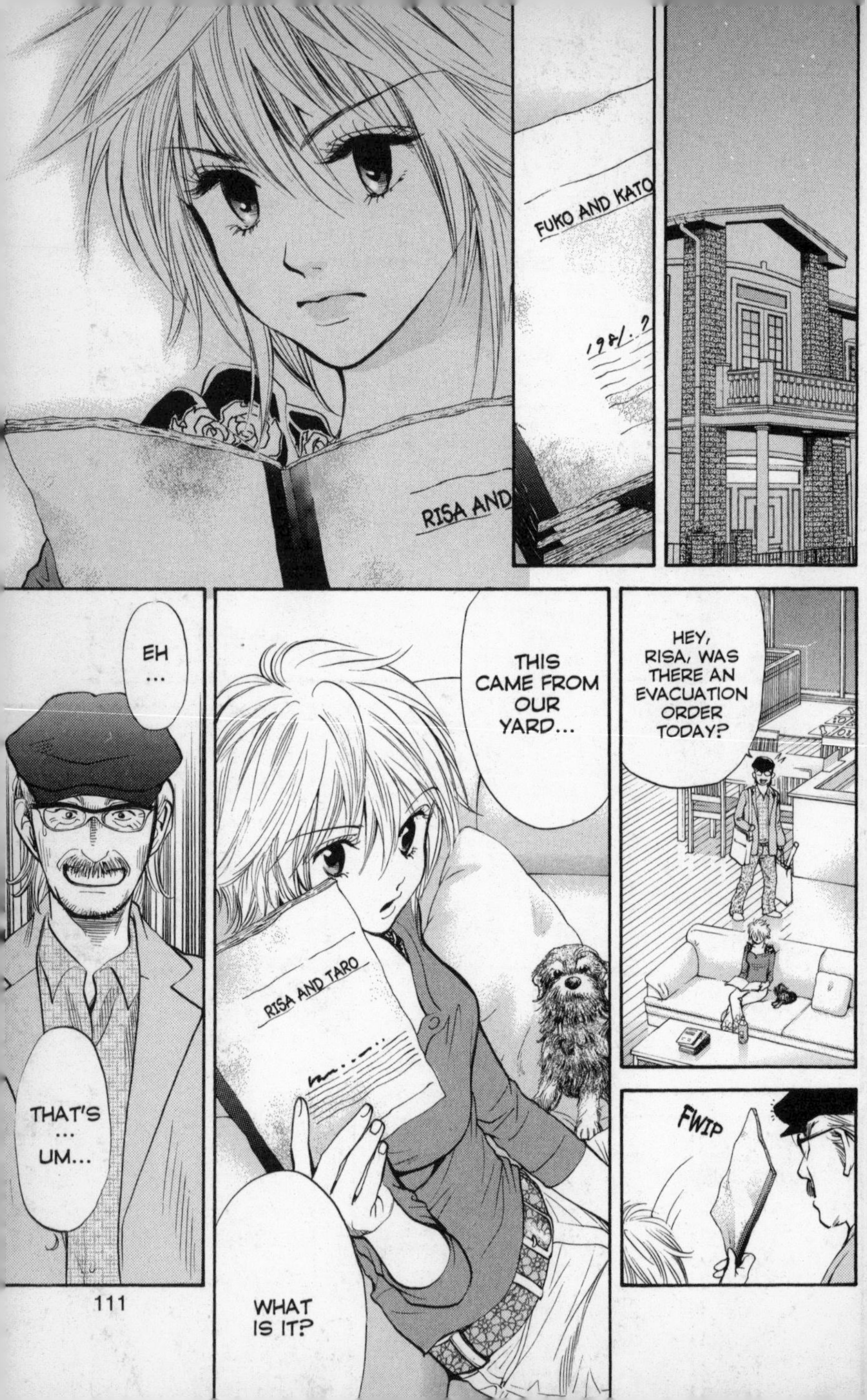
FUKO AND KATO
RISA AND
HEY, RISA, WAS THERE AN EVACUATION ORDER TODAY?
FWIP
THIS CAME FROM OUR YARD...
RISA AND TARO
WHAT IS IT?
EH ...
THAT'S ... UM...

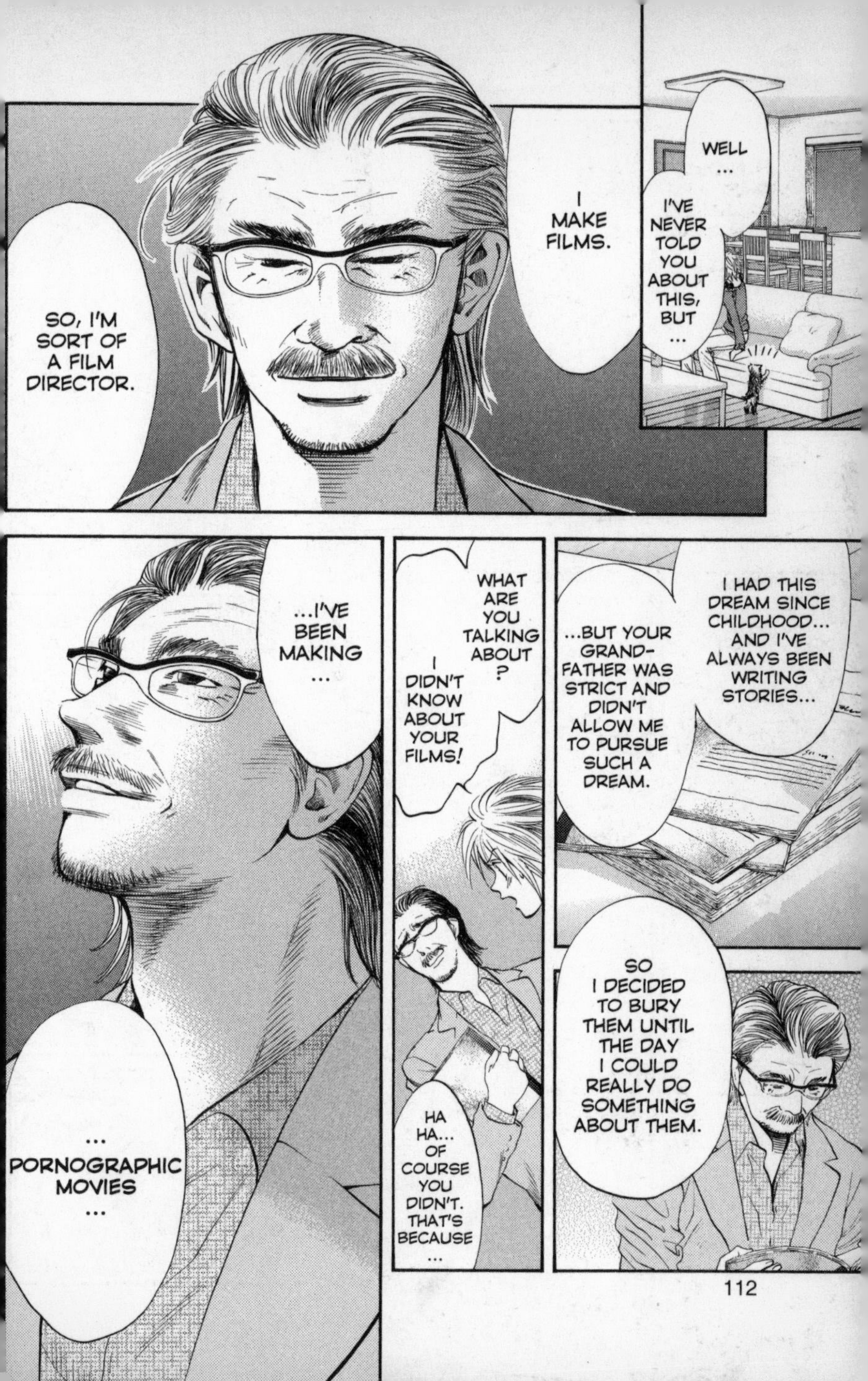
WELL ...
I'VE NEVER TOLD YOU ABOUT THIS, BUT ...
I MAKE FILMS.
SO, I'M SORT OF A FILM DIRECTOR.
I HAD THIS DREAM SINCE CHILDHOOD... AND I'VE ALWAYS BEEN WRITING STORIES...
...BUT YOUR GRAND-FATHER WAS STRICT AND DIDN'T ALLOW ME TO PURSUE SUCH A DREAM.
SO I DECIDED TO BURY THEM UNTIL THE DAY I COULD REALLY DO SOMETHING ABOUT THEM.
WHAT ARE YOU TALKING ABOUT ?
I DIDN'T KNOW ABOUT YOUR FILMS!
HA HA... OF COURSE YOU DIDN'T. THAT'S BECAUSE ...
...I'VE BEEN MAKING ...
... PORNOGRAPHIC MOVIES ...

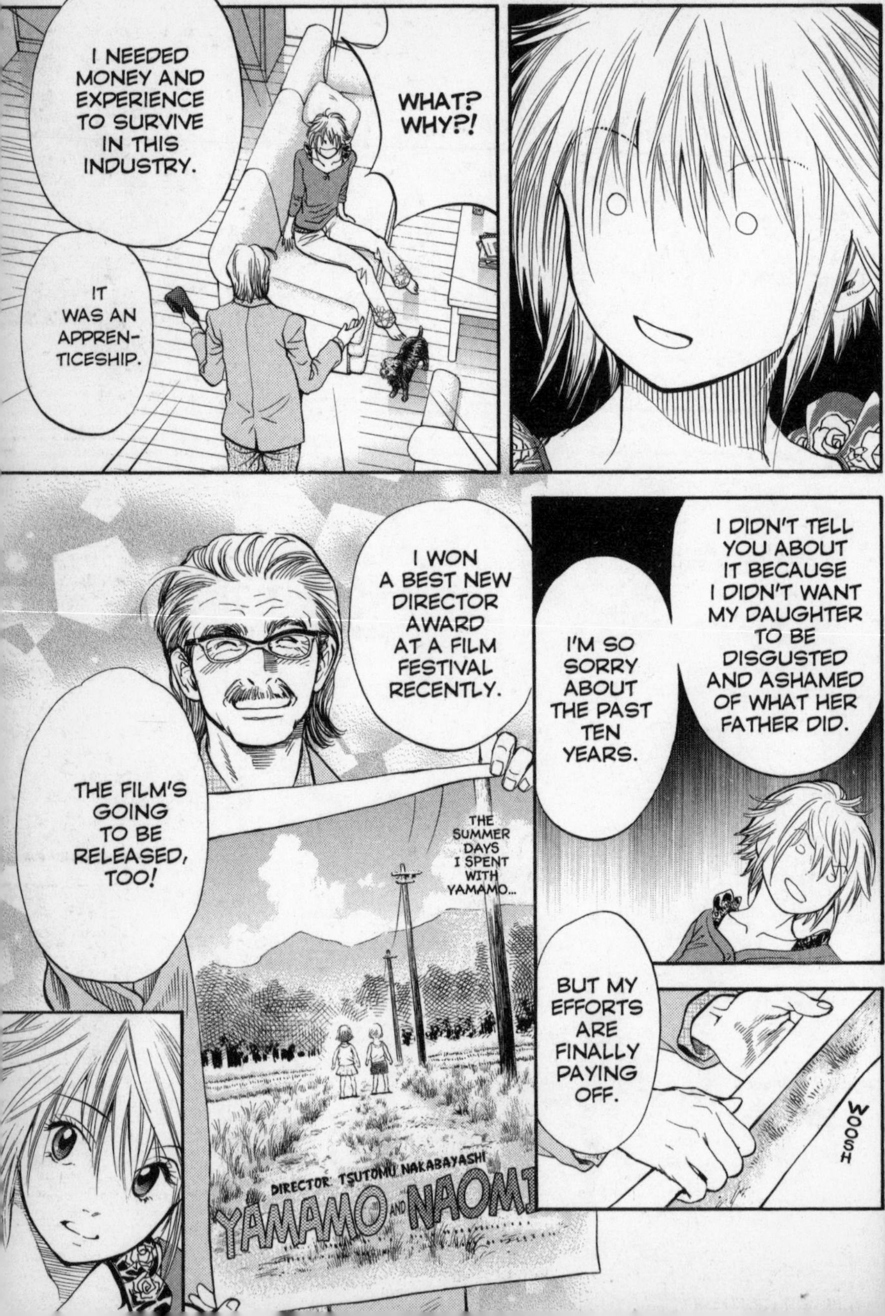
WHAT? WHY?!
I NEEDED MONEY AND EXPERIENCE TO SURVIVE IN THIS INDUSTRY.
IT WAS AN APPRENTICESHIP.
I DIDN'T TELL YOU ABOUT IT BECAUSE I DIDN'T WANT MY DAUGHTER TO BE DISGUSTED AND ASHAMED OF WHAT HER FATHER DID.
I'M SO SORRY ABOUT THE PAST TEN YEARS.
BUT MY EFFORTS ARE FINALLY PAYING OFF.
WOOSH
I WON A BEST NEW DIRECTOR AWARD AT A FILM FESTIVAL RECENTLY.
THE FILM'S GOING TO BE RELEASED, TOO!
THE SUMMER DAYS I SPENT WITH YAMAMO...
DIRECTOR: TSUTOMU NAKABAYASHI
YAMAMO AND NAOMI

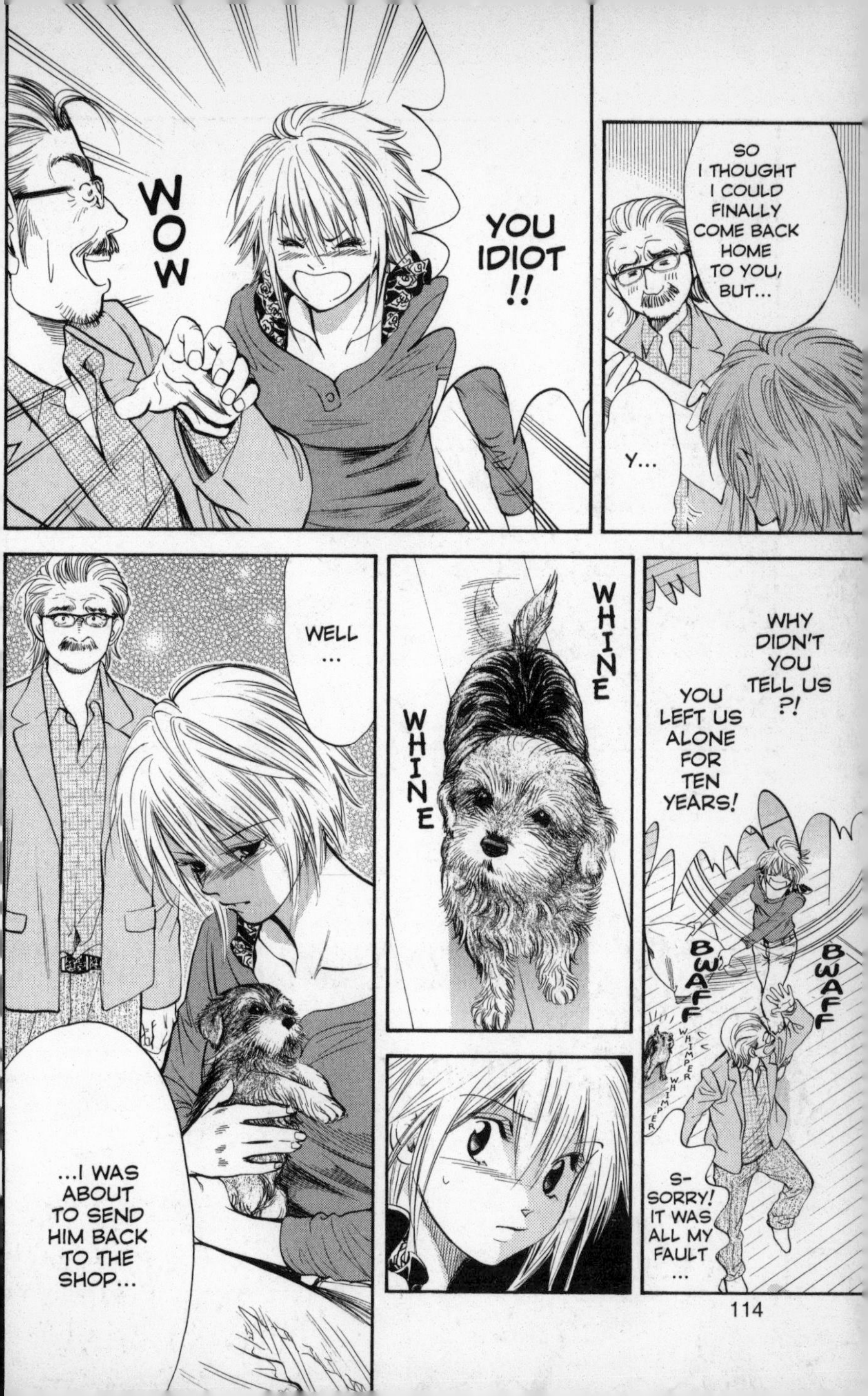
SO I THOUGHT I COULD FINALLY COME BACK HOME TO YOU, BUT...
Y...
YOU IDIOT!!
WOW
WHY DIDN'T YOU TELL US?!
YOU LEFT US ALONE FOR TEN YEARS!
BWAFF
BWAFF
WHIMPER
WHIMPER
S-SORRY! IT WAS ALL MY FAULT...
WHINE
WHINE
WELL...
...I WAS ABOUT TO SEND HIM BACK TO THE SHOP...

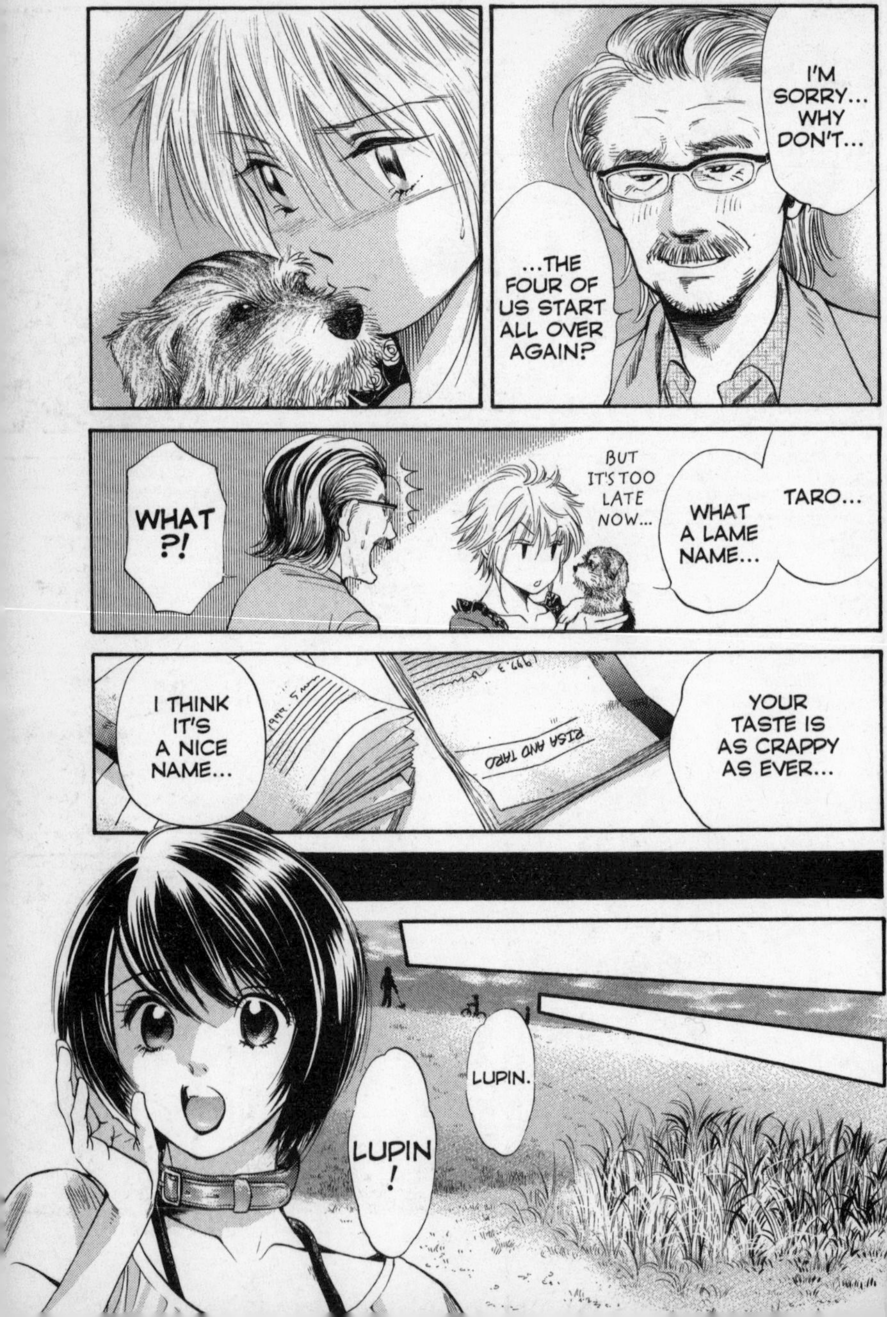
I'M SORRY... WHY DON'T...
...THE FOUR OF US START ALL OVER AGAIN?
TARO...
WHAT A LAME NAME...
BUT IT'S TOO LATE NOW...
WHAT ?!
YOUR TASTE IS AS CRAPPY AS EVER...
RISA AND TARO
I THINK IT'S A NICE NAME...
LUPIN.
LUPIN!

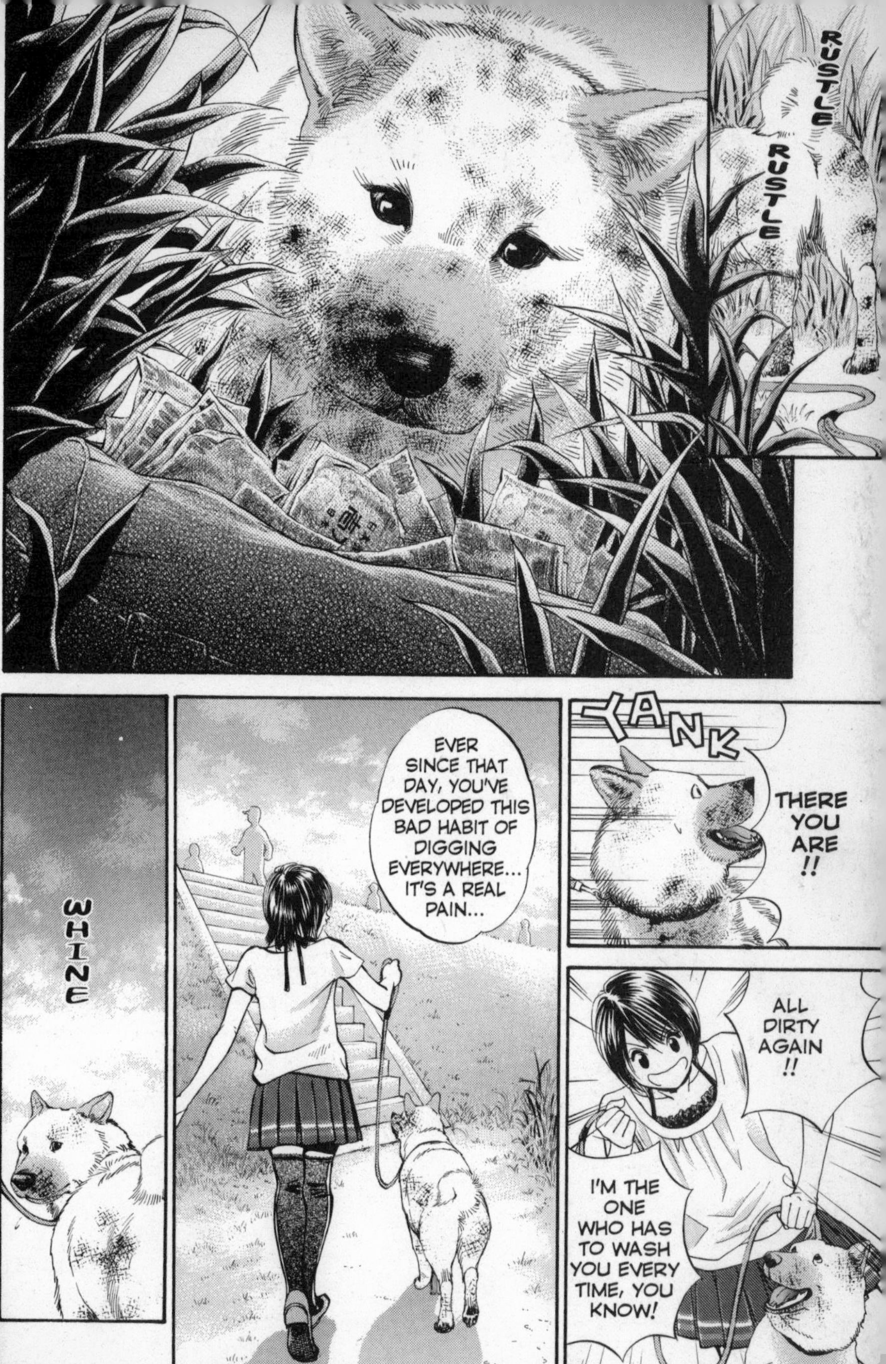
RUSTLE
RUSTLE
YANK
THERE YOU ARE!!
ALL DIRTY AGAIN!!
I'M THE ONE WHO HAS TO WASH YOU EVERY TIME, YOU KNOW!
EVER SINCE THAT DAY, YOU'VE DEVELOPED THIS BAD HABIT OF DIGGING EVERYWHERE... IT'S A REAL PAIN...
WHINE

CHAPTER 59: THE THREESOME

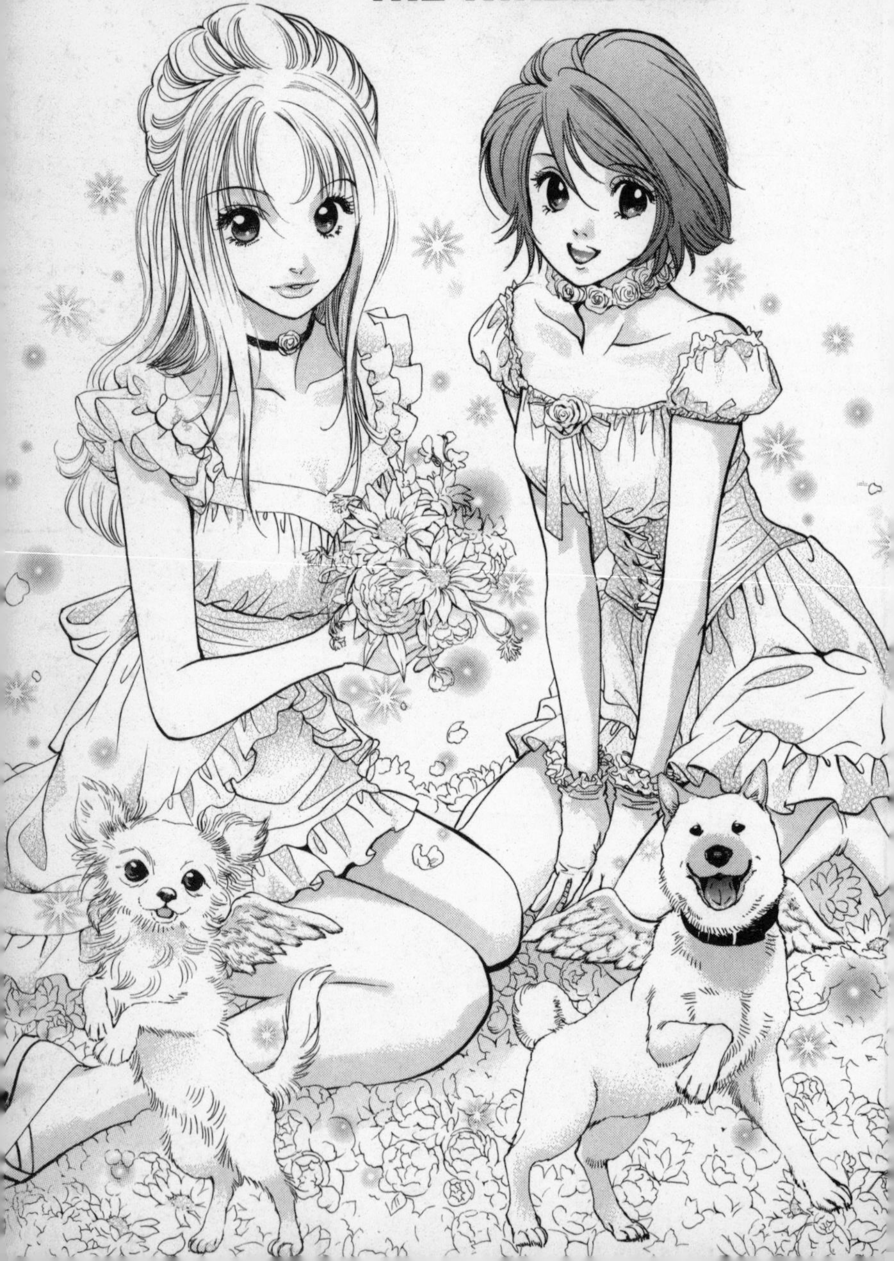

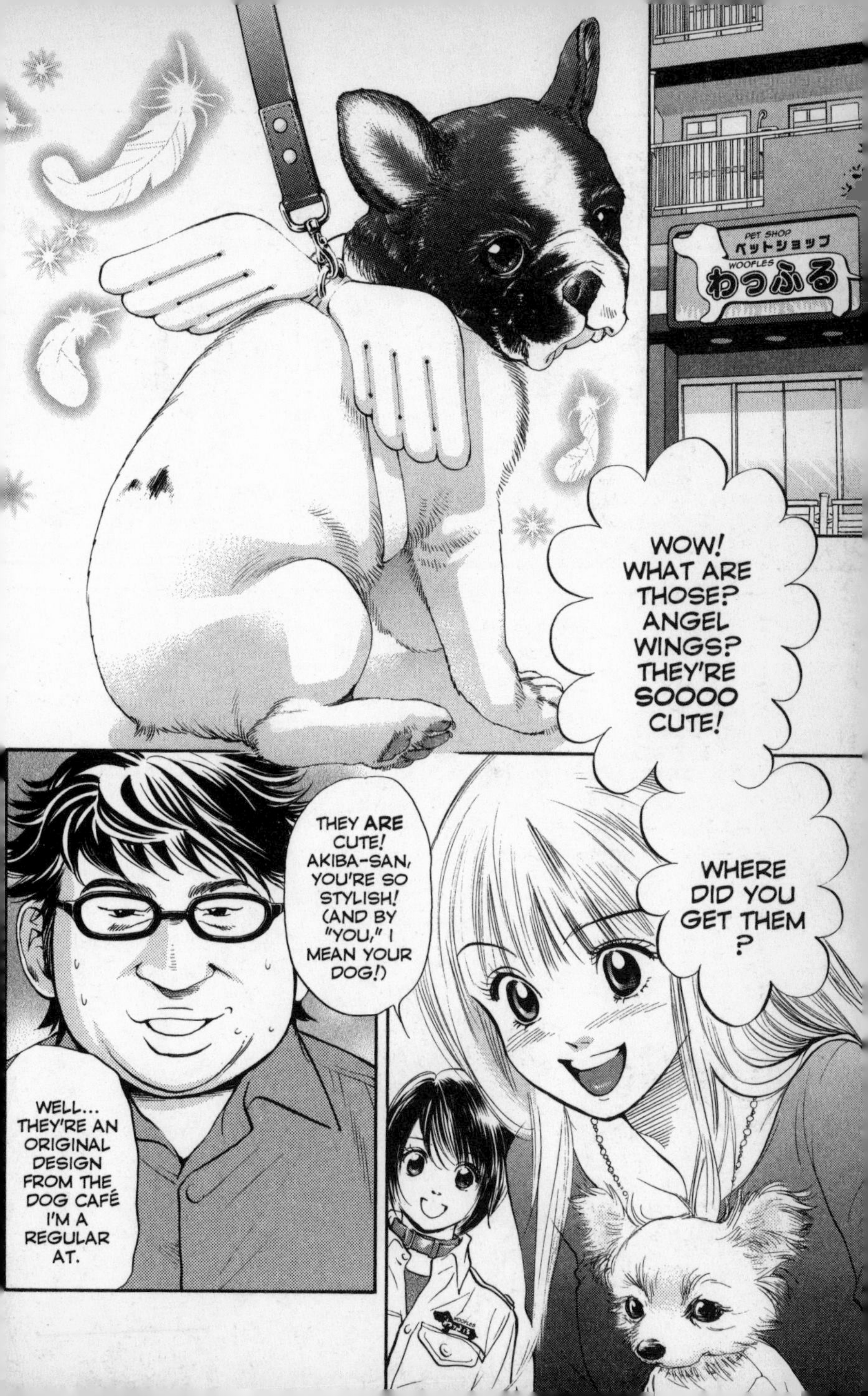
PET SHOP
ペットショップ
WOOPLES
わっふる
WOW! WHAT ARE THOSE? ANGEL WINGS? THEY'RE SOOOO CUTE!
WHERE DID YOU GET THEM?
THEY ARE CUTE! AKIBA-SAN, YOU'RE SO STYLISH! (AND BY "YOU," I MEAN YOUR DOG!)
WELL... THEY'RE AN ORIGINAL DESIGN FROM THE DOG CAFÉ I'M A REGULAR AT.

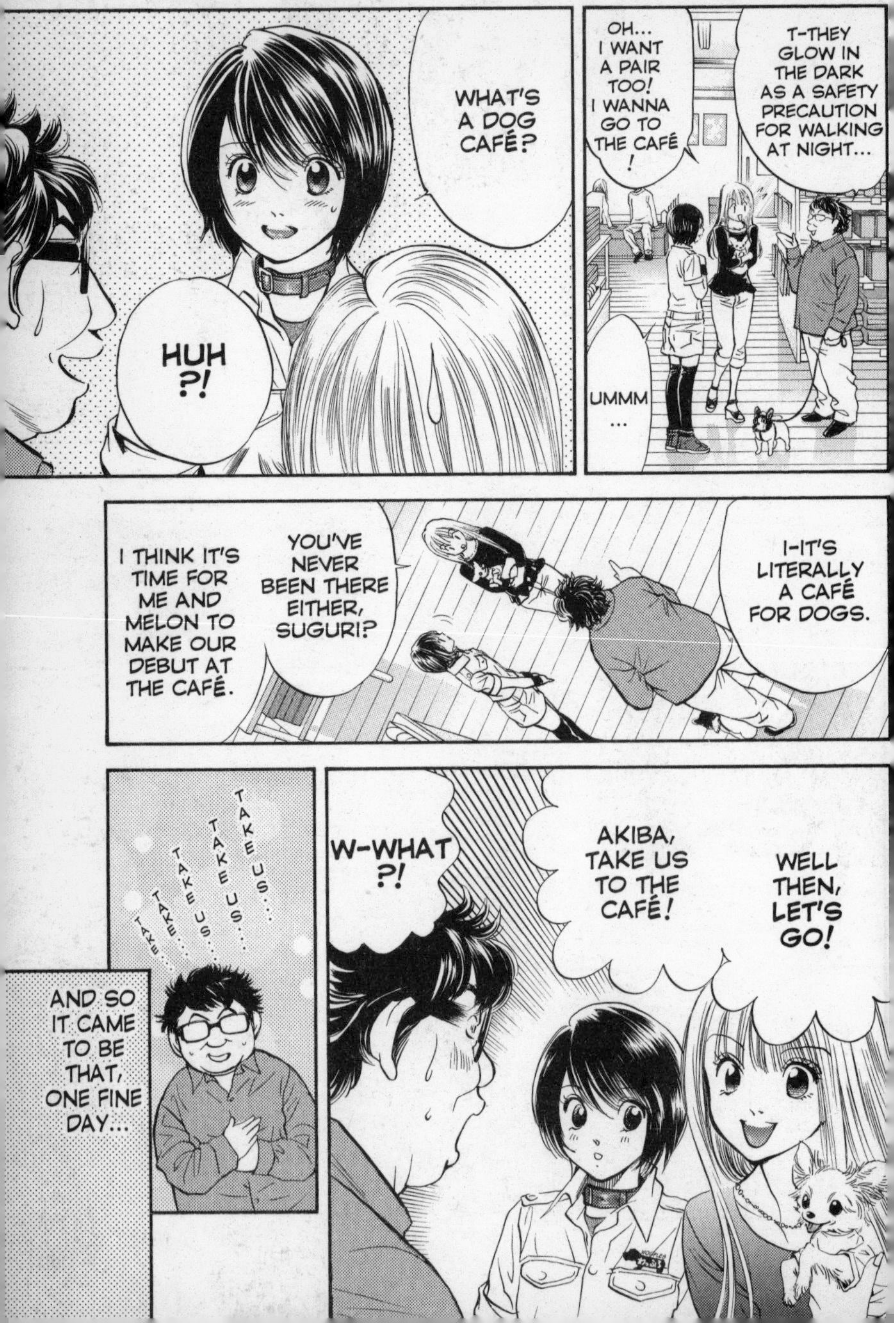
T-THEY GLOW IN THE DARK AS A SAFETY PRECAUTION FOR WALKING AT NIGHT...
OH... I WANT A PAIR TOO! I WANNA GO TO THE CAFÉ!
UMMM...
WHAT'S A DOG CAFÉ?
HUH?!
I-IT'S LITERALLY A CAFÉ FOR DOGS.
YOU'VE NEVER BEEN THERE EITHER, SUGURI?
I THINK IT'S TIME FOR ME AND MELON TO MAKE OUR DEBUT AT THE CAFÉ.
WELL THEN, LET'S GO!
AKIBA, TAKE US TO THE CAFÉ!
W-WHAT?!
TAKE US...
TAKE US...
TAKE US...
TAKE...
TAKE...
AND SO IT CAME TO BE THAT, ONE FINE DAY...

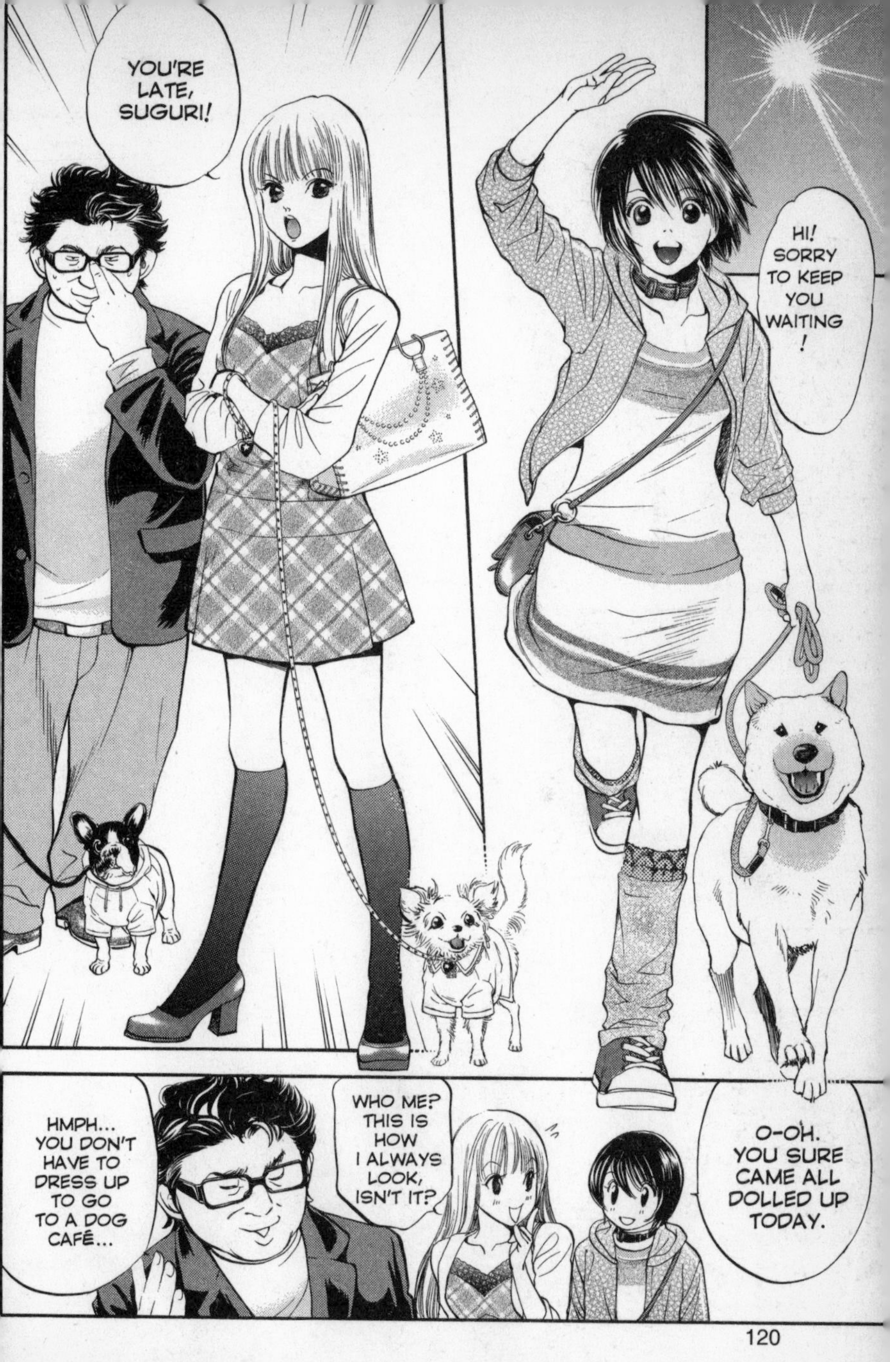
HI! SORRY TO KEEP YOU WAITING!
YOU'RE LATE, SUGURI!
O-OH. YOU SURE CAME ALL DOLLED UP TODAY.
WHO ME? THIS IS HOW I ALWAYS LOOK, ISN'T IT?
HMPH... YOU DON'T HAVE TO DRESS UP TO GO TO A DOG CAFÉ...

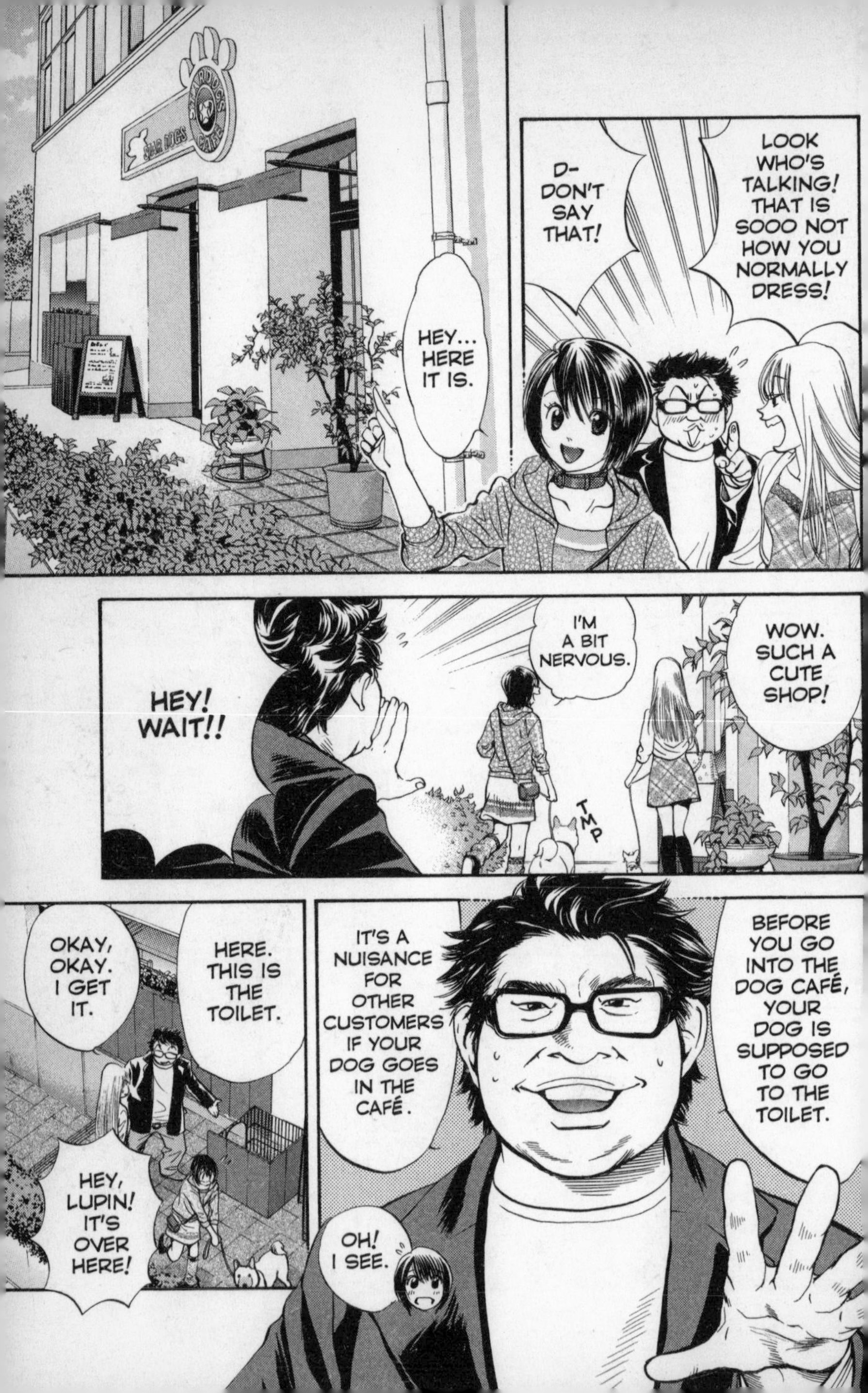
LOOK WHO'S TALKING! THAT IS SOOO NOT HOW YOU NORMALLY DRESS!
D- DON'T SAY THAT!
HEY... HERE IT IS.
STAR DOGS
WOW. SUCH A CUTE SHOP!
I'M A BIT NERVOUS.
TMP
HEY! WAIT!!
BEFORE YOU GO INTO THE DOG CAFÉ, YOUR DOG IS SUPPOSED TO GO TO THE TOILET.
IT'S A NUISANCE FOR OTHER CUSTOMERS IF YOUR DOG GOES IN THE CAFÉ.
OH! I SEE.
HERE. THIS IS THE TOILET.
OKAY, OKAY. I GET IT.
HEY, LUPIN! IT'S OVER HERE!

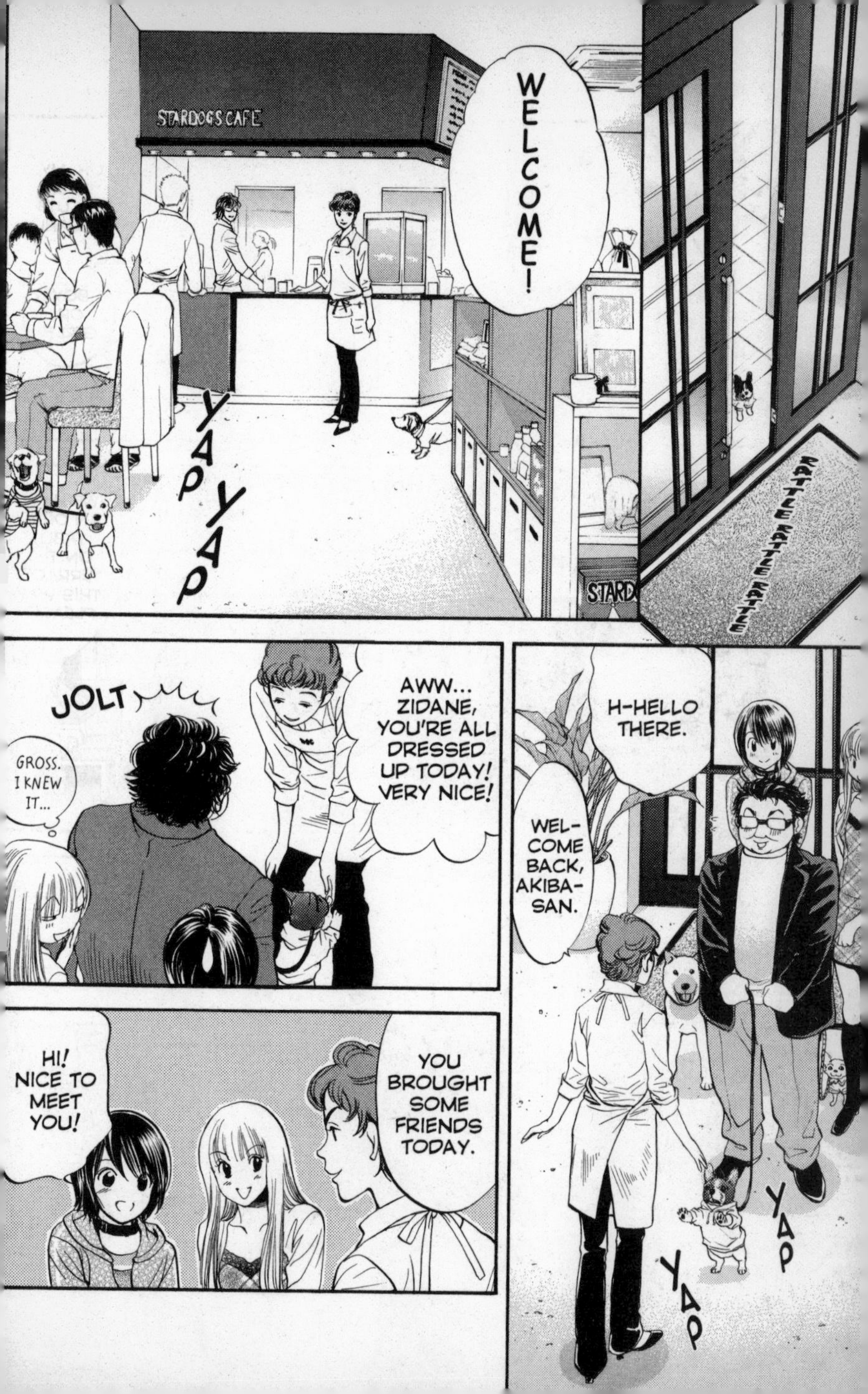
STARDOGS CAFE
WELCOME!
RATTLE RATTLE RATTLE
YAP YAP YAP
H-HELLO THERE.
WEL-COME BACK, AKIBA-SAN.
YAP YAP
AWW... ZIDANE, YOU'RE ALL DRESSED UP TODAY! VERY NICE!
JOLT
GROSS. I KNEW IT...
YOU BROUGHT SOME FRIENDS TODAY.
HI! NICE TO MEET YOU!

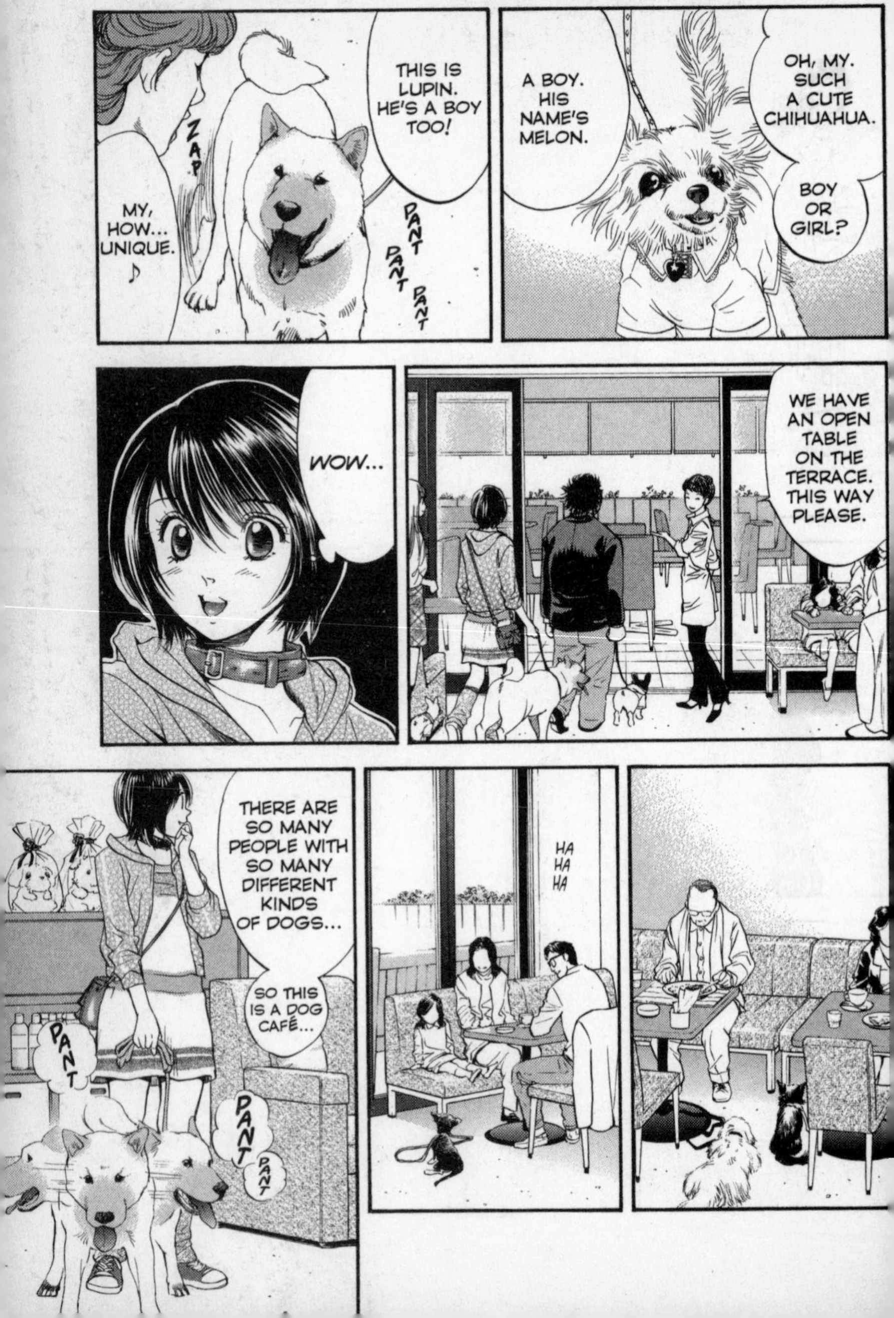
OH, MY. SUCH A CUTE CHIHUAHUA.
BOY OR GIRL?
A BOY. HIS NAME'S MELON.
THIS IS LUPIN. HE'S A BOY TOO!
ZAP
PANT PANT PANT
MY, HOW... UNIQUE. ♪
WE HAVE AN OPEN TABLE ON THE TERRACE. THIS WAY PLEASE.
WOW...
HA HA HA
THERE ARE SO MANY PEOPLE WITH SO MANY DIFFERENT KINDS OF DOGS...
SO THIS IS A DOG CAFÉ...
PANT
PANT PANT

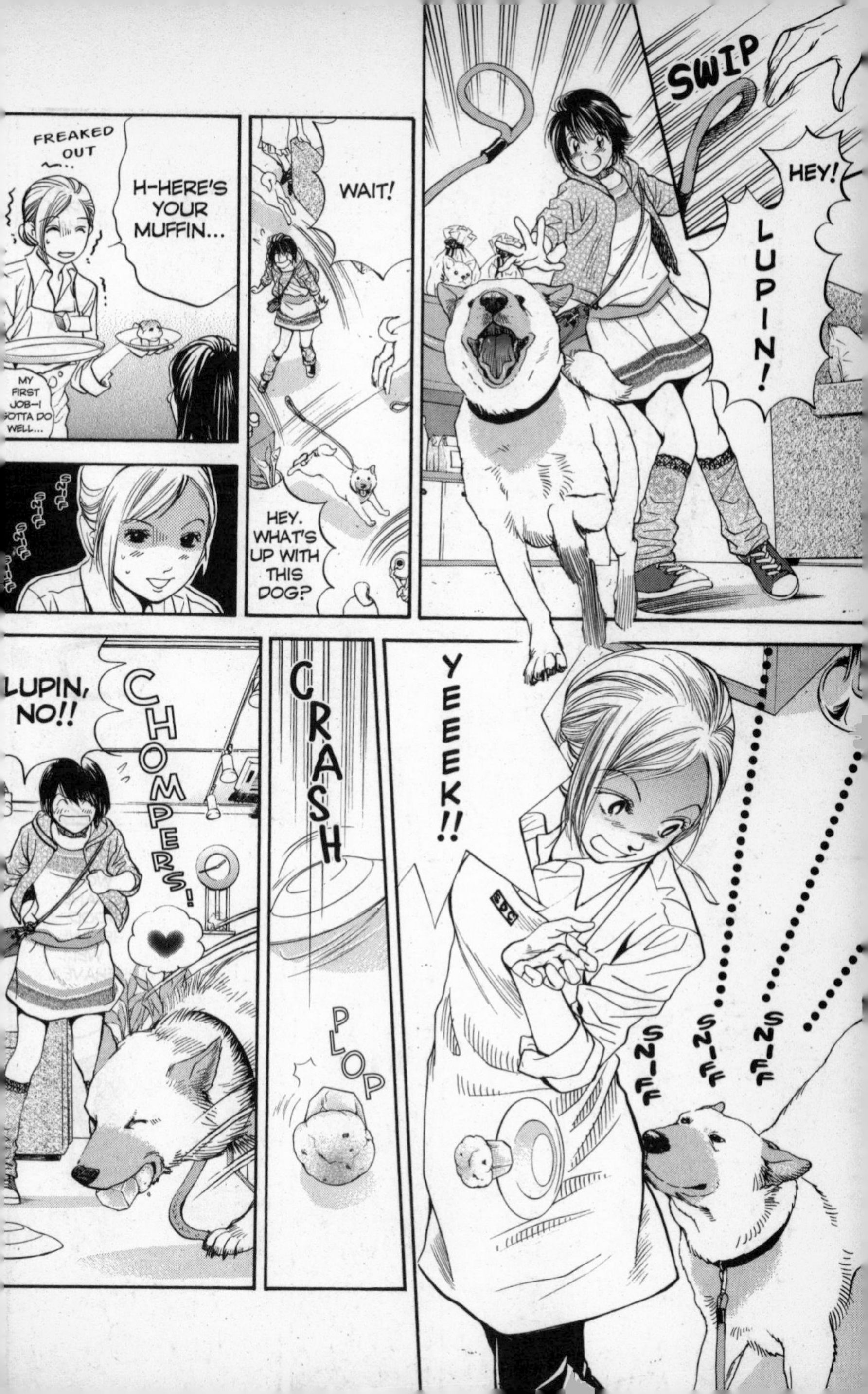
SWIP
HEY!
LUPIN!
WAIT!
HEY. WHAT'S UP WITH THIS DOG?
FREAKED OUT ~...
H-HERE'S YOUR MUFFIN...
MY FIRST JOB—I GOTTA DO WELL...
SNIFF SNIFF SNIFF SNIFF
YEEEK!!
SNIFF SNIFF SNIFF
CRASH
PLOP
LUPIN, NO!!
CHOMPERS!

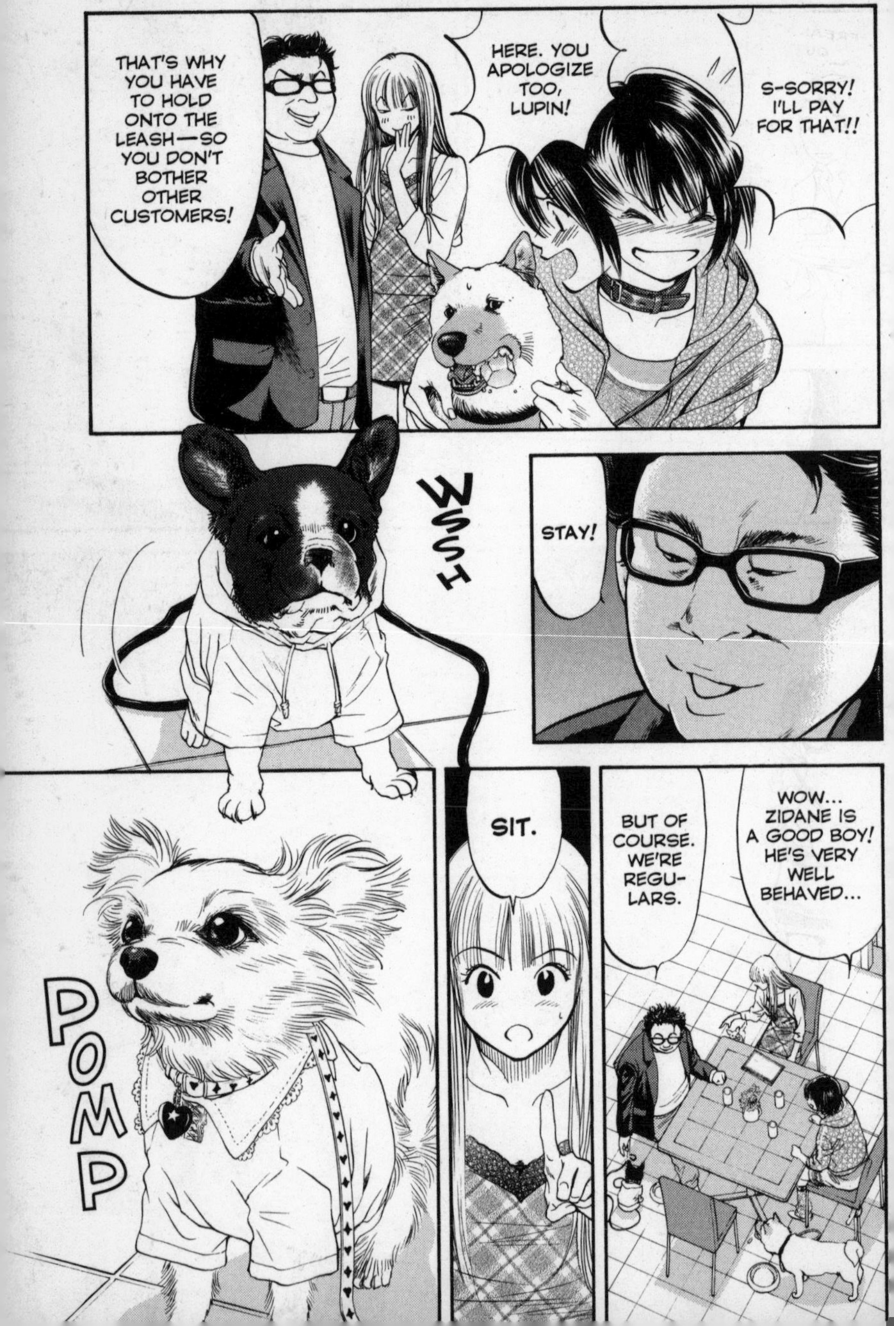
S-SORRY! I'LL PAY FOR THAT!!
HERE. YOU APOLOGIZE TOO, LUPIN!
THAT'S WHY YOU HAVE TO HOLD ONTO THE LEASH—SO YOU DON'T BOTHER OTHER CUSTOMERS!
STAY!
WSSH
WOW... ZIDANE IS A GOOD BOY! HE'S VERY WELL BEHAVED...
BUT OF COURSE. WE'RE REGU-LARS.
SIT.
POMP

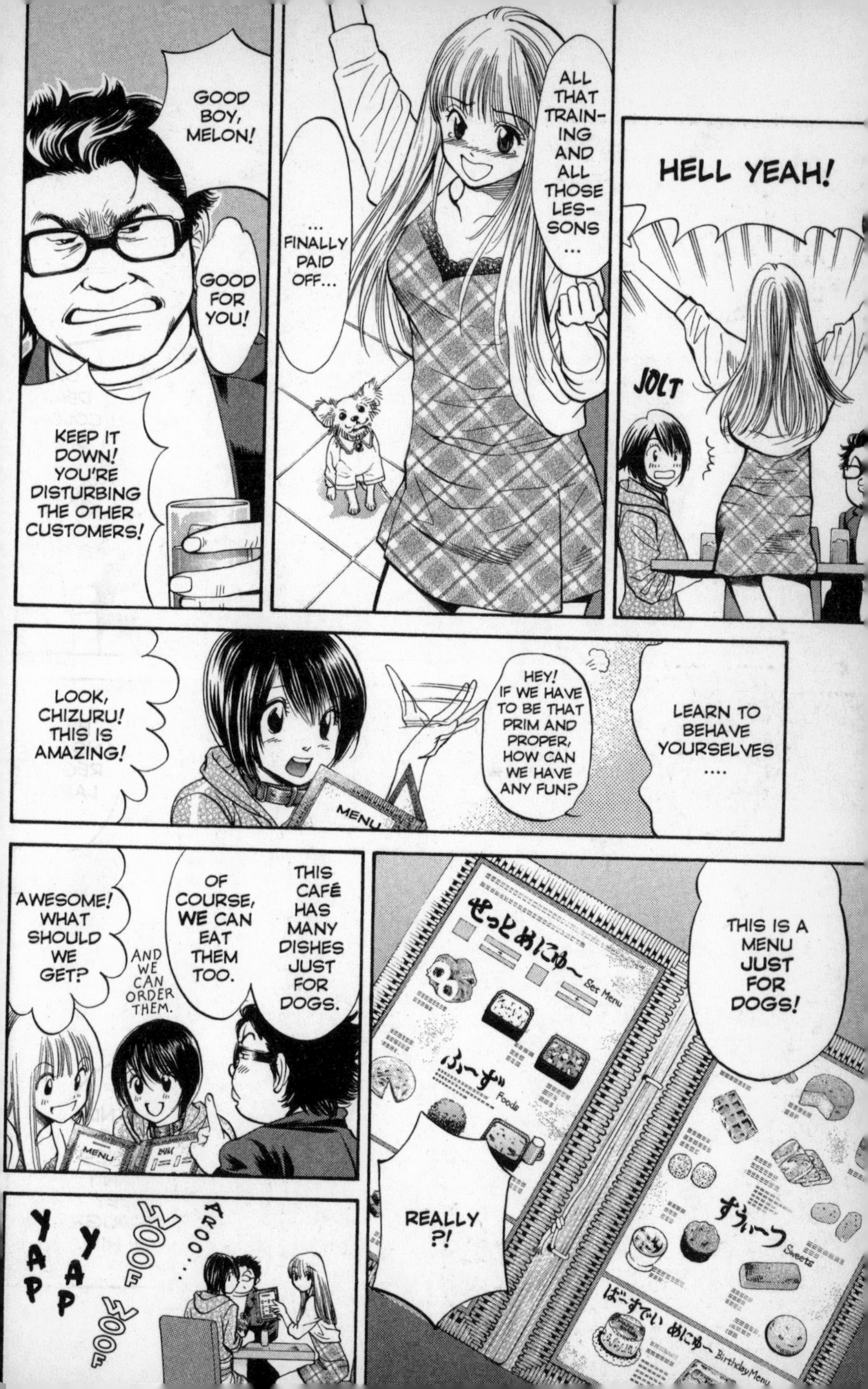
HELL YEAH!
JOLT
ALL THAT TRAINING AND ALL THOSE LESSONS...
...FINALLY PAID OFF...
GOOD BOY, MELON!
GOOD FOR YOU!
KEEP IT DOWN! YOU'RE DISTURBING THE OTHER CUSTOMERS!
LEARN TO BEHAVE YOURSELVES....
HEY! IF WE HAVE TO BE THAT PRIM AND PROPER, HOW CAN WE HAVE ANY FUN?
MENU
LOOK, CHIZURU! THIS IS AMAZING!
THIS IS A MENU JUST FOR DOGS!
せっとめにゅ～ Set Menu
ふ～ず Foods
すうぃ～つ Sweets
ば～すでい めにゅ～ BirthdayMenu
REALLY?!
THIS CAFÉ HAS MANY DISHES JUST FOR DOGS.
OF COURSE, WE CAN EAT THEM TOO.
AND WE CAN ORDER THEM.
AWESOME! WHAT SHOULD WE GET?
MENU
...ARROO
WOOF WOOF
WOOF WOOF
YAP YAP

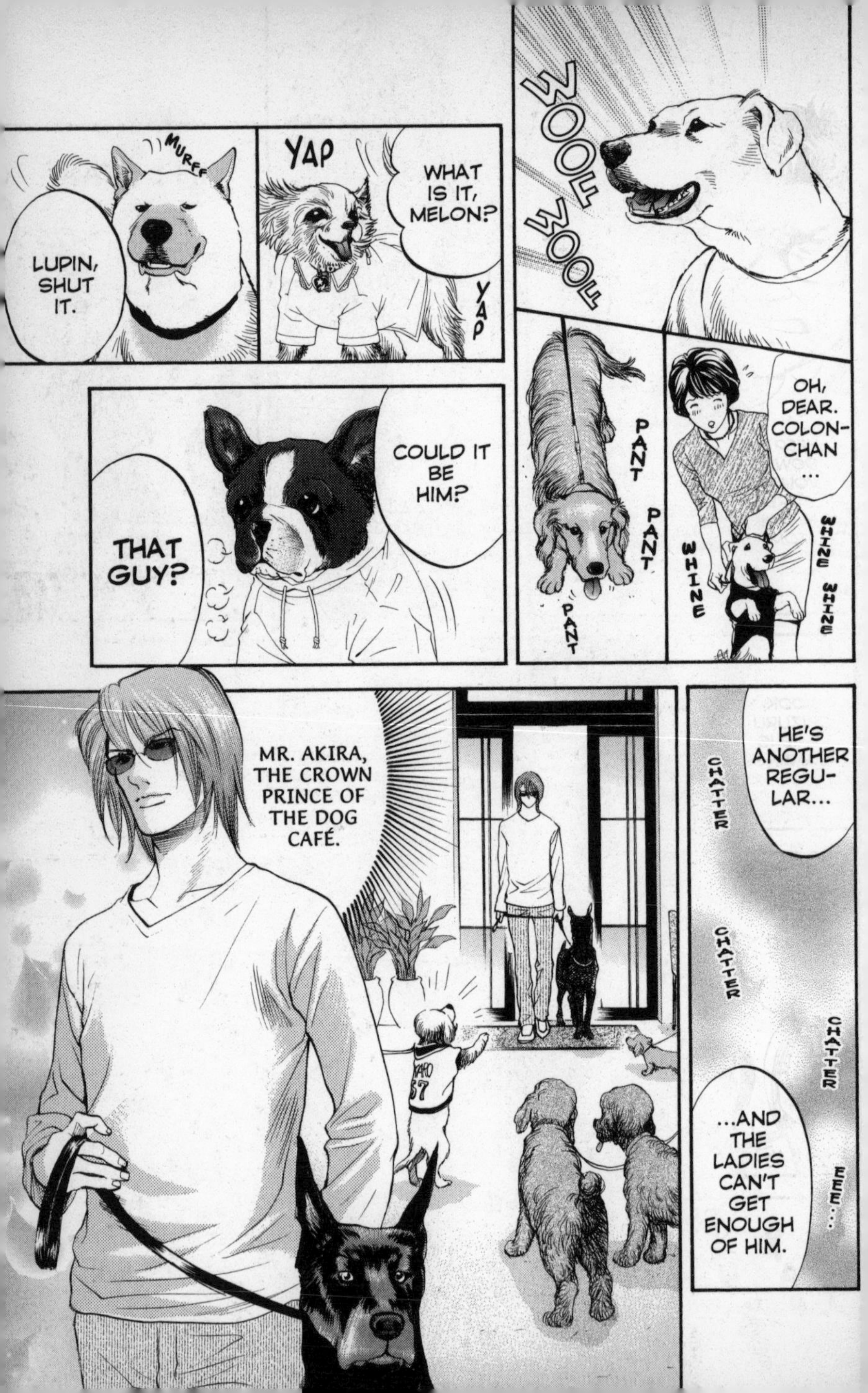
WOOF WOOF
YAP
WHAT IS IT, MELON?
YAP
MURFF
LUPIN, SHUT IT.
OH, DEAR. COLON-CHAN...
WHINE
WHINE WHINE
PANT PANT
PANT
COULD IT BE HIM?
THAT GUY?
HE'S ANOTHER REGULAR...
CHATTER
CHATTER
CHATTER
...AND THE LADIES CAN'T GET ENOUGH OF HIM.
EEE...
MR. AKIRA, THE CROWN PRINCE OF THE DOG CAFÉ.

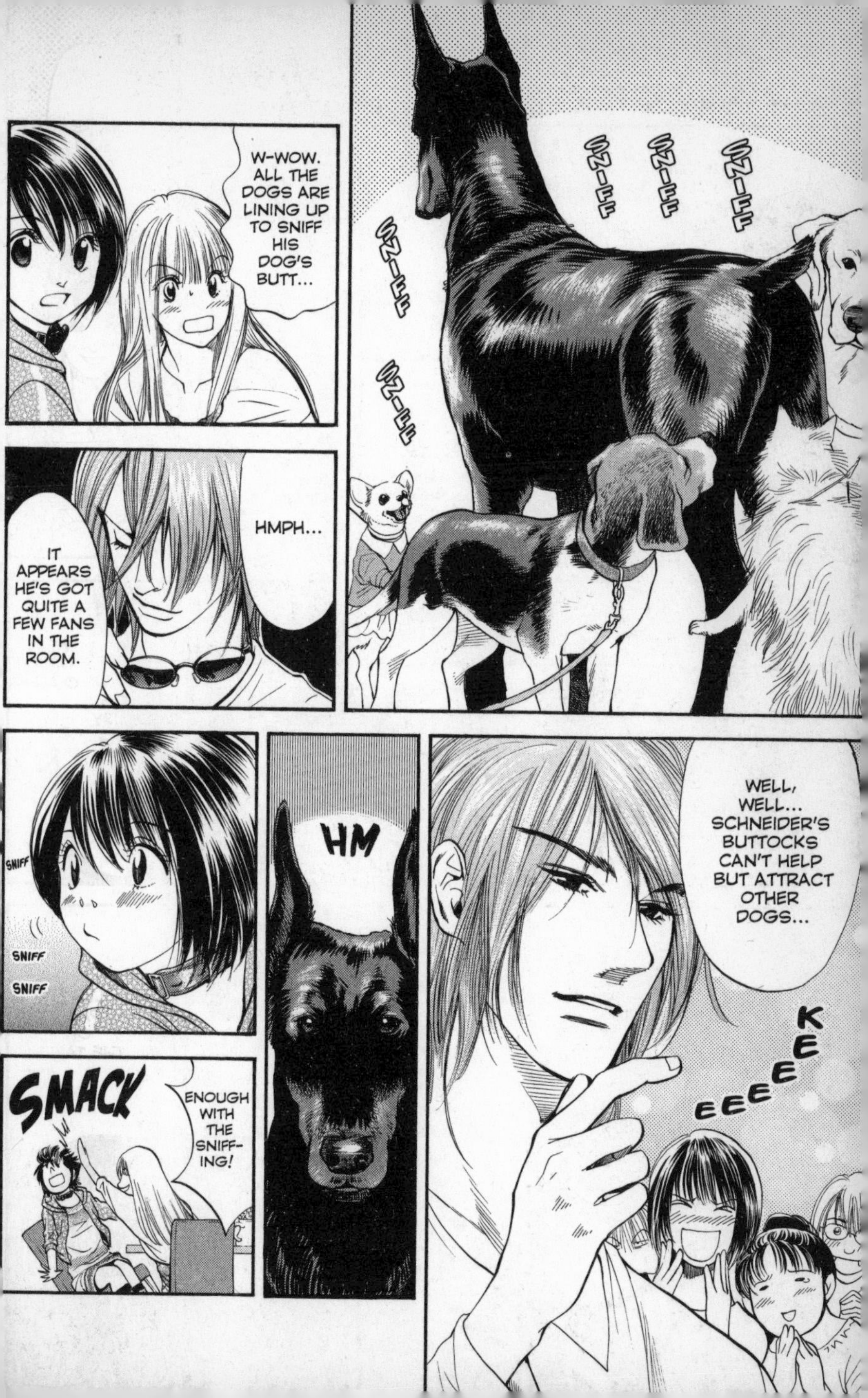
SNIFF
SNIFF
SNIFF
SNIFF
SNIFF
W-WOW. ALL THE DOGS ARE LINING UP TO SNIFF HIS DOG'S BUTT...
HMPH...
IT APPEARS HE'S GOT QUITE A FEW FANS IN THE ROOM.
WELL, WELL... SCHNEIDER'S BUTTOCKS CAN'T HELP BUT ATTRACT OTHER DOGS...
KEEEEEE
HM
SNIFF
SNIFF
SNIFF
SMACK
ENOUGH WITH THE SNIFF-ING!

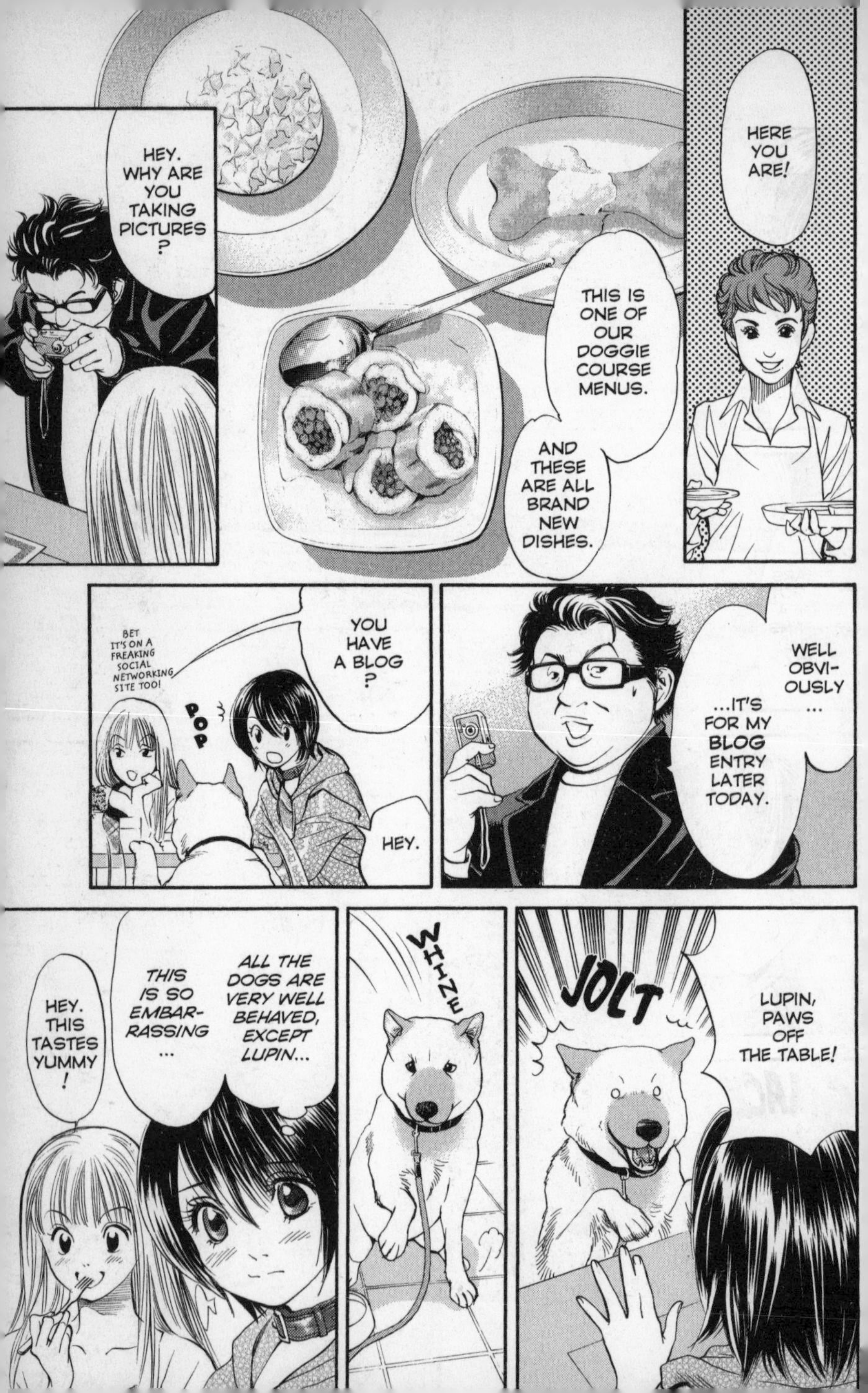
HERE YOU ARE!
THIS IS ONE OF OUR DOGGIE COURSE MENUS.
AND THESE ARE ALL BRAND NEW DISHES.
HEY. WHY ARE YOU TAKING PICTURES?
WELL OBVIOUSLY...
...IT'S FOR MY BLOG ENTRY LATER TODAY.
YOU HAVE A BLOG?
BET IT'S ON A FREAKING SOCIAL NETWORKING SITE TOO!
POP
HEY.
JOLT
LUPIN, PAWS OFF THE TABLE!
WHINE
ALL THE DOGS ARE VERY WELL BEHAVED, EXCEPT LUPIN...
THIS IS SO EMBARRASSING...
HEY. THIS TASTES YUMMY!

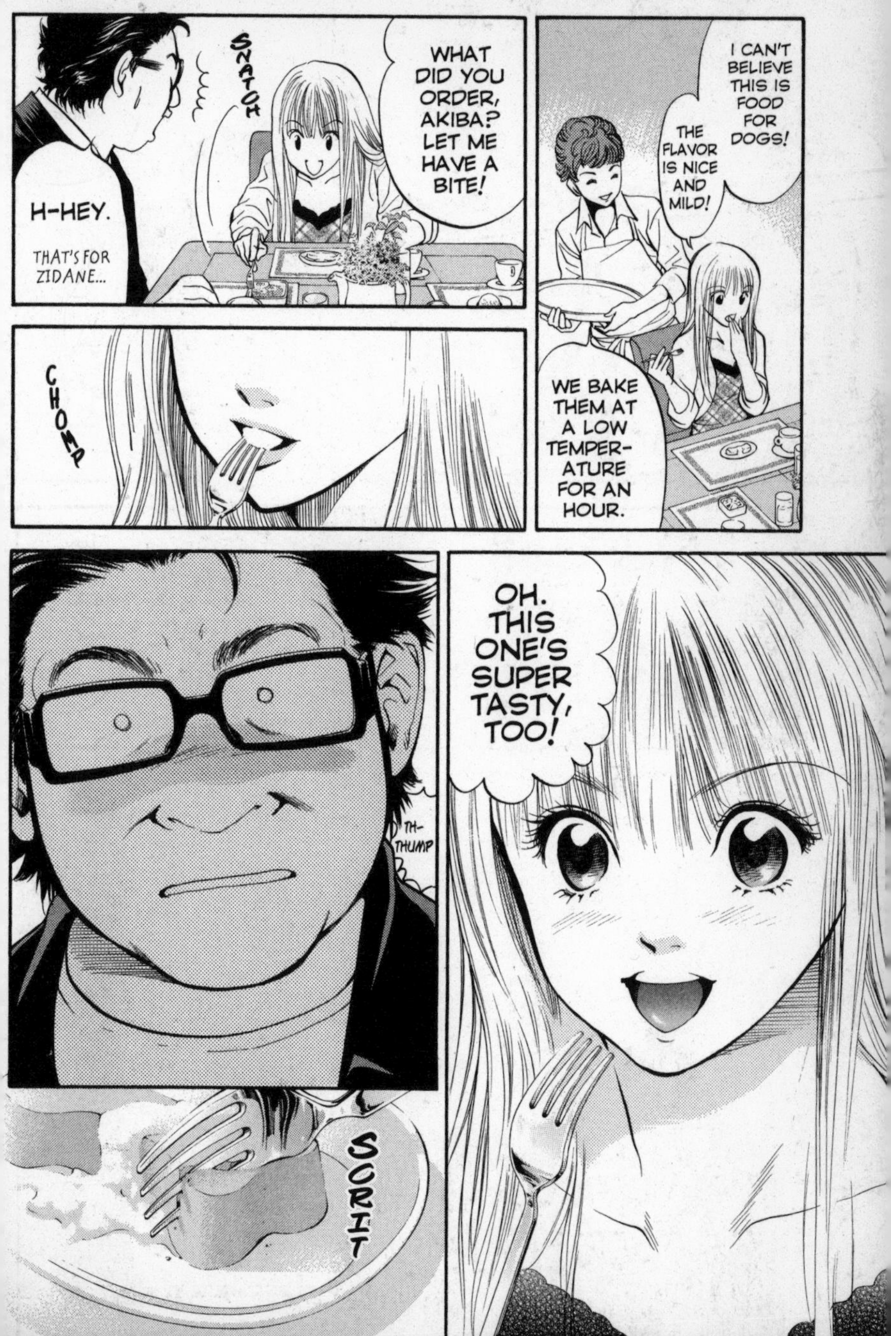
I CAN'T BELIEVE THIS IS FOOD FOR DOGS!
THE FLAVOR IS NICE AND MILD!
WE BAKE THEM AT A LOW TEMPERATURE FOR AN HOUR.
WHAT DID YOU ORDER, AKIBA? LET ME HAVE A BITE!
SNATCH
H-HEY.
THAT'S FOR ZIDANE...
CHOMP
OH. THIS ONE'S SUPER TASTY, TOO!
TH-THUMP
SCRIT

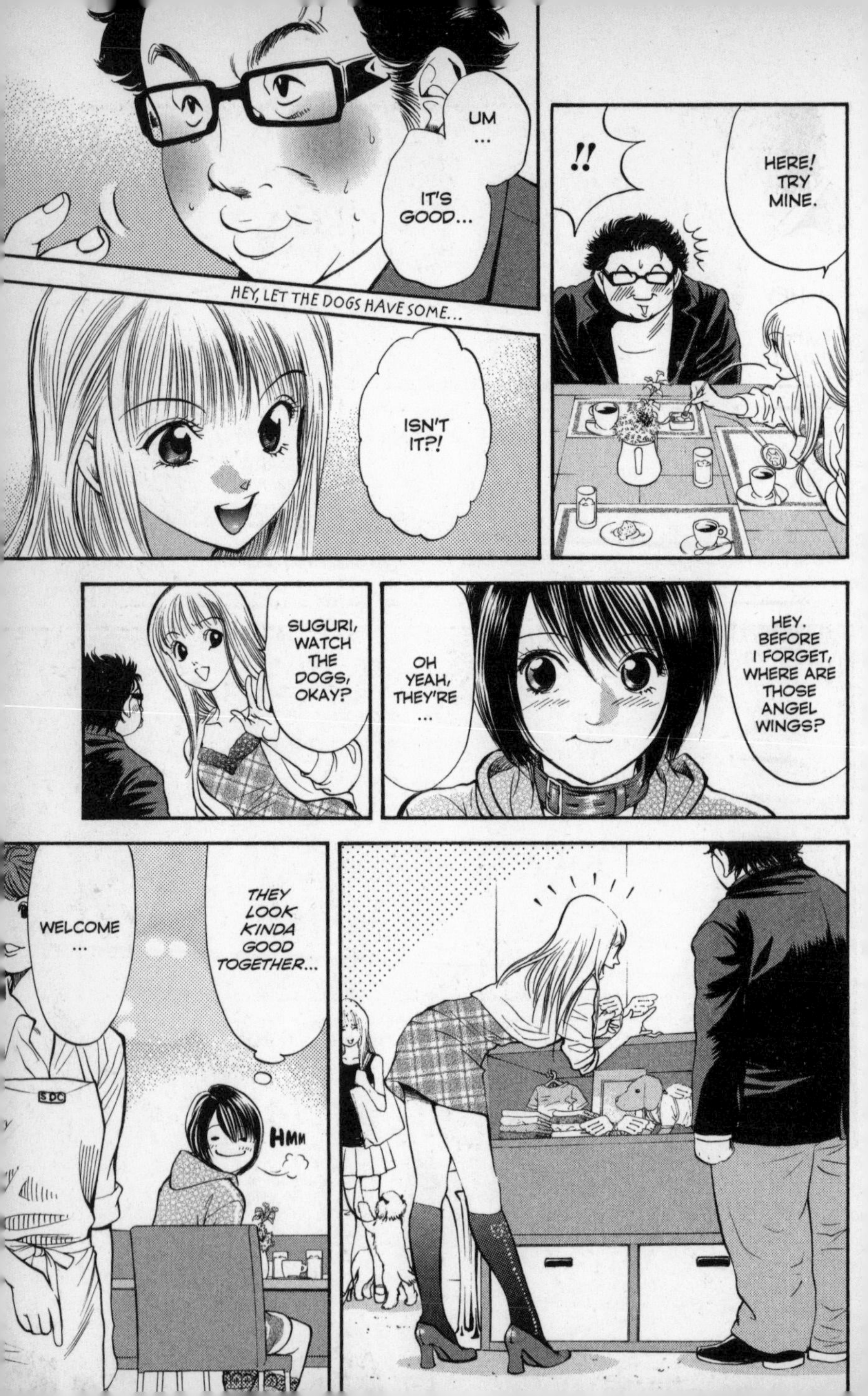
HERE! TRY MINE.
!!
UM ...
IT'S GOOD...
HEY, LET THE DOGS HAVE SOME...
ISN'T IT?!
HEY. BEFORE I FORGET, WHERE ARE THOSE ANGEL WINGS?
OH YEAH, THEY'RE ...
SUGURI, WATCH THE DOGS, OKAY?
THEY LOOK KINDA GOOD TOGETHER...
WELCOME ...
SDC
HMM

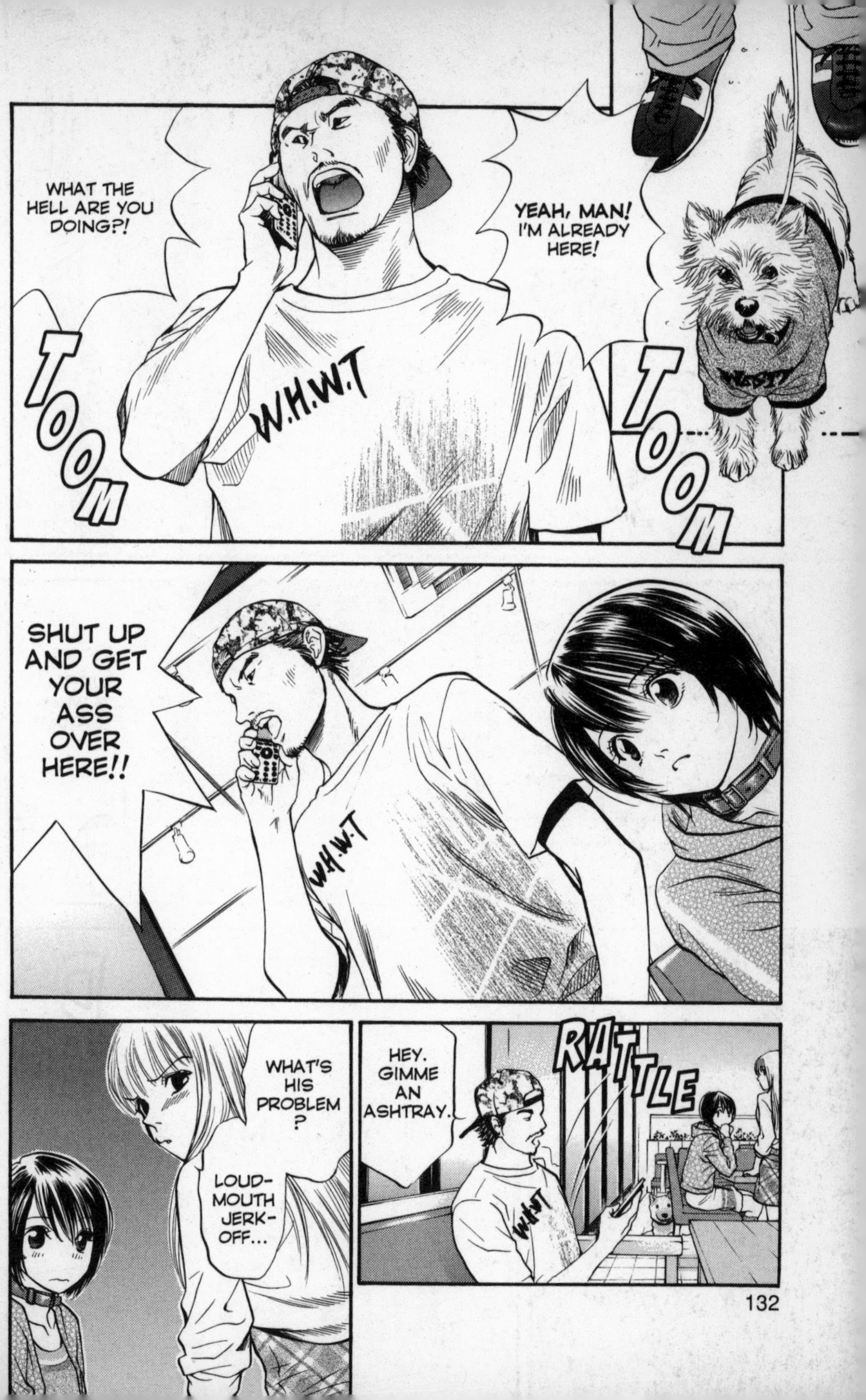
YEAH, MAN! I'M ALREADY HERE!
TOOM
WHAT THE HELL ARE YOU DOING?!
TOOM
SHUT UP AND GET YOUR ASS OVER HERE!!
RATTLE
HEY. GIMME AN ASHTRAY.
WHAT'S HIS PROBLEM?
LOUD-MOUTH JERK-OFF...

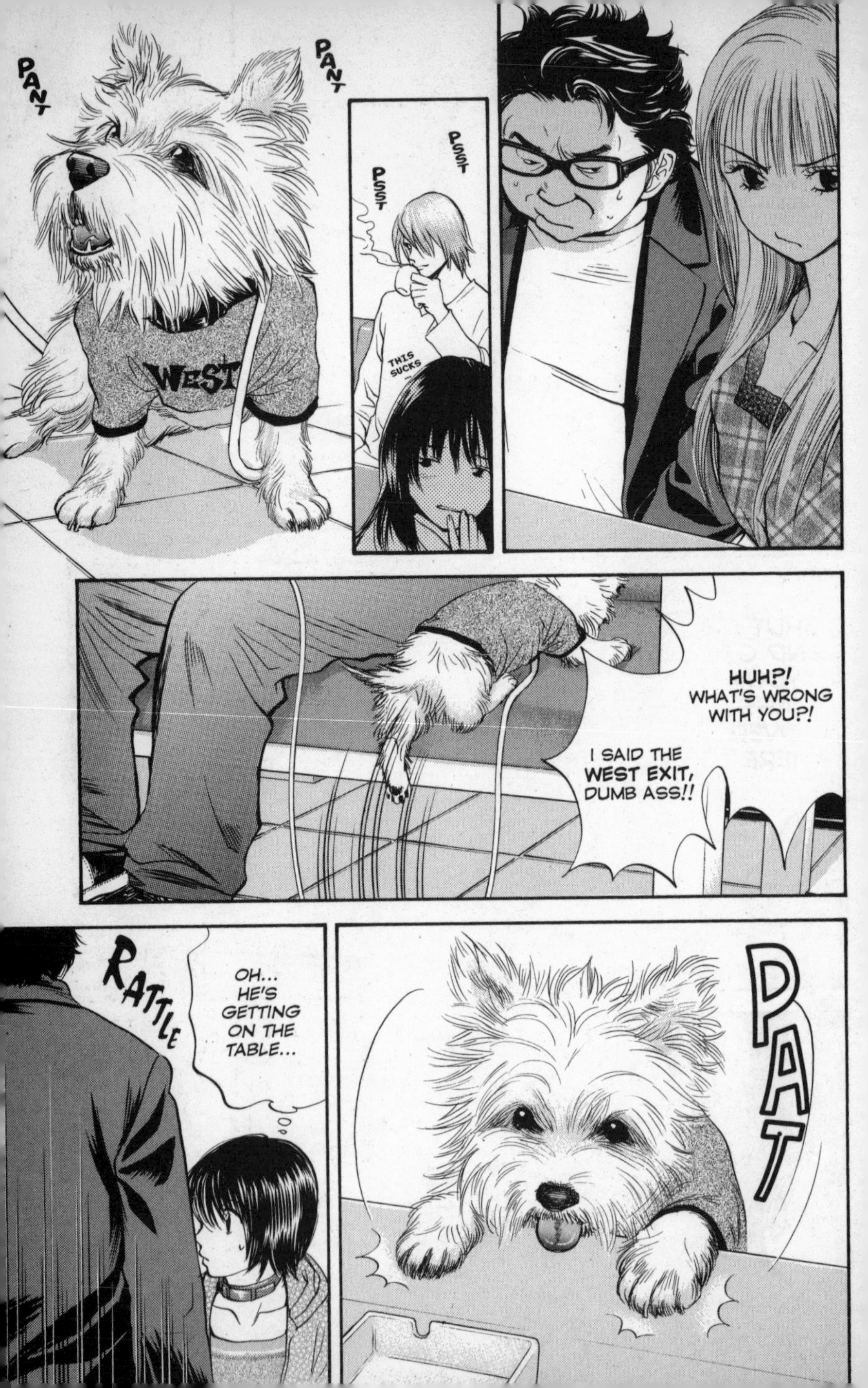
PSST
PSST
THIS SUCKS
PANT
PANT
WEST
HUH?! WHAT'S WRONG WITH YOU?!
I SAID THE WEST EXIT, DUMB ASS!!
PAT
OH... HE'S GETTING ON THE TABLE...
RATTLE

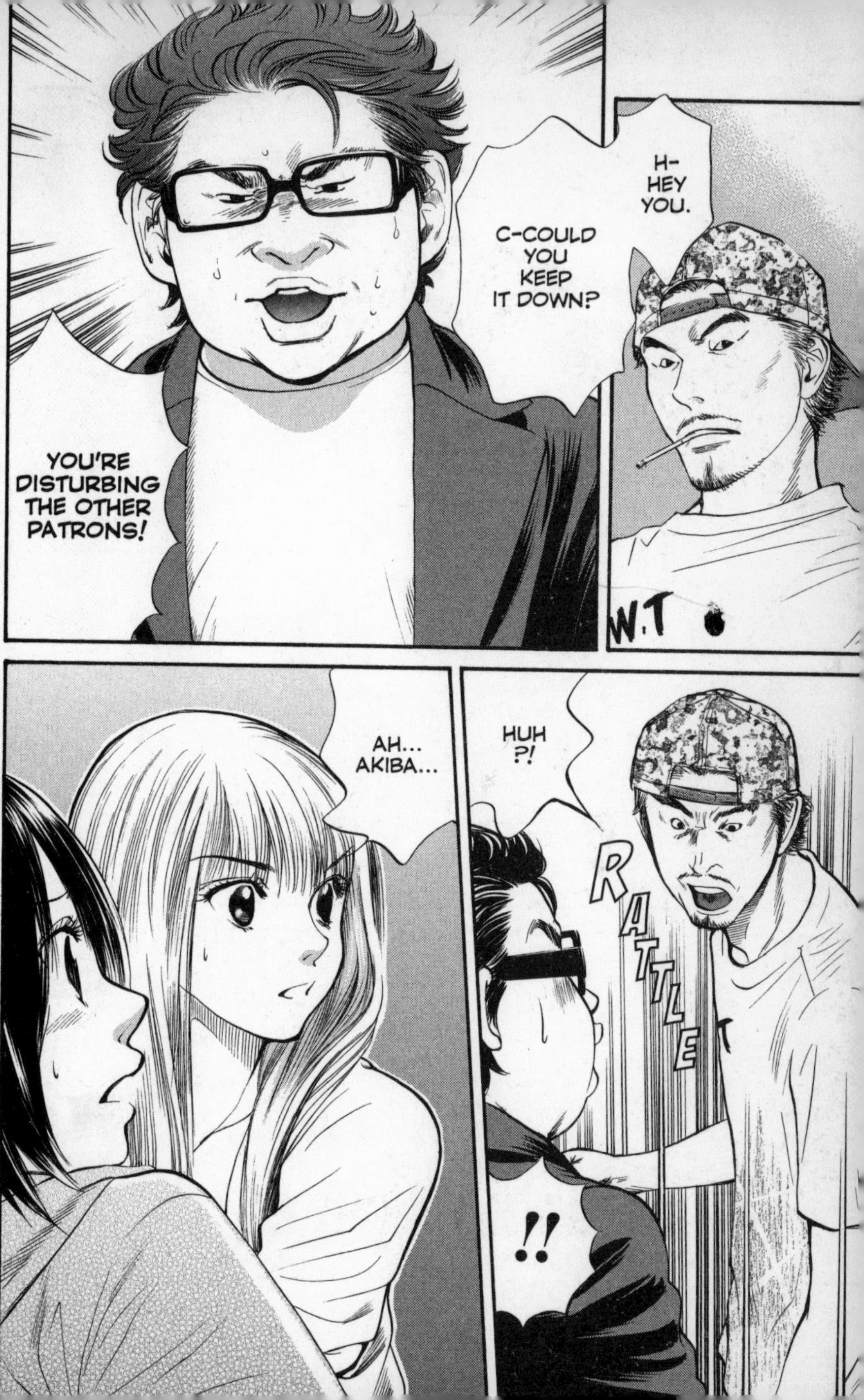
H- HEY YOU.
C-COULD YOU KEEP IT DOWN?
YOU'RE DISTURBING THE OTHER PATRONS!
HUH ?!
RATTLE
!!
AH... AKIBA...

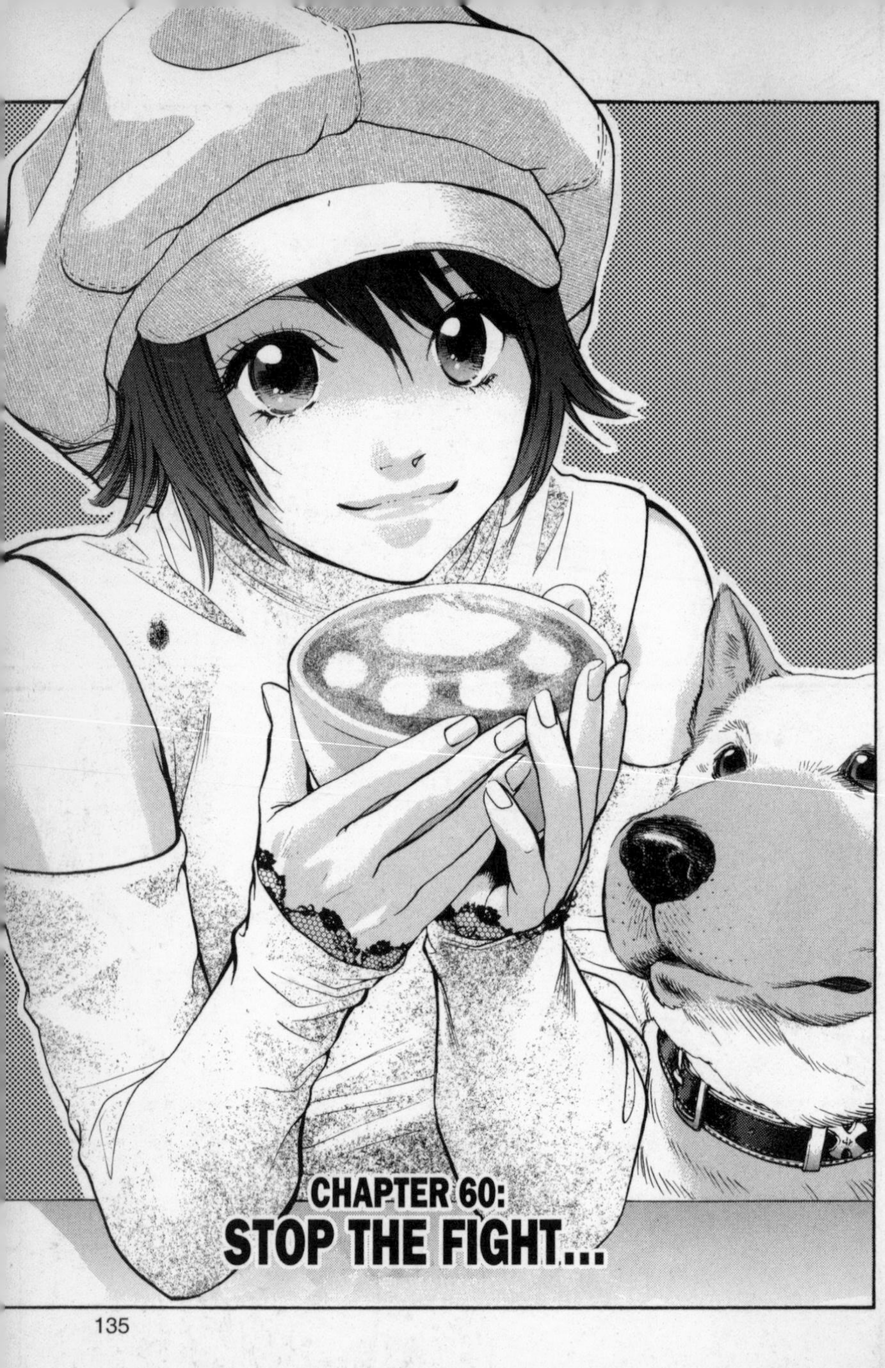
CHAPTER 60:
STOP THE FIGHT...

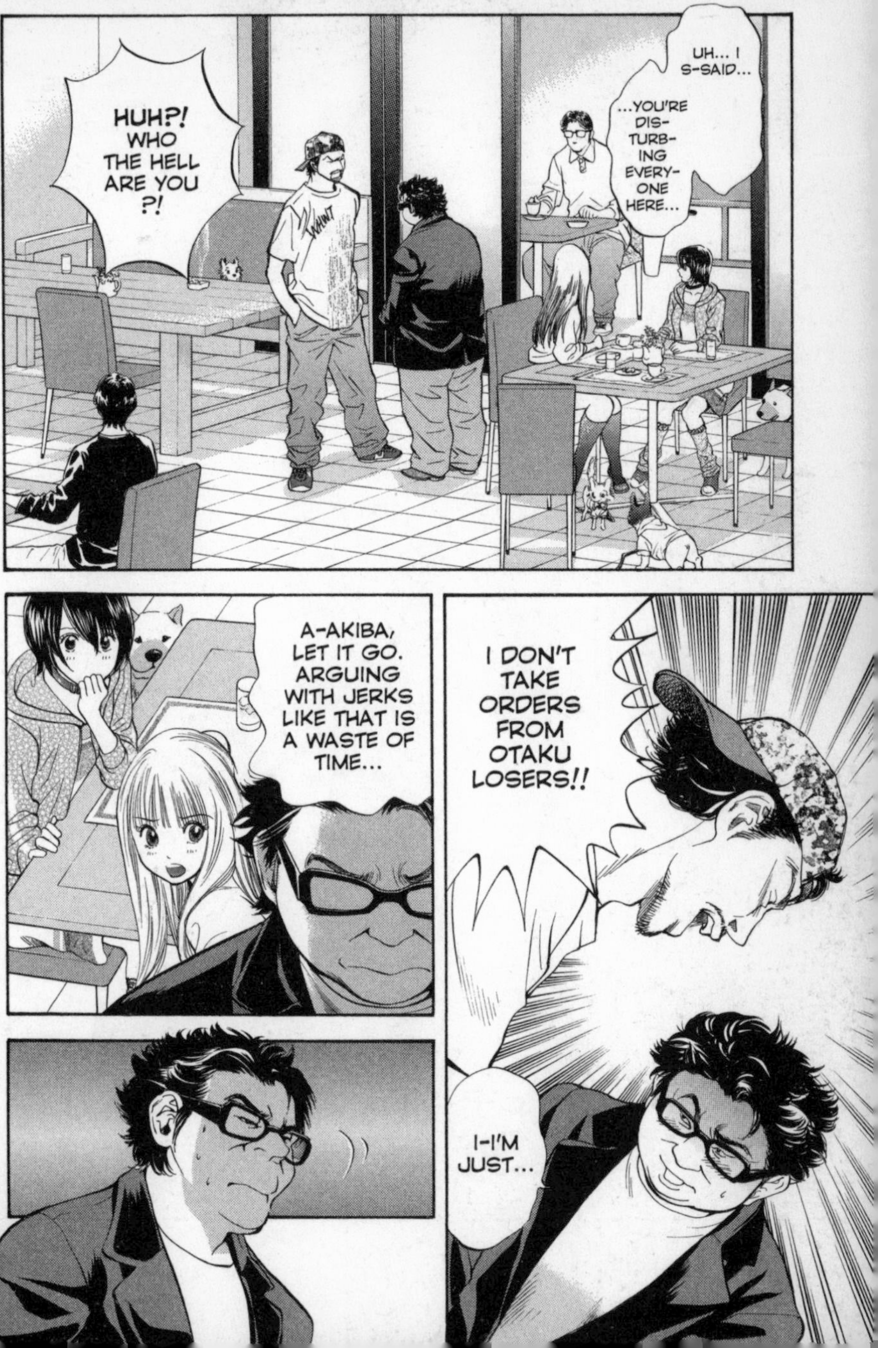
UH... I S-SAID...
...YOU'RE DISTURBING EVERYONE HERE...
HUH?! WHO THE HELL ARE YOU?!
I DON'T TAKE ORDERS FROM OTAKU LOSERS!!
A-AKIBA, LET IT GO. ARGUING WITH JERKS LIKE THAT IS A WASTE OF TIME...
I-I'M JUST...

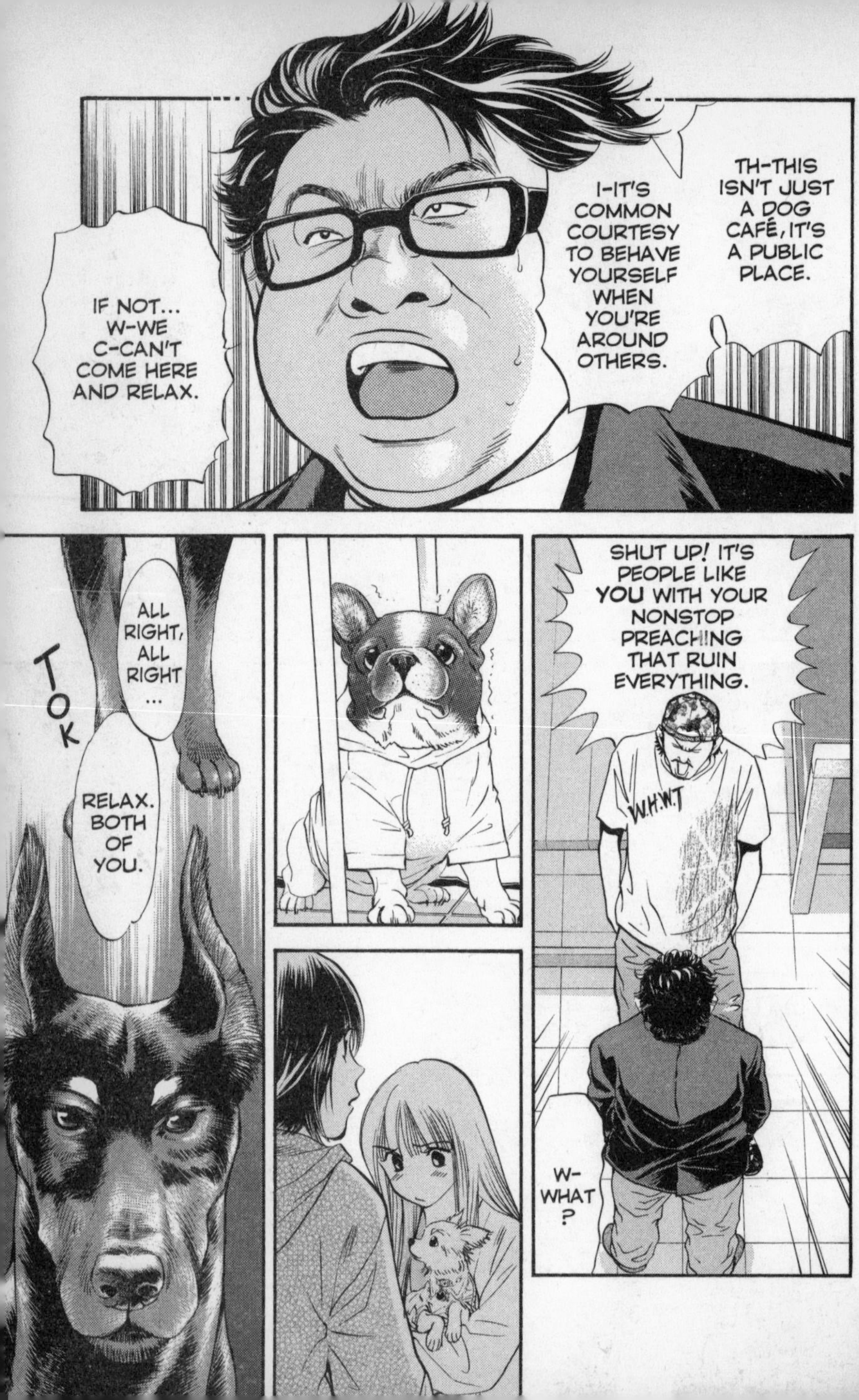
TH-THIS ISN'T JUST A DOG CAFÉ, IT'S A PUBLIC PLACE.
I-IT'S COMMON COURTESY TO BEHAVE YOURSELF WHEN YOU'RE AROUND OTHERS.
IF NOT... W-WE C-CAN'T COME HERE AND RELAX.
SHUT UP! IT'S PEOPLE LIKE YOU WITH YOUR NONSTOP PREACHING THAT RUIN EVERYTHING.
W.H.W.T
W- WHAT ?
ALL RIGHT, ALL RIGHT ...
TOK
RELAX. BOTH OF YOU.

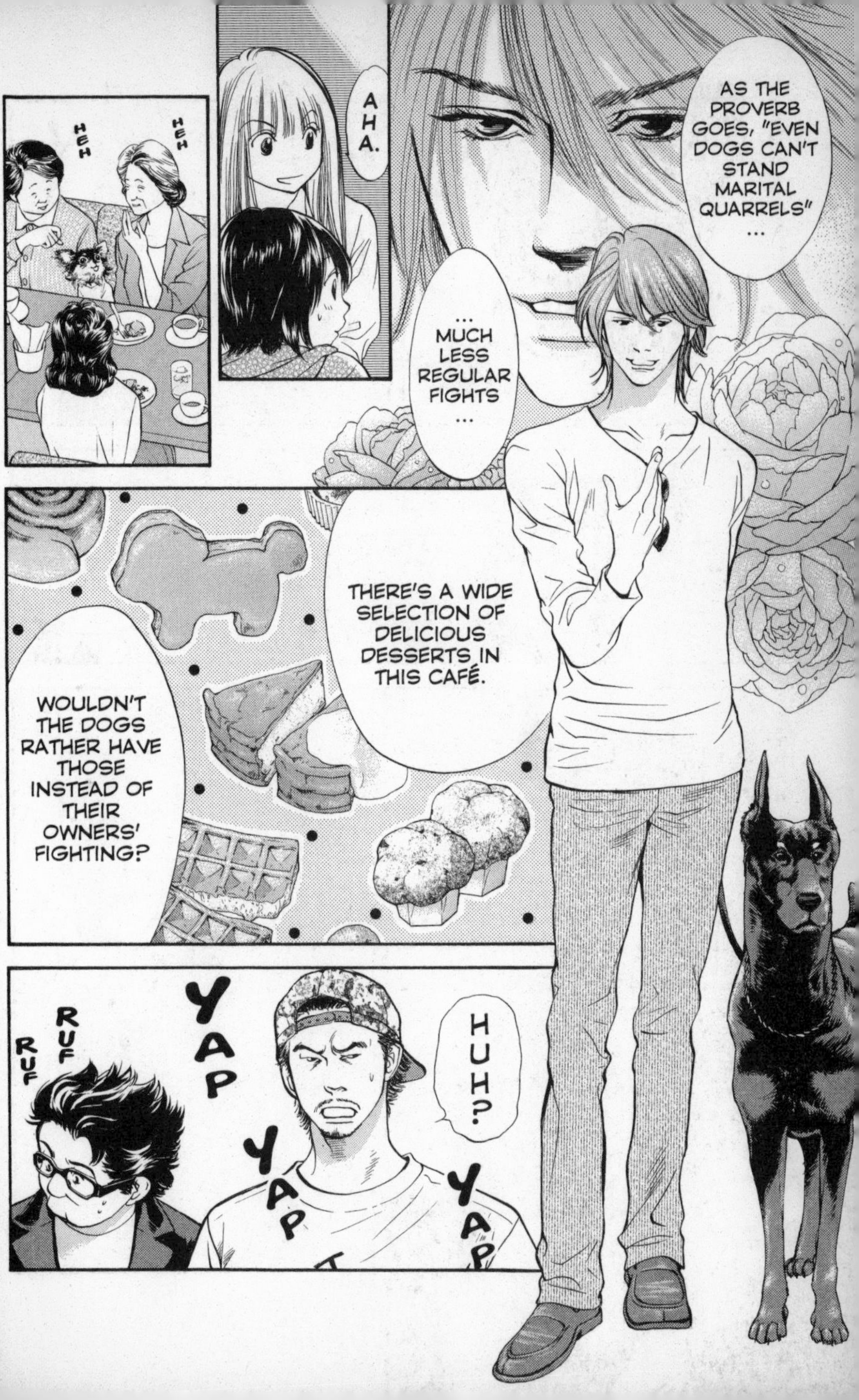
AS THE PROVERB GOES, "EVEN DOGS CAN'T STAND MARITAL QUARRELS" ...
... MUCH LESS REGULAR FIGHTS ...
AHA.
HEH
HEH
THERE'S A WIDE SELECTION OF DELICIOUS DESSERTS IN THIS CAFÉ.
WOULDN'T THE DOGS RATHER HAVE THOSE INSTEAD OF THEIR OWNERS' FIGHTING?
HUH?
YAP
YAP
YAP
YAP
YAP
YAP
RUF
RUF

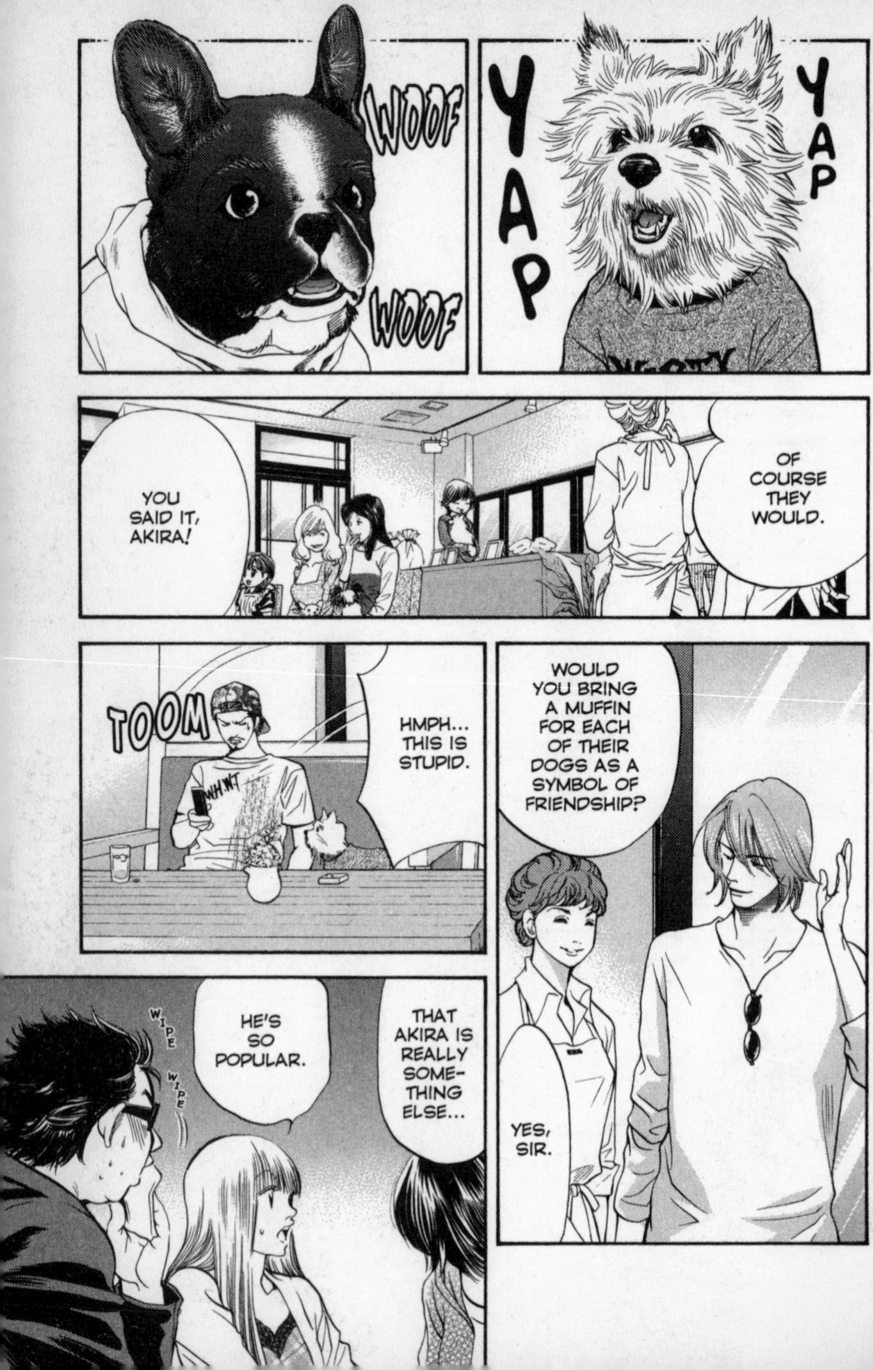
YAP YAP
YAP YAP
WOOF
WOOF
OF COURSE THEY WOULD.
YOU SAID IT, AKIRA!
WOULD YOU BRING A MUFFIN FOR EACH OF THEIR DOGS AS A SYMBOL OF FRIENDSHIP?
YES, SIR.
HMPH... THIS IS STUPID.
TOOM
THAT AKIRA IS REALLY SOMETHING ELSE...
HE'S SO POPULAR.
WIPE
WIPE

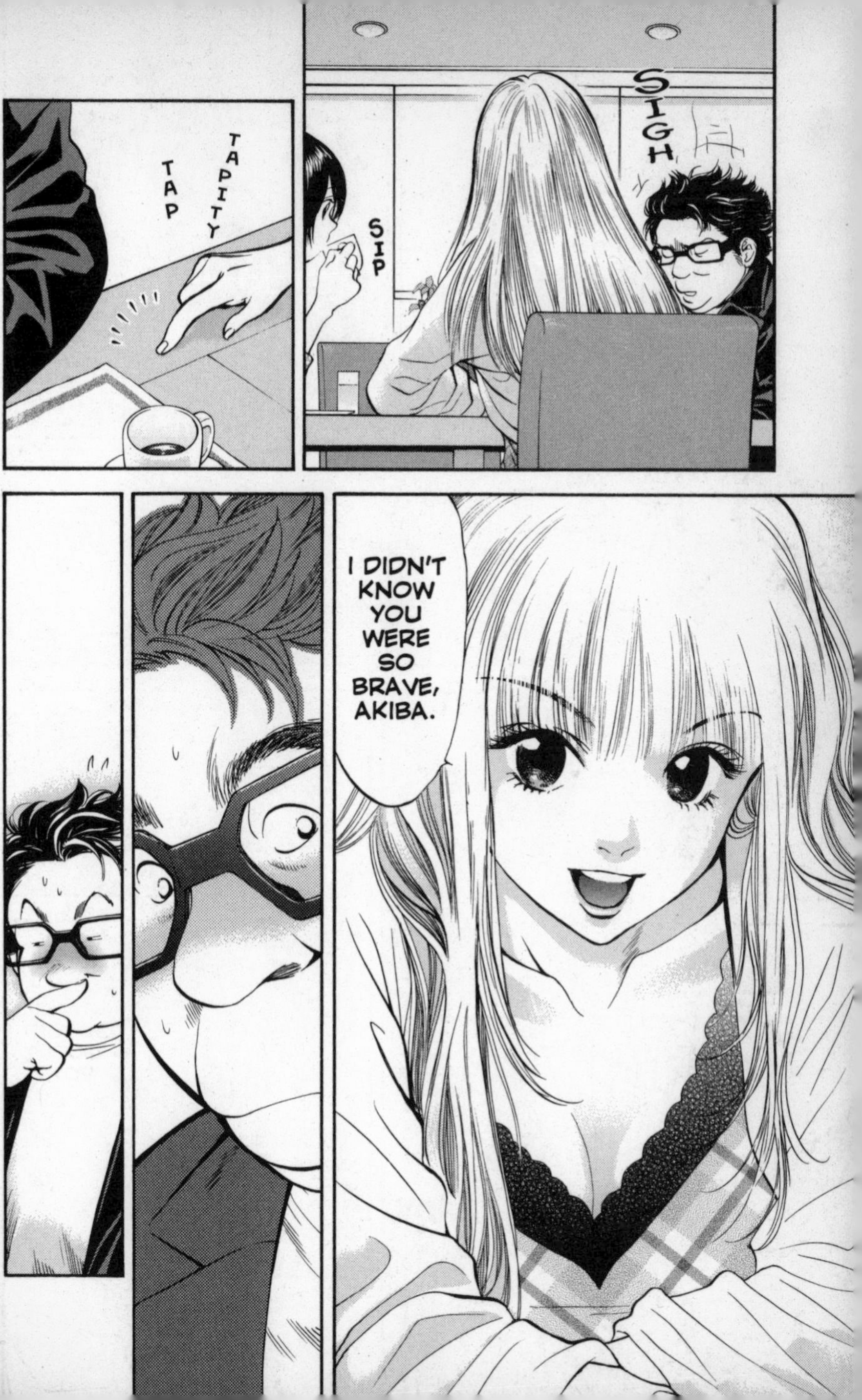
SIGH
SIP
TAPITY
TAP
I DIDN'T KNOW YOU WERE SO BRAVE, AKIBA.

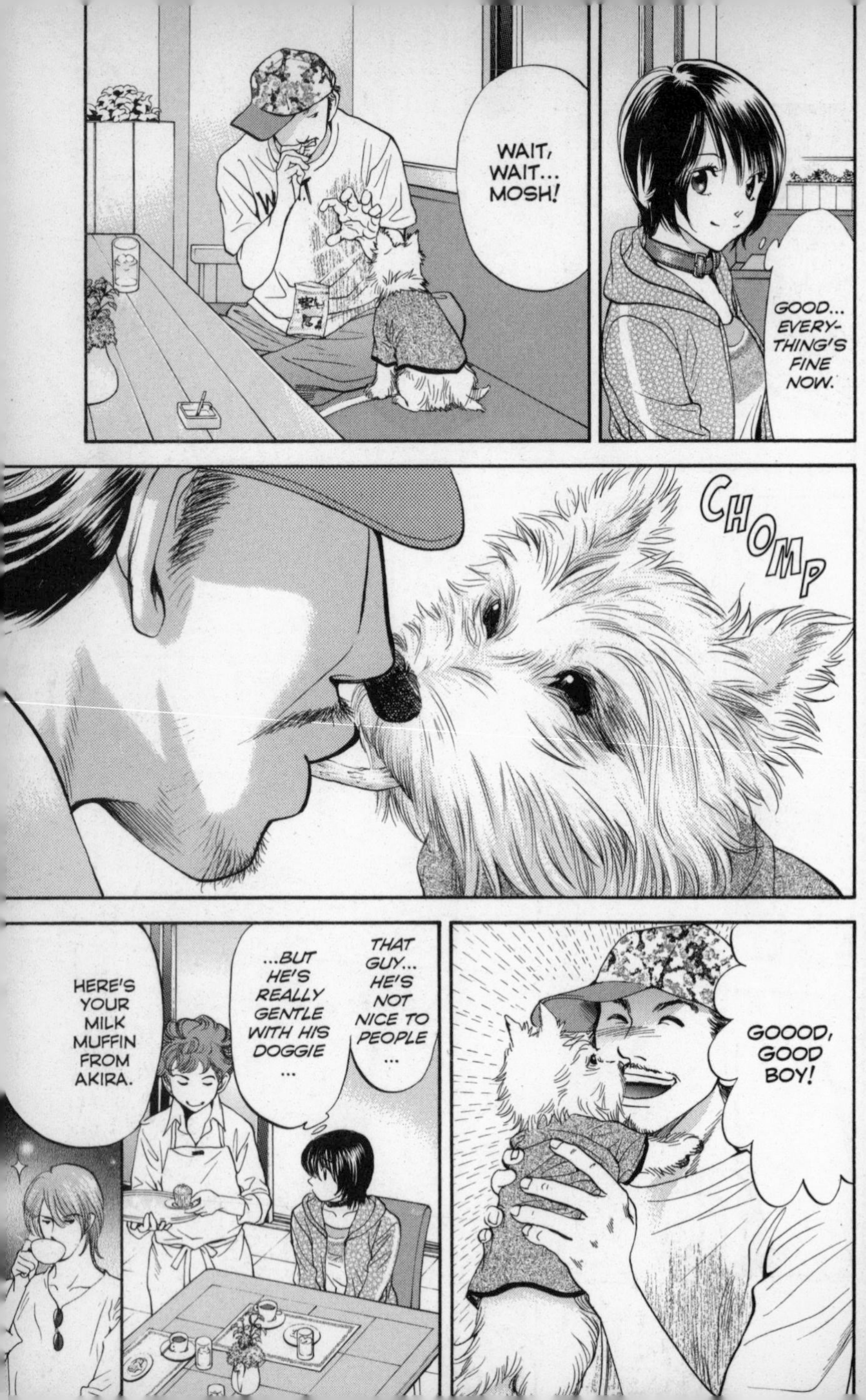
GOOD... EVERY-THING'S FINE NOW.
WAIT, WAIT... MOSH!
CHOMP
GOOOD, GOOD BOY!
THAT GUY... HE'S NOT NICE TO PEOPLE ...
...BUT HE'S REALLY GENTLE WITH HIS DOGGIE ...
HERE'S YOUR MILK MUFFIN FROM AKIRA.

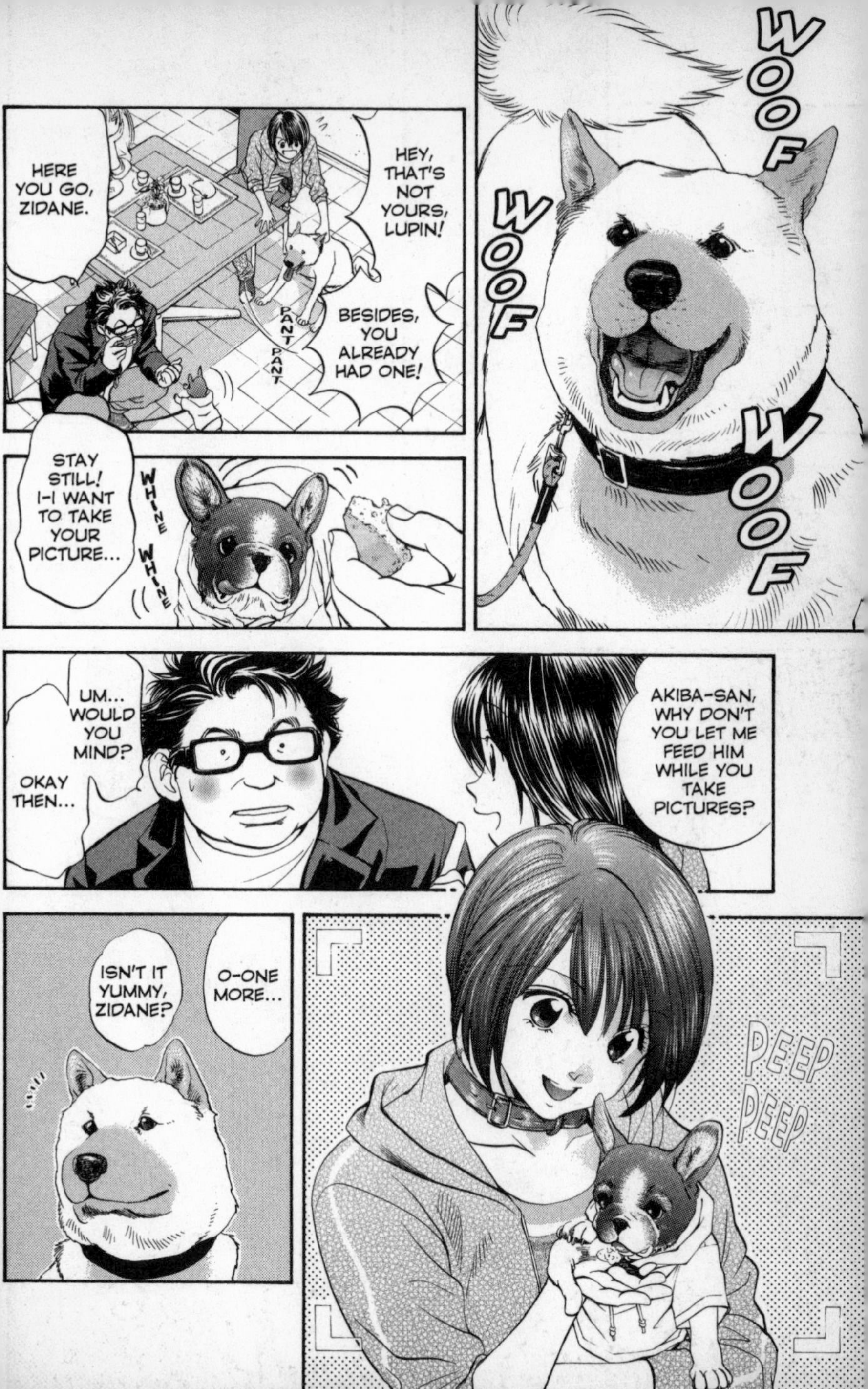
WOOF
WOOF
WOOF
HEY, THAT'S NOT YOURS, LUPIN!
BESIDES, YOU ALREADY HAD ONE!
PANT PANT
HERE YOU GO, ZIDANE.
WHINE WHINE
STAY STILL! I-I WANT TO TAKE YOUR PICTURE...
AKIBA-SAN, WHY DON'T YOU LET ME FEED HIM WHILE YOU TAKE PICTURES?
UM... WOULD YOU MIND?
OKAY THEN...
PEEP PEEP
O-ONE MORE...
ISN'T IT YUMMY, ZIDANE?

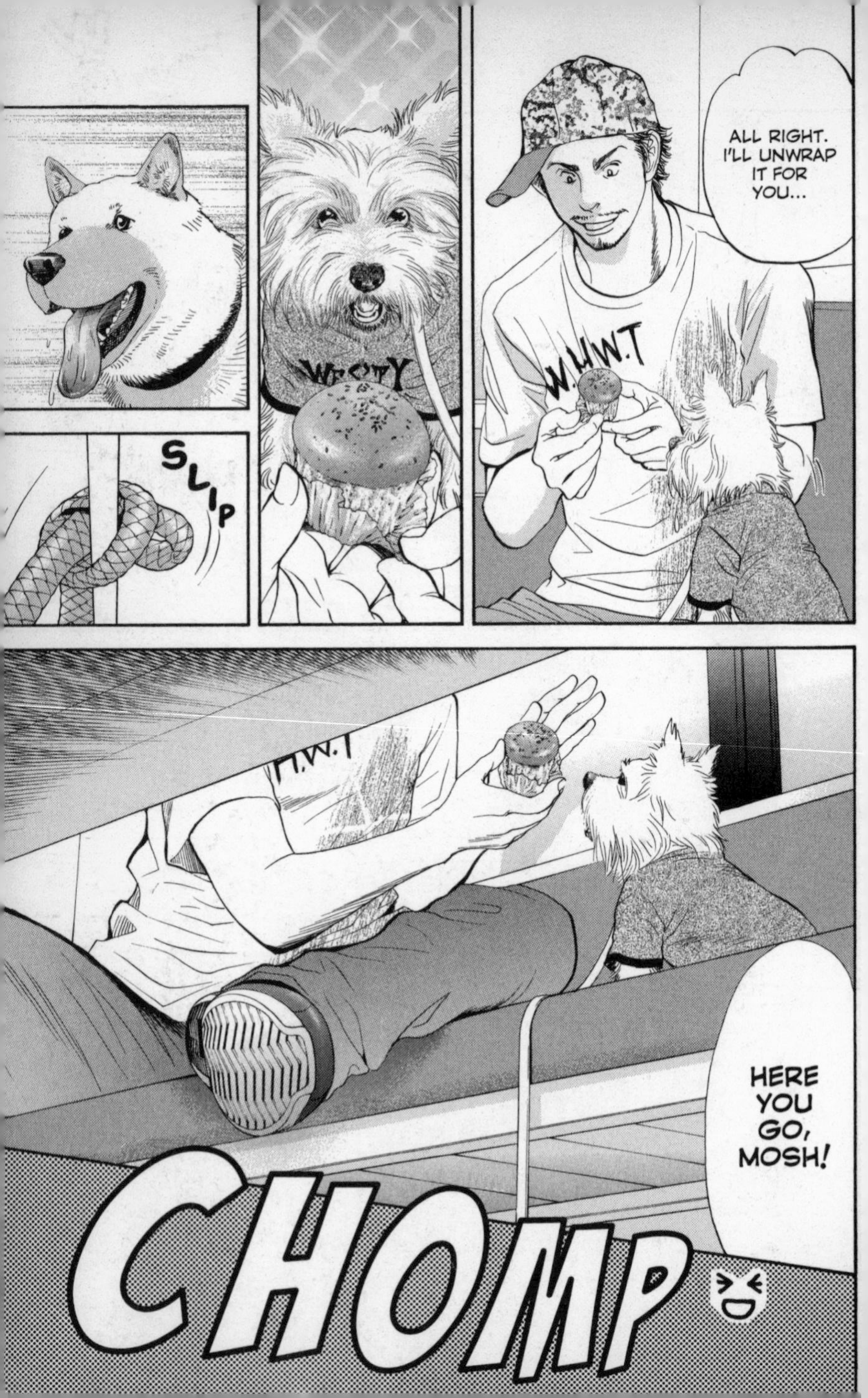
ALL RIGHT. I'LL UNWRAP IT FOR YOU...
SLIP
HERE YOU GO, MOSH!
CHOMP

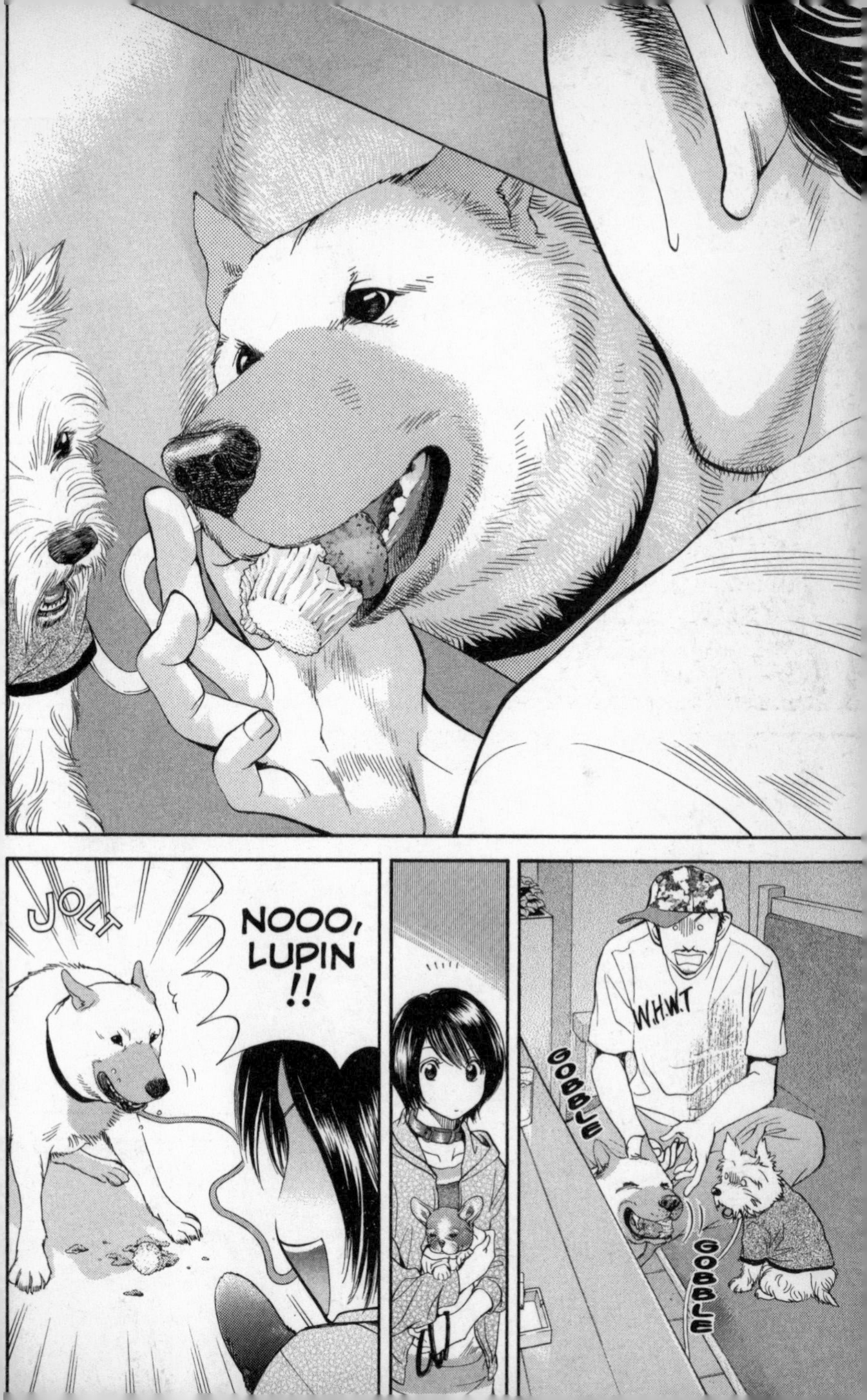

W.H.W.T
GOBBLE
GOBBLE
JOLT
NOOO, LUPIN !!

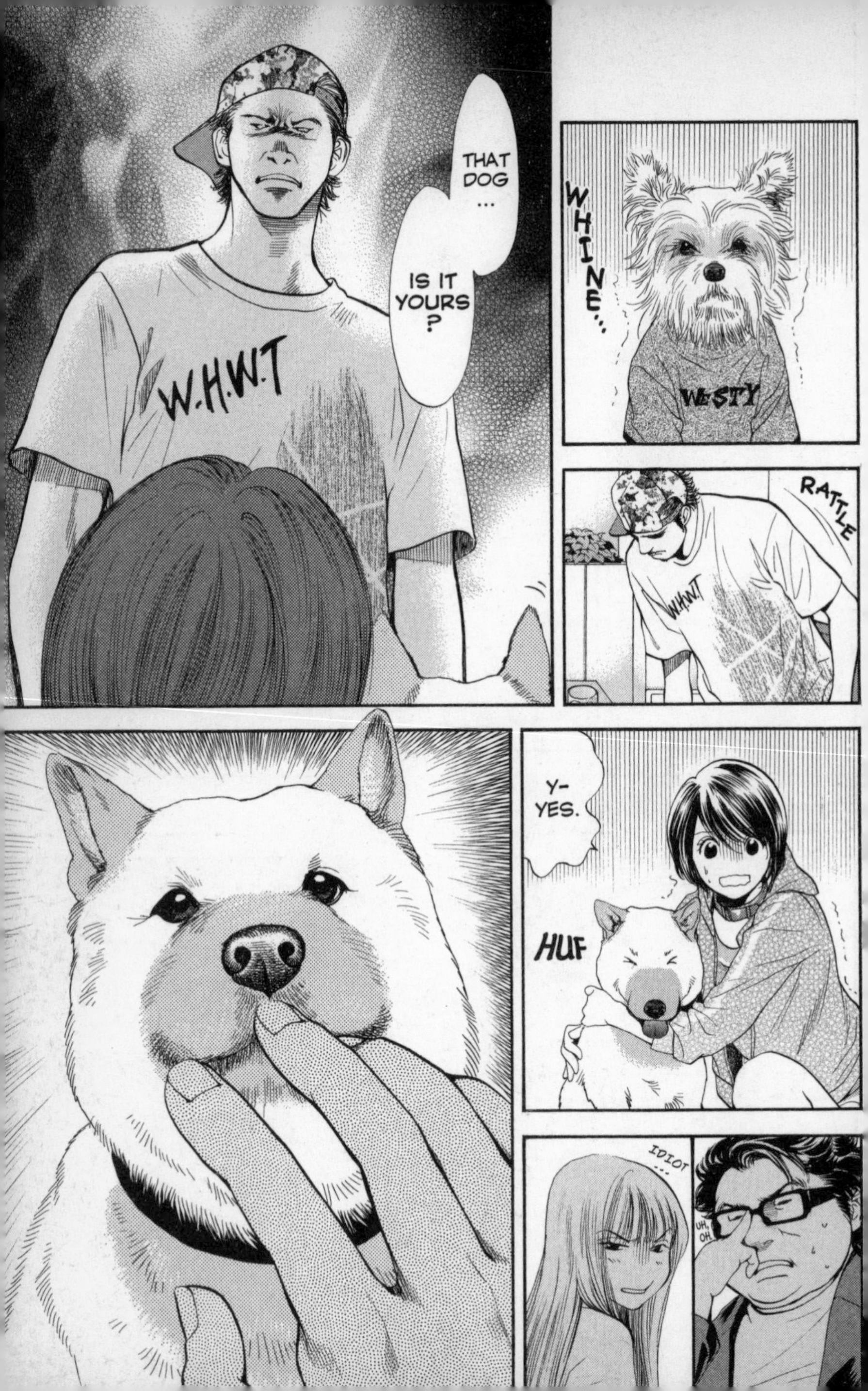
WHINE...
WESTY
RATTLE
W.H.W.T
THAT DOG ...
IS IT YOURS ?
W.H.W.T
Y-YES.
HUF
IDIOT ...
UH, OH.

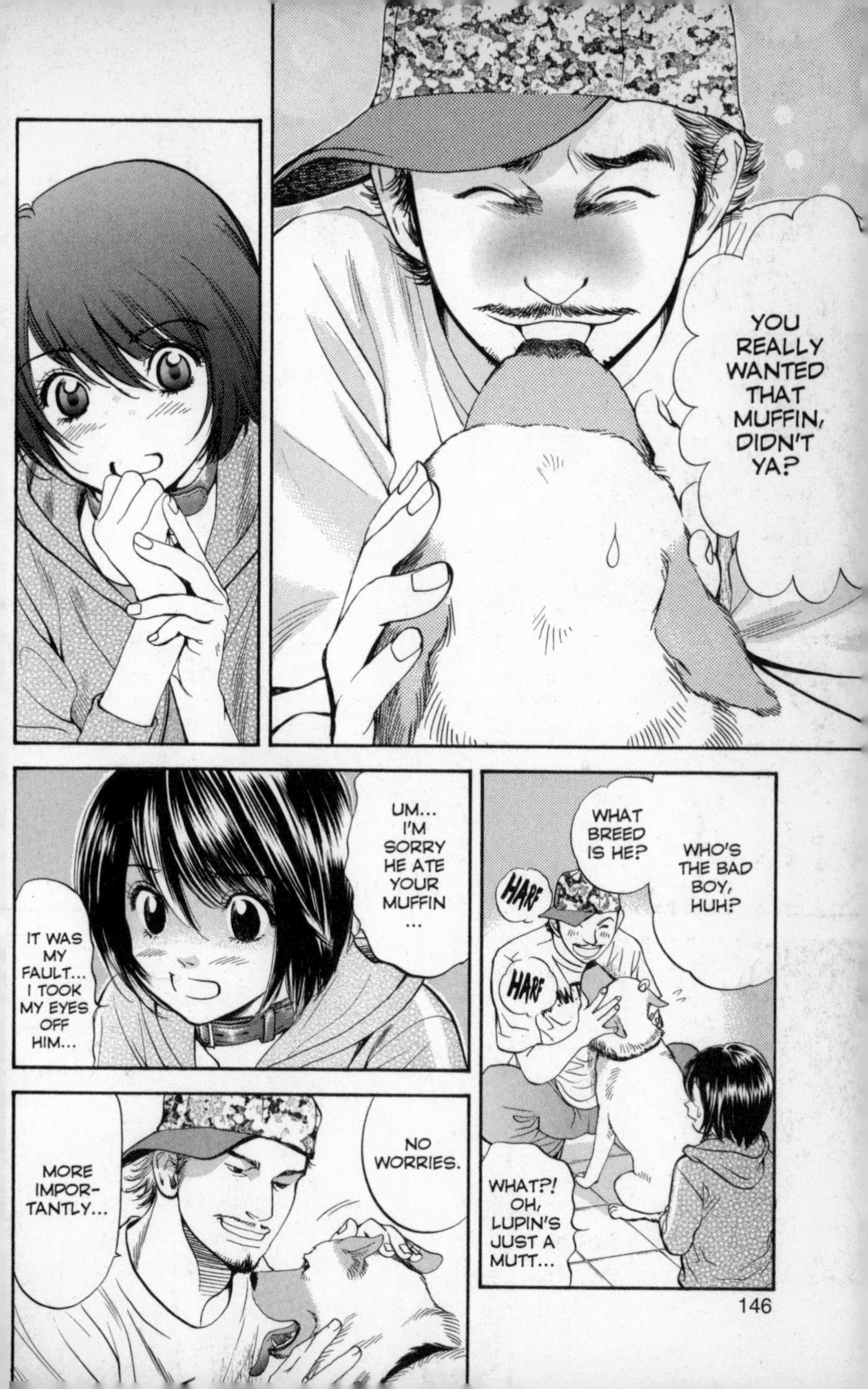
YOU REALLY WANTED THAT MUFFIN, DIDN'T YA?
WHO'S THE BAD BOY, HUH?
WHAT BREED IS HE?
HARF
HARF
WHAT?! OH, LUPIN'S JUST A MUTT...
UM... I'M SORRY HE ATE YOUR MUFFIN ...
IT WAS MY FAULT... I TOOK MY EYES OFF HIM...
NO WORRIES.
MORE IMPOR-TANTLY...

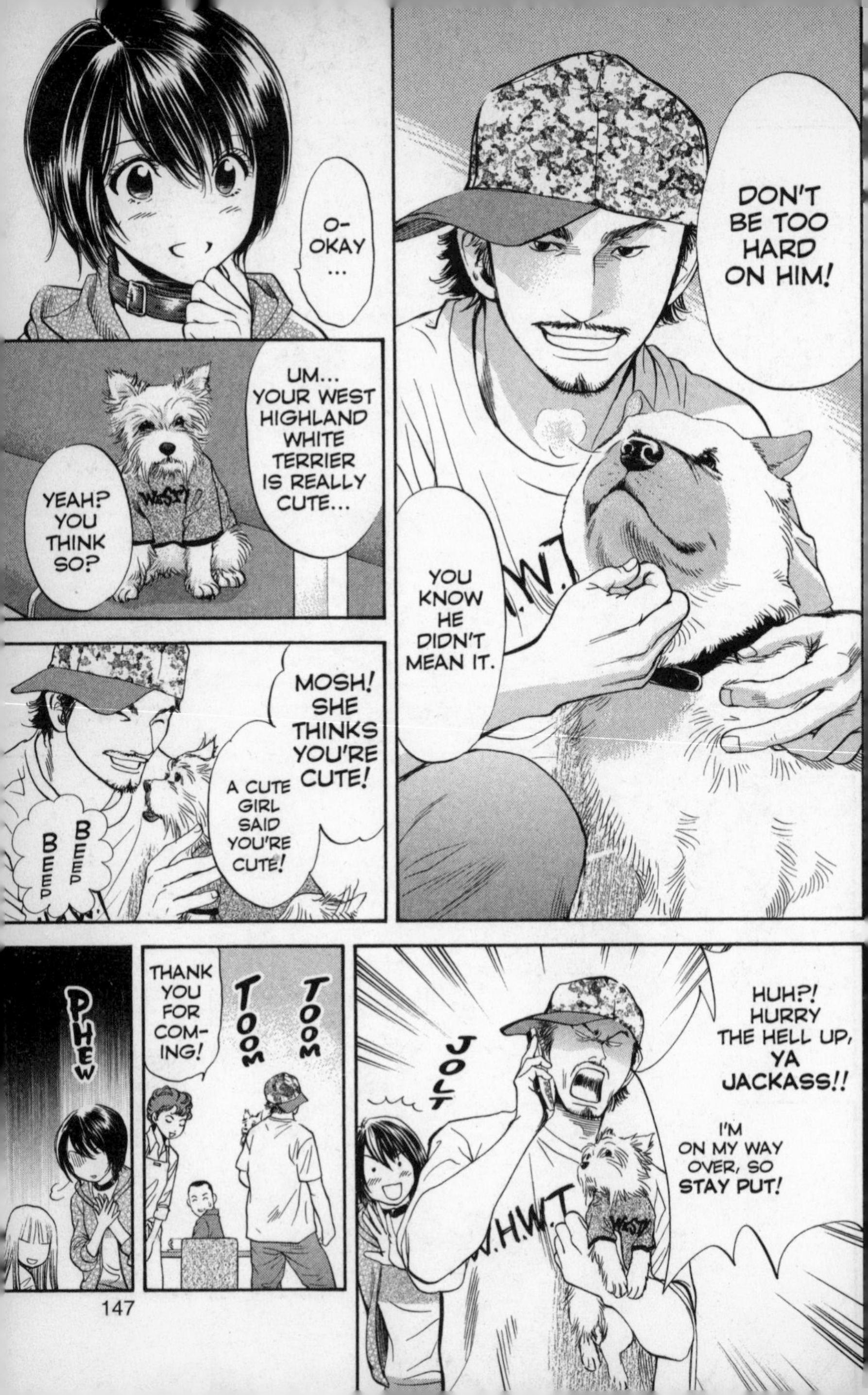
DON'T BE TOO HARD ON HIM!
YOU KNOW HE DIDN'T MEAN IT.
O-OKAY ...
UM... YOUR WEST HIGHLAND WHITE TERRIER IS REALLY CUTE...
YEAH? YOU THINK SO?
MOSH! SHE THINKS YOU'RE CUTE!
A CUTE GIRL SAID YOU'RE CUTE!
BEEP
BEEP
HUH?! HURRY THE HELL UP, YA JACKASS!!
I'M ON MY WAY OVER, SO STAY PUT!
JOLT
TOOM
TOOM
THANK YOU FOR COM-ING!
PHEW

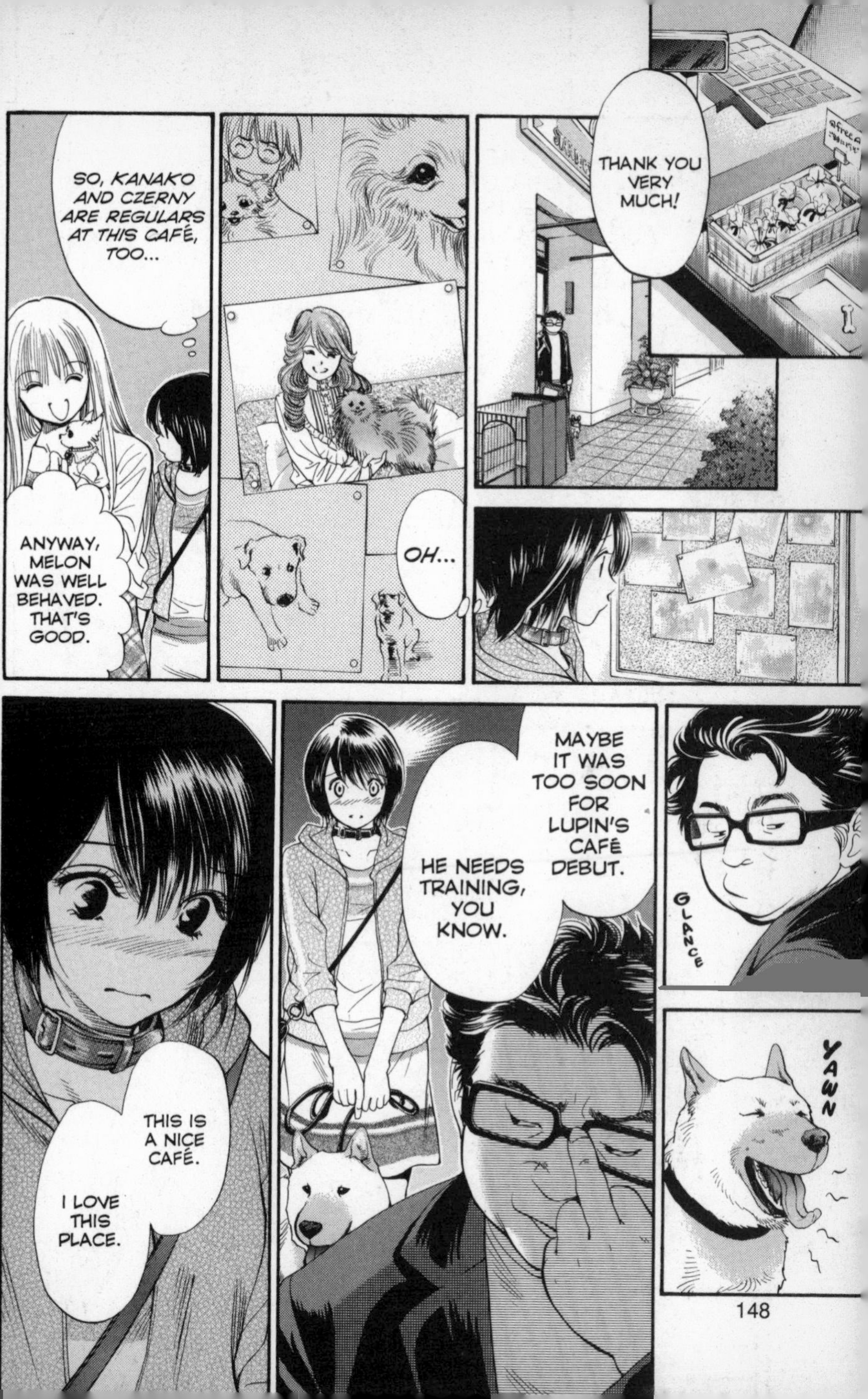
THANK YOU VERY MUCH!
OH...
SO, KANAKO AND CZERNY ARE REGULARS AT THIS CAFÉ, TOO...
ANYWAY, MELON WAS WELL BEHAVED. THAT'S GOOD.
GLANCE
YAWN
MAYBE IT WAS TOO SOON FOR LUPIN'S CAFÉ DEBUT.
HE NEEDS TRAINING, YOU KNOW.
THIS IS A NICE CAFÉ.
I LOVE THIS PLACE.

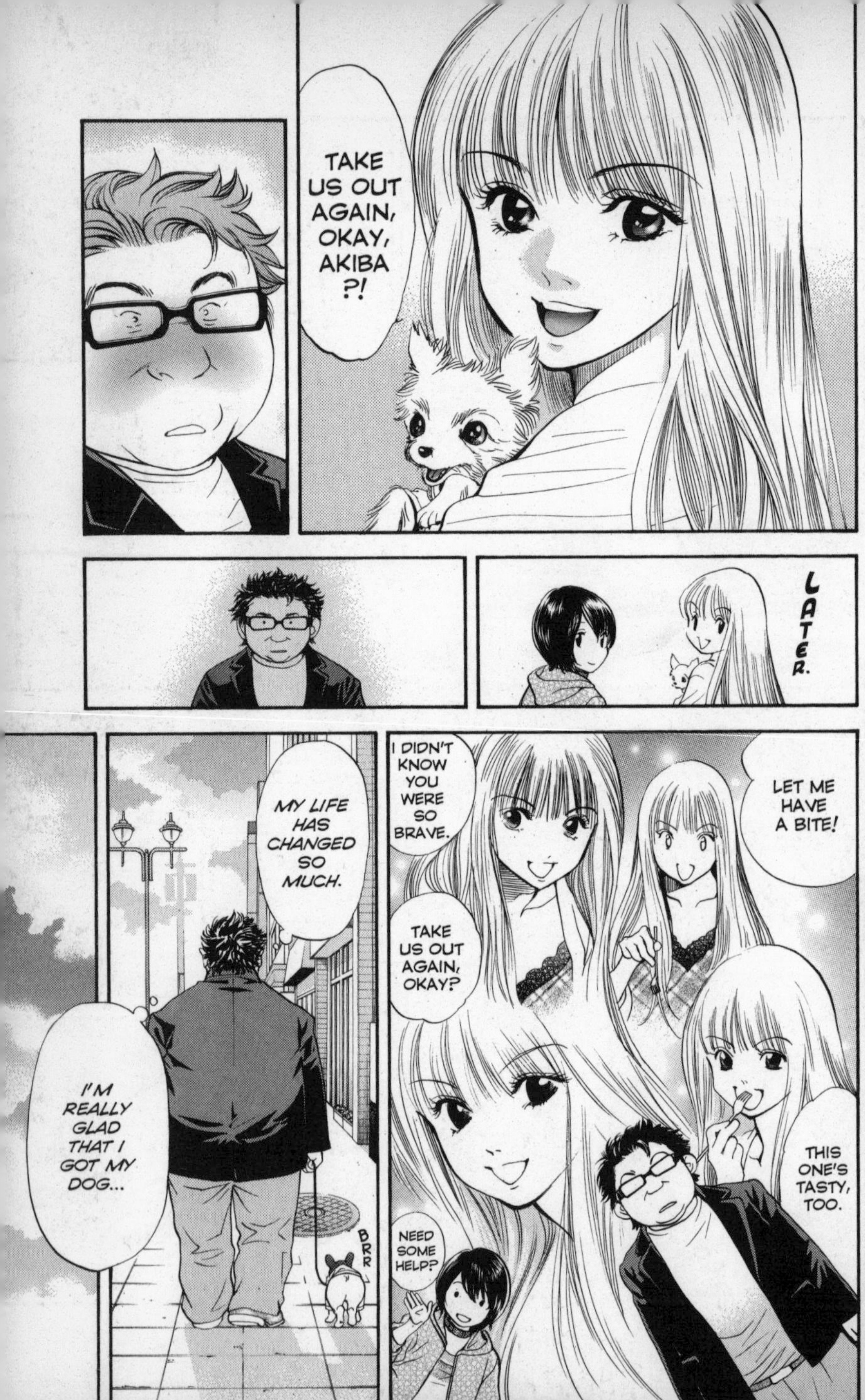
TAKE US OUT AGAIN, OKAY, AKIBA ?!
LATER.
LET ME HAVE A BITE!
I DIDN'T KNOW YOU WERE SO BRAVE.
TAKE US OUT AGAIN, OKAY?
THIS ONE'S TASTY, TOO.
NEED SOME HELP?
MY LIFE HAS CHANGED SO MUCH.
BRR
I'M REALLY GLAD THAT I GOT MY DOG...

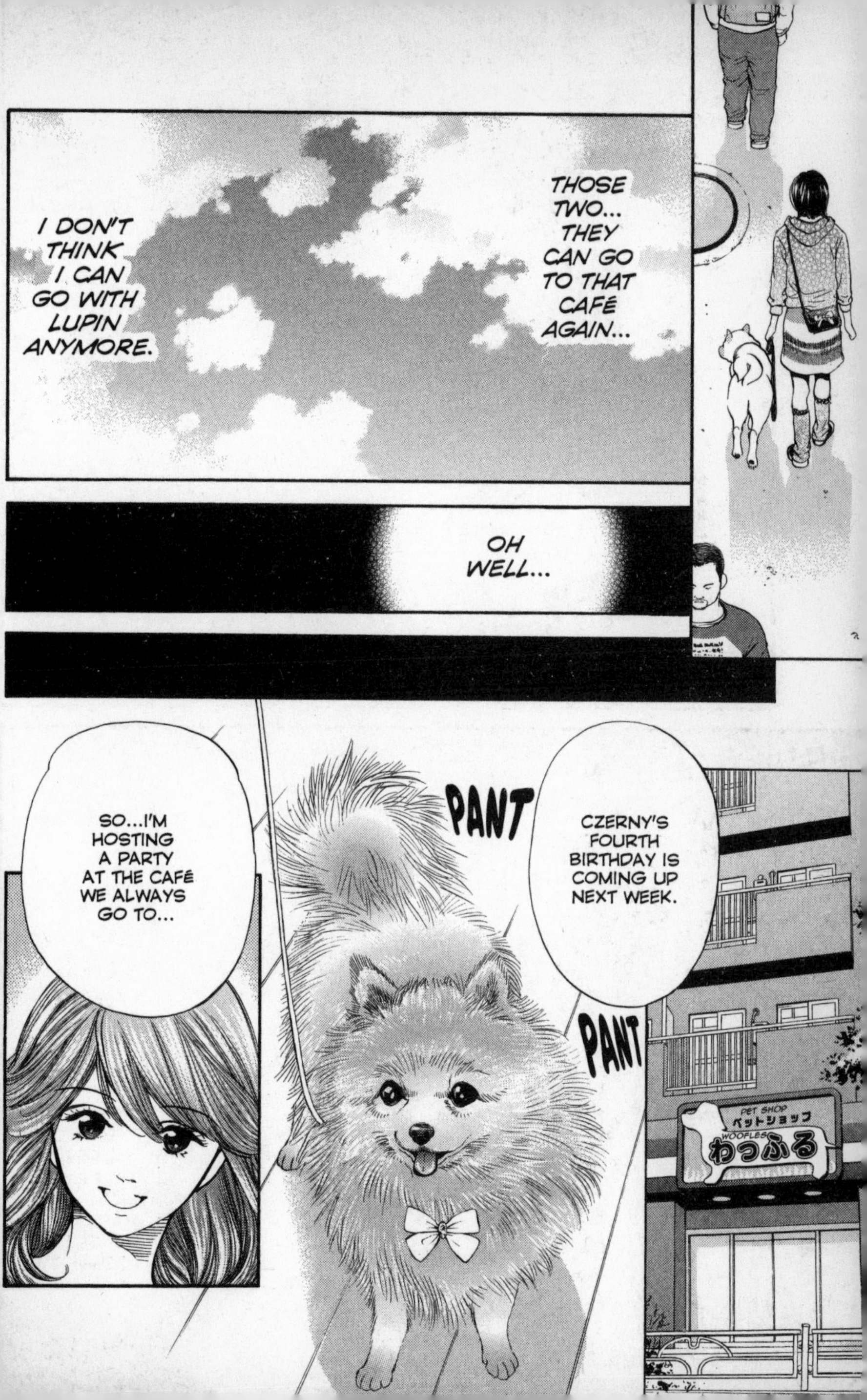
THOSE TWO... THEY CAN GO TO THAT CAFÉ AGAIN...
I DON'T THINK I CAN GO WITH LUPIN ANYMORE.
OH WELL...
CZERNY'S FOURTH BIRTHDAY IS COMING UP NEXT WEEK.
PANT
SO...I'M HOSTING A PARTY AT THE CAFÉ WE ALWAYS GO TO...
PANT
PET SHOP
ペットショップ
WOOFLES
わつふる

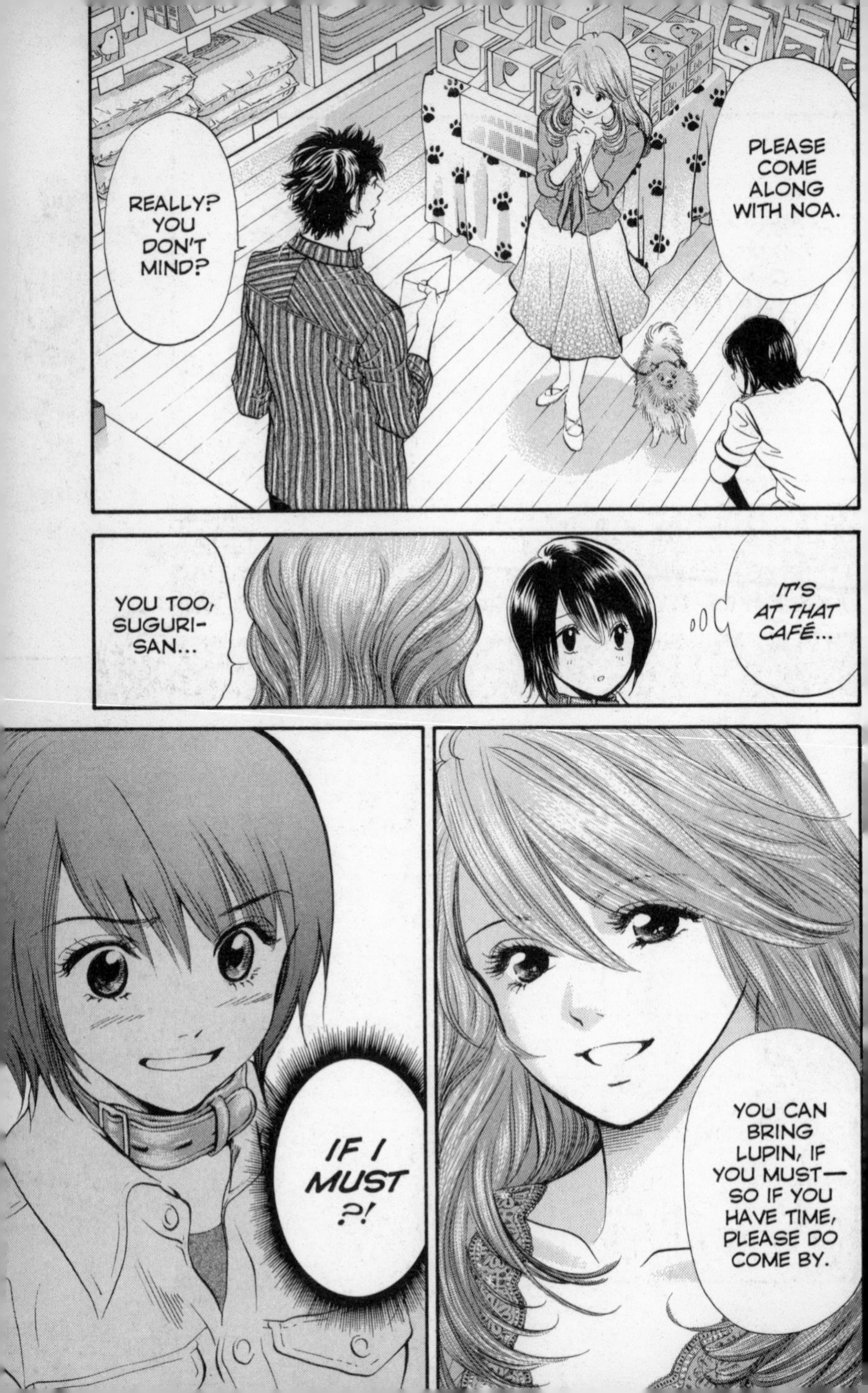
PLEASE COME ALONG WITH NOA.
REALLY? YOU DON'T MIND?
IT'S AT THAT CAFÉ...
YOU TOO, SUGURI-SAN...
YOU CAN BRING LUPIN, IF YOU MUST— SO IF YOU HAVE TIME, PLEASE DO COME BY.
IF I MUST?!

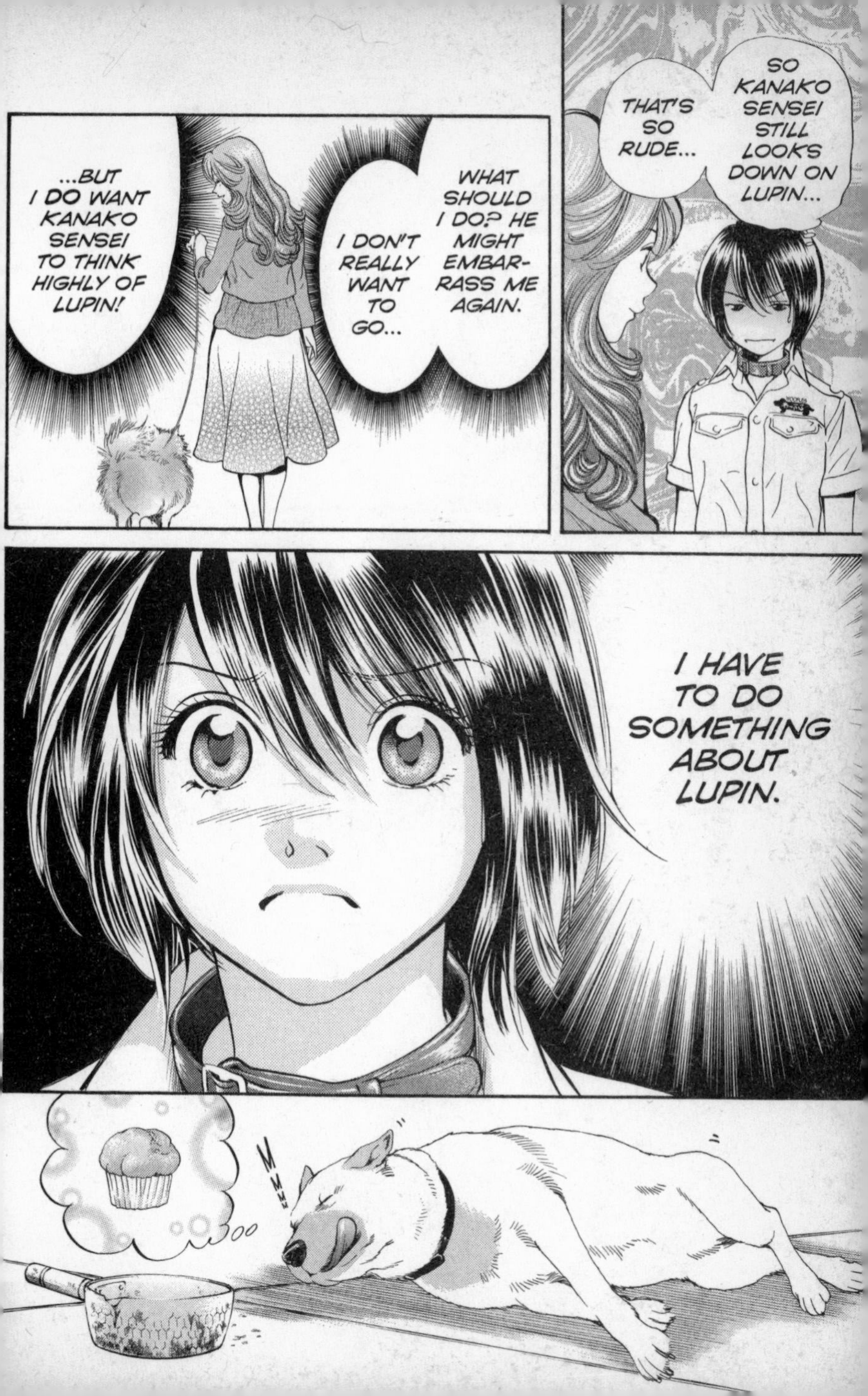
SO KANAKO SENSEI STILL LOOKS DOWN ON LUPIN...
THAT'S SO RUDE...
WHAT SHOULD I DO? HE MIGHT EMBARRASS ME AGAIN.
I DON'T REALLY WANT TO GO...
...BUT I DO WANT KANAKO SENSEI TO THINK HIGHLY OF LUPIN!
I HAVE TO DO SOMETHING ABOUT LUPIN.

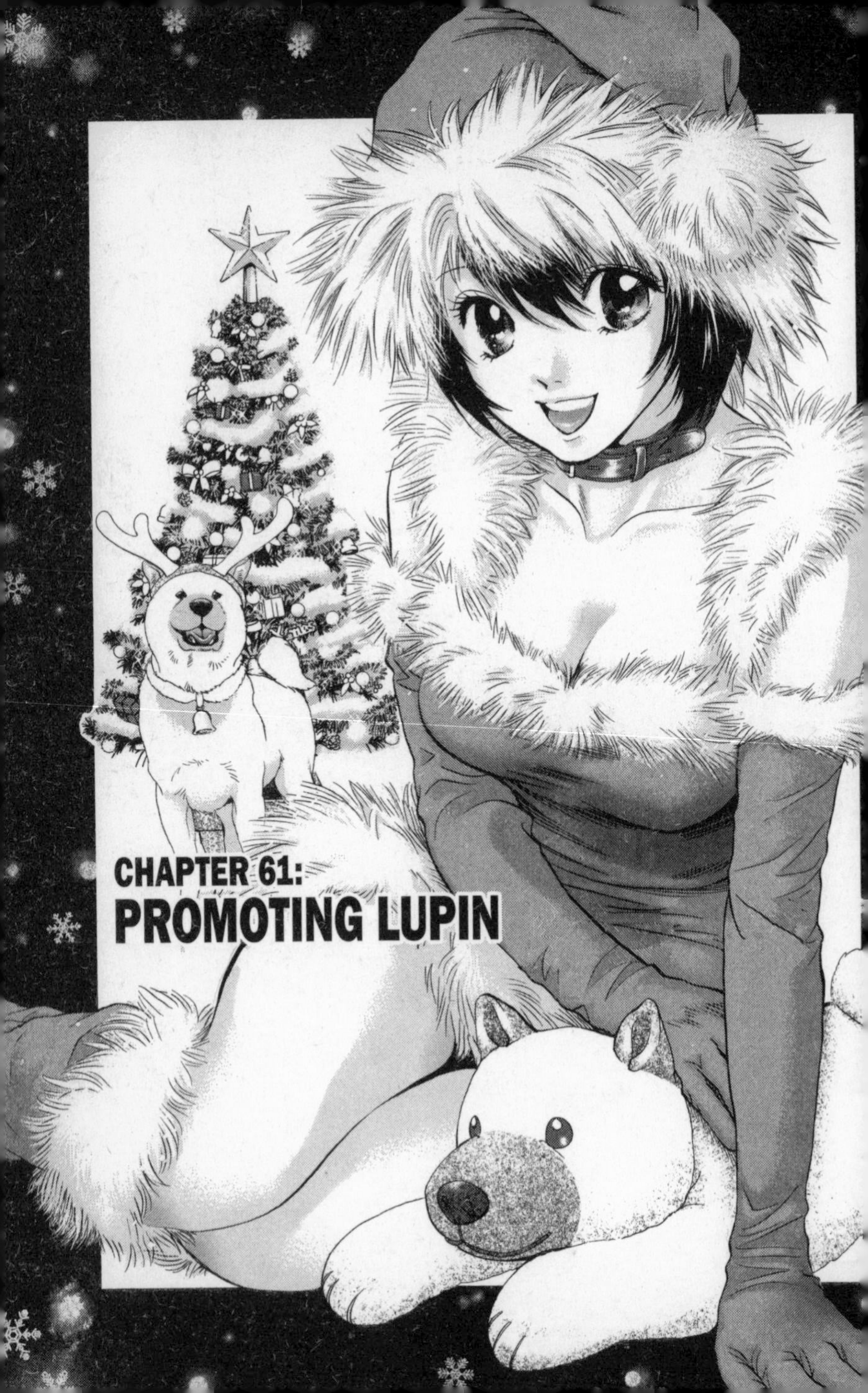
CHAPTER 61:
PROMOTING LUPIN

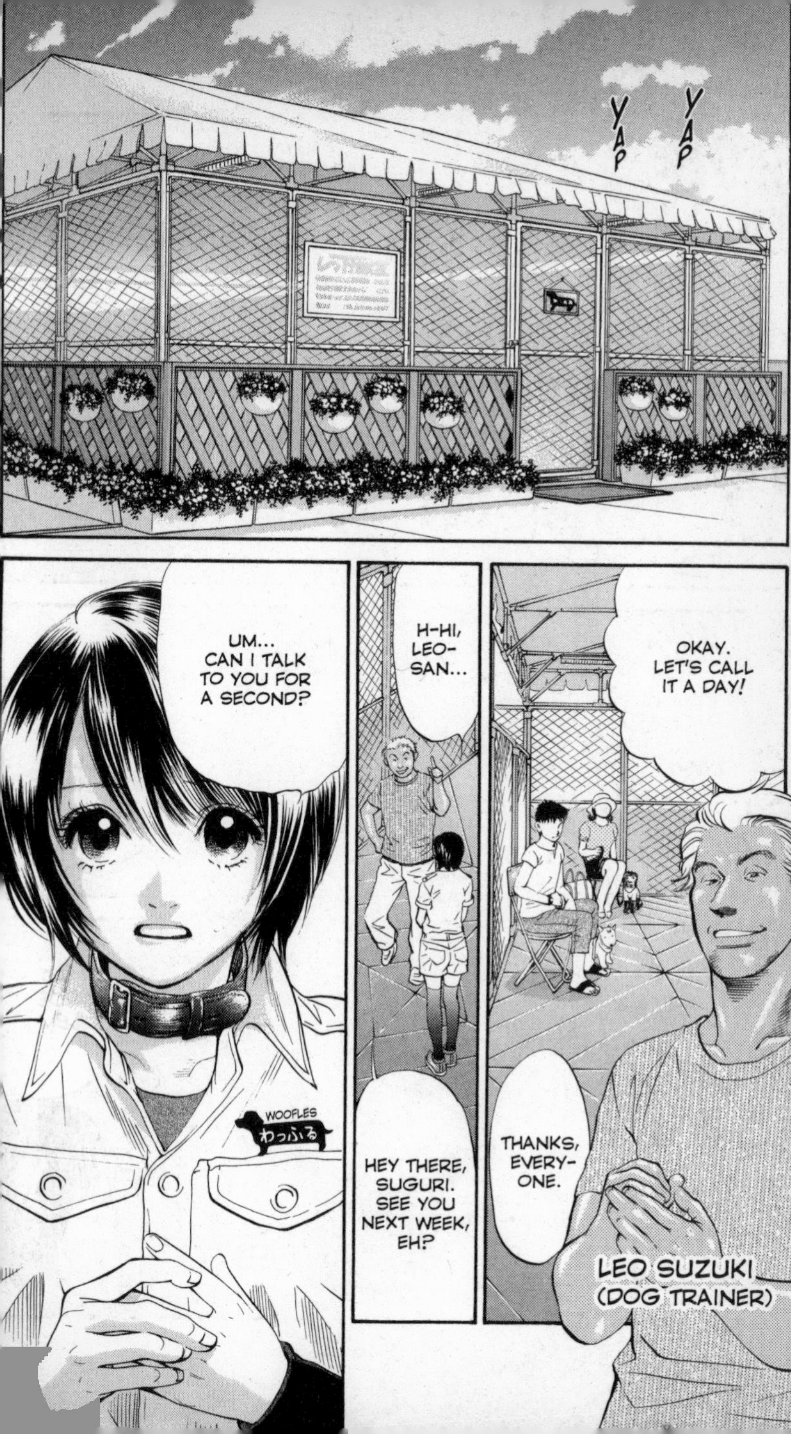
YAP YAP
OKAY. LET'S CALL IT A DAY!
THANKS, EVERY-ONE.
LEO SUZUKI (DOG TRAINER)
H-HI, LEO-SAN...
HEY THERE, SUGURI. SEE YOU NEXT WEEK, EH?
UM... CAN I TALK TO YOU FOR A SECOND?
WOOFLES
わっふる

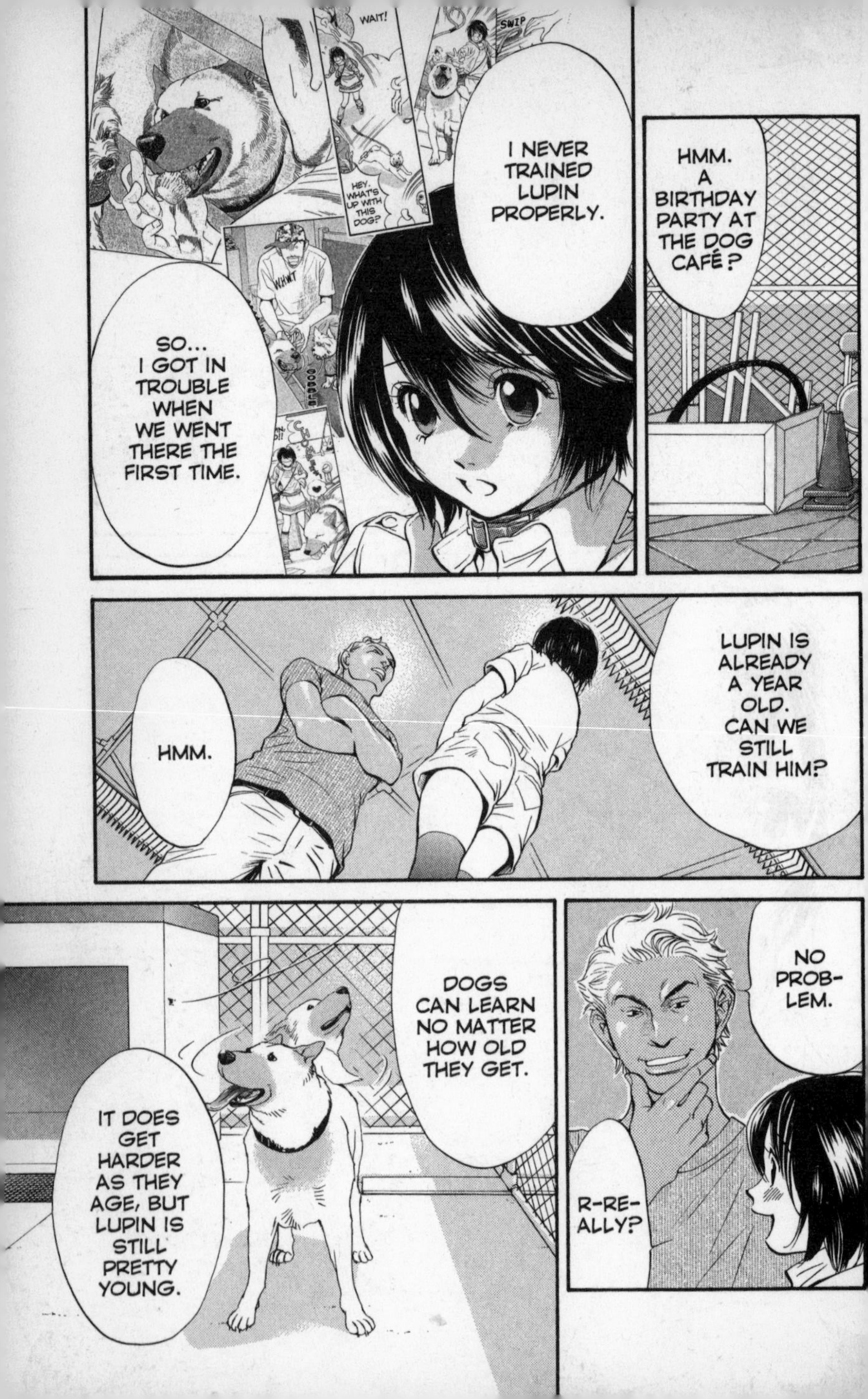
HMM. A BIRTHDAY PARTY AT THE DOG CAFÉ?
SWIP
WAIT!
I NEVER TRAINED LUPIN PROPERLY.
HEY, WHAT'S UP WITH THIS DOG?
SO... I GOT IN TROUBLE WHEN WE WENT THERE THE FIRST TIME.
LUPIN IS ALREADY A YEAR OLD. CAN WE STILL TRAIN HIM?
HMM.
NO PROB-LEM.
R-RE-ALLY?
DOGS CAN LEARN NO MATTER HOW OLD THEY GET.
IT DOES GET HARDER AS THEY AGE, BUT LUPIN IS STILL PRETTY YOUNG.

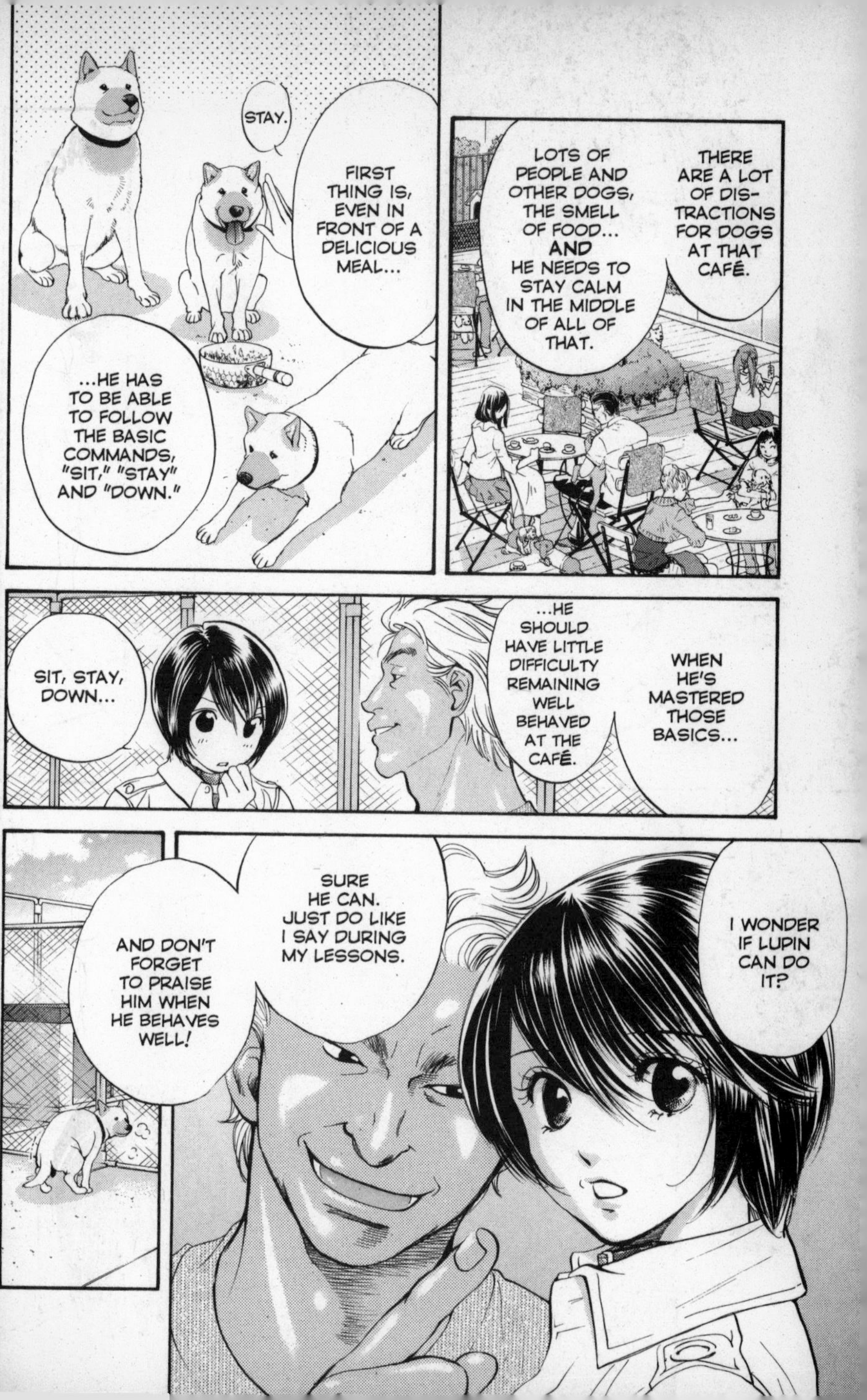
THERE ARE A LOT OF DIS-TRACTIONS FOR DOGS AT THAT CAFÉ.
LOTS OF PEOPLE AND OTHER DOGS, THE SMELL OF FOOD... AND HE NEEDS TO STAY CALM IN THE MIDDLE OF ALL OF THAT.
FIRST THING IS, EVEN IN FRONT OF A DELICIOUS MEAL...
STAY.
...HE HAS TO BE ABLE TO FOLLOW THE BASIC COMMANDS, "SIT," "STAY" AND "DOWN."
WHEN HE'S MASTERED THOSE BASICS...
...HE SHOULD HAVE LITTLE DIFFICULTY REMAINING WELL BEHAVED AT THE CAFÉ.
SIT, STAY, DOWN...
I WONDER IF LUPIN CAN DO IT?
SURE HE CAN. JUST DO LIKE I SAY DURING MY LESSONS.
AND DON'T FORGET TO PRAISE HIM WHEN HE BEHAVES WELL!

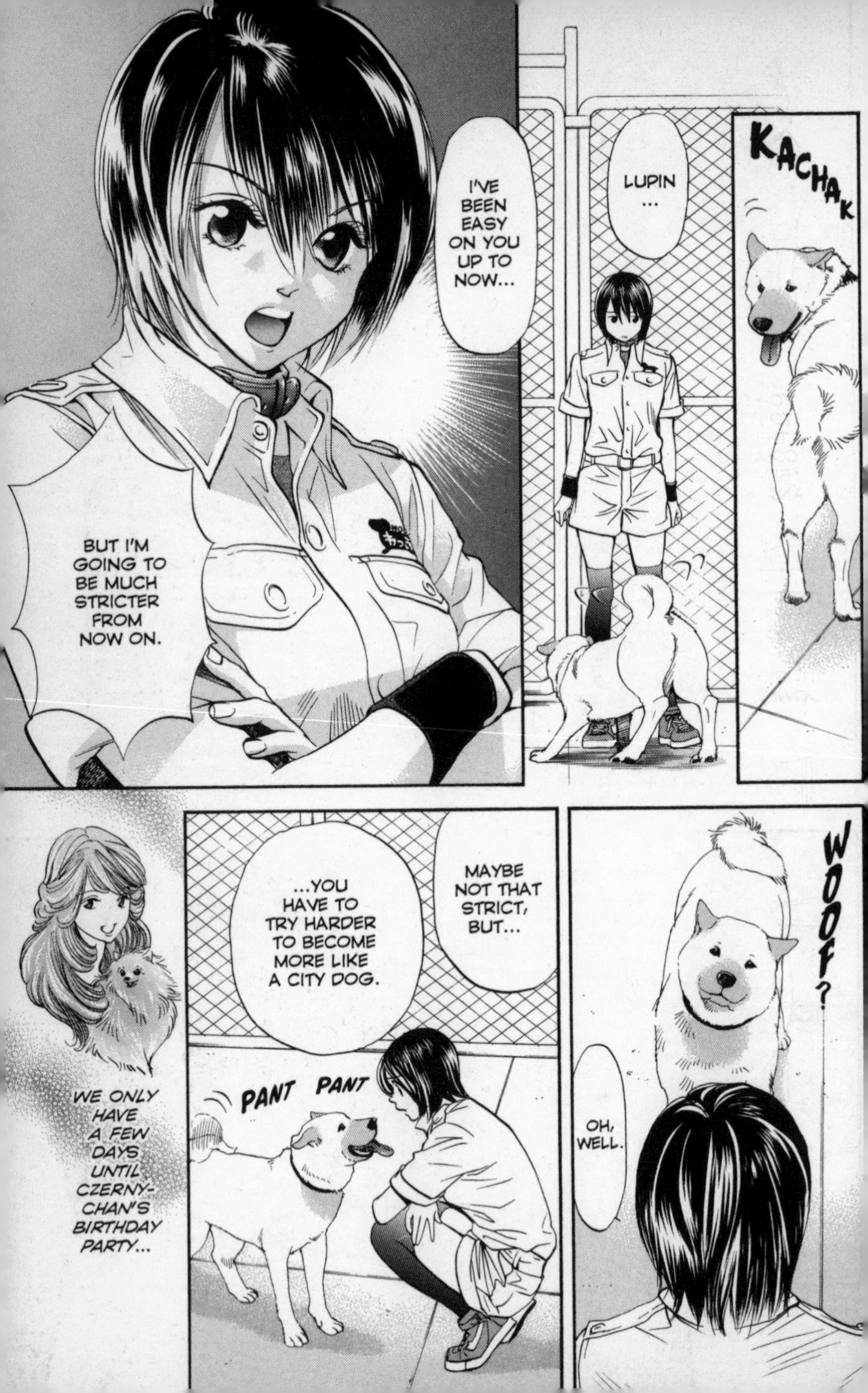
KACHAK
LUPIN...
I'VE BEEN EASY ON YOU UP TO NOW...
BUT I'M GOING TO BE MUCH STRICTER FROM NOW ON.
WOOF?
OH, WELL.
MAYBE NOT THAT STRICT, BUT...
...YOU HAVE TO TRY HARDER TO BECOME MORE LIKE A CITY DOG.
PANT PANT
WE ONLY HAVE A FEW DAYS UNTIL CZERNY-CHAN'S BIRTHDAY PARTY...

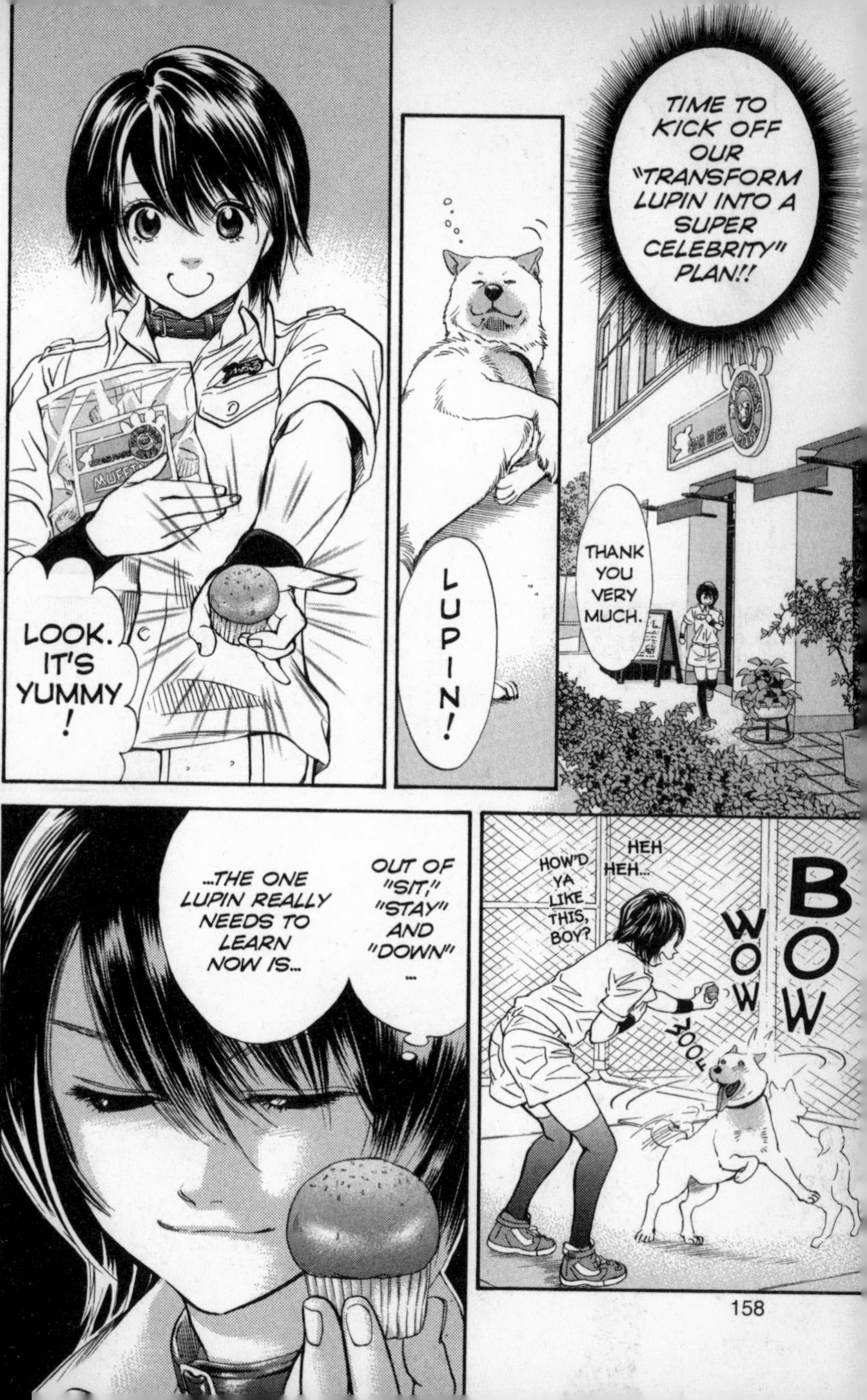
TIME TO KICK OFF OUR "TRANSFORM LUPIN INTO A SUPER CELEBRITY" PLAN!!
THANK YOU VERY MUCH.
LUPIN!
LOOK. IT'S YUMMY!
BOW WOW
WOW WOW
HEH HEH...
HOW'D YA LIKE THIS, BOY?
WOOF
OUT OF "SIT," "STAY" AND "DOWN"...
...THE ONE LUPIN REALLY NEEDS TO LEARN NOW IS...

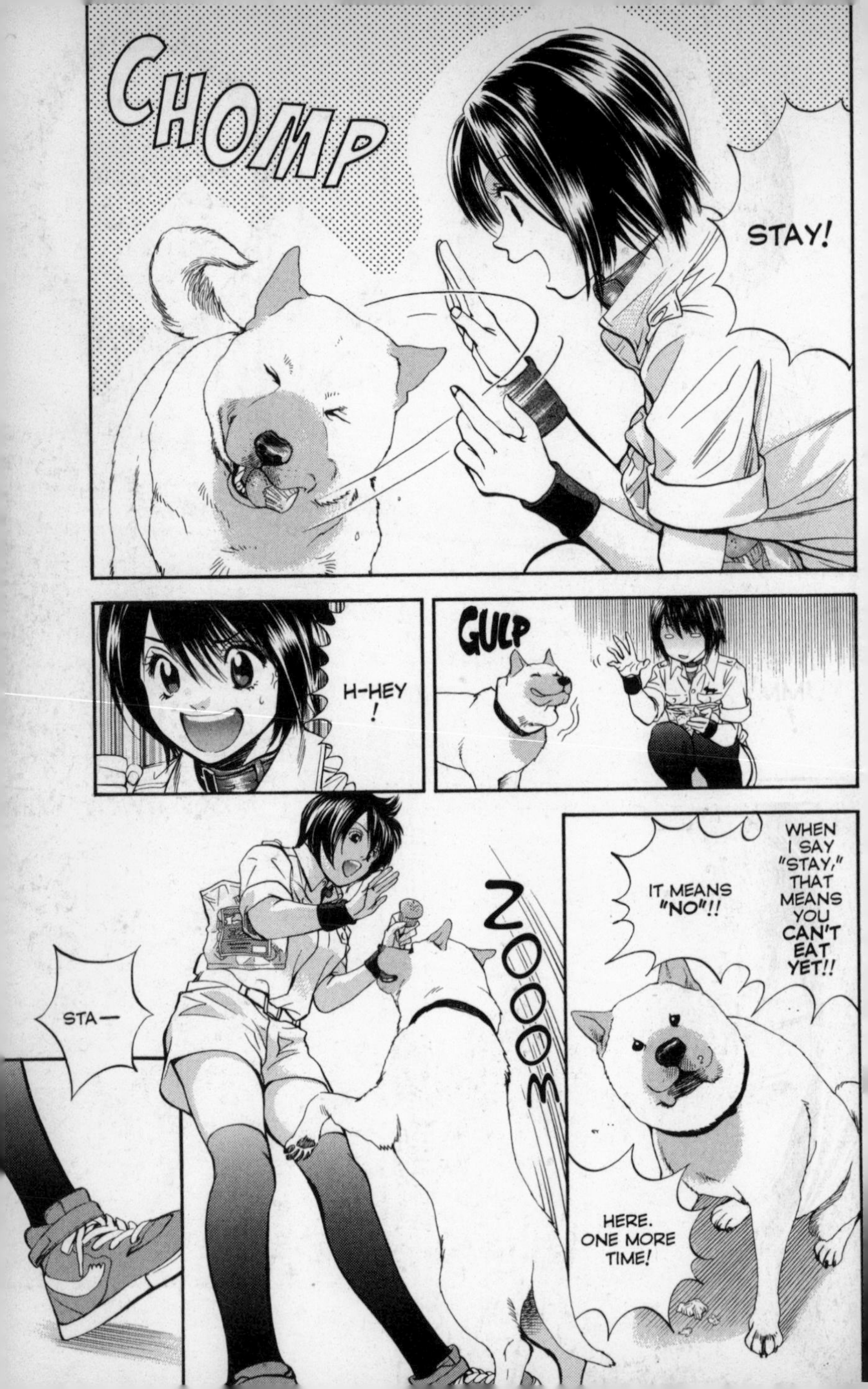
STAY!
CHOMP
GULP
H-HEY!
WHEN I SAY "STAY," THAT MEANS YOU CAN'T EAT YET!!
IT MEANS "NO"!!
HERE. ONE MORE TIME!
ZOOOOM
STA—

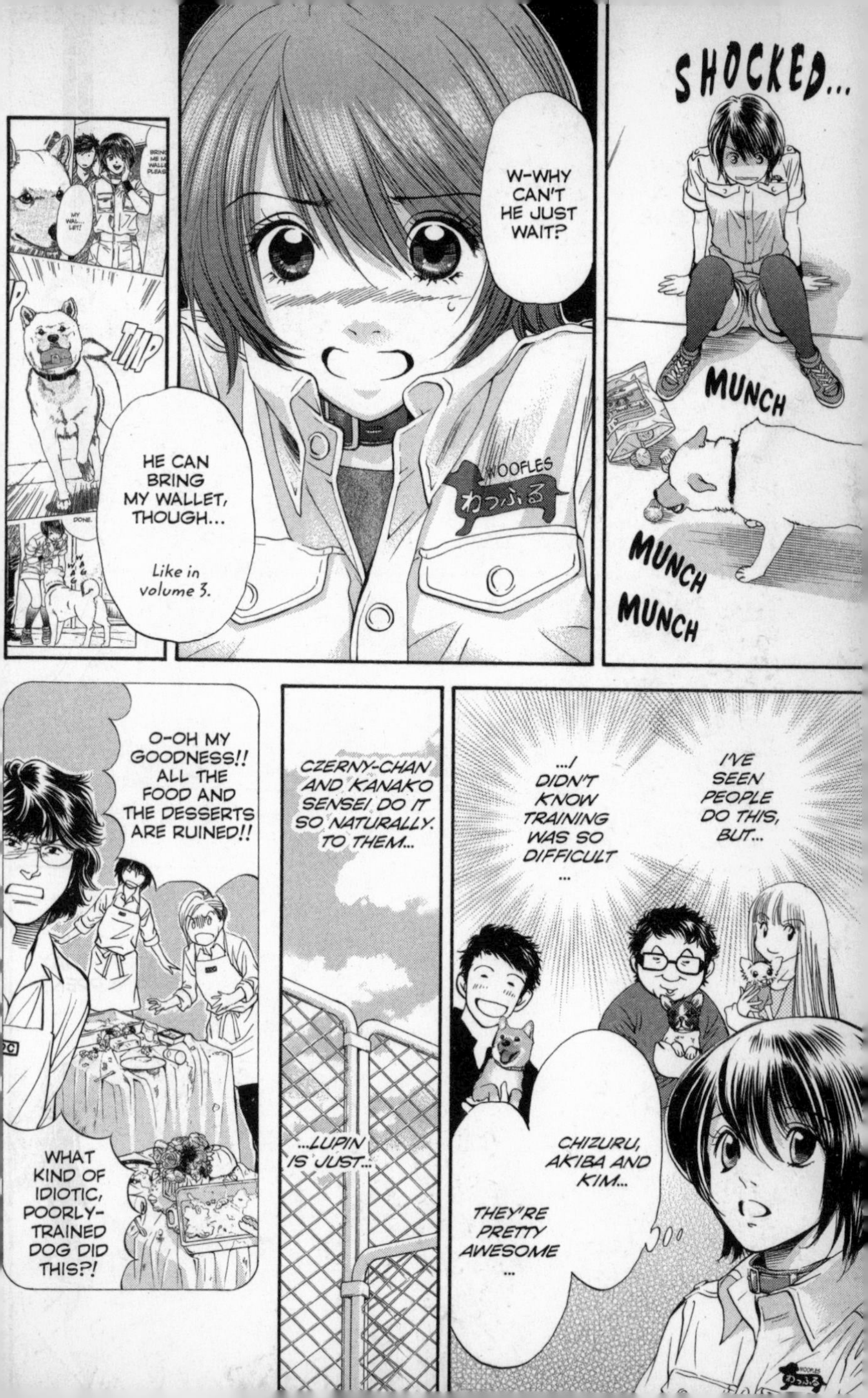
SHOCKED...
MUNCH
MUNCH
MUNCH
MUNCH
W-WHY CAN'T HE JUST WAIT?
WOOFLES
わっふる
MY WAL... LET!
TAP
DONE.
WAG WAG
HE CAN BRING MY WALLET, THOUGH...
Like in volume 3.
I'VE SEEN PEOPLE DO THIS, BUT...
...I DIDN'T KNOW TRAINING WAS SO DIFFICULT...
CHIZURU, AKIBA AND KIM...
THEY'RE PRETTY AWESOME...
CZERNY-CHAN AND KANAKO SENSEI DO IT SO NATURALLY. TO THEM...
...LUPIN IS JUST...
O-OH MY GOODNESS!! ALL THE FOOD AND THE DESSERTS ARE RUINED!!
WHAT KIND OF IDIOTIC, POORLY-TRAINED DOG DID THIS?!

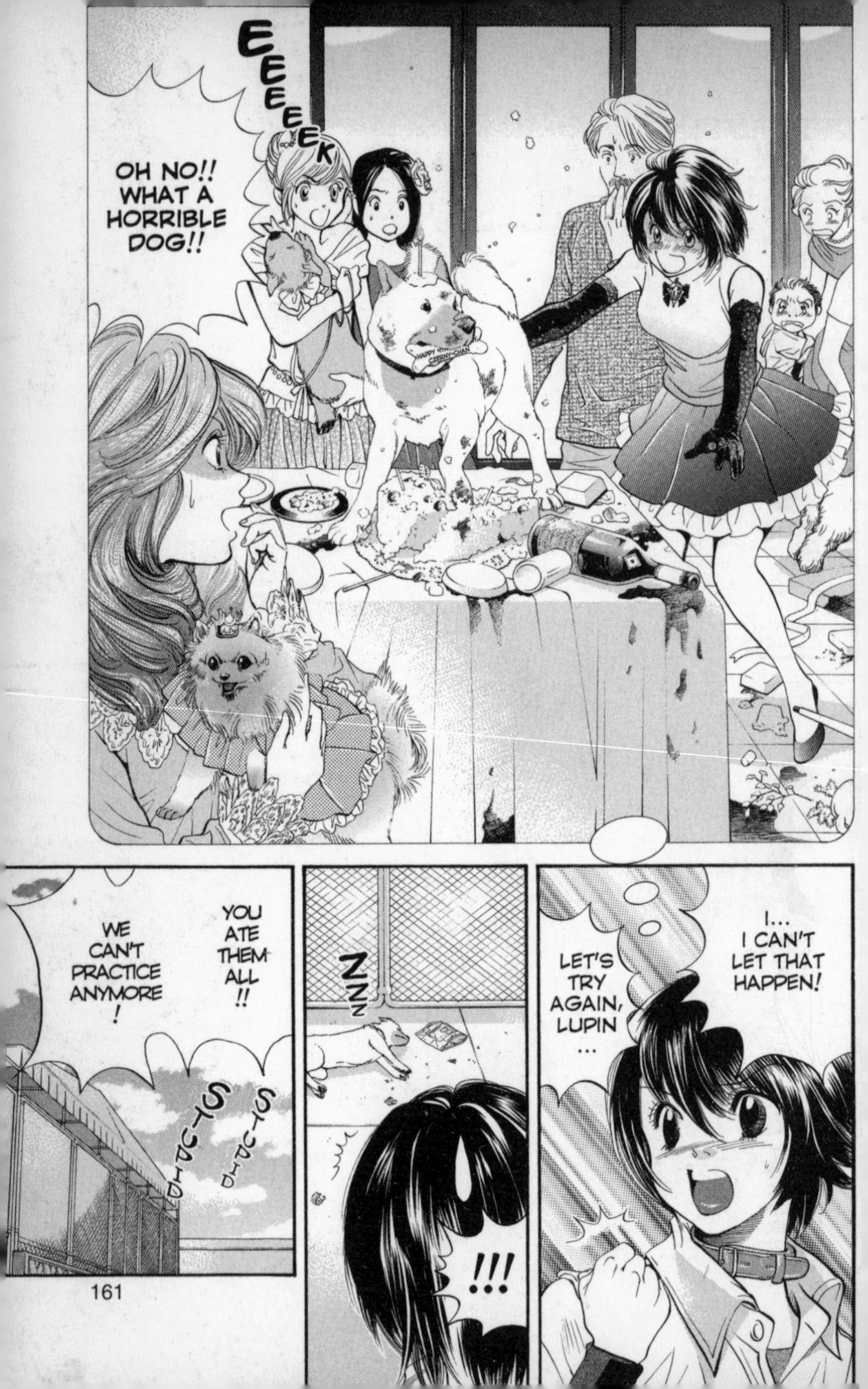
EEEEEK
OH NO!! WHAT A HORRIBLE DOG!!
I... I CAN'T LET THAT HAPPEN!
LET'S TRY AGAIN, LUPIN ...
ZZZ
!!!
YOU ATE THEM ALL!!
WE CAN'T PRACTICE ANYMORE!
STUPID
STUPID

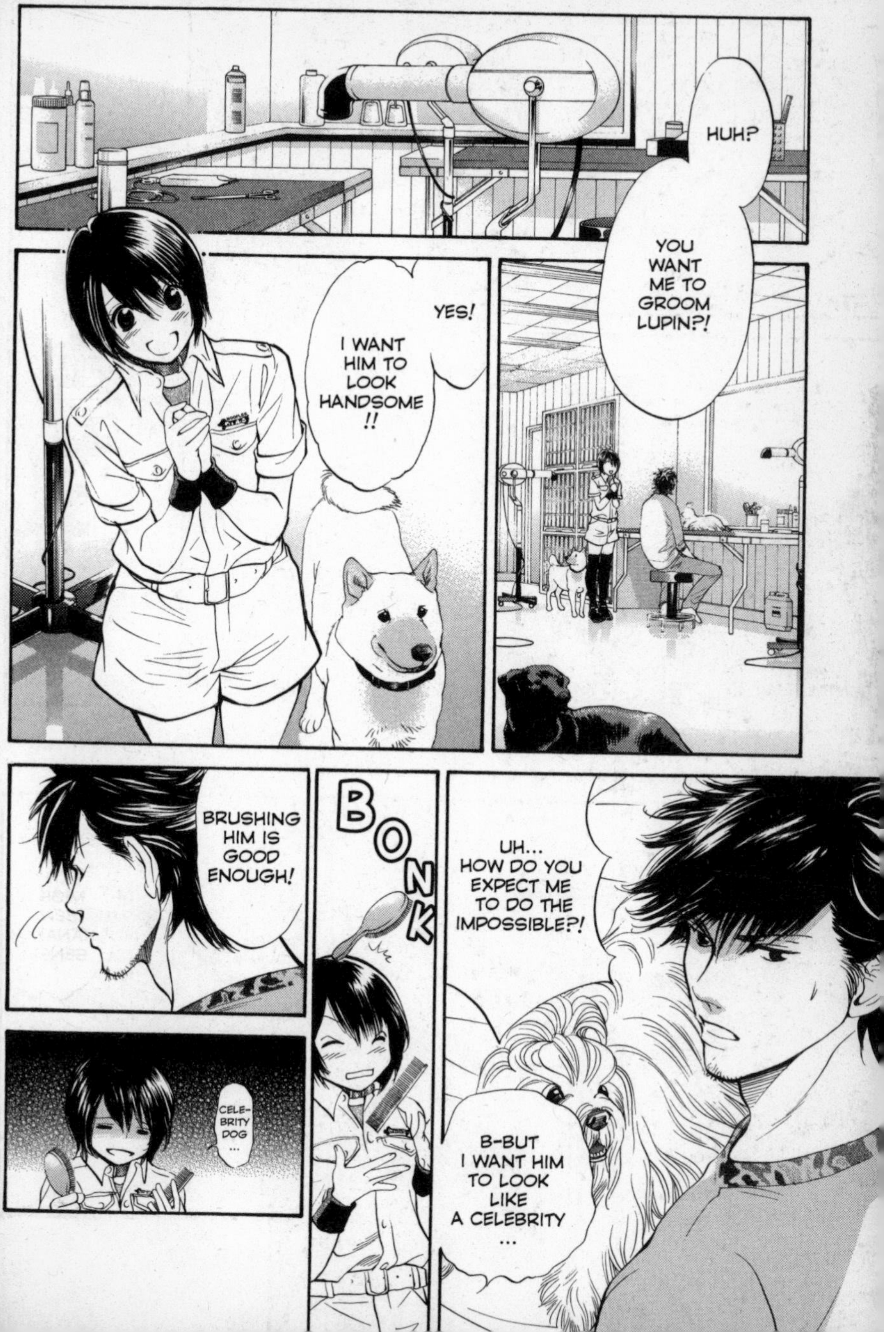
HUH?
YOU WANT ME TO GROOM LUPIN?!
YES! I WANT HIM TO LOOK HANDSOME!!
UH... HOW DO YOU EXPECT ME TO DO THE IMPOSSIBLE?!
B-BUT I WANT HIM TO LOOK LIKE A CELEBRITY...
BONK
BRUSHING HIM IS GOOD ENOUGH!
CELEBRITY DOG...

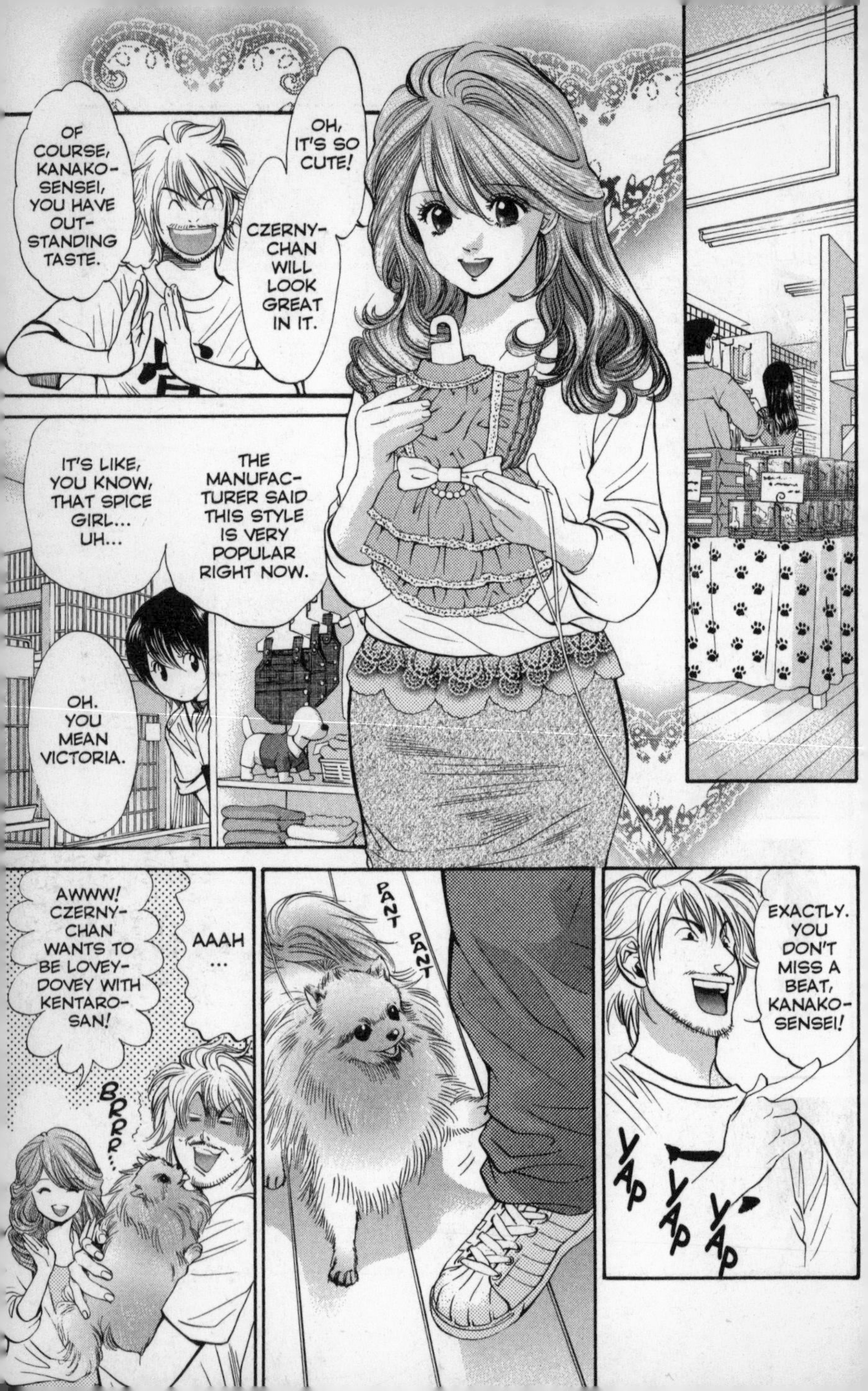
OH, IT'S SO CUTE!
CZERNY-CHAN WILL LOOK GREAT IN IT.
OF COURSE, KANAKO-SENSEI, YOU HAVE OUT-STANDING TASTE.
THE MANUFAC-TURER SAID THIS STYLE IS VERY POPULAR RIGHT NOW.
IT'S LIKE, YOU KNOW, THAT SPICE GIRL... UH...
OH. YOU MEAN VICTORIA.
EXACTLY. YOU DON'T MISS A BEAT, KANAKO-SENSEI!
YAP YAP YAP
PANT PANT
AAAH...
AWWW! CZERNY-CHAN WANTS TO BE LOVEY-DOVEY WITH KENTARO-SAN!
BRRR...

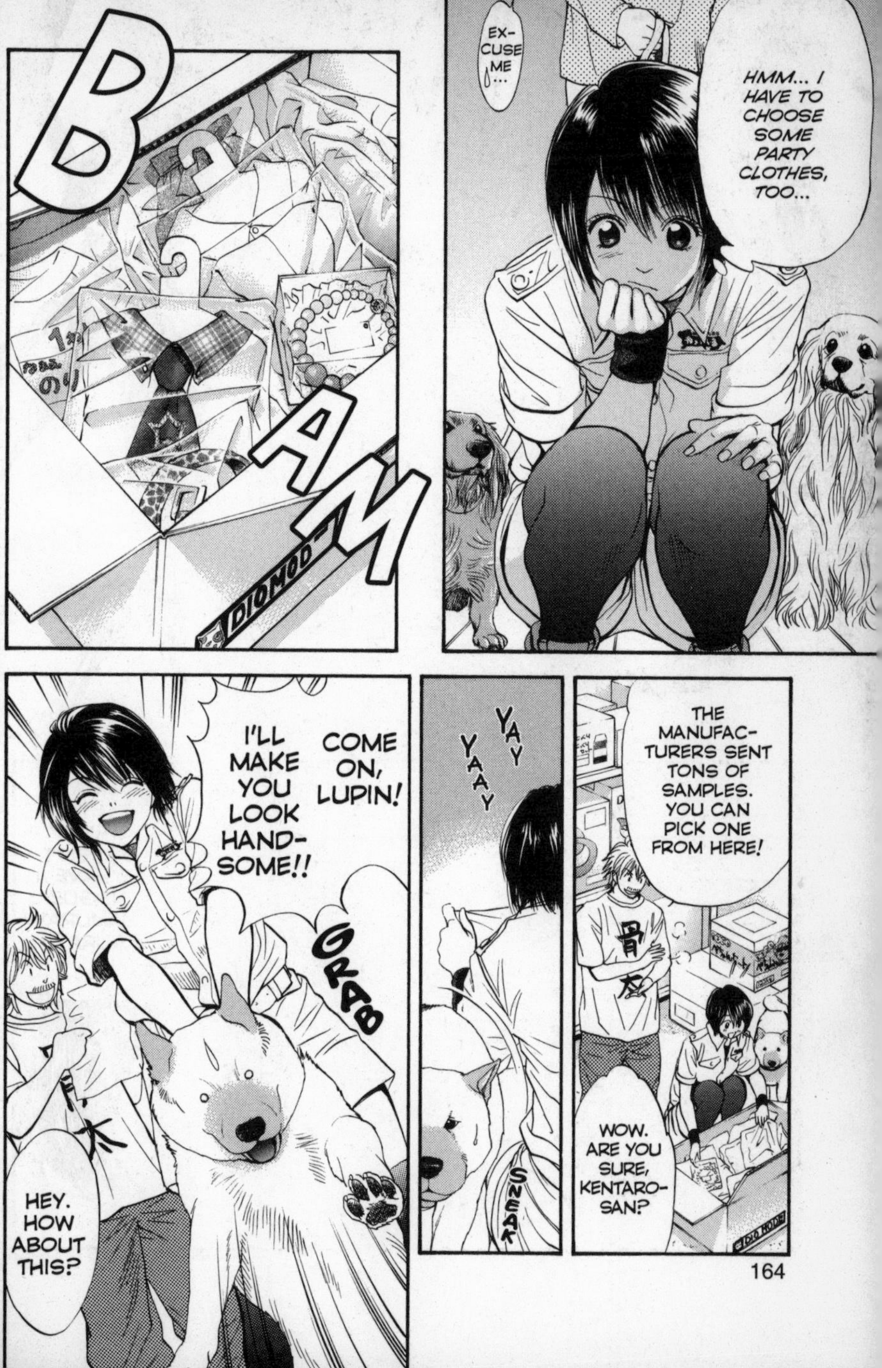
HMM... I HAVE TO CHOOSE SOME PARTY CLOTHES, TOO...
EX-CUSE ME...
BAM
DIOMODE
THE MANUFACTURERS SENT TONS OF SAMPLES. YOU CAN PICK ONE FROM HERE!
WOW. ARE YOU SURE, KENTARO-SAN?
YAY
YAAAY
SNEAK
COME ON, LUPIN!
I'LL MAKE YOU LOOK HANDSOME!!
GRAB
HEY. HOW ABOUT THIS?

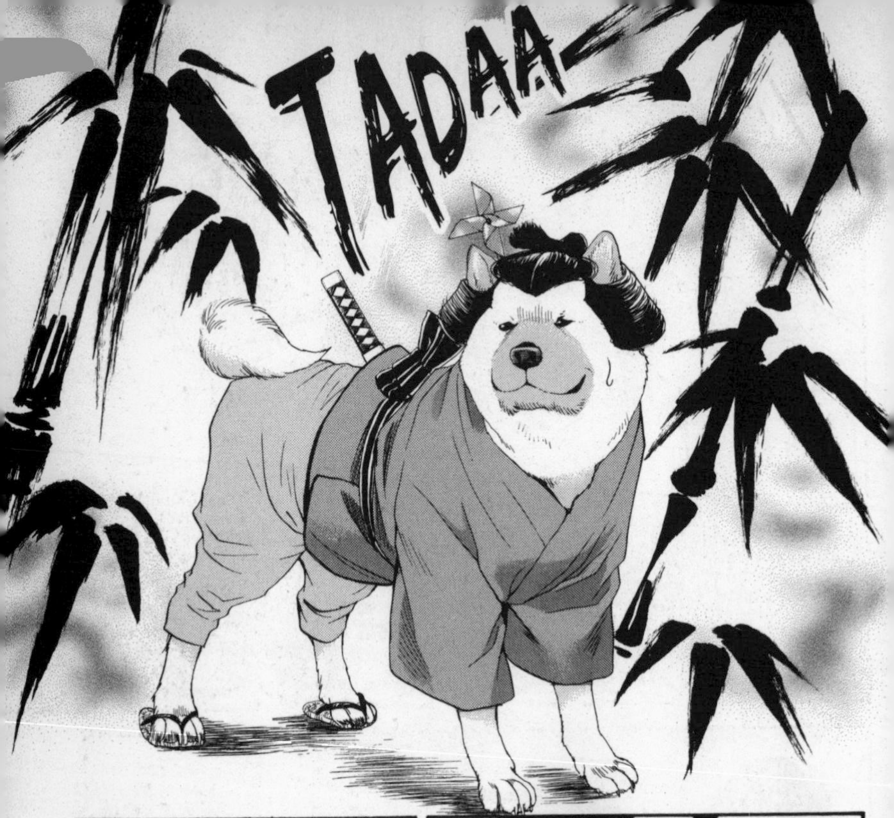
TADAA-

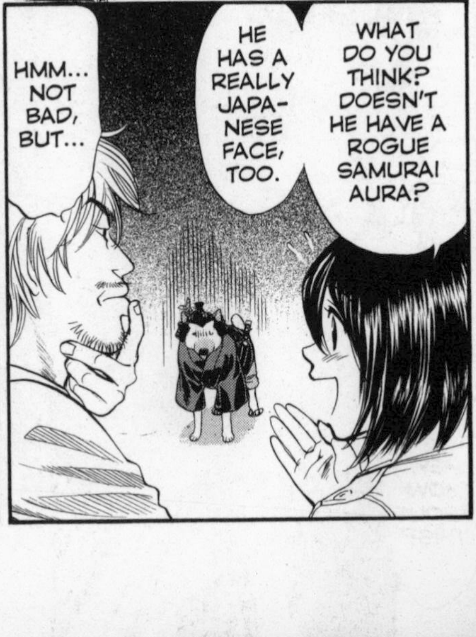
WHAT DO YOU THINK? DOESN'T HE HAVE A ROGUE SAMURAI AURA?
HE HAS A REALLY JAPA-NESE FACE, TOO.
HMM... NOT BAD, BUT...

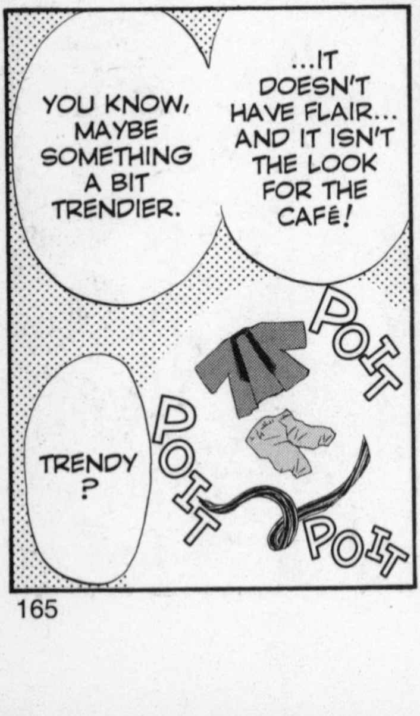
...IT DOESN'T HAVE FLAIR... AND IT ISN'T THE LOOK FOR THE CAFÉ!
YOU KNOW, MAYBE SOMETHING A BIT TRENDIER.
POIT
POIT
POIT
POIT
TRENDY?

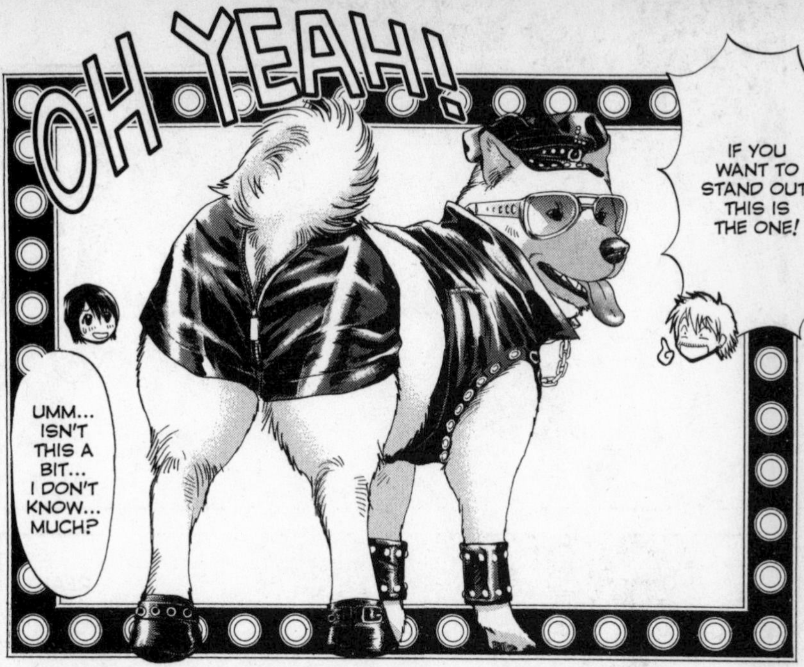
IF YOU WANT TO STAND OUT, THIS IS THE ONE!
OH YEAH!
UMM... ISN'T THIS A BIT... I DON'T KNOW... MUCH?

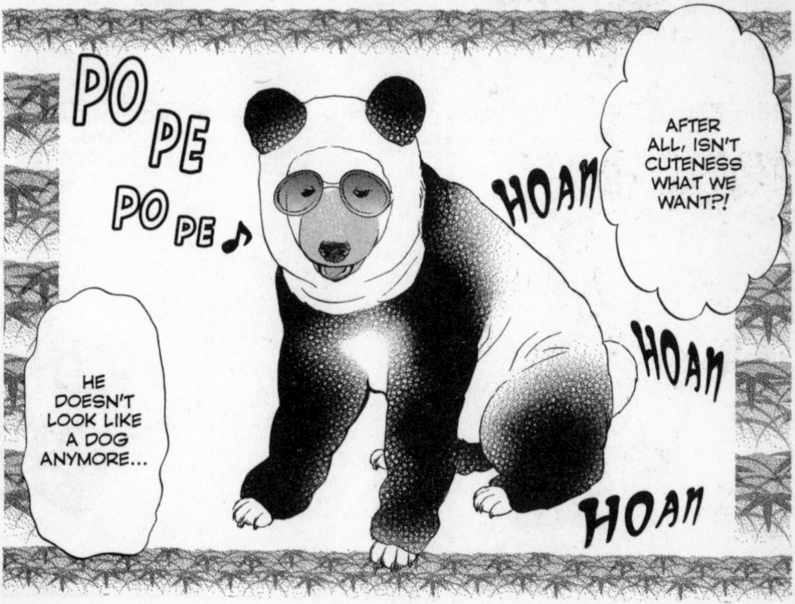
AFTER ALL, ISN'T CUTENESS WHAT WE WANT?!
HOAN
HOAN
HOAN
PO PE
PO PE♪
HE DOESN'T LOOK LIKE A DOG ANYMORE...

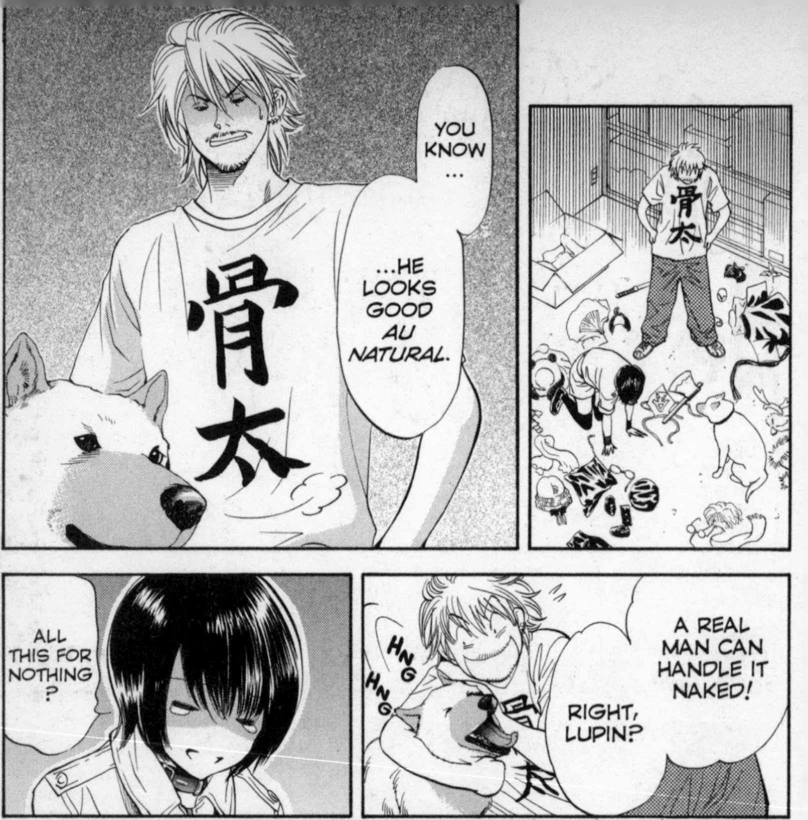
YOU KNOW ...
...HE LOOKS GOOD *AU NATURAL.*
A REAL MAN CAN HANDLE IT NAKED!
RIGHT, LUPIN?
HNG HNG
ALL THIS FOR NOTHING?

* T-SHIRT: *HONEBUTO* (KANJI CHARACTERS FOR "BONE" AND "THICK," MEANING A PERSON/ANIMAL THAT'S BIG-BONED AND STURDY).

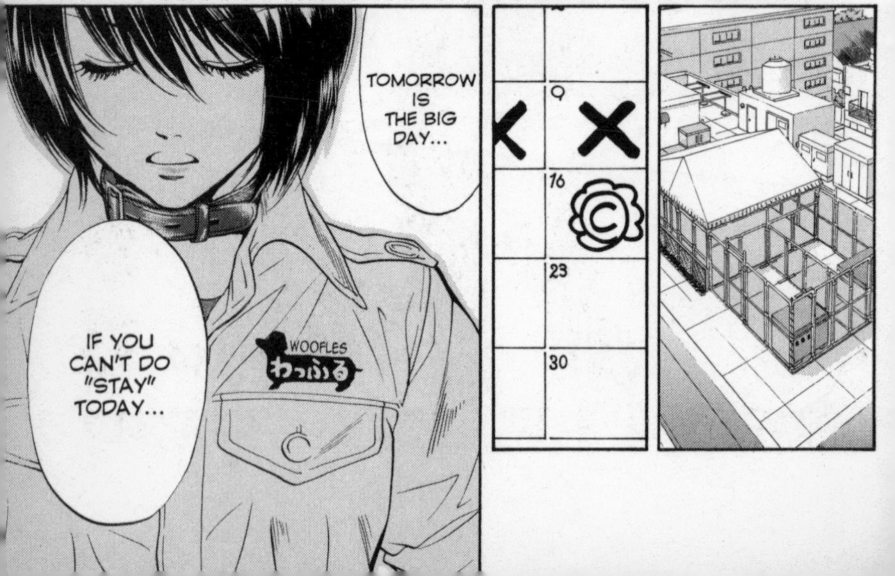
9
16
23
30
TOMORROW IS THE BIG DAY...
WOOFLES
わっふる
IF YOU CAN'T DO "STAY" TODAY...

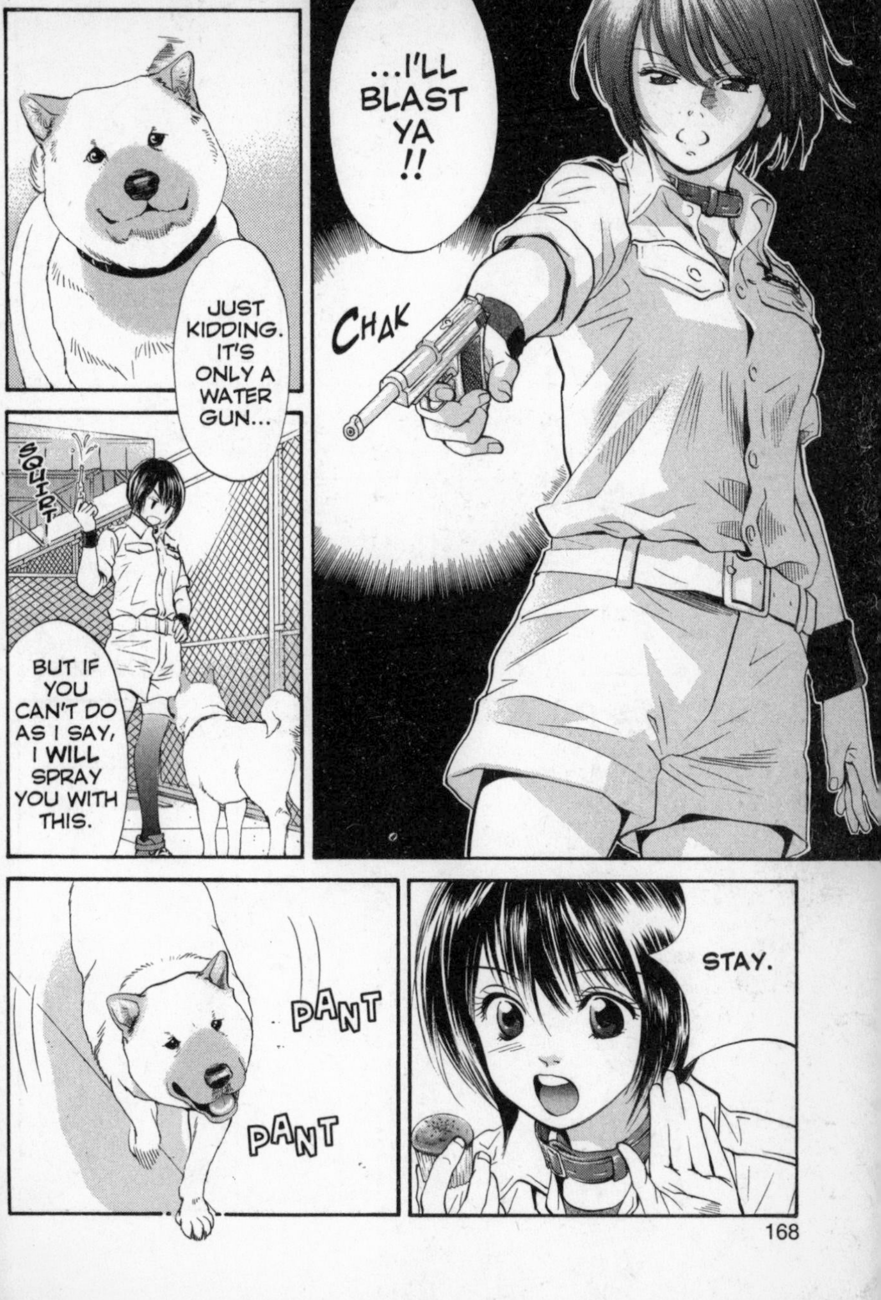
...I'LL BLAST YA!!
CHAK
JUST KIDDING. IT'S ONLY A WATER GUN...
SQUIRT
BUT IF YOU CAN'T DO AS I SAY, I WILL SPRAY YOU WITH THIS.
STAY.
PANT
PANT

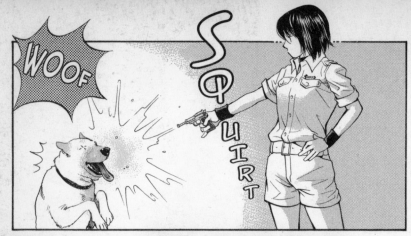

WOOF

SQUIRT

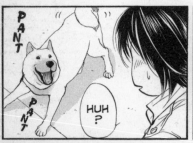

PANT

PANT

HUH?

I— I REALLY DON'T WANT TO DO THIS...

BUT...

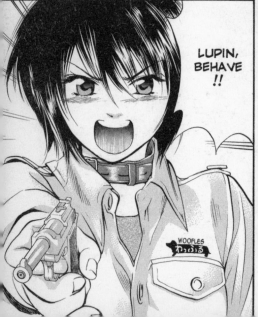

LUPIN, BEHAVE!!

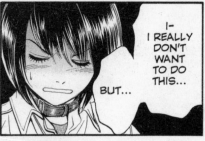

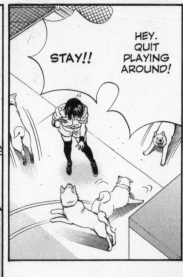

STAY!!

HEY. QUIT PLAYING AROUND!

WOOFLES
わっふる

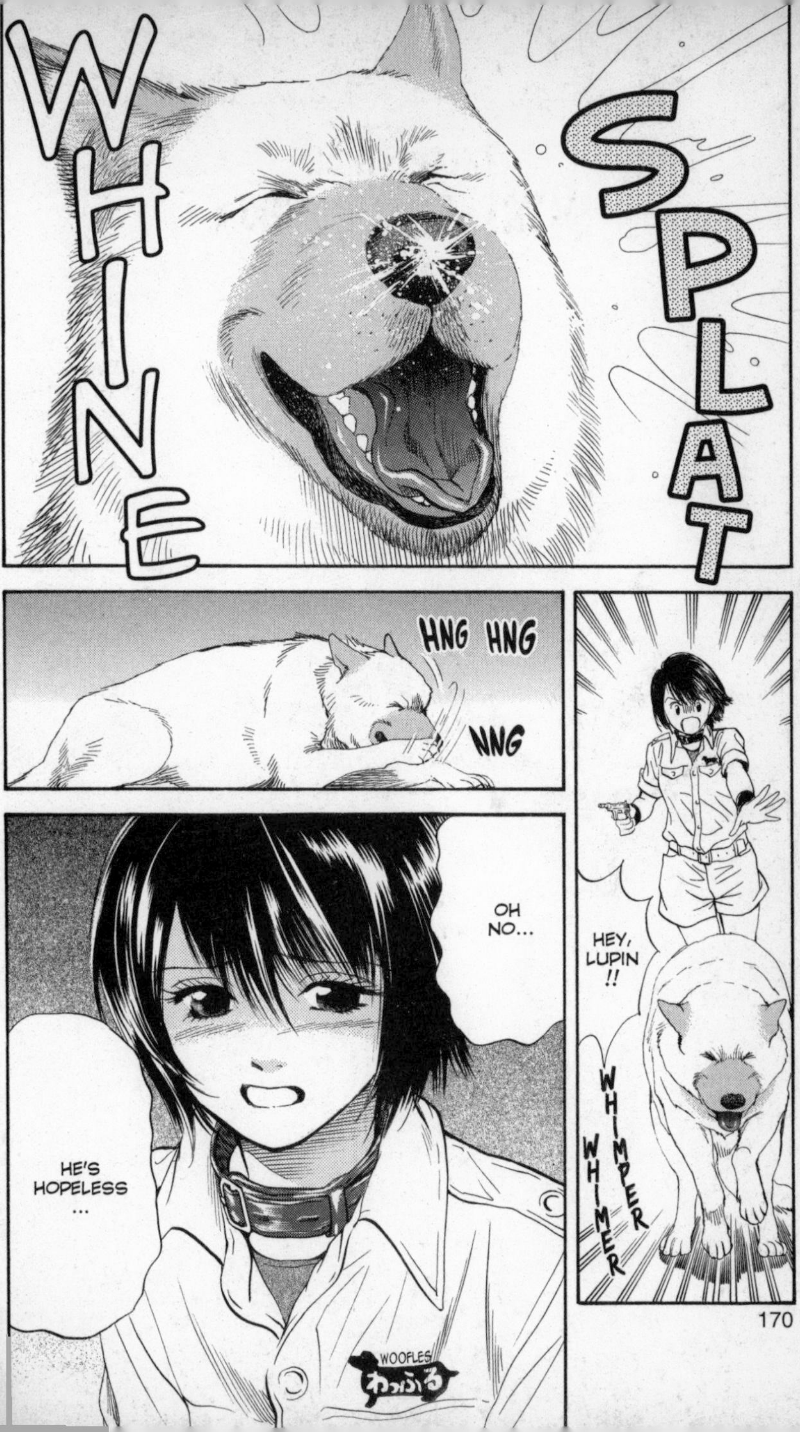
SPLAT
WHINE
HEY, LUPIN !!
WHIMPER WHIMPER
HNG HNG
NNG
OH NO...
HE'S HOPELESS ...
WOOFLES
わっふる

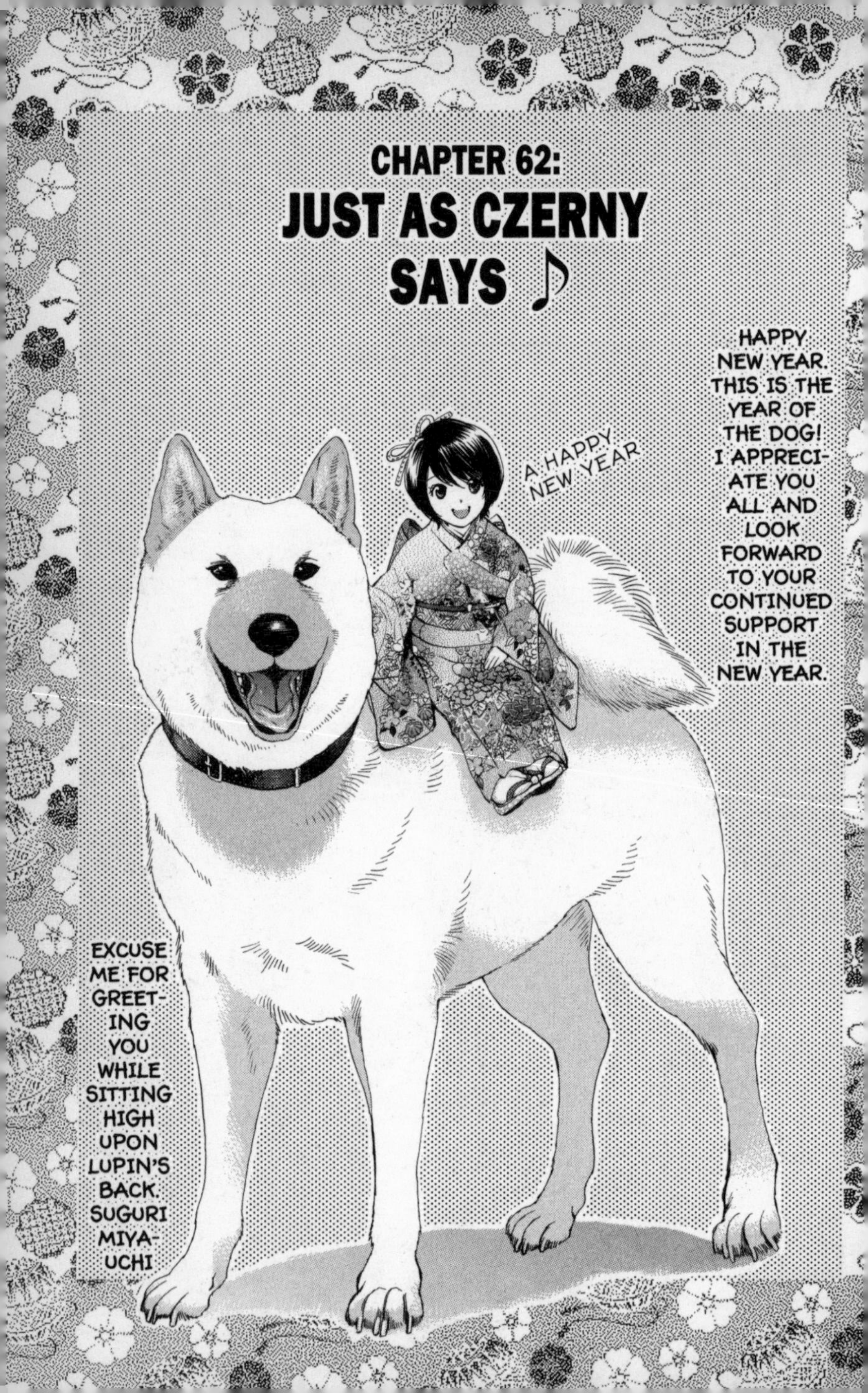
CHAPTER 62:
JUST AS CZERNY SAYS ♪
HAPPY NEW YEAR. THIS IS THE YEAR OF THE DOG! I APPRECIATE YOU ALL AND LOOK FORWARD TO YOUR CONTINUED SUPPORT IN THE NEW YEAR.
A HAPPY NEW YEAR
EXCUSE ME FOR GREETING YOU WHILE SITTING HIGH UPON LUPIN'S BACK. SUGURI MIYAUCHI

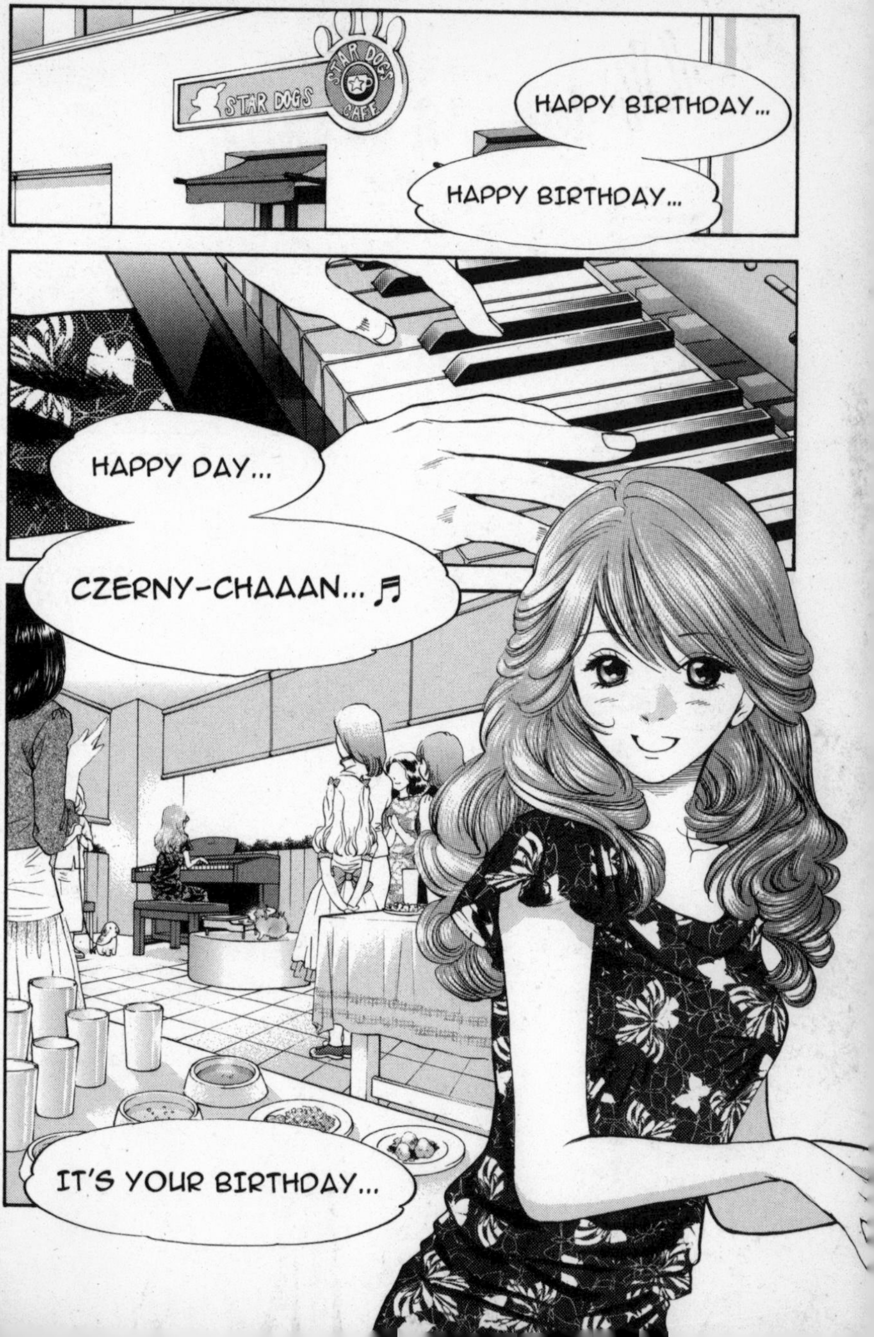
STAR DOGS
STAR DOGS CAFE
HAPPY BIRTHDAY...
HAPPY BIRTHDAY...
HAPPY DAY...
CZERNY-CHAAAN... ♬
IT'S YOUR BIRTHDAY...

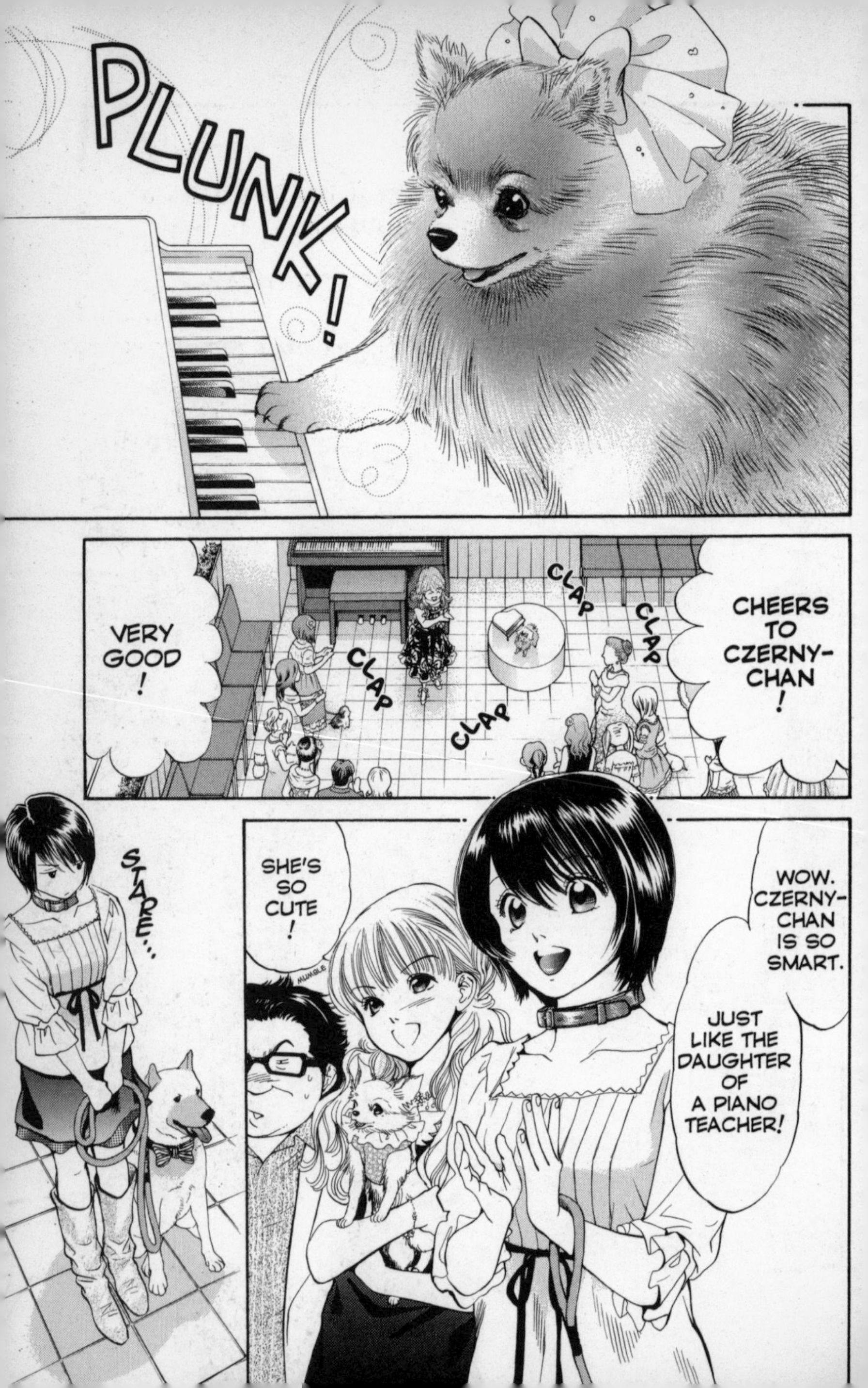
PLUNK!
CHEERS TO CZERNY-CHAN!
CLAP
CLAP
CLAP
CLAP
VERY GOOD!
WOW. CZERNY-CHAN IS SO SMART.
JUST LIKE THE DAUGHTER OF A PIANO TEACHER!
SHE'S SO CUTE!
MUMBLE
STARE...

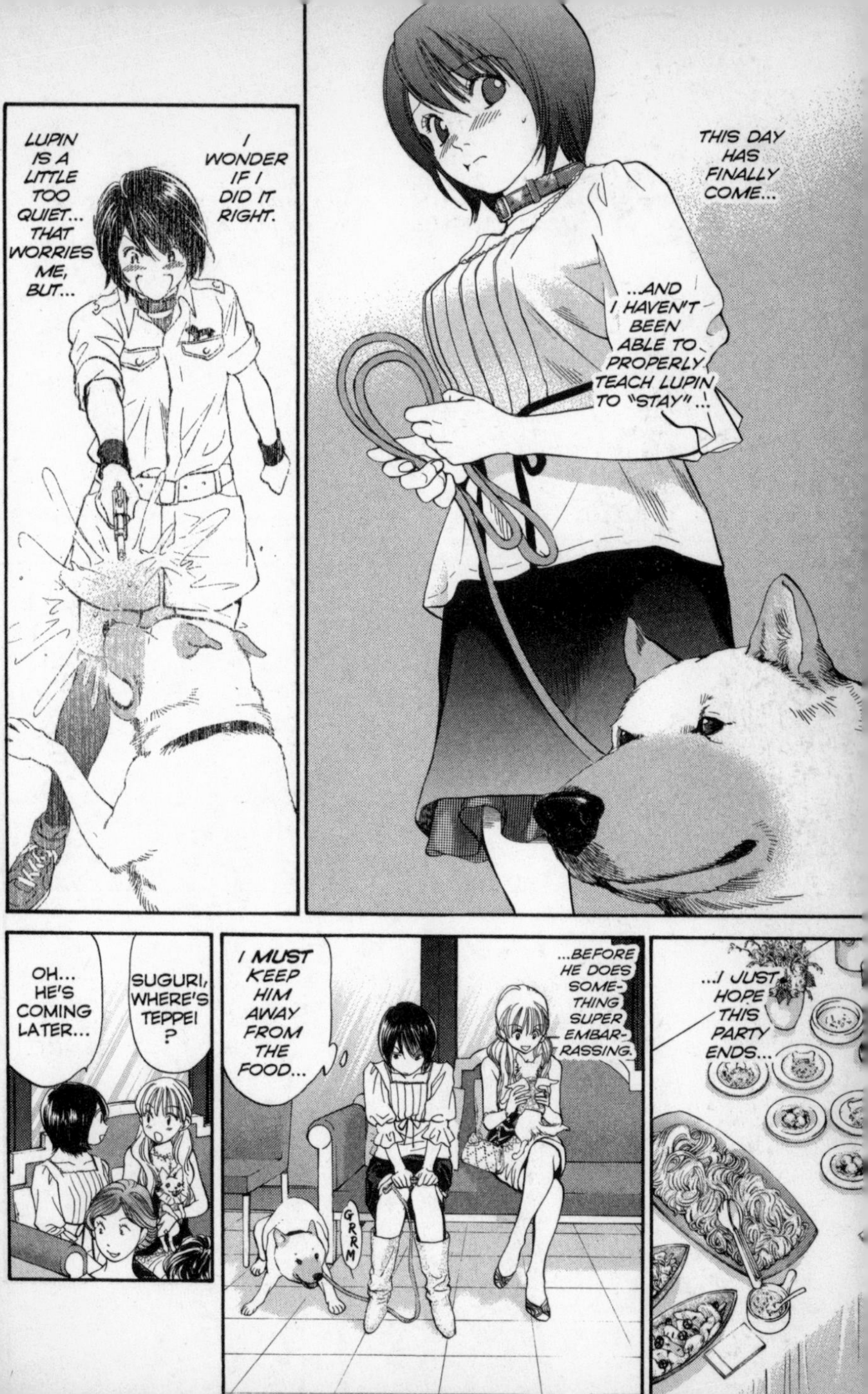
THIS DAY HAS FINALLY COME...
...AND I HAVEN'T BEEN ABLE TO PROPERLY TEACH LUPIN TO "STAY"...
I WONDER IF I DID IT RIGHT.
LUPIN IS A LITTLE TOO QUIET... THAT WORRIES ME, BUT...
...I JUST HOPE THIS PARTY ENDS...
...BEFORE HE DOES SOME-THING SUPER EMBAR-RASSING.
I MUST KEEP HIM AWAY FROM THE FOOD...
GRRM
SUGURI, WHERE'S TEPPEI?
OH... HE'S COMING LATER...

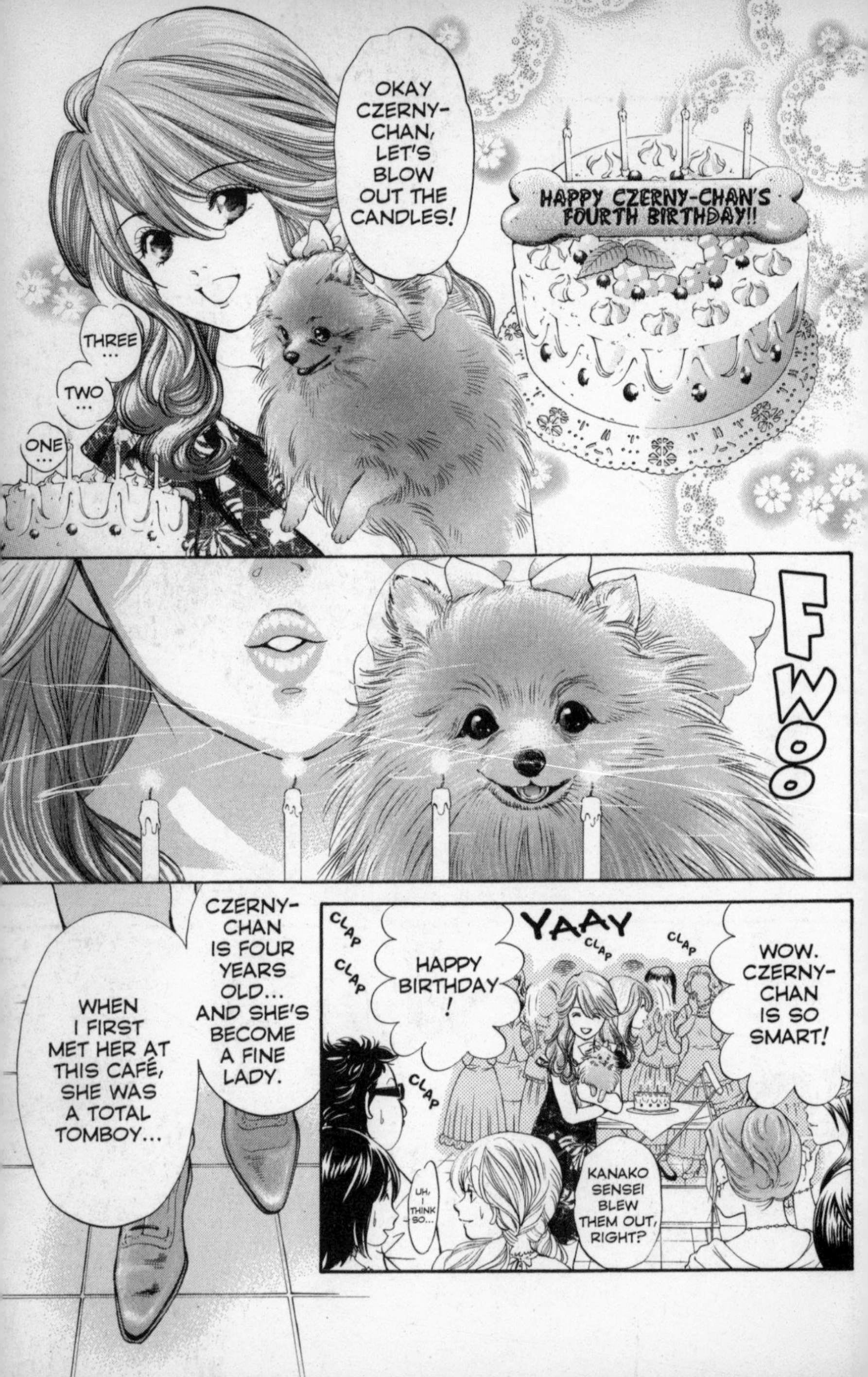
HAPPY CZERNY-CHAN'S FOURTH BIRTHDAY!!
OKAY CZERNY-CHAN, LET'S BLOW OUT THE CANDLES!
THREE...
TWO...
ONE...
FWOO
WOW. CZERNY-CHAN IS SO SMART!
CLAP
YAAY
CLAP
HAPPY BIRTHDAY!
CLAP
CLAP
CLAP
KANAKO SENSEI BLEW THEM OUT, RIGHT?
UH, I THINK SO...
CZERNY-CHAN IS FOUR YEARS OLD... AND SHE'S BECOME A FINE LADY.
WHEN I FIRST MET HER AT THIS CAFÉ, SHE WAS A TOTAL TOMBOY...

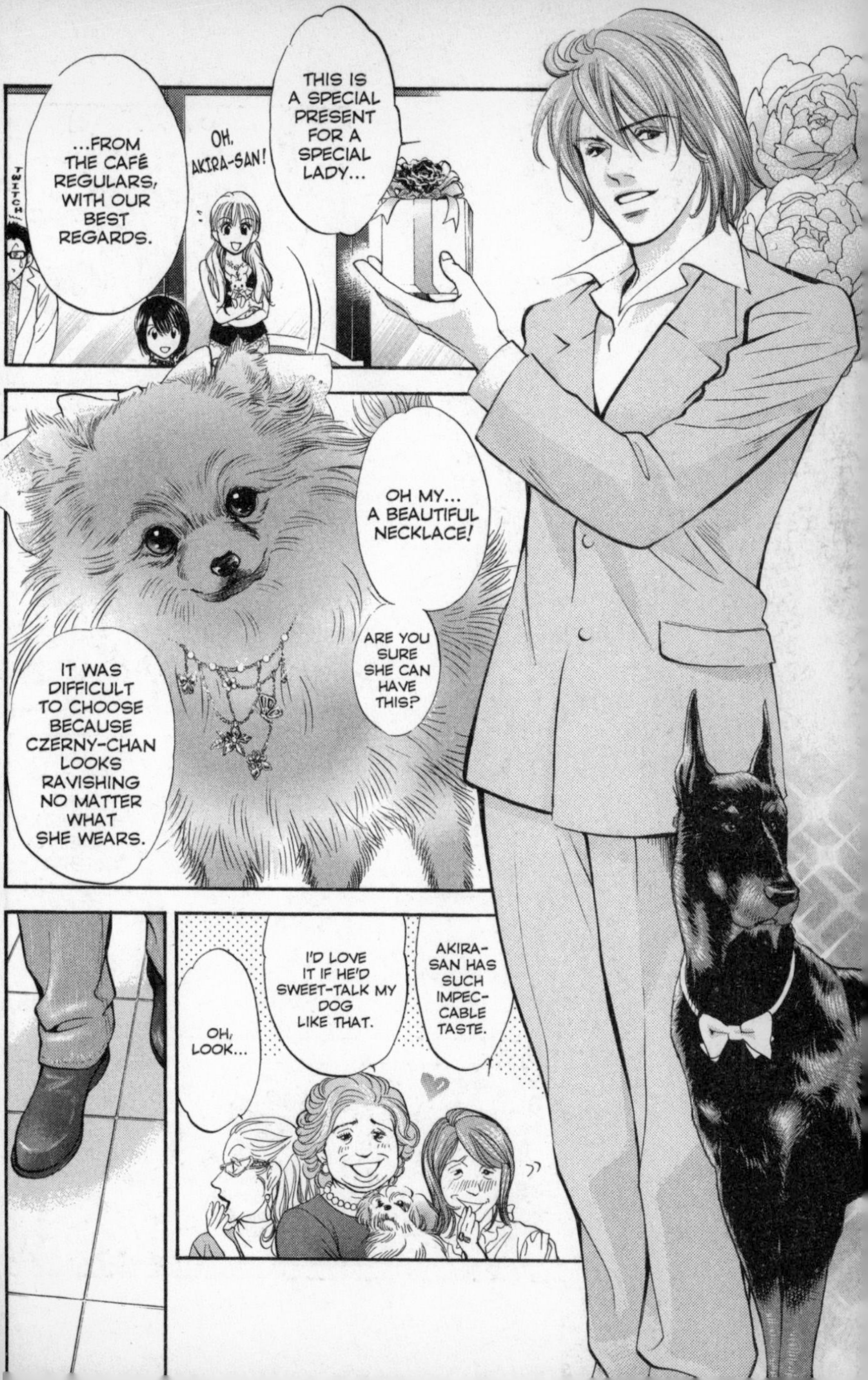
THIS IS A SPECIAL PRESENT FOR A SPECIAL LADY...
OH, AKIRA-SAN!
...FROM THE CAFÉ REGULARS, WITH OUR BEST REGARDS.
TWITCH
OH MY... A BEAUTIFUL NECKLACE!
ARE YOU SURE SHE CAN HAVE THIS?
IT WAS DIFFICULT TO CHOOSE BECAUSE CZERNY-CHAN LOOKS RAVISHING NO MATTER WHAT SHE WEARS.
AKIRA-SAN HAS SUCH IMPECCABLE TASTE.
I'D LOVE IT IF HE'D SWEET-TALK MY DOG LIKE THAT.
OH, LOOK...

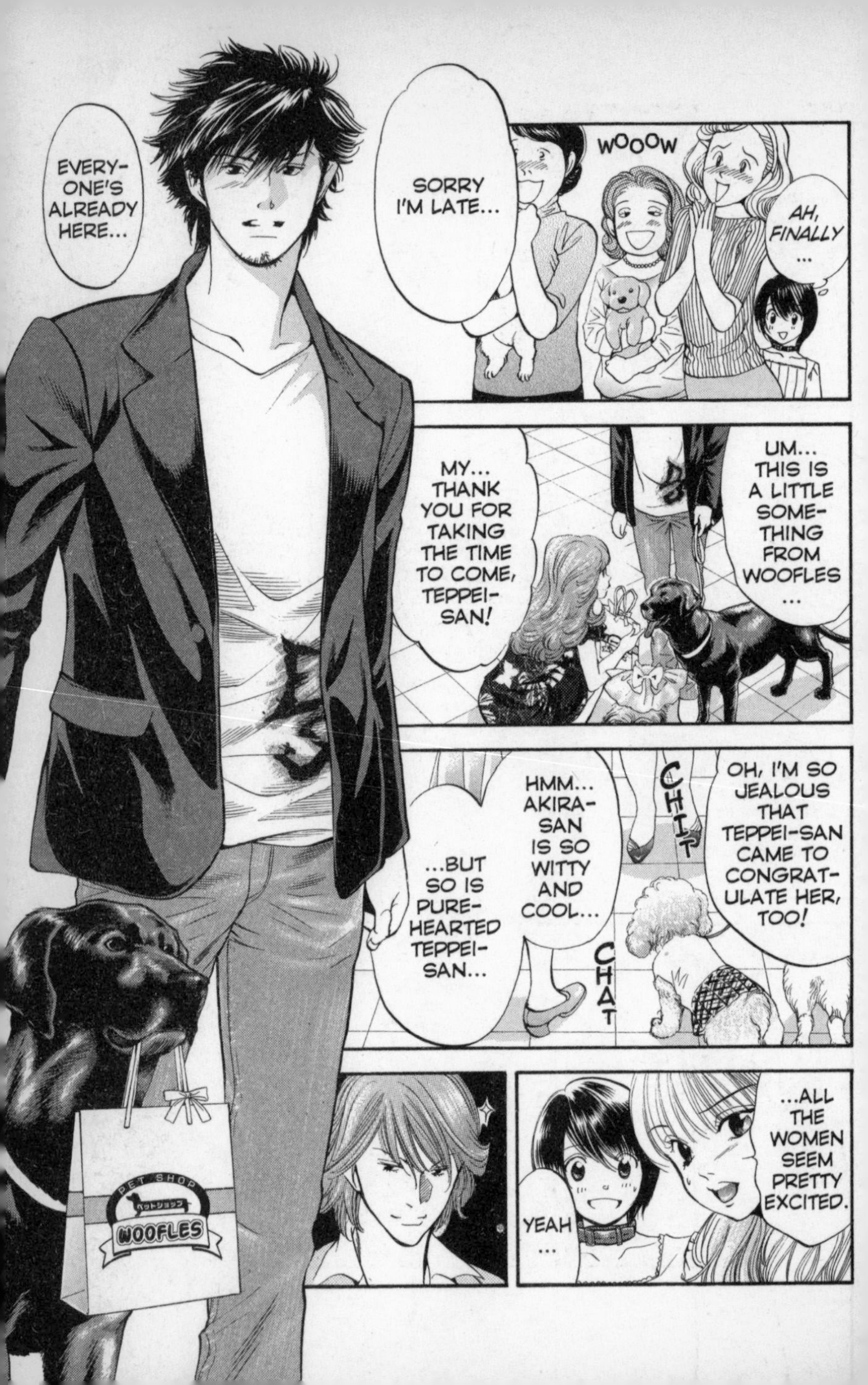
WOOOW
AH, FINALLY...
UM... THIS IS A LITTLE SOME-THING FROM WOOFLES...
MY... THANK YOU FOR TAKING THE TIME TO COME, TEPPEI-SAN!
OH, I'M SO JEALOUS THAT TEPPEI-SAN CAME TO CONGRAT-ULATE HER, TOO!
CHIT
HMM... AKIRA-SAN IS SO WITTY AND COOL...
CHAT
...BUT SO IS PURE-HEARTED TEPPEI-SAN...
...ALL THE WOMEN SEEM PRETTY EXCITED.
YEAH...
SORRY I'M LATE...
EVERY-ONE'S ALREADY HERE...
PET SHOP
WOOFLES

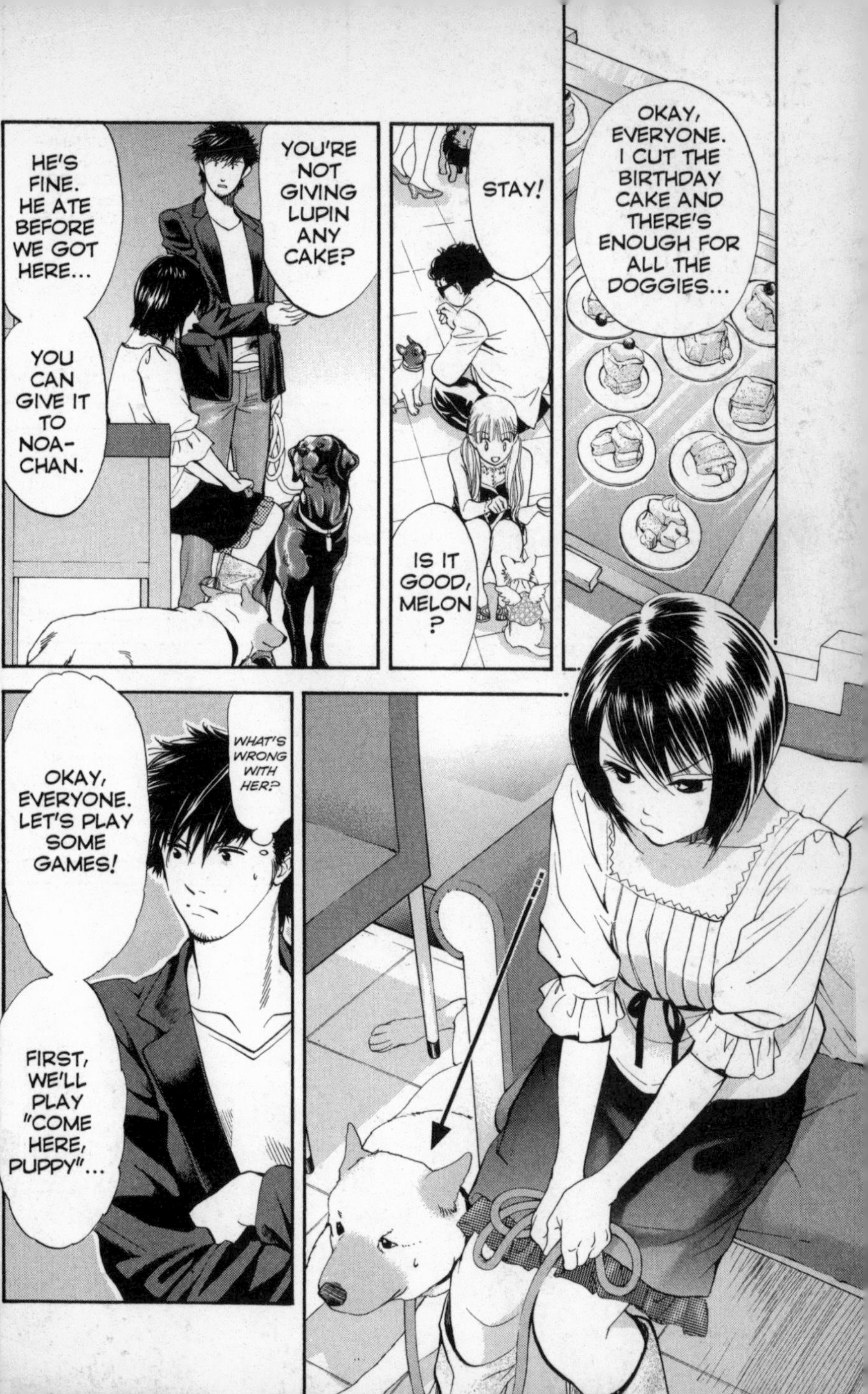
OKAY, EVERYONE. I CUT THE BIRTHDAY CAKE AND THERE'S ENOUGH FOR ALL THE DOGGIES...
STAY!
IS IT GOOD, MELON?
YOU'RE NOT GIVING LUPIN ANY CAKE?
HE'S FINE. HE ATE BEFORE WE GOT HERE...
YOU CAN GIVE IT TO NOA-CHAN.
WHAT'S WRONG WITH HER?
OKAY, EVERYONE. LET'S PLAY SOME GAMES!
FIRST, WE'LL PLAY "COME HERE, PUPPY"...

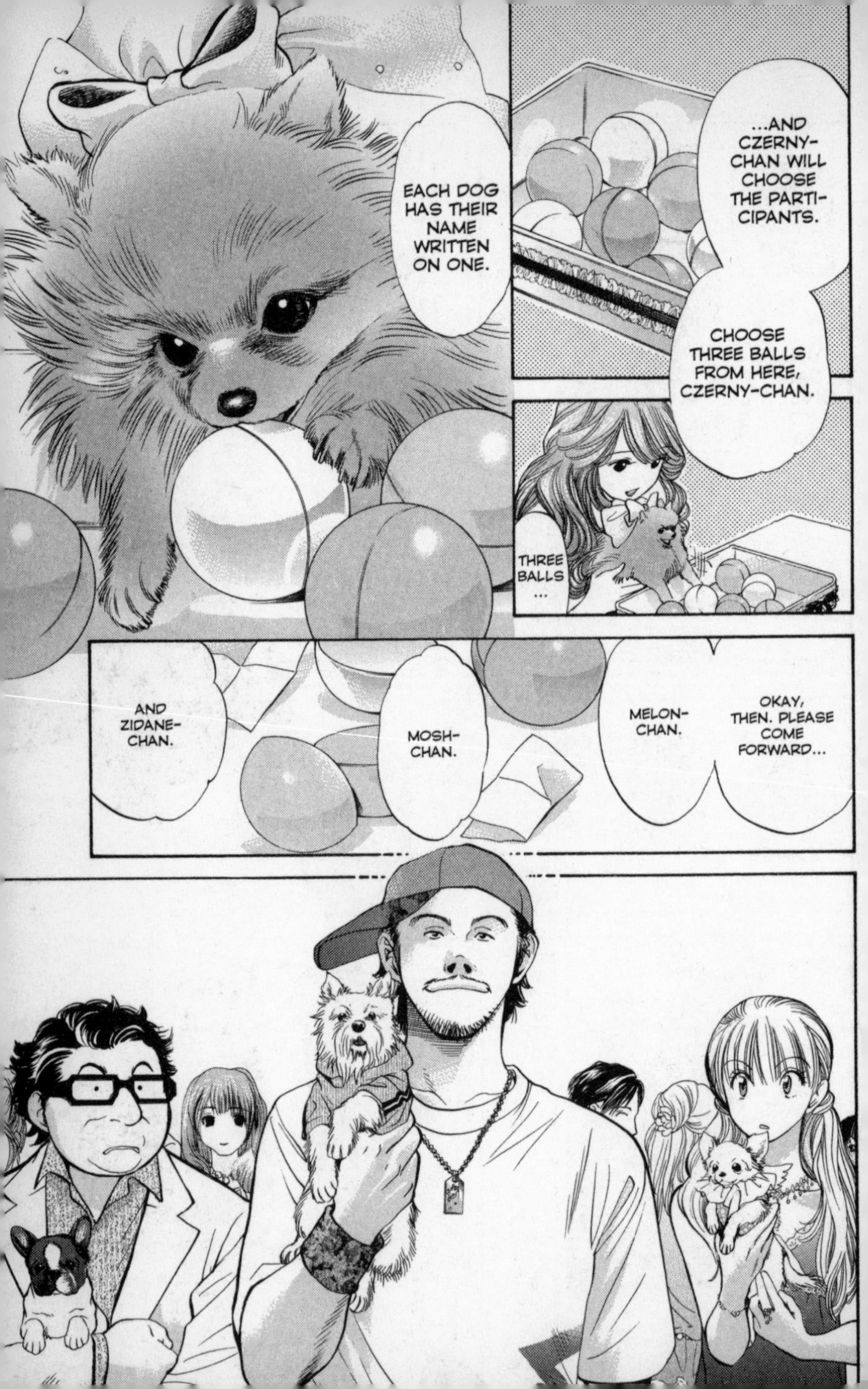
...AND CZERNY-CHAN WILL CHOOSE THE PARTI-CIPANTS.
CHOOSE THREE BALLS FROM HERE, CZERNY-CHAN.
THREE BALLS ...
EACH DOG HAS THEIR NAME WRITTEN ON ONE.
OKAY, THEN. PLEASE COME FORWARD...
MELON-CHAN.
MOSH-CHAN.
AND ZIDANE-CHAN.

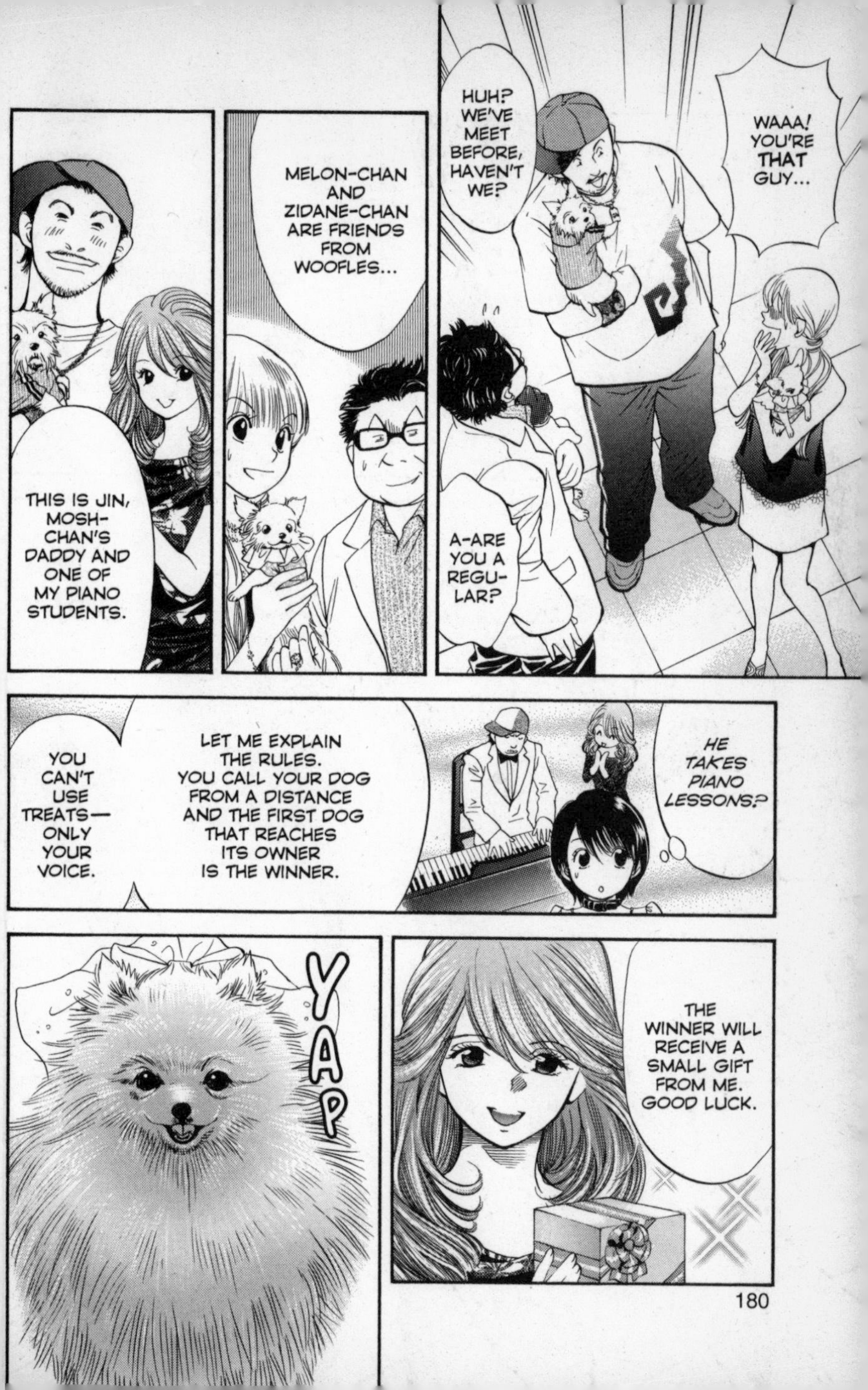
WAAA! YOU'RE THAT GUY...
HUH? WE'VE MEET BEFORE, HAVEN'T WE?
A-ARE YOU A REGULAR?
MELON-CHAN AND ZIDANE-CHAN ARE FRIENDS FROM WOOFLES...
THIS IS JIN, MOSH-CHAN'S DADDY AND ONE OF MY PIANO STUDENTS.
HE TAKES PIANO LESSONS?
LET ME EXPLAIN THE RULES. YOU CALL YOUR DOG FROM A DISTANCE AND THE FIRST DOG THAT REACHES ITS OWNER IS THE WINNER.
YOU CAN'T USE TREATS— ONLY YOUR VOICE.
THE WINNER WILL RECEIVE A SMALL GIFT FROM ME. GOOD LUCK.
YAP

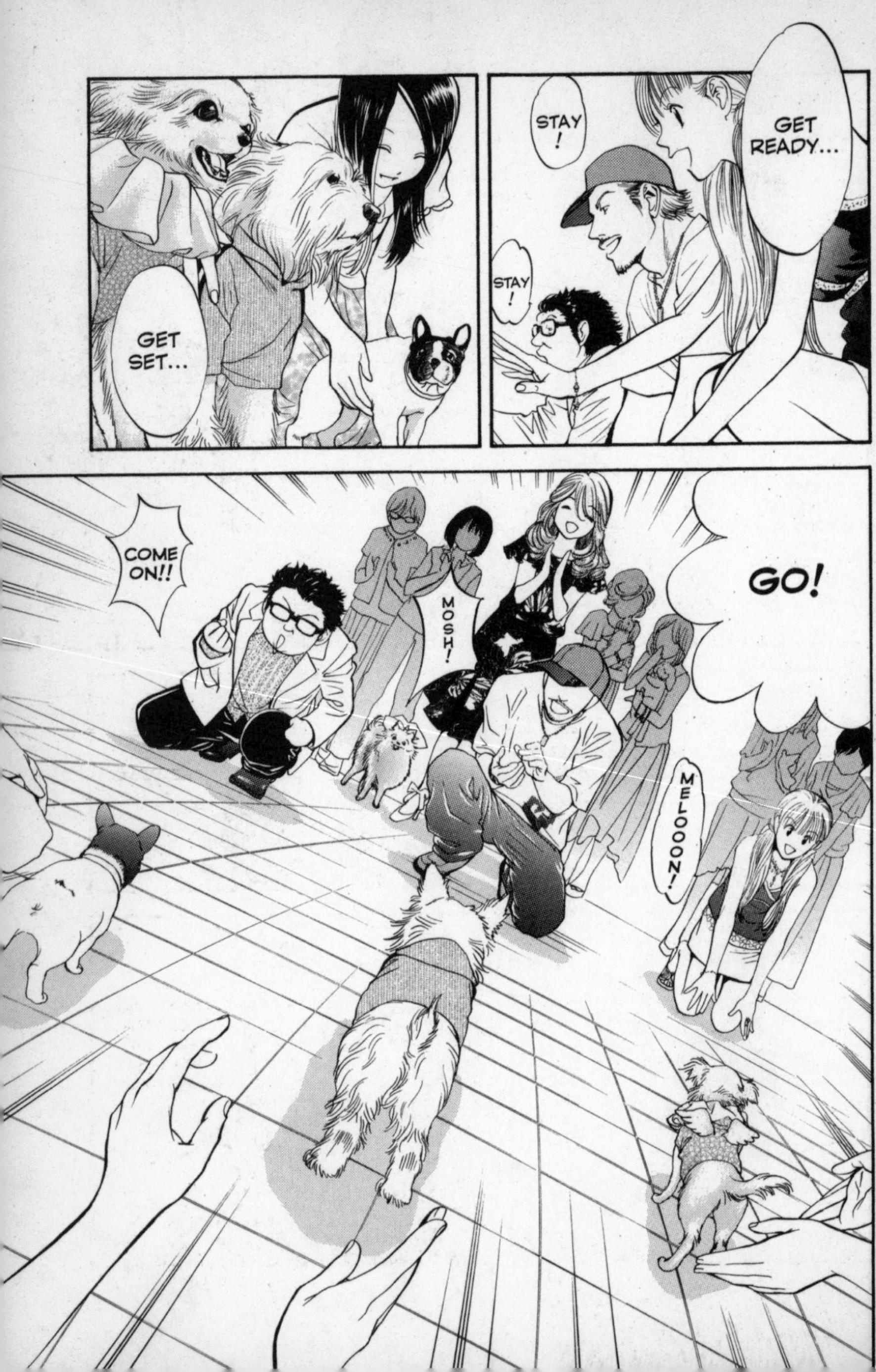
GET READY...
STAY!
STAY!
GET SET...
GO!
MELOOOON!
MOSH!
COME ON!!

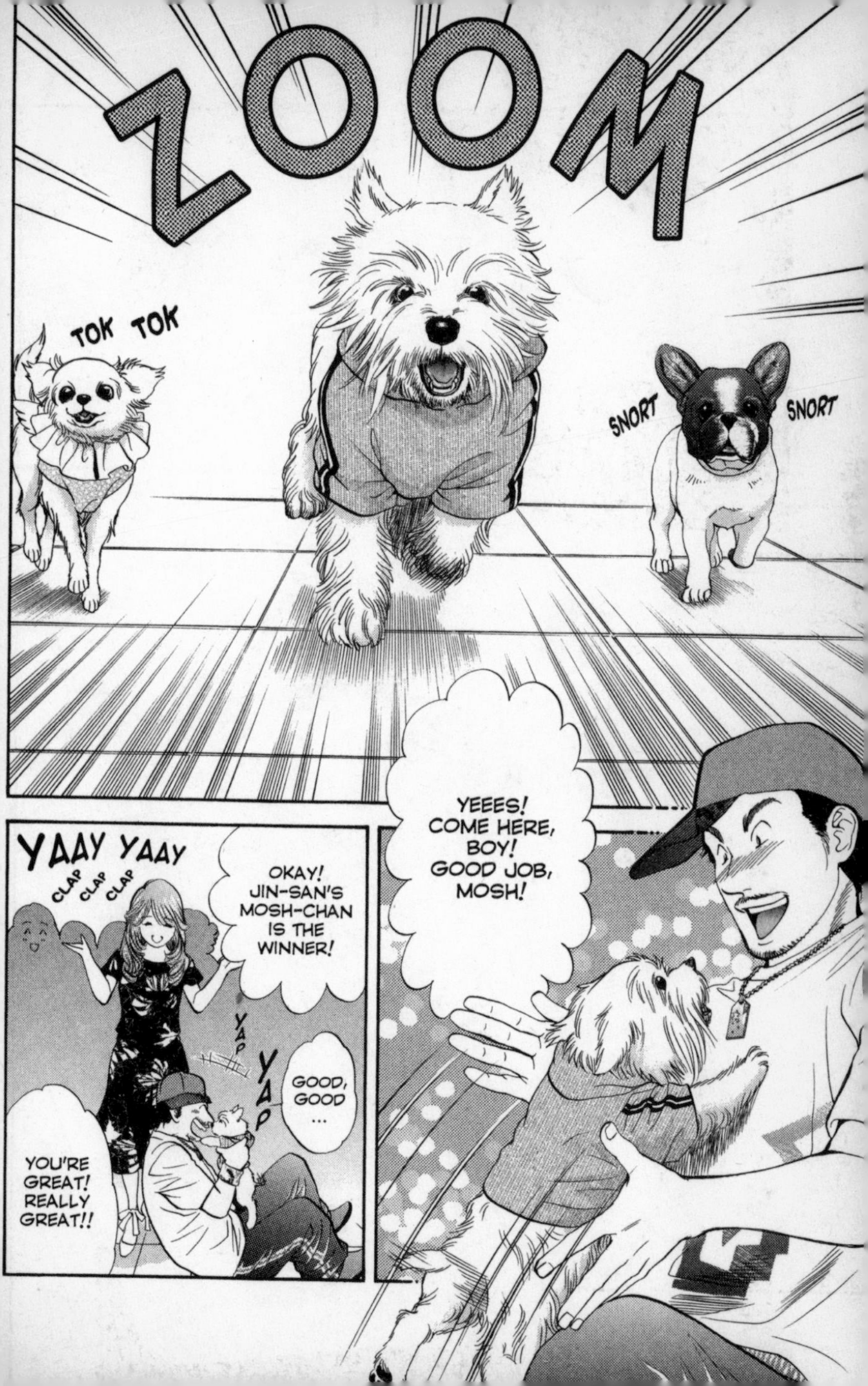
ZOOM
SNORT SNORT
TOK TOK
YEEES! COME HERE, BOY! GOOD JOB, MOSH!
OKAY! JIN-SAN'S MOSH-CHAN IS THE WINNER!
YAAY YAAY
CLAP CLAP CLAP
YAP YAP
GOOD, GOOD ...
YOU'RE GREAT! REALLY GREAT!!

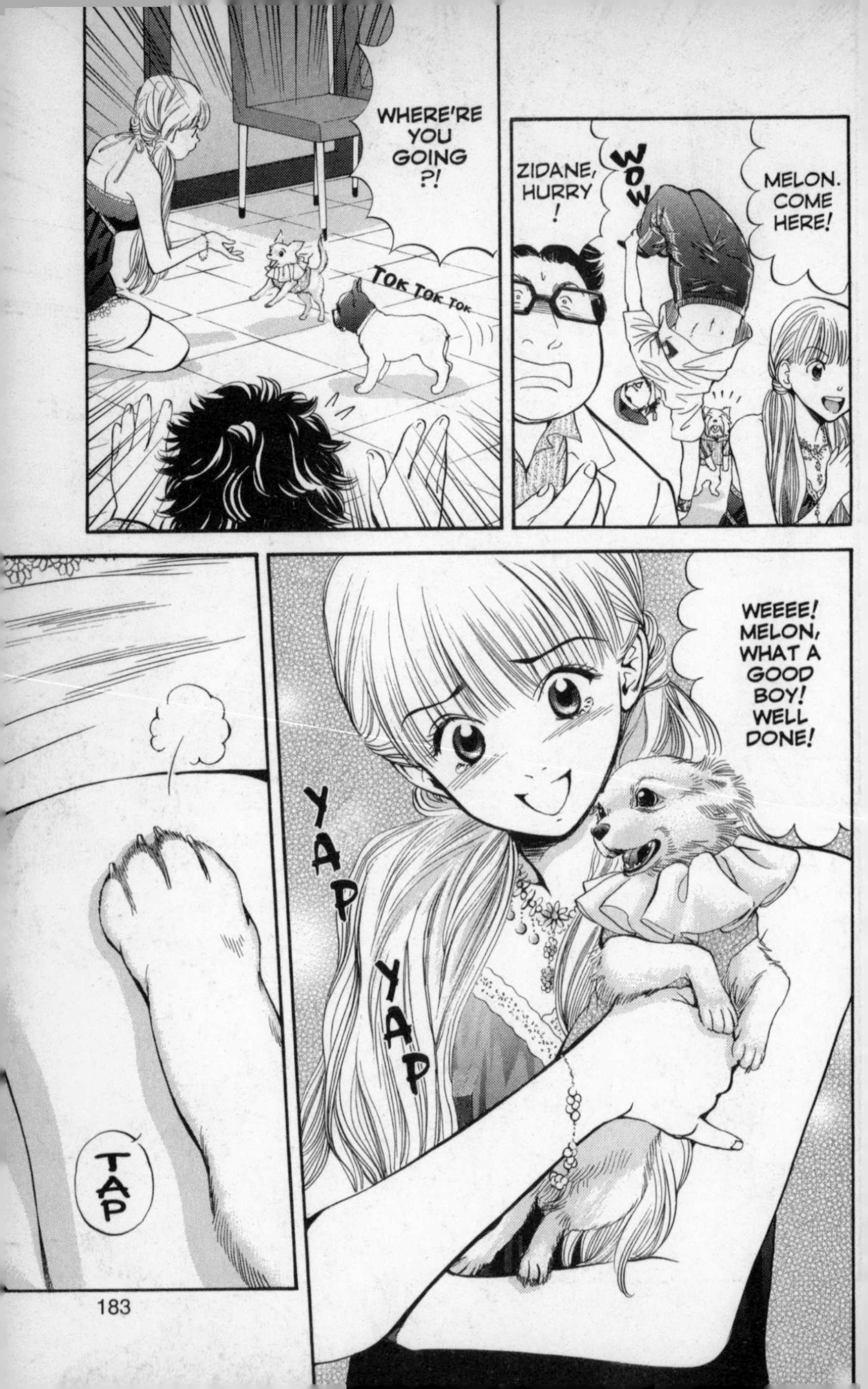
MELON. COME HERE!
WOW
ZIDANE, HURRY!
WHERE'RE YOU GOING?!
TOK TOK TOK
WEEEE! MELON, WHAT A GOOD BOY! WELL DONE!
YAP YAP
YAP YAP
TAP

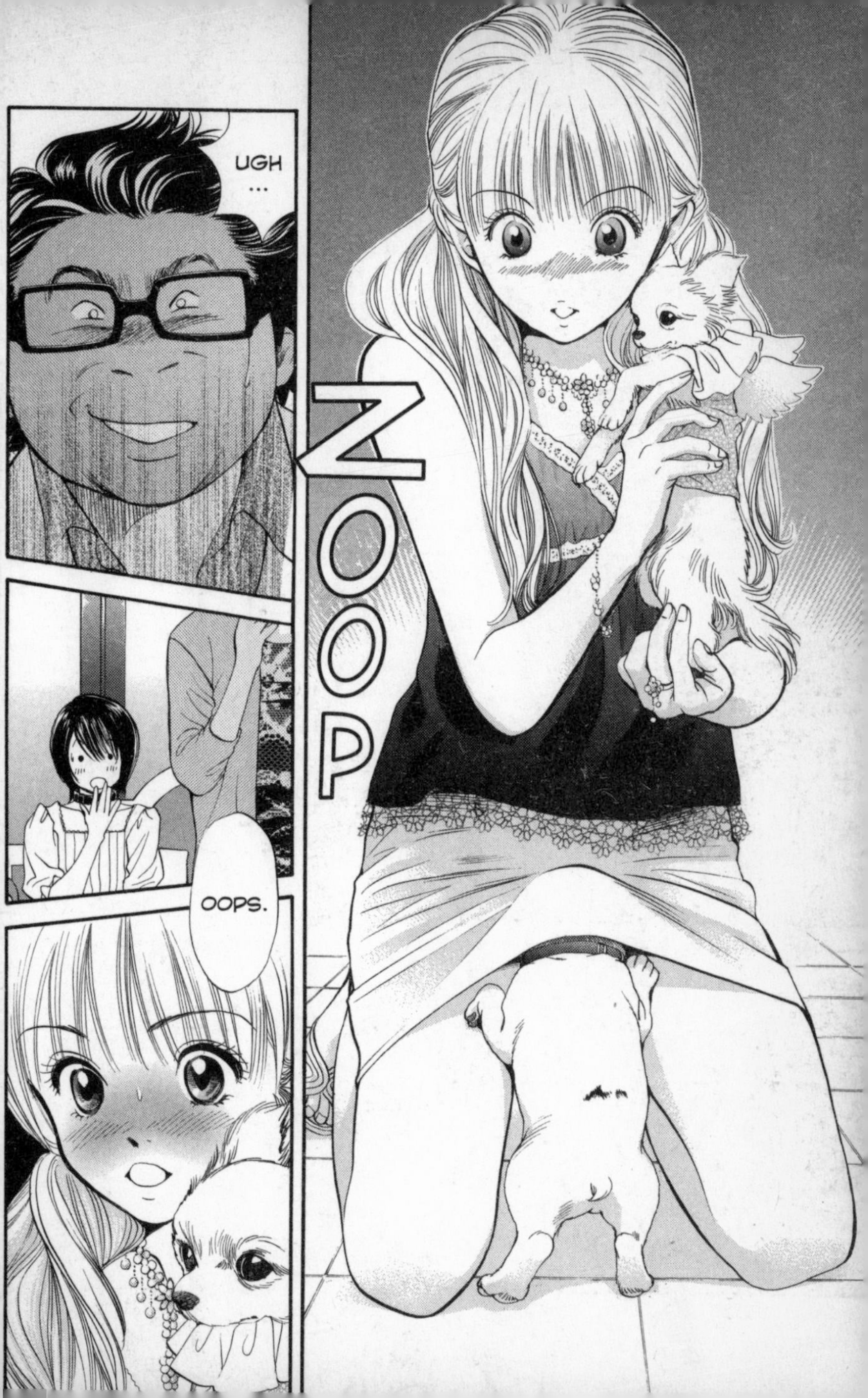
ZOOP
UGH ...
OOPS.

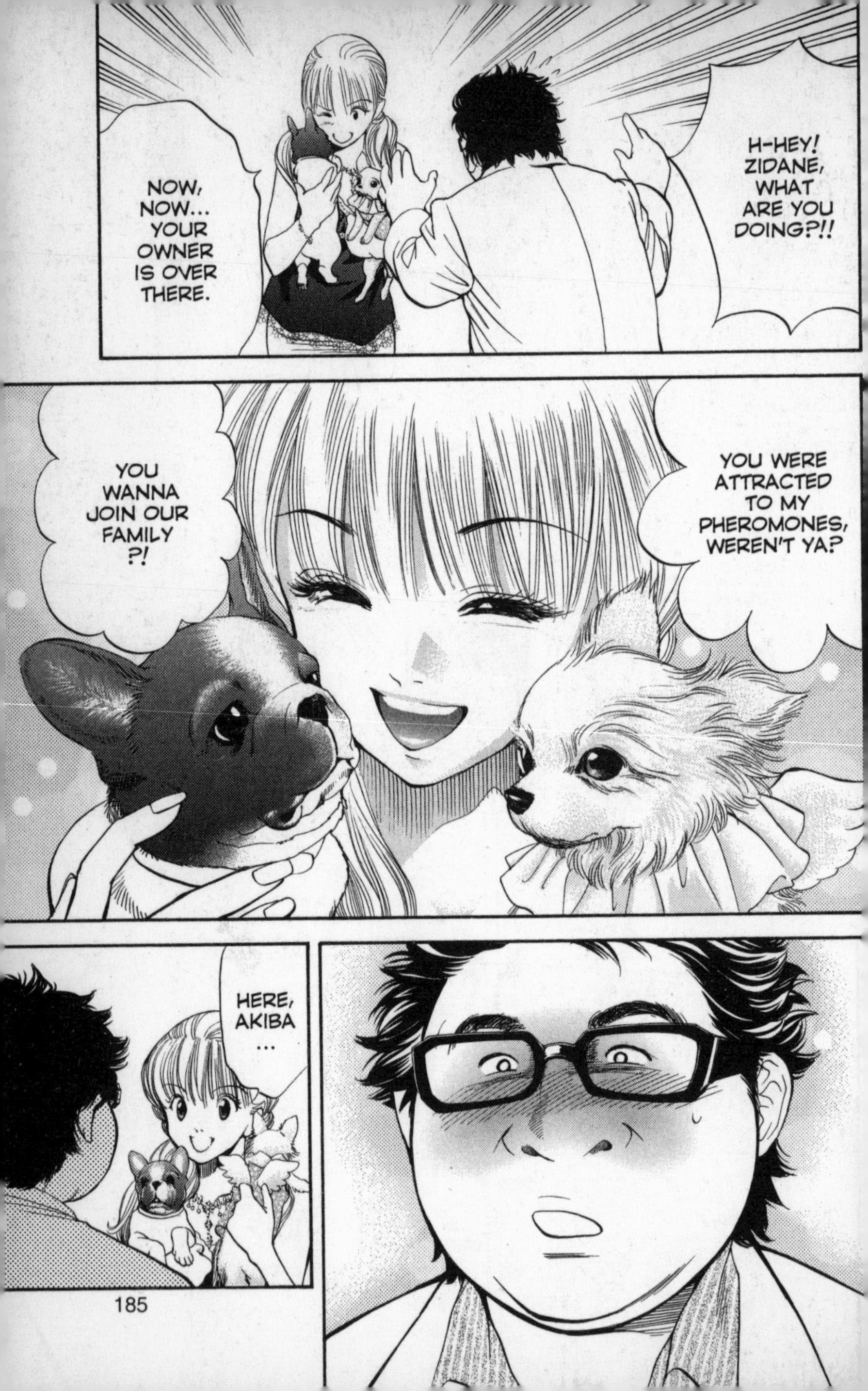
H-HEY! ZIDANE, WHAT ARE YOU DOING?!!
NOW, NOW... YOUR OWNER IS OVER THERE.
YOU WERE ATTRACTED TO MY PHEROMONES, WEREN'T YA?
YOU WANNA JOIN OUR FAMILY ?!
HERE, AKIBA ...

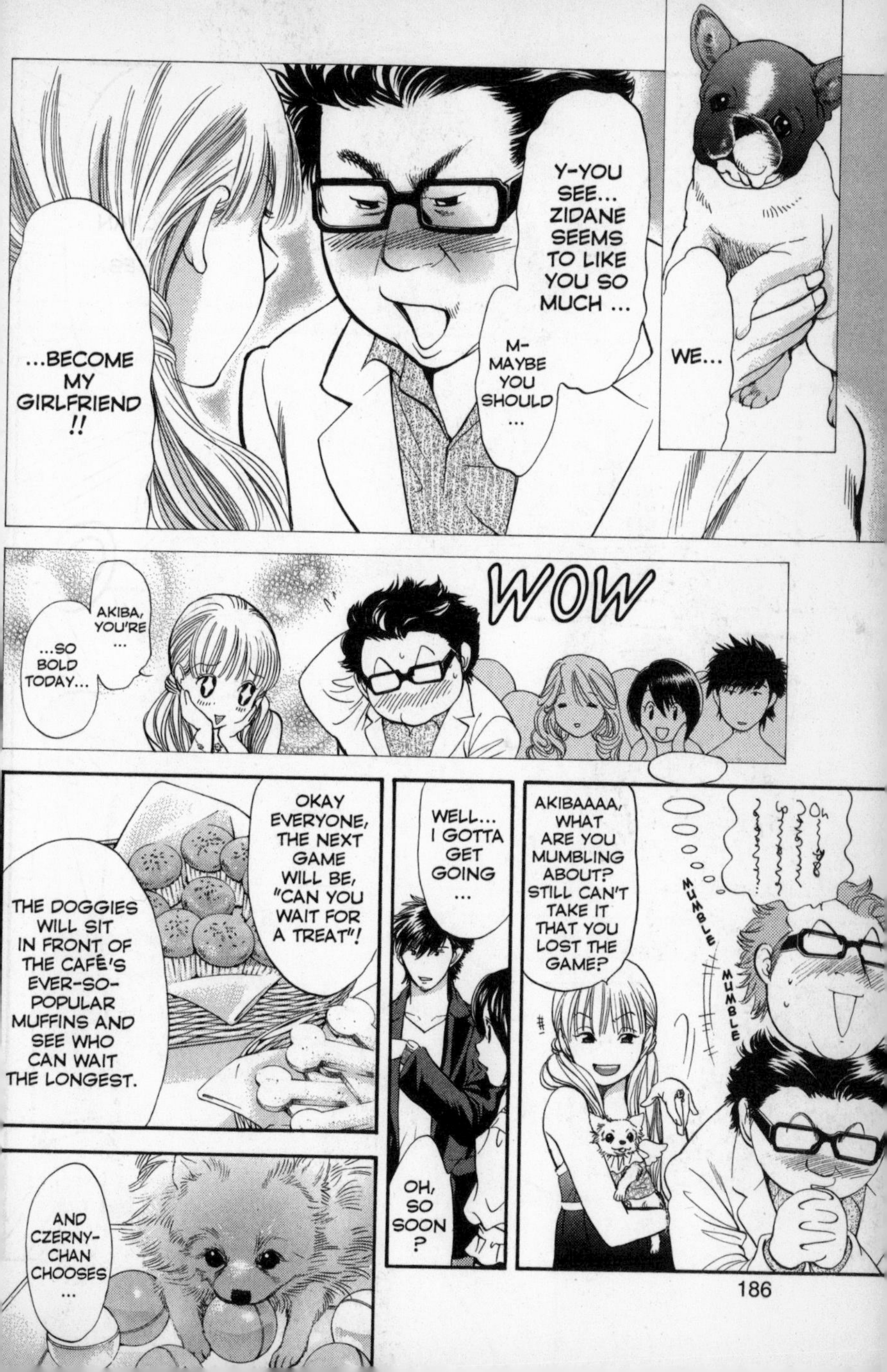
WE...
Y-YOU SEE... ZIDANE SEEMS TO LIKE YOU SO MUCH ...
M-MAYBE YOU SHOULD ...
...BECOME MY GIRLFRIEND !!
WOW
AKIBA, YOU'RE ...
...SO BOLD TODAY...
MUMBLE
MUMBLE
AKIBAAAA, WHAT ARE YOU MUMBLING ABOUT? STILL CAN'T TAKE IT THAT YOU LOST THE GAME?
WELL... I GOTTA GET GOING ...
OH, SO SOON ?
OKAY EVERYONE, THE NEXT GAME WILL BE, "CAN YOU WAIT FOR A TREAT"!
THE DOGGIES WILL SIT IN FRONT OF THE CAFÉ'S EVER-SO-POPULAR MUFFINS AND SEE WHO CAN WAIT THE LONGEST.
AND CZERNY-CHAN CHOOSES ...

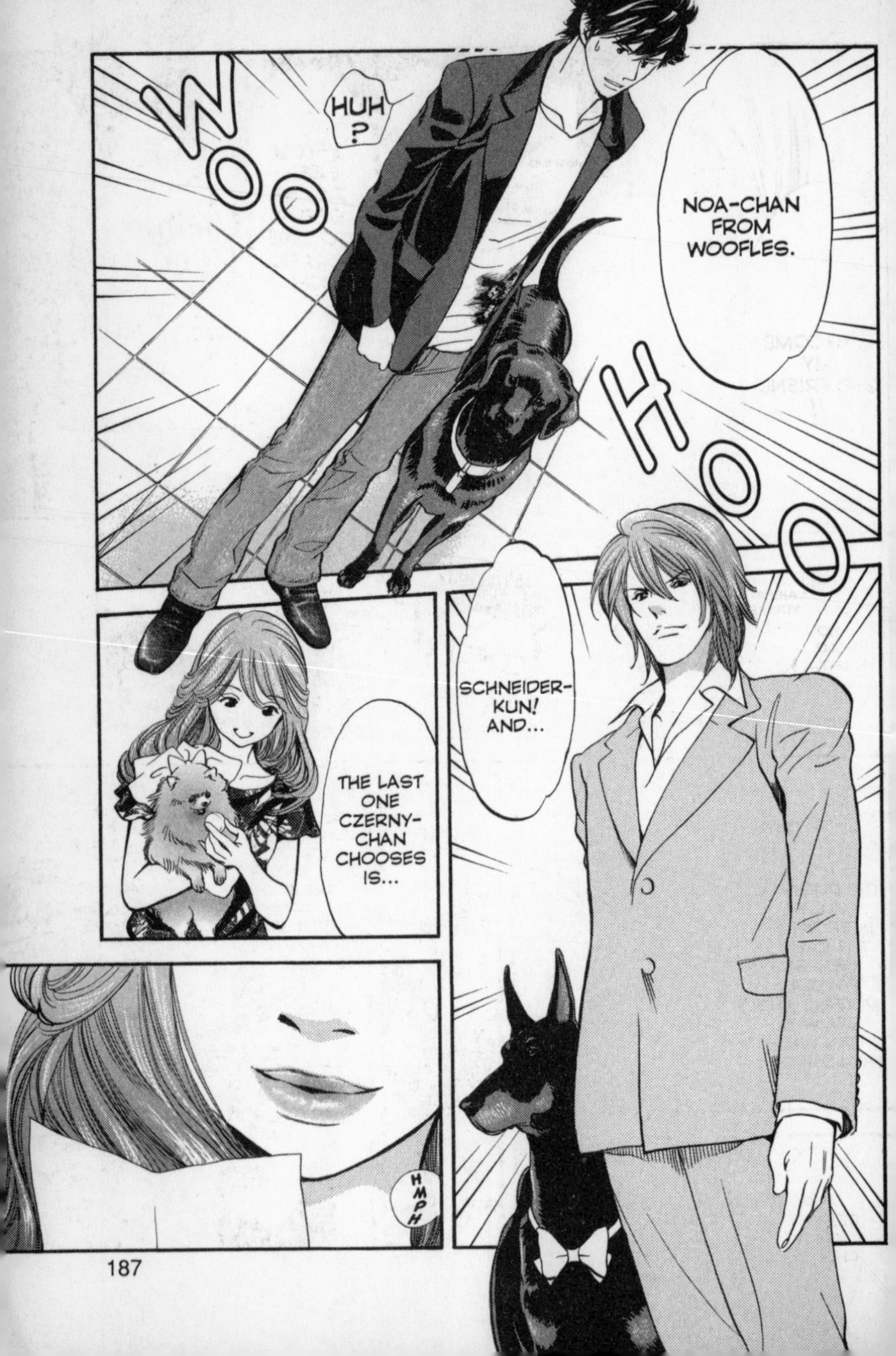
NOA-CHAN FROM WOOFLES.
WOO
HUH?
HOOO
SCHNEIDER-KUN! AND...
THE LAST ONE CZERNY-CHAN CHOOSES IS...
HMPH

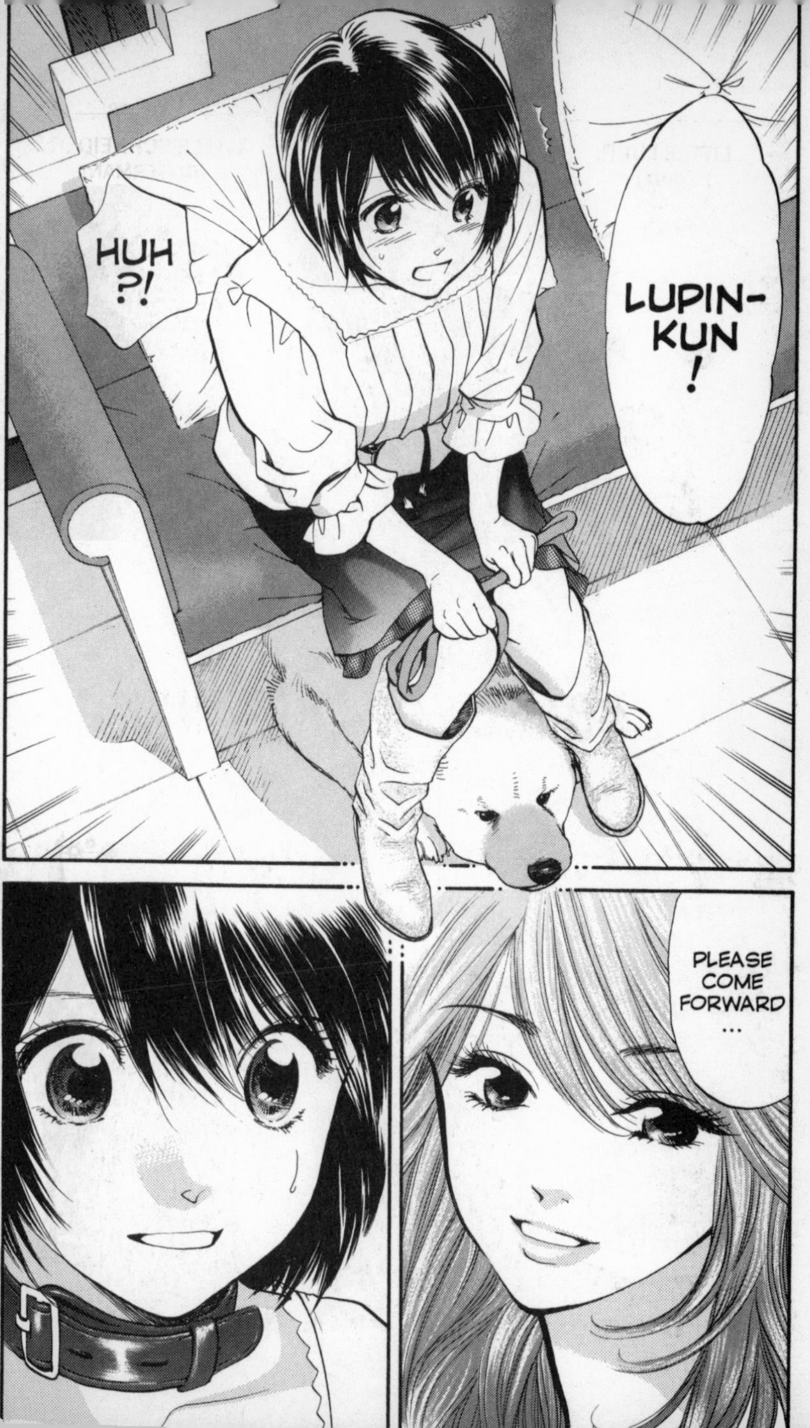
LUPIN-KUN!
HUH?!
PLEASE COME FORWARD ...

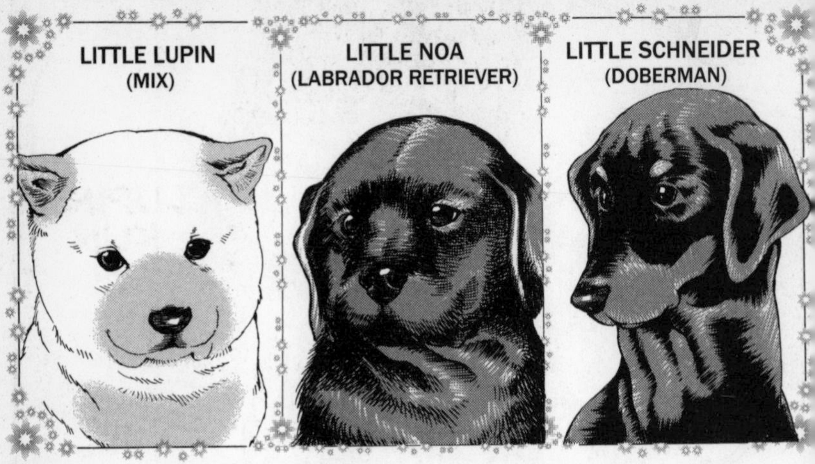
LITTLE SCHNEIDER
(DOBERMAN)
LITTLE NOA
(LABRADOR RETRIEVER)
LITTLE LUPIN
(MIX)

CHAPTER 63:
SCARED OF MUFFIN?!

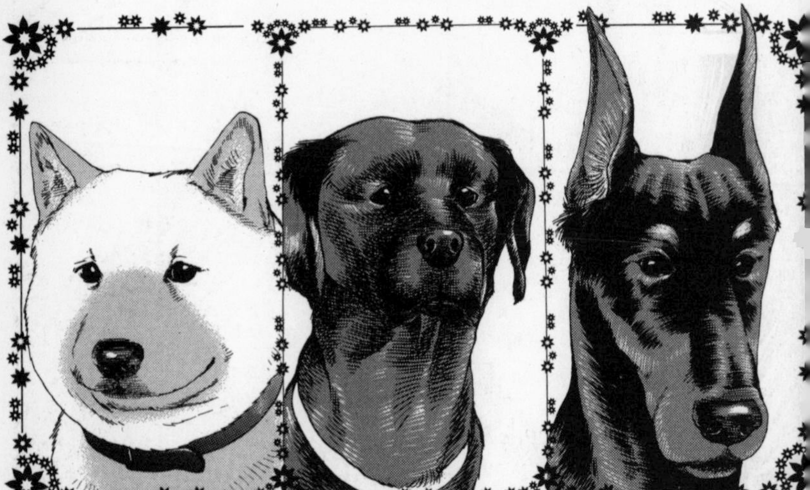

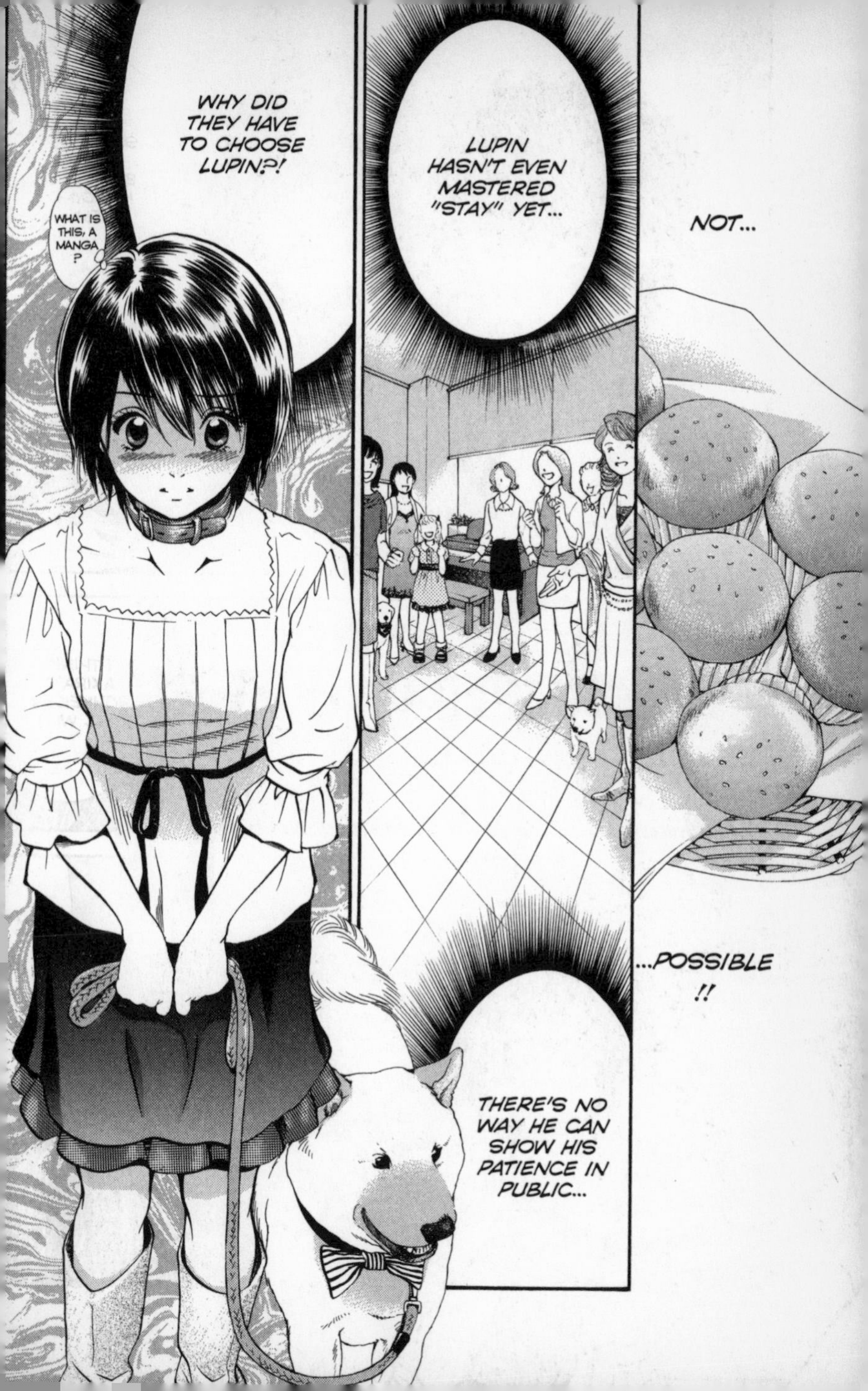
NOT...
...POSSIBLE !!
LUPIN HASN'T EVEN MASTERED "STAY" YET...
THERE'S NO WAY HE CAN SHOW HIS PATIENCE IN PUBLIC...
WHY DID THEY HAVE TO CHOOSE LUPIN?!
WHAT IS THIS, A MANGA ?

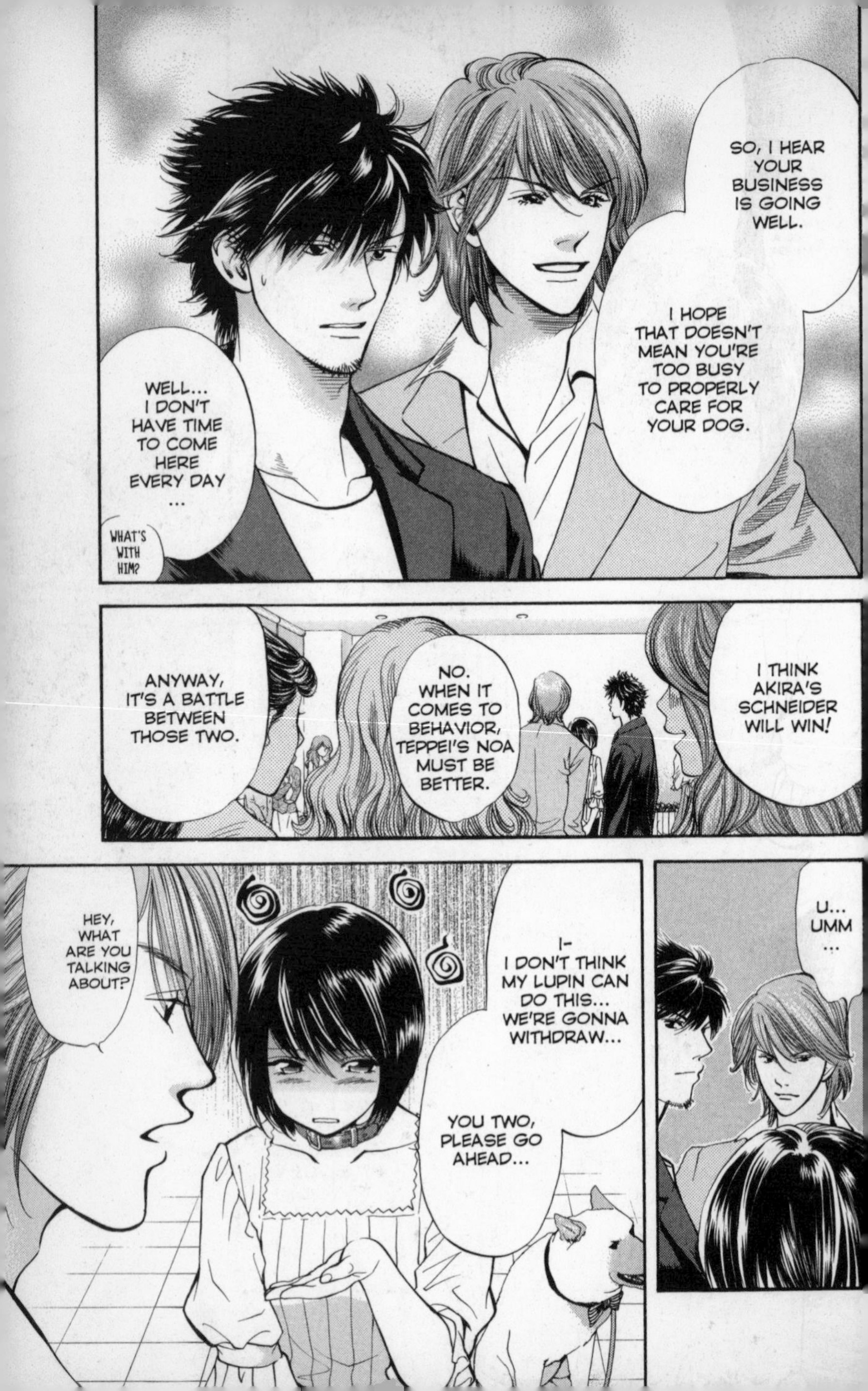
SO, I HEAR YOUR BUSINESS IS GOING WELL.
I HOPE THAT DOESN'T MEAN YOU'RE TOO BUSY TO PROPERLY CARE FOR YOUR DOG.
WELL... I DON'T HAVE TIME TO COME HERE EVERY DAY ...
WHAT'S WITH HIM?
I THINK AKIRA'S SCHNEIDER WILL WIN!
NO. WHEN IT COMES TO BEHAVIOR, TEPPEI'S NOA MUST BE BETTER.
ANYWAY, IT'S A BATTLE BETWEEN THOSE TWO.
U... UMM ...
I- I DON'T THINK MY LUPIN CAN DO THIS... WE'RE GONNA WITHDRAW...
YOU TWO, PLEASE GO AHEAD...
HEY, WHAT ARE YOU TALKING ABOUT?

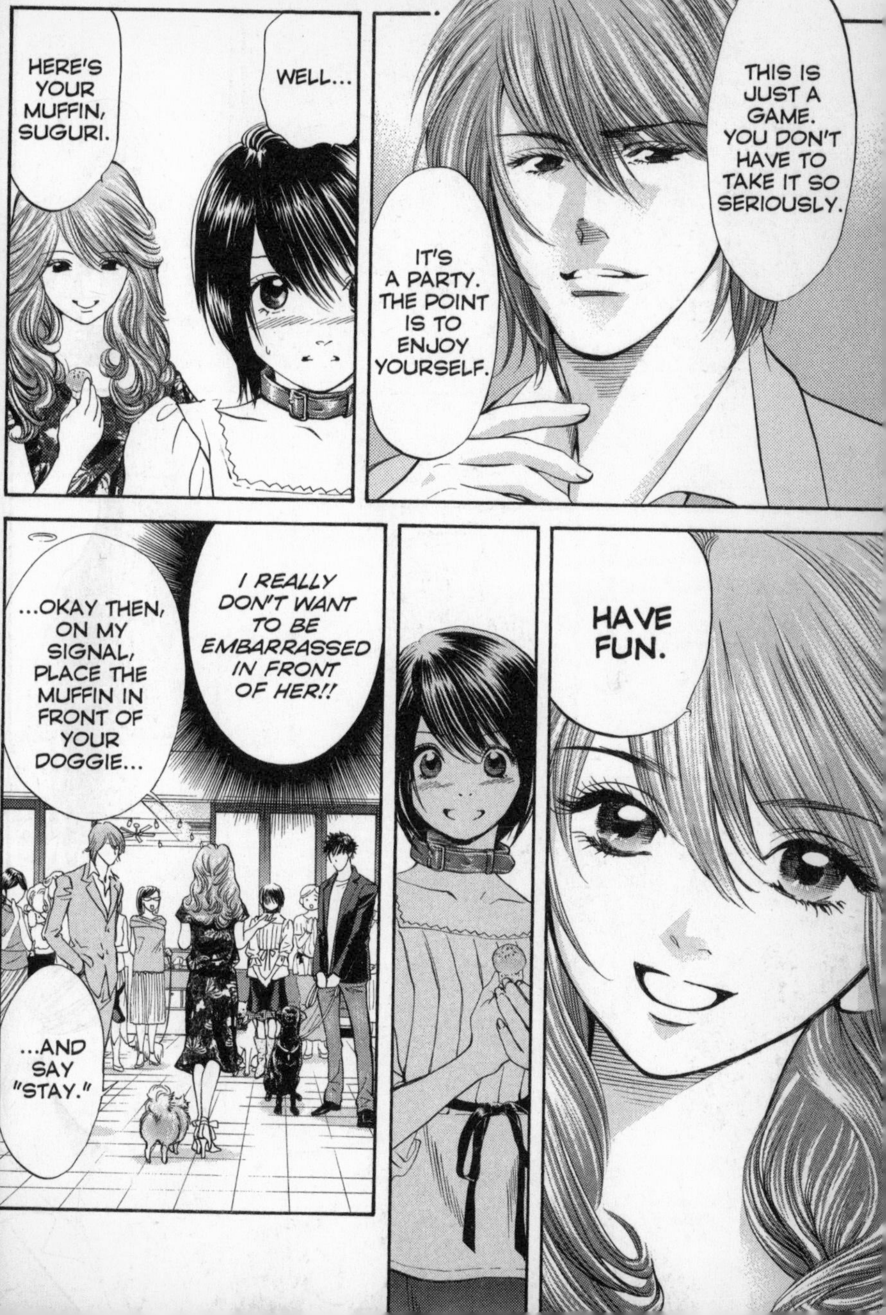
THIS IS JUST A GAME. YOU DON'T HAVE TO TAKE IT SO SERIOUSLY.
IT'S A PARTY. THE POINT IS TO ENJOY YOURSELF.
WELL...
HERE'S YOUR MUFFIN, SUGURI.
HAVE FUN.
I REALLY DON'T WANT TO BE EMBARRASSED IN FRONT OF HER!!
...OKAY THEN, ON MY SIGNAL, PLACE THE MUFFIN IN FRONT OF YOUR DOGGIE...
...AND SAY "STAY."

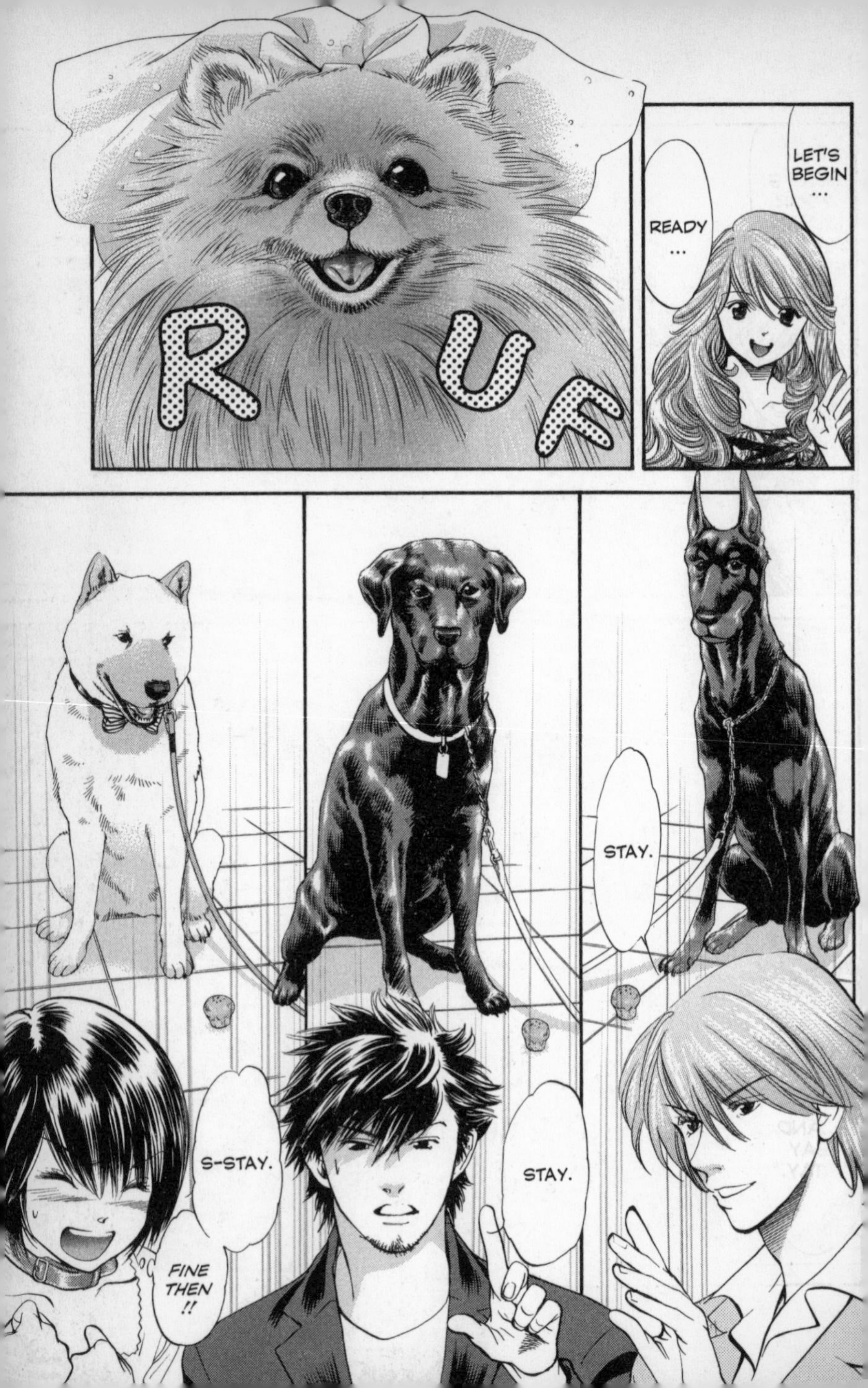

LET'S BEGIN ...
READY ...
RUF
STAY.
STAY.
S-STAY.
FINE THEN !!

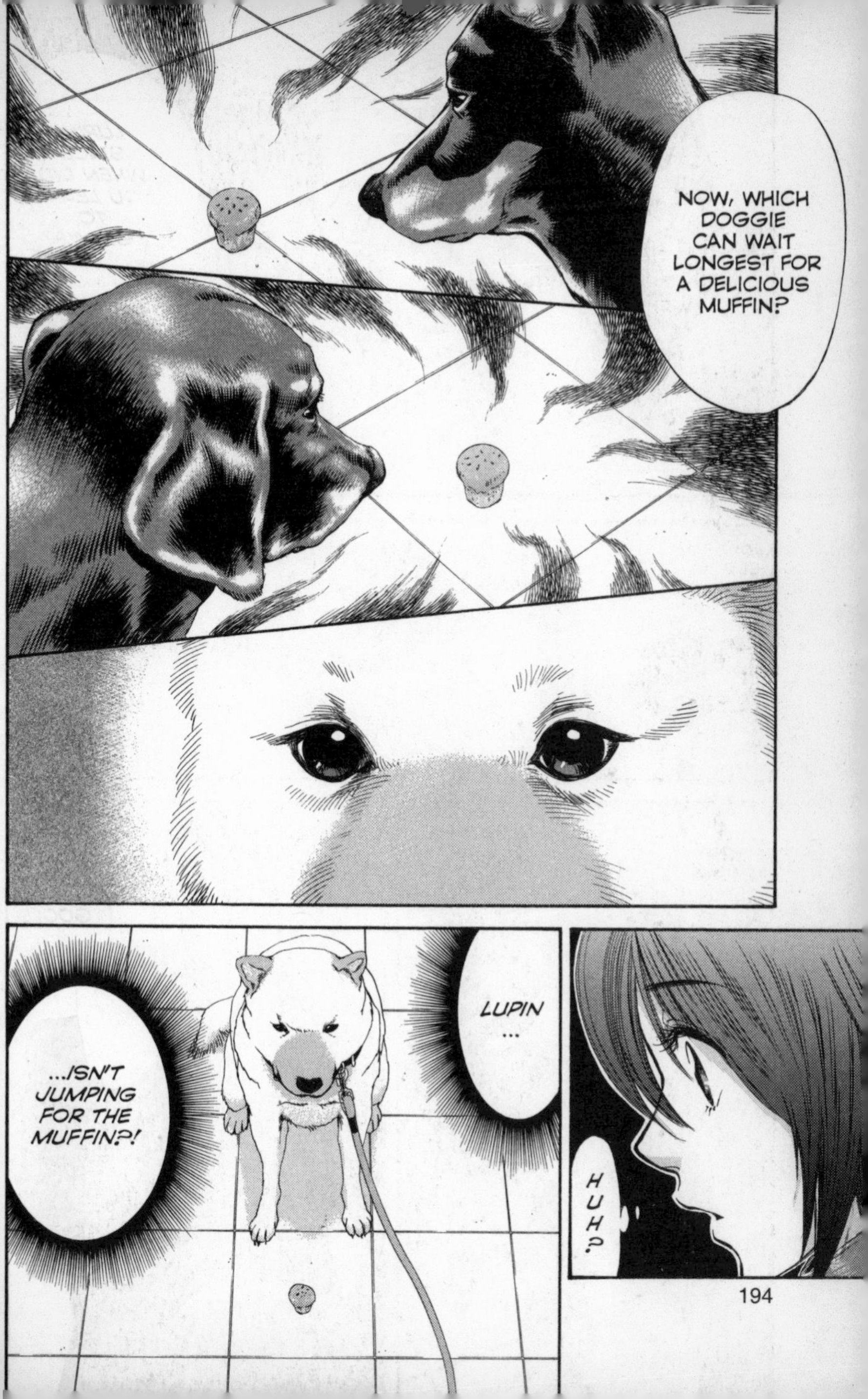
NOW, WHICH DOGGIE CAN WAIT LONGEST FOR A DELICIOUS MUFFIN?
HUH?
LUPIN ...
...ISN'T JUMPING FOR THE MUFFIN?!

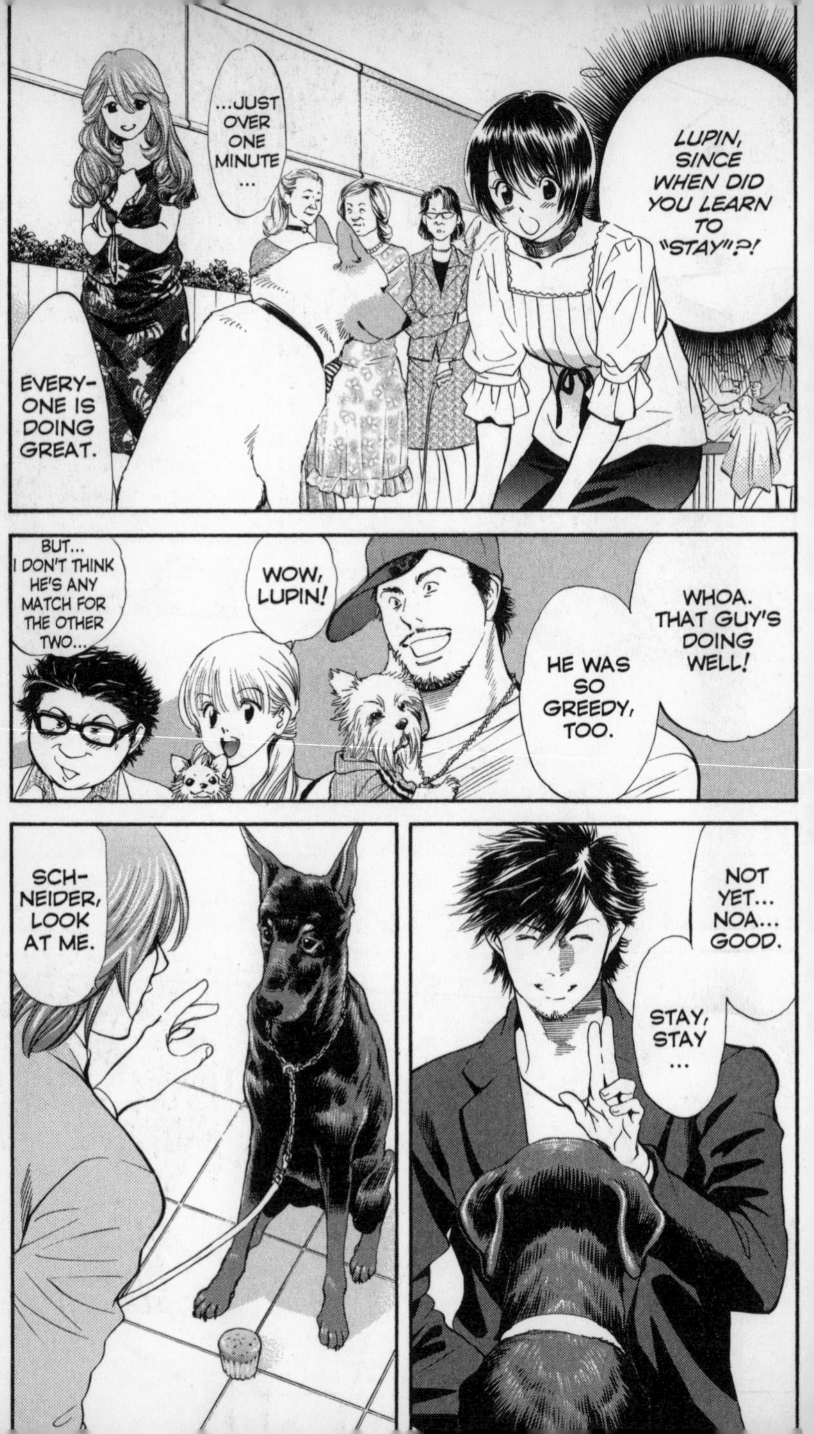
LUPIN, SINCE WHEN DID YOU LEARN TO "STAY"?!
...JUST OVER ONE MINUTE ...
EVERY-ONE IS DOING GREAT.
WHOA. THAT GUY'S DOING WELL!
HE WAS SO GREEDY, TOO.
WOW, LUPIN!
BUT... I DON'T THINK HE'S ANY MATCH FOR THE OTHER TWO...
NOT YET... NOA... GOOD.
STAY, STAY ...
SCH-NEIDER, LOOK AT ME.

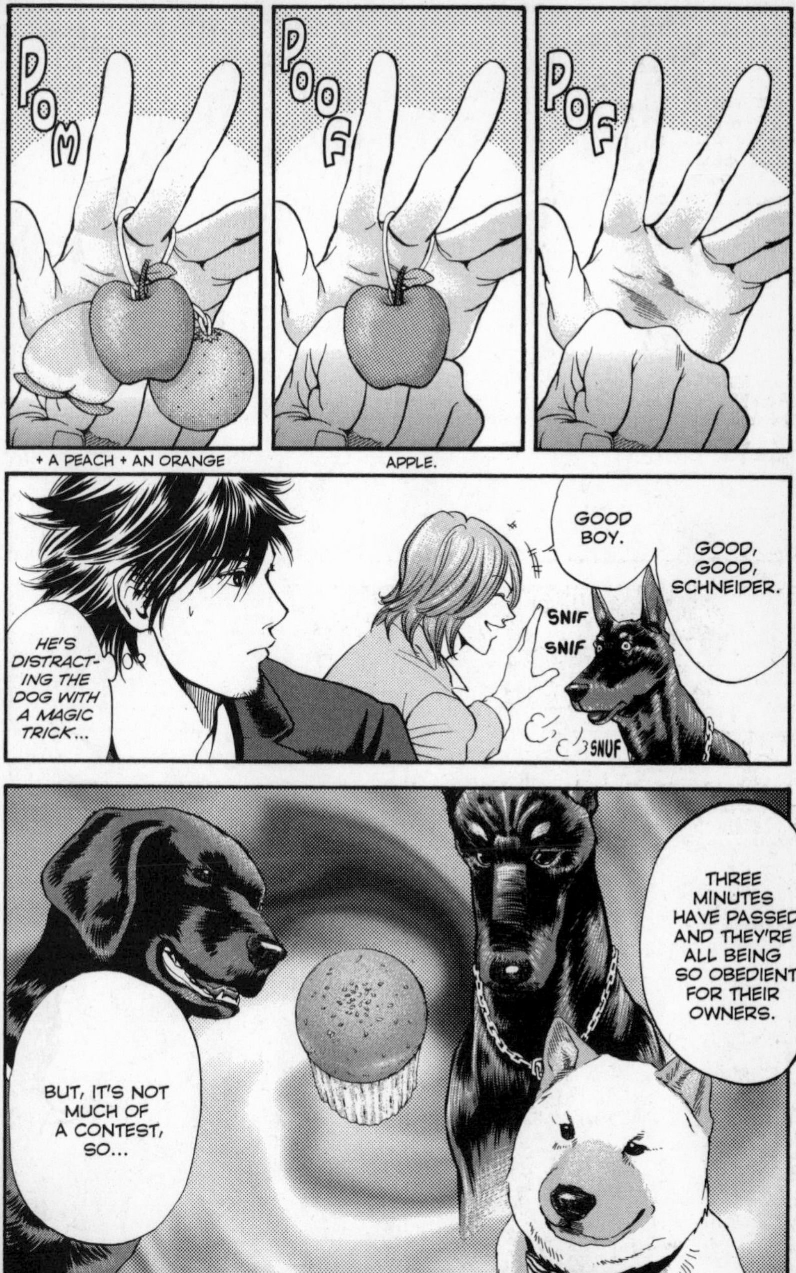

POF
POOF
APPLE.
POM
+ A PEACH + AN ORANGE
GOOD, GOOD, SCHNEIDER.
GOOD BOY.
SNIF SNIF
SNUF
HE'S DISTRACT-ING THE DOG WITH A MAGIC TRICK...
THREE MINUTES HAVE PASSED AND THEY'RE ALL BEING SO OBEDIENT FOR THEIR OWNERS.
BUT, IT'S NOT MUCH OF A CONTEST, SO...

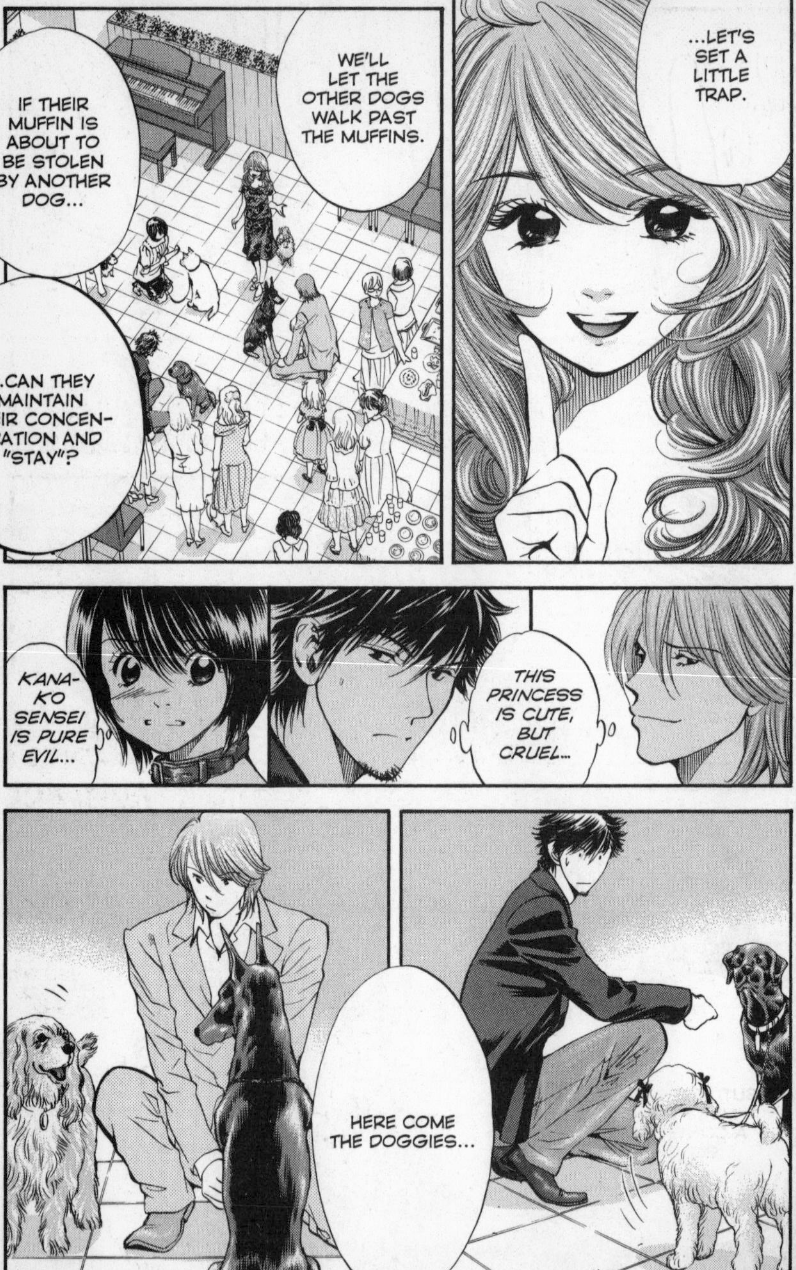
...LET'S SET A LITTLE TRAP.
WE'LL LET THE OTHER DOGS WALK PAST THE MUFFINS.
IF THEIR MUFFIN IS ABOUT TO BE STOLEN BY ANOTHER DOG...
...CAN THEY MAINTAIN THEIR CONCENTRATION AND "STAY"?
THIS PRINCESS IS CUTE, BUT CRUEL...
KANAKO SENSEI IS PURE EVIL...
HERE COME THE DOGGIES...

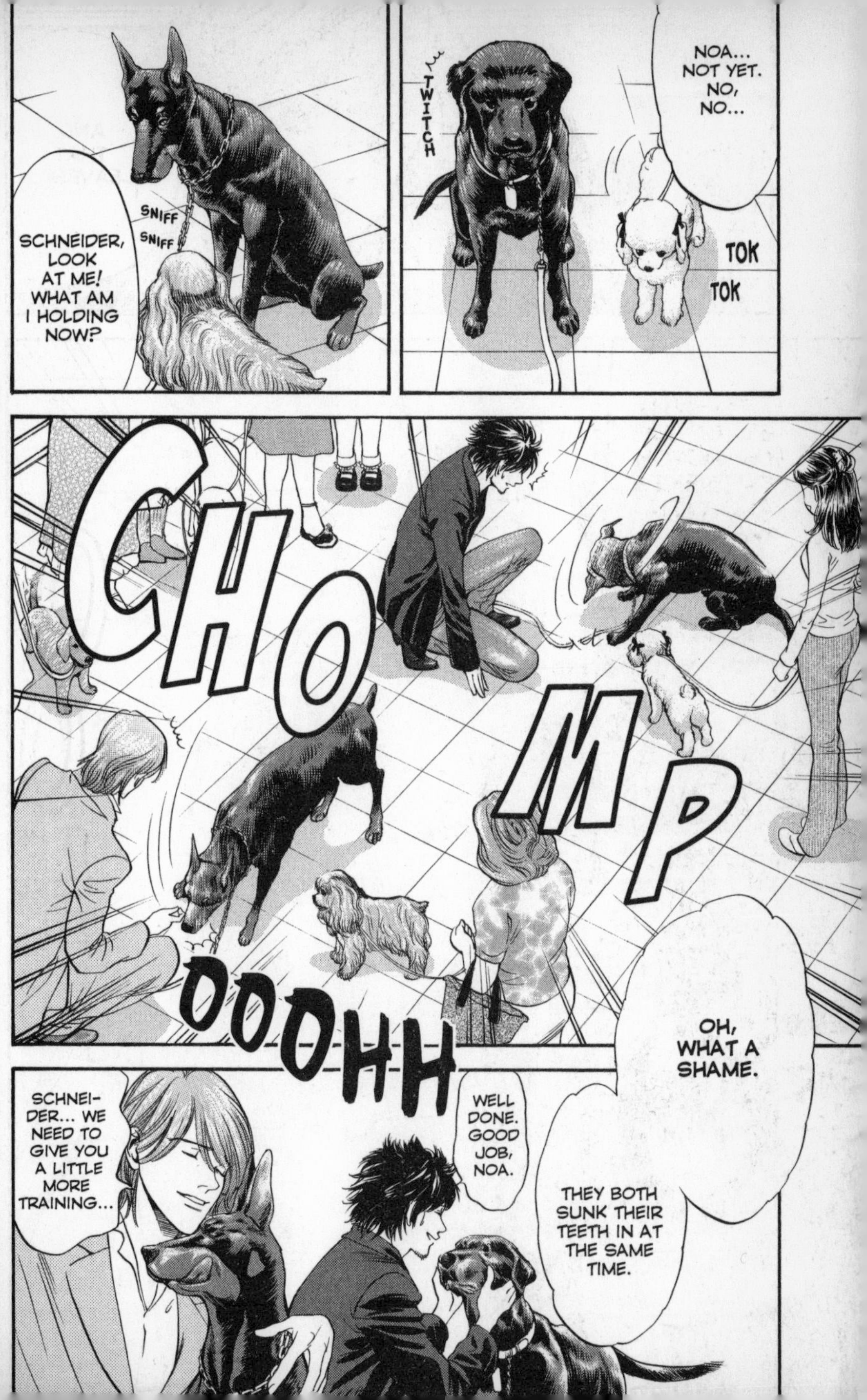
NOA... NOT YET. NO, NO...
TWITCH
TOK
TOK
SNIFF
SNIFF
SCHNEIDER, LOOK AT ME! WHAT AM I HOLDING NOW?
CHOMP
OOOOHH
OH, WHAT A SHAME.
THEY BOTH SUNK THEIR TEETH IN AT THE SAME TIME.
WELL DONE. GOOD JOB, NOA.
SCHNEI-DER... WE NEED TO GIVE YOU A LITTLE MORE TRAINING...

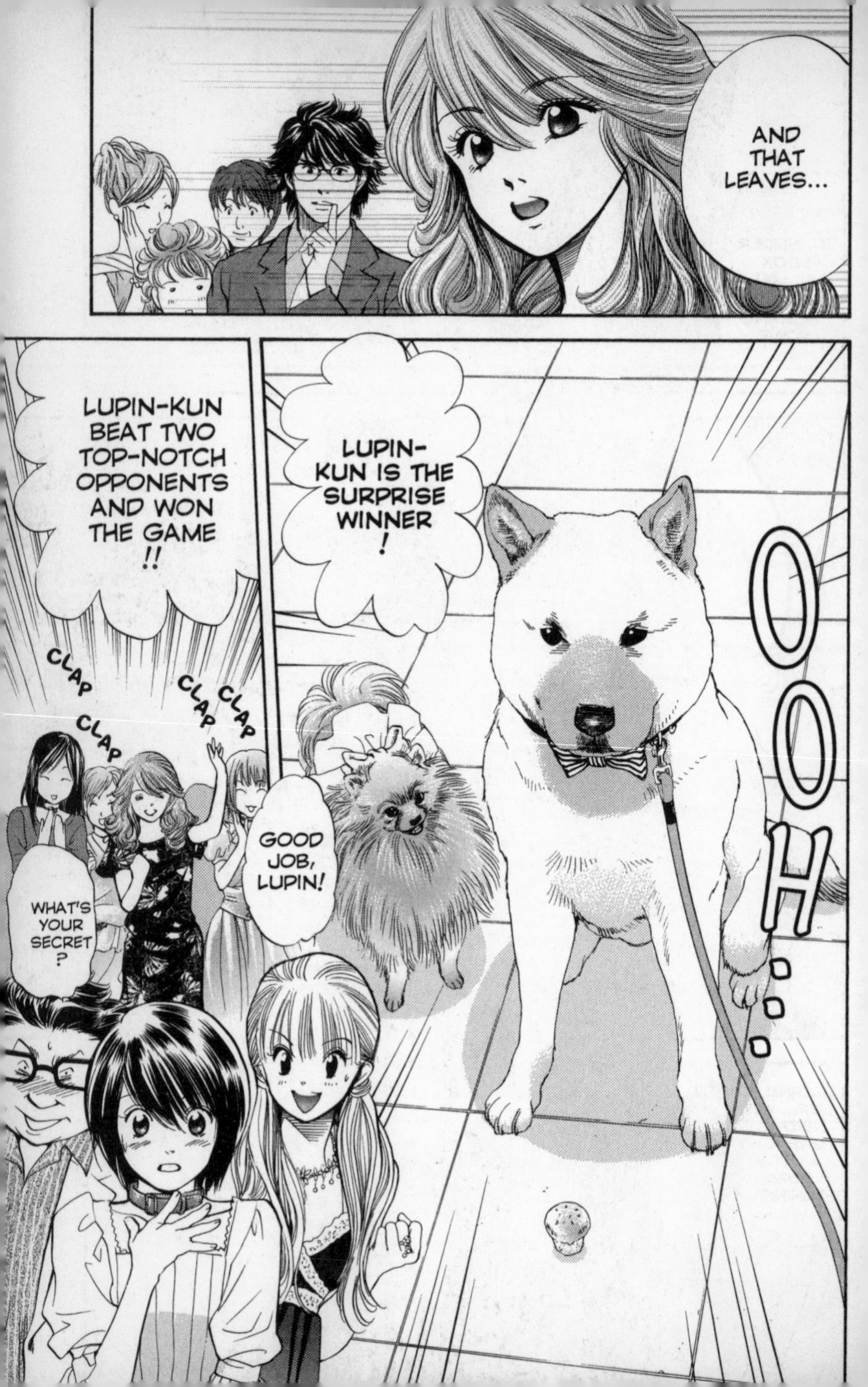
AND THAT LEAVES...
OOOH...
LUPIN-KUN IS THE SURPRISE WINNER!
LUPIN-KUN BEAT TWO TOP-NOTCH OPPONENTS AND WON THE GAME!!
CLAP CLAP CLAP CLAP
GOOD JOB, LUPIN!
WHAT'S YOUR SECRET?

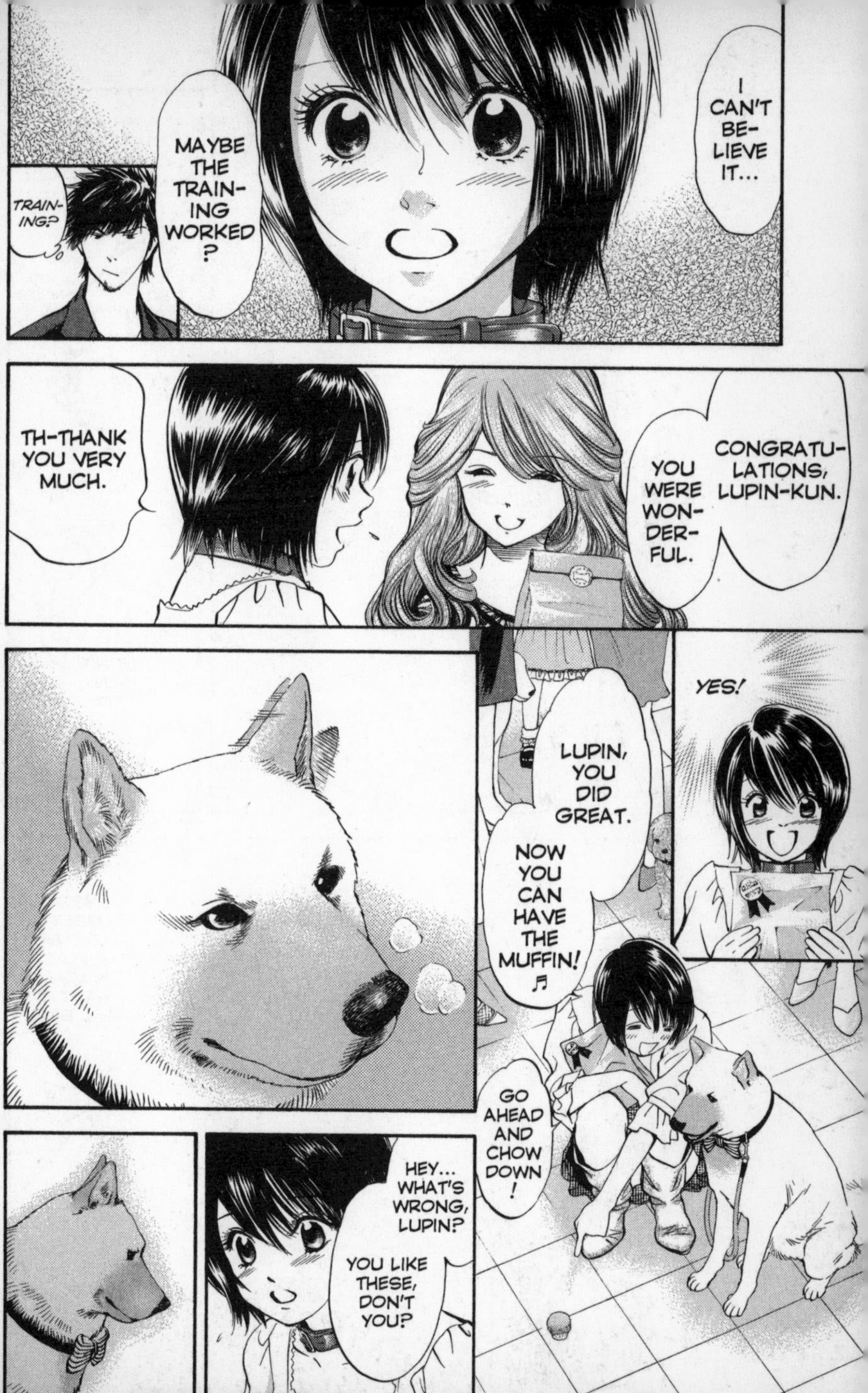
I CAN'T BE-LIEVE IT...
MAYBE THE TRAIN-ING WORKED?
TRAIN-ING?
CONGRATU-LATIONS, LUPIN-KUN.
YOU WERE WON-DER-FUL.
TH-THANK YOU VERY MUCH.
YES!
LUPIN, YOU DID GREAT.
NOW YOU CAN HAVE THE MUFFIN! ♬
GO AHEAD AND CHOW DOWN!
HEY... WHAT'S WRONG, LUPIN?
YOU LIKE THESE, DON'T YOU?

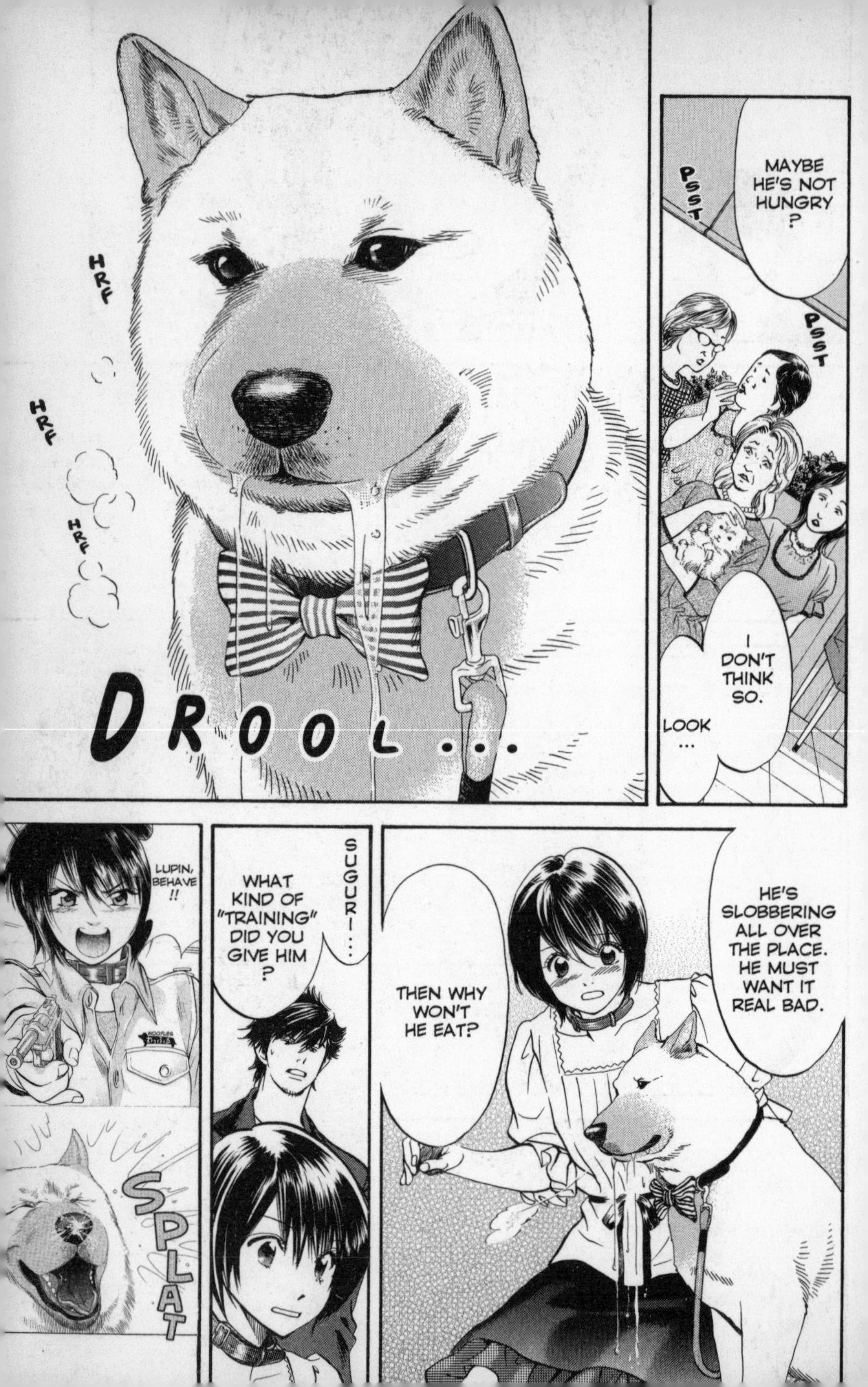
PSST
MAYBE HE'S NOT HUNGRY ?
PSST
I DON'T THINK SO.
LOOK ...
HRF
HRF
HRF
DROOL...
HE'S SLOBBERING ALL OVER THE PLACE. HE MUST WANT IT REAL BAD.
THEN WHY WON'T HE EAT?
SUGURI...
WHAT KIND OF "TRAINING" DID YOU GIVE HIM ?
LUPIN, BEHAVE !!
SPLAT

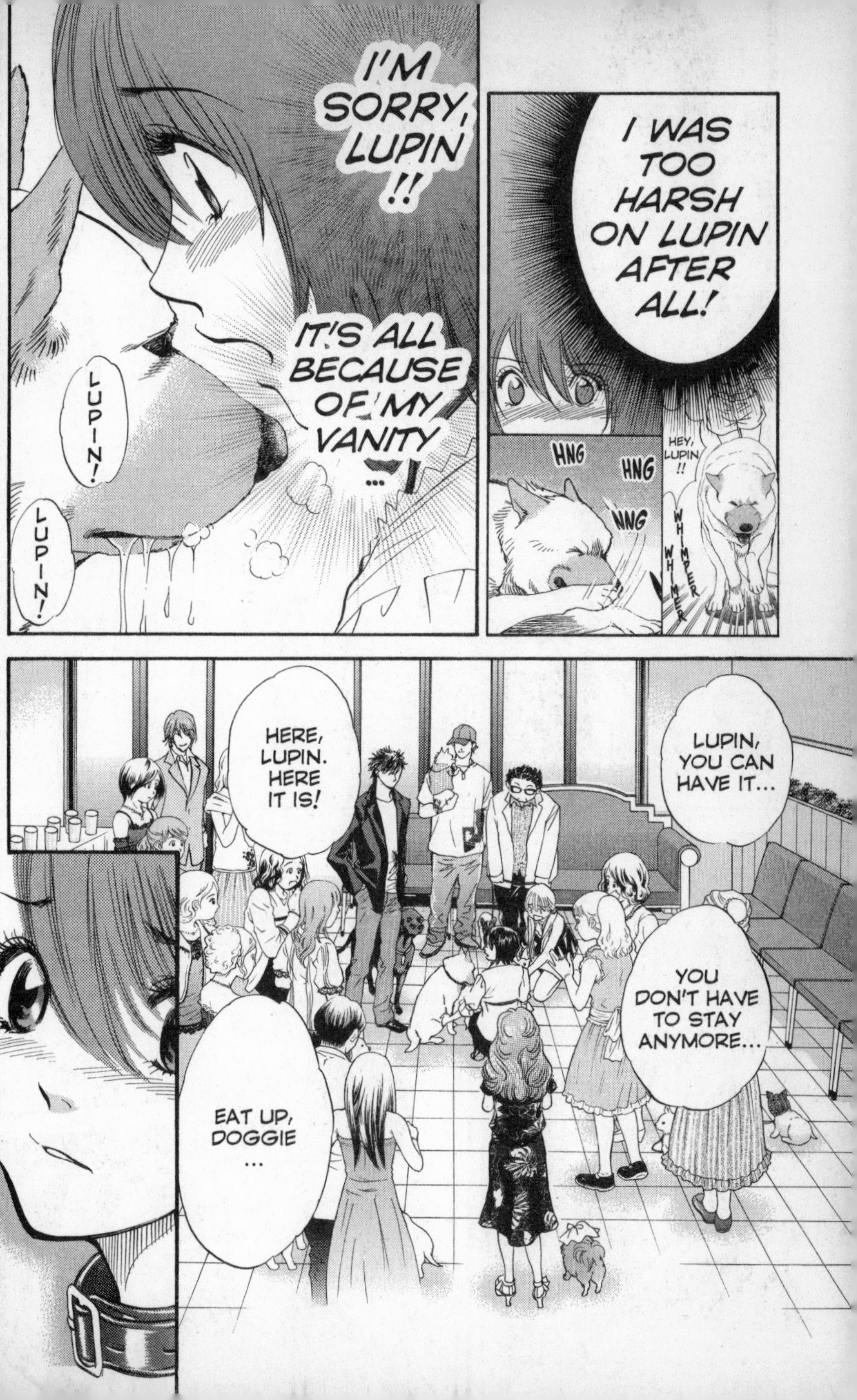
I WAS TOO HARSH ON LUPIN AFTER ALL!
HEY, LUPIN!!
WHIMPER
WHIMPER
HNG
HNG
NNG
I'M SORRY, LUPIN!!
IT'S ALL BECAUSE OF MY VANITY...
LUPIN!
LUPIN!
LUPIN, YOU CAN HAVE IT...
YOU DON'T HAVE TO STAY ANYMORE...
HERE, LUPIN. HERE IT IS!
EAT UP, DOGGIE...

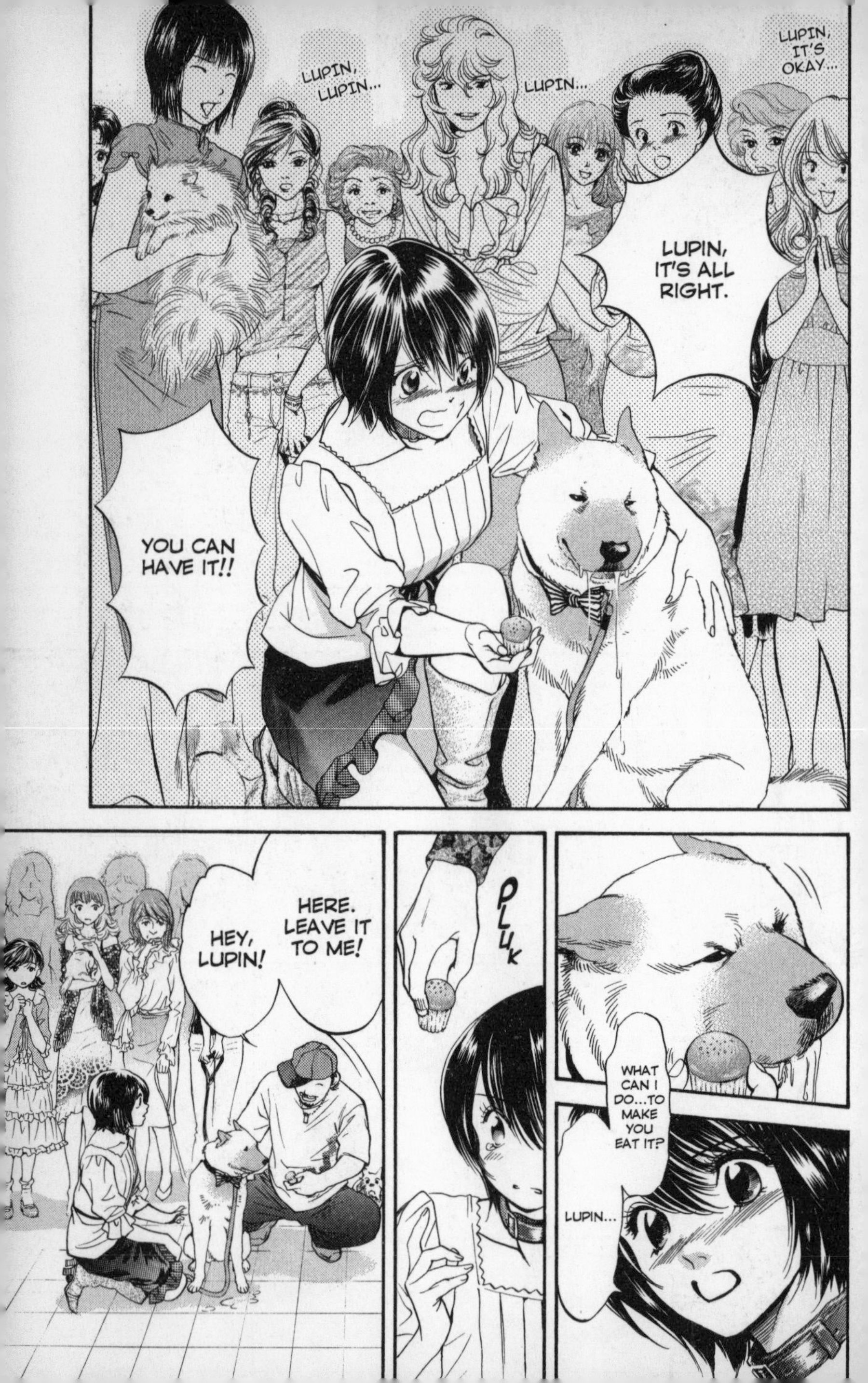
LUPIN, IT'S OKAY...
LUPIN...
LUPIN, LUPIN...
LUPIN, IT'S ALL RIGHT.
YOU CAN HAVE IT!!
WHAT CAN I DO...TO MAKE YOU EAT IT?
LUPIN...
PLUK
HERE. LEAVE IT TO ME!
HEY, LUPIN!

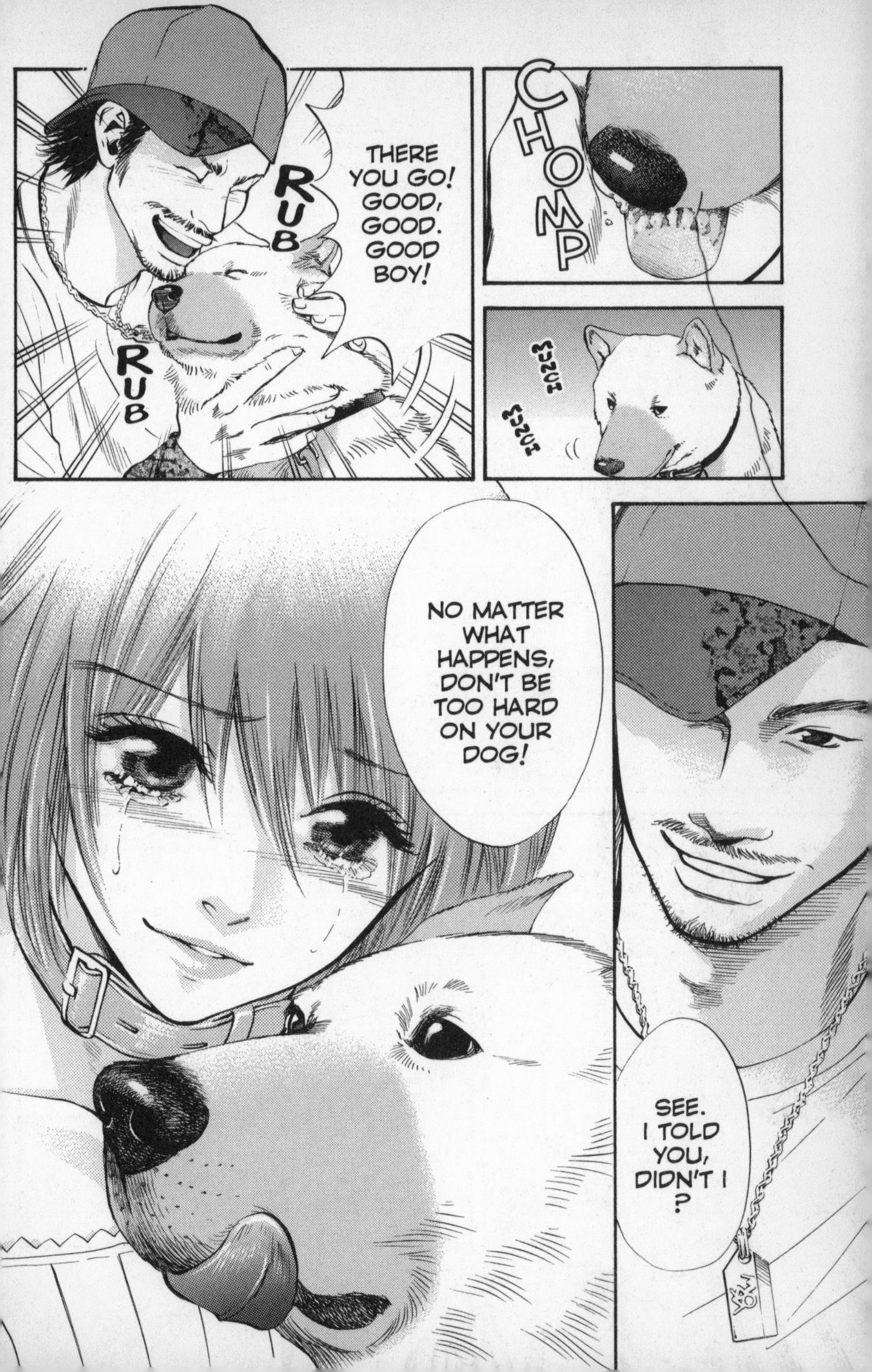
CHOMP
MUNCH MUNCH
THERE YOU GO! GOOD, GOOD. GOOD BOY!
RUB RUB
SEE. I TOLD YOU, DIDN'T I ?
NO MATTER WHAT HAPPENS, DON'T BE TOO HARD ON YOUR DOG!

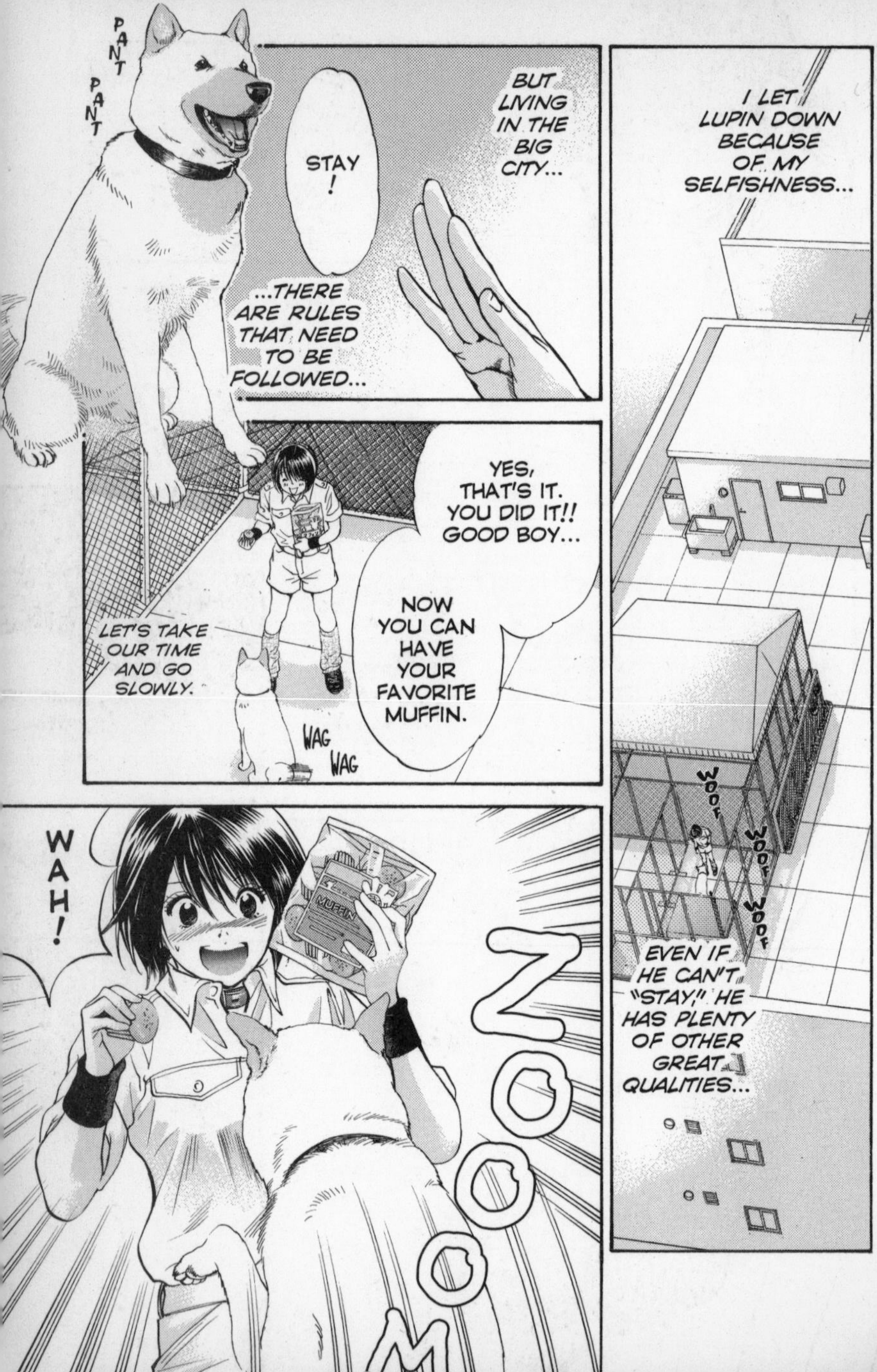
I LET LUPIN DOWN BECAUSE OF MY SELFISHNESS...
WOOF
WOOF
WOOF
EVEN IF HE CAN'T "STAY," HE HAS PLENTY OF OTHER GREAT QUALITIES...
BUT LIVING IN THE BIG CITY...
STAY!
...THERE ARE RULES THAT NEED TO BE FOLLOWED...
PANT PANT
YES, THAT'S IT. YOU DID IT!! GOOD BOY...
NOW YOU CAN HAVE YOUR FAVORITE MUFFIN.
WAG WAG
LET'S TAKE OUR TIME AND GO SLOWLY.
ZOOOM
MUFFIN
WAH!

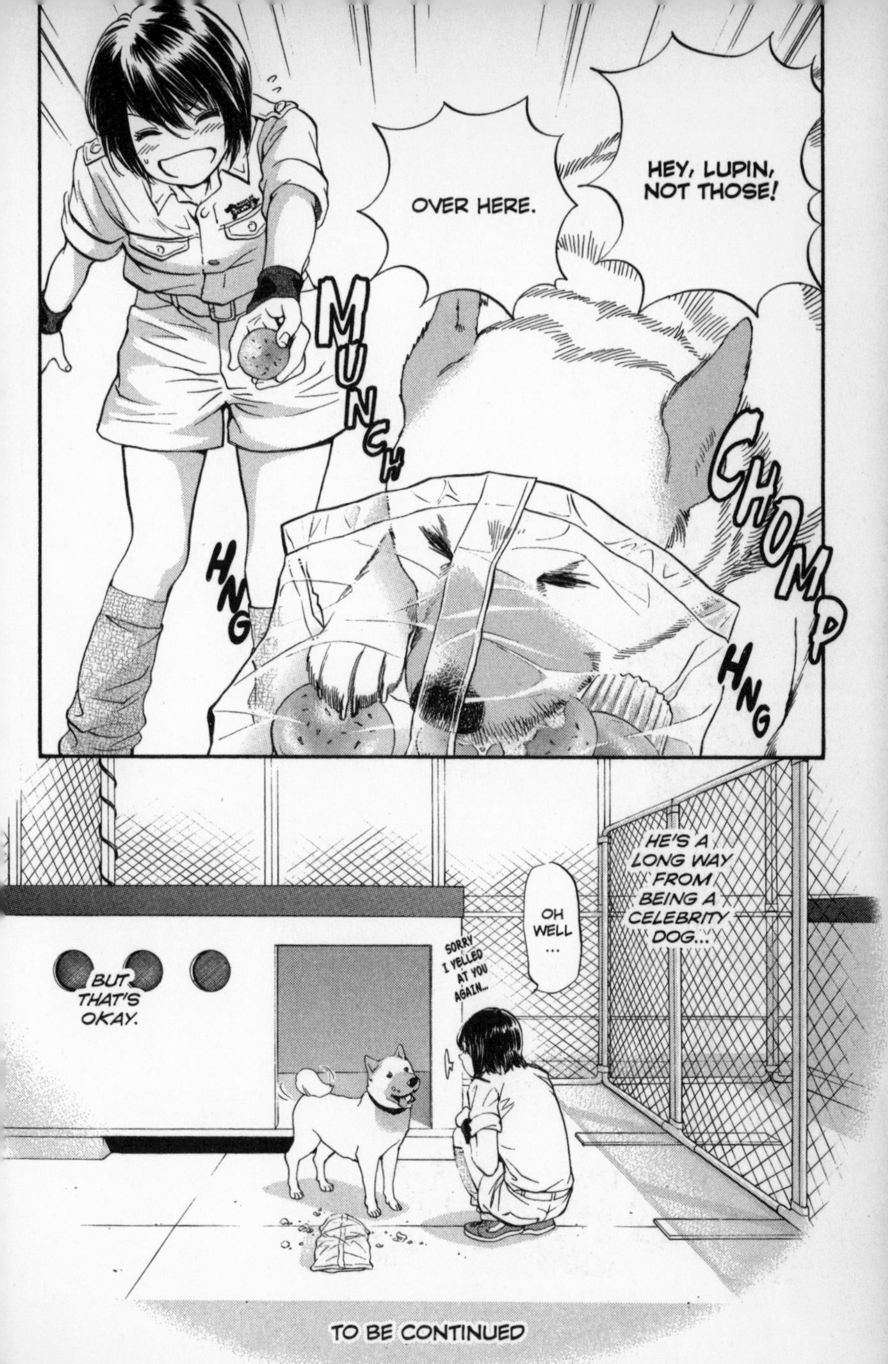
HEY, LUPIN, NOT THOSE!
OVER HERE.
CHOMP
HNG
MUNCH
HNG
HE'S A LONG WAY FROM BEING A CELEBRITY DOG...
OH WELL ...
SORRY I YELLED AT YOU AGAIN...
BUT THAT'S OKAY.
TO BE CONTINUED

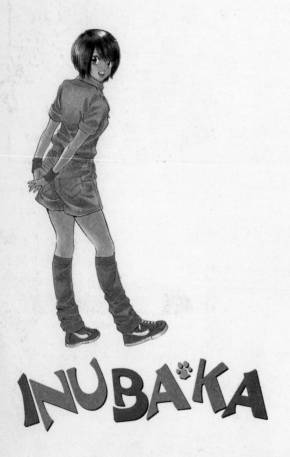

INUBA✦KA

INUBAKA

Everybody's Crazy for Dogs!

From Holee-san in Tokyo

🐾 Tiara-chan (Miniature Dachshund)

This dog-loving woman bought a dog without telling her husband. She kept the dog at her parents' for a while and later brought it home to ask her husband if she could keep it. Seeing how cute the dog was, the husband wished that they could have kept the dog from the start.

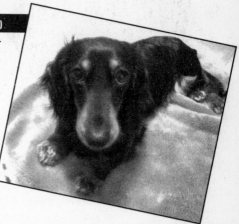

Yukiya Sakuragi

A tactical victory for the wife? But there is no way you can say, "No, we can't keep it" in front of a dog this cute. It must have been even cuter when it was a puppy! The husband must regret not having been able to see the best of its cute puppy years.

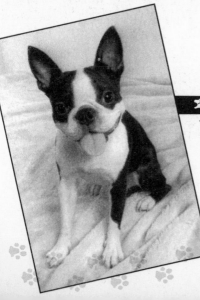

From Sakamoto-san in Tokyo

🐾 Tora-kun (Boston Terrier)

Tora turns four this July. The owner loves the feeling of its cheeks, so Tora-kun is kissed there all the time.

Yukiya Sakuragi

Great face (lol). Boston Terriers have a smiley face that makes us smile too! I want to feel its floppy skin...

From Takahashi-san in Shiga prefecture

Pepe-kun (Mutt)

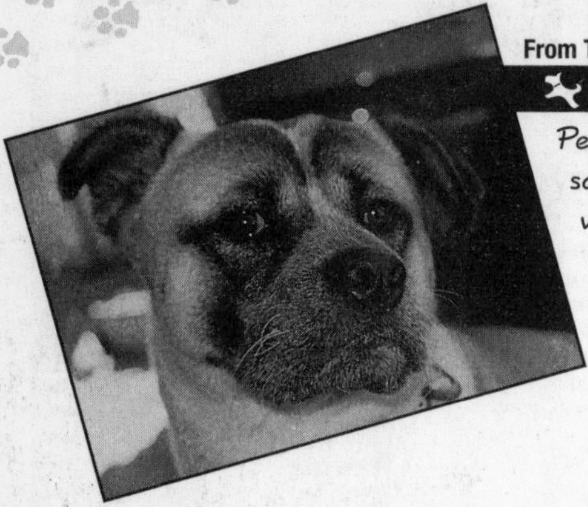

People say that his face is scary when we're out for walks, but he loves the cats that have been living with him since he was a puppy. A talent for making friends is a good quality for dogs too!

Yukiya Sakuragi

He may look scary at first, but he actually likes cuties just like Lupin does! Um… actually, Lupin just likes cute female dogs…Sorry (lol). The mongrel I had before hated cats. It must be really nice having dogs and cats be friends.

From Saeki-san in Osaka

Ryu-kun (Miniature Dachshund)

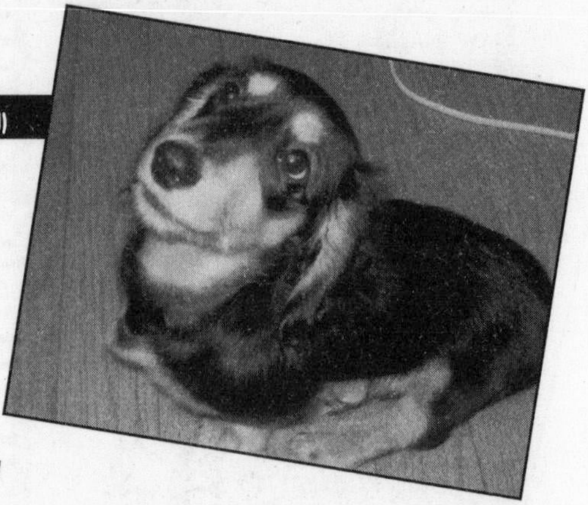

The father of the family used to hate animals, including dogs. They got Ryu because the kids nagged him for a dog. But now he loves the dog even more than the kids do... He's definitely crazy for dogs!

Yukiya Sakuragi

Even if people say that they don't like them, I think it's just because they don't know dogs. When lovely eyes like these look up at you, there's no way you can say that you dislike them!

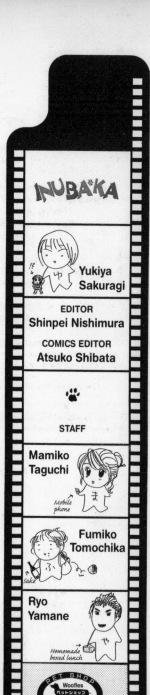

INUBAKA

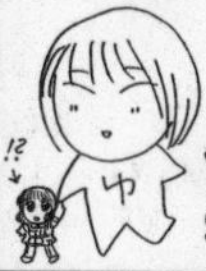
!?

Yukiya Sakuragi

EDITOR
Shinpei Nishimura

COMICS EDITOR
Atsuko Shibata

STAFF

Mamiko Taguchi

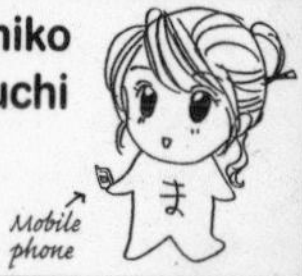
Mobile phone

Fumiko Tomochika

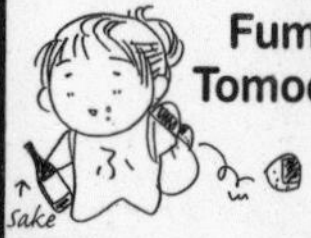
Sake

Ryo Yamane

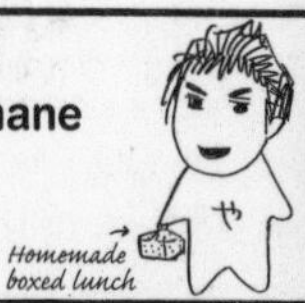
Homemade boxed lunch

PET SHOP Woofles ペットショップ わっふる

Toshiaki Kato

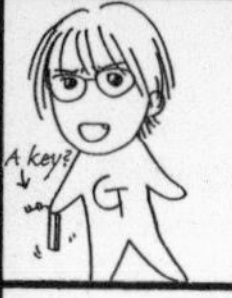
A key?

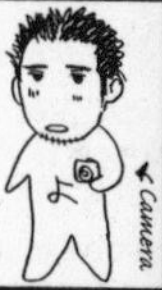
Camera

Yuzo Warabi

Noriko Takahashi

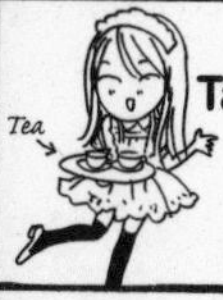
Tea

Susumu Takeda

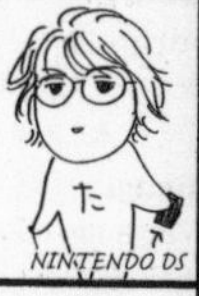
NINTENDO DS

Akira Iwaya

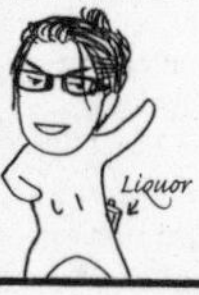
Liquor

Tomoe Ishido

Yoichi Miyoshi

SPECIAL THANKS TO
YUKIYA'S FAMILY AND BLANC

DAIKEI DESIGN ROOM
SEIJI KOBAYASHI

THIS CREDIT PAGE SHOWS SKETCHES OF EACH STAFF MEMBER THAT SAKURAGI-SENSEI DREW ON THE ENVELOPE FOR THE FINALIZED MANGA MANUSCRIPT. EVERYONE IS DRAWN WITH AN ITEM STRONGLY RELATED TO THEIR PERSONALITY.

THANK YOU!!

Inubaka
Crazy for Dogs
Vol. #6
VIZ Media Edition

**Story and Art by
Yukiya Sakuragi**

Translation/Hidemi Hachitori, HC Language Solutions, Inc.
English Adaptation/Ian Reid, HC Language Solutions, Inc.
Touch-up Art & Lettering/HudsonYards
Cover and Interior Design/Hidemi Sahara
Editor/Ian Robertson

Editor in Chief, Books/Alvin Lu
Editor in Chief, Magazines/Marc Weidenbaum
VP of Publishing Licensing/Rika Inouye
VP of Sales/Gonzalo Ferreyra
Sr. VP of Marketing/Liza Coppola
Publisher/Hyoe Narita

Printed in the U.S.A.

Published by VIZ Media, LLC
P.O. Box 77010
San Francisco, CA 94107

10 9 8 7 6 5 4 3 2 1
First printing, December 2007

**www.viz.com
store.viz.com**

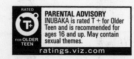

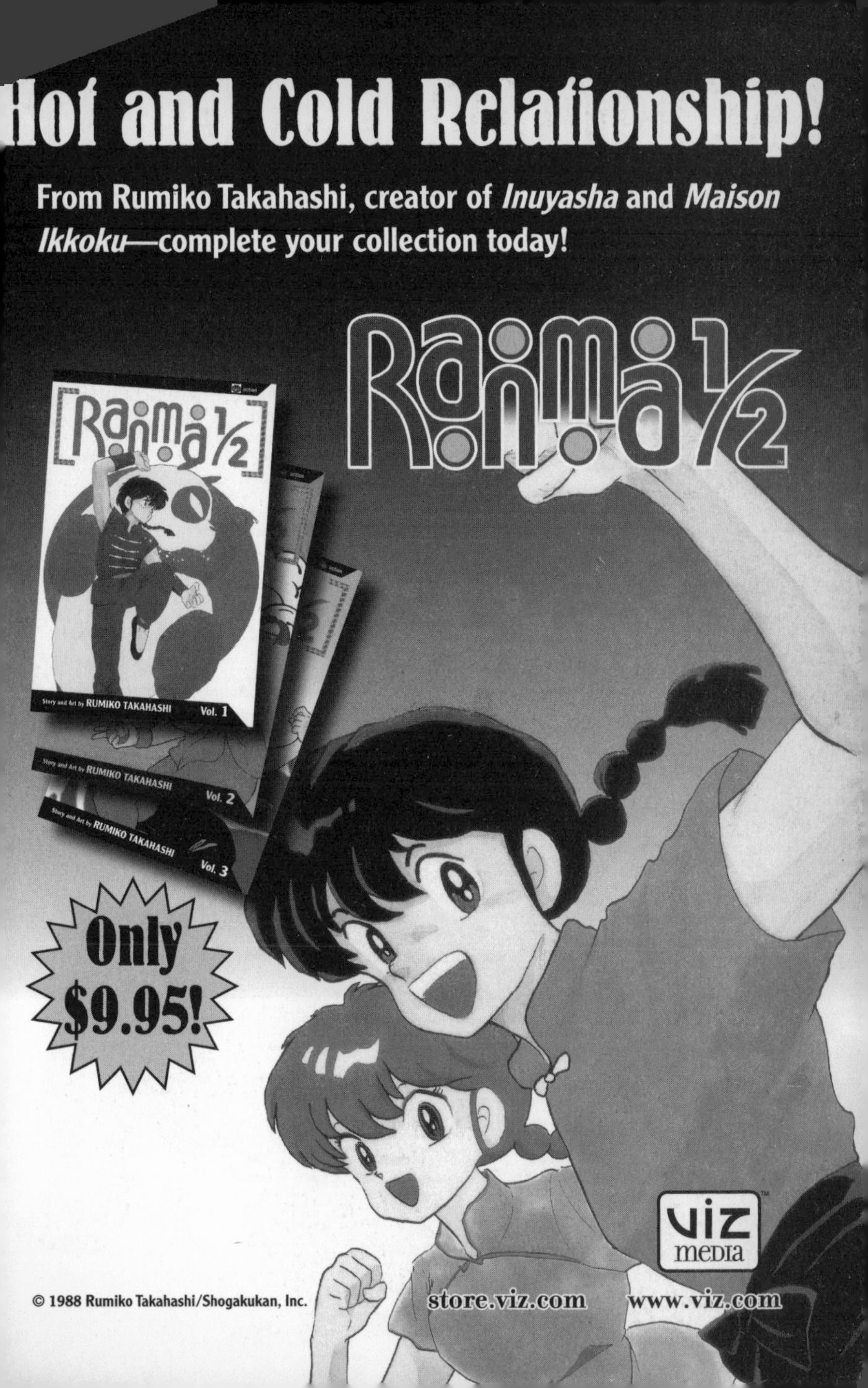
Hot and Cold Relationship!
From Rumiko Takahashi, creator of *Inuyasha* and *Maison Ikkoku*—complete your collection today!
Ranma 1/2
Ranma 1/2
Story and Art by RUMIKO TAKAHASHI Vol. 1
Story and Art by RUMIKO TAKAHASHI Vol. 2
Story and Art by RUMIKO TAKAHASHI Vol. 3
Only $9.95!
VIZ media
© 1988 Rumiko Takahashi/Shogakukan, Inc.
store.viz.com
www.viz.com

A Comedy that Redefines a

Due to an unfortunate accident, when martial artist Ranma gets splashed with cold water, he becomes a buxom young girl! Hot water reverses the effect, but when blamed for offenses both real and imagined, and pursued by lovesick suitors of both genders, what's a half-boy, half-girl to do?

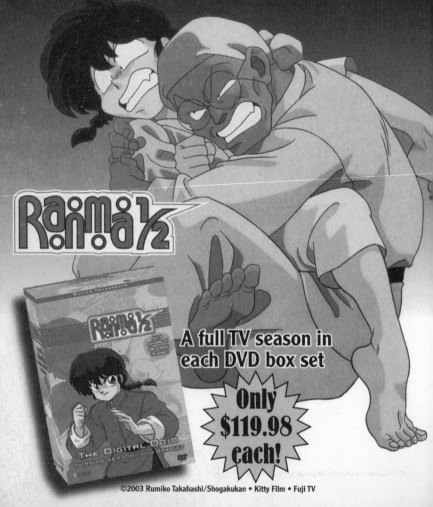

A full TV season in each DVD box set

Only $119.98 each!

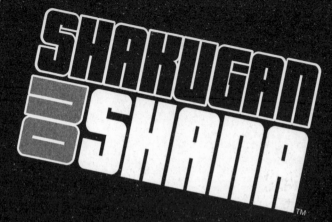
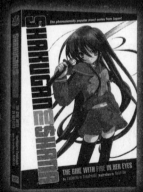
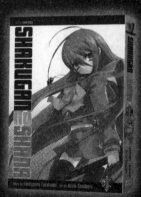

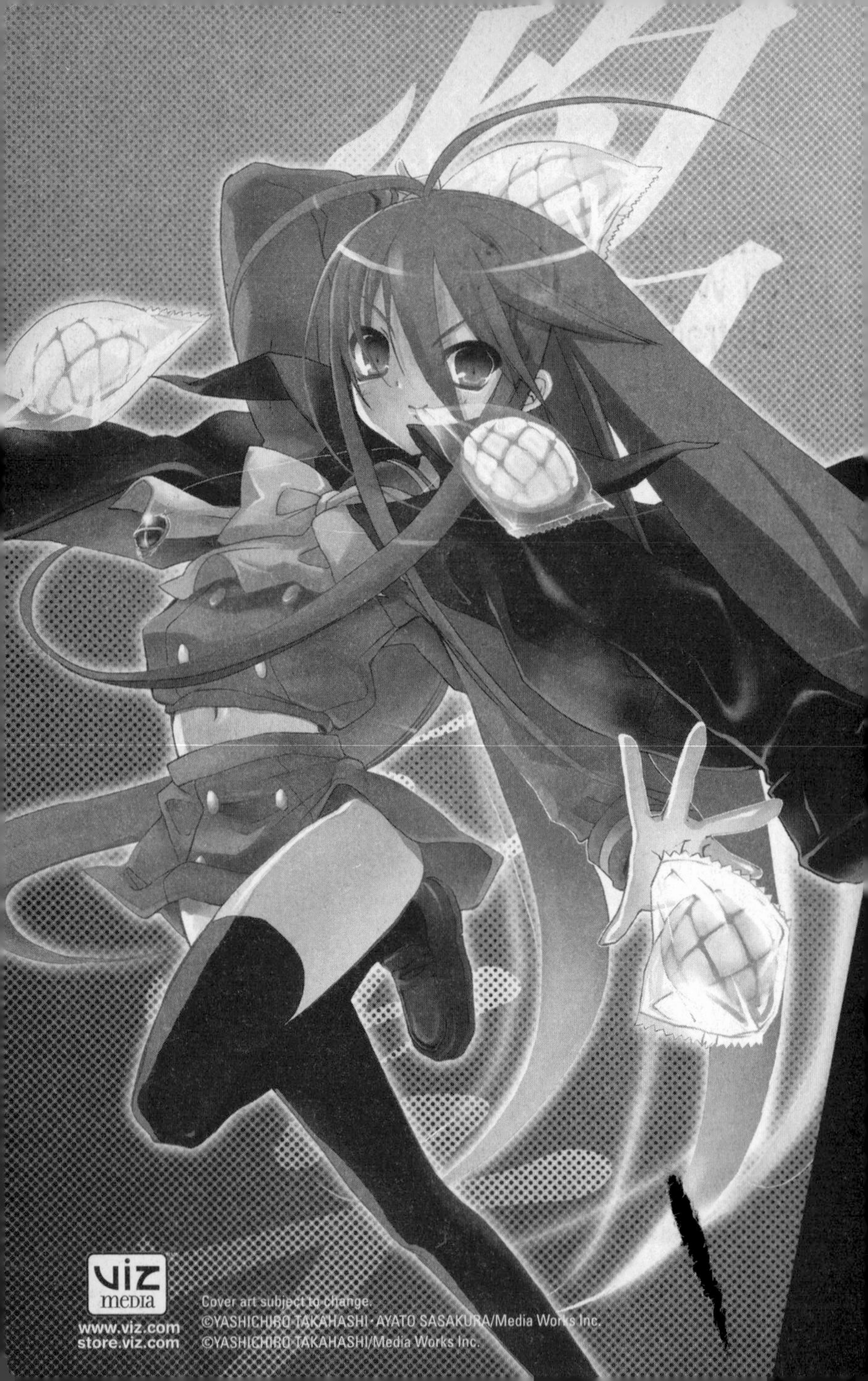

LOVE MAN
LET US KNOW WHAT YOU THINK!

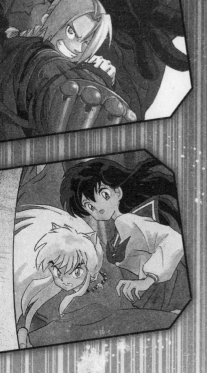

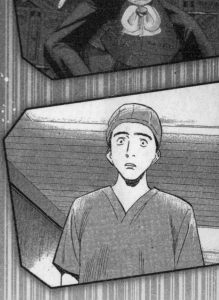

HELP US MAKE THE MANGA
YOU LOVE BETTER!

FEB 2014